Lecture Notes in Computer Science 5959

Commenced Publication in 1973
Founding and Former Series Editors:
Gerhard Goos, Juris Hartmanis, and Jan van Leeuwen

Editorial Board

David Hutchison
   Lancaster University, UK

Takeo Kanade
   Carnegie Mellon University, Pittsburgh, PA, USA
Josef Kittler
   University of Surrey, Guildford, UK
Jon M. Kleinberg
   Cornell University, Ithaca, NY, USA
Alfred Kobsa
   University of California, Irvine, CA, USA
Friedemann Mattern
   ETH Zurich, Switzerland
John C. Mitchell
   Stanford University, CA, USA
Moni Naor
   Weizmann Institute of Science, Rehovot, Israel
Oscar Nierstrasz
   University of Bern, Switzerland
C. Pandu Rangan
   Indian Institute of Technology, Madras, India
Bernhard Steffen
   TU Dortmund University, Germany
Madhu Sudan
   Microsoft Research, Cambridge, MA, USA
Demetri Terzopoulos
   University of California, Los Angeles, CA, USA
Doug Tygar
   University of California, Berkeley, CA, USA
Gerhard Weikum
   Max-Planck Institute of Computer Science, Saarbruecken, Germany

Bernadette Charron-Bost
Fernando Pedone
André Schiper (Eds.)

Replication

Theory and Practice

 Springer

Volume Editors

Bernadette Charron-Bost
École Polytechnique, CNRS
Laboratoire d'Informatique (LIX)
91128 Palaiseau CEDEX, France
E-mail: charron@lix.polytechnique.fr

Fernando Pedone
Università della Svizzera italiana (USI)
Facoltà di Scienze informatiche
Via Giuseppe Buffi 6, 6900 Lugano, Switzerland
E-mail: fernando.pedone@usi.ch

André Schiper
École Polytechnique Fédérale de Lausanne (EPFL)
School of Computer and Communication Sciences
Station 14, 1015 Lausanne, Switzerland
E-mail: andre.schiper@epfl.ch

Cover illustration: M.C. Escher's "Symmetry Drawing E126"
© 2010 The M.C. Escher Company–Holland. All rights reserved.
www.mcescher.com

Library of Congress Control Number: 2009941316

CR Subject Classification (1998): H.2-4, H.2.4, C.4, C.2.4, E.3, E.1

LNCS Sublibrary: SL 1 – Theoretical Computer Science and General Issues

ISSN	0302-9743
ISBN-10	3-642-11293-5 Springer Berlin Heidelberg New York
ISBN-13	978-3-642-11293-5 Springer Berlin Heidelberg New York

springer.com

© Springer-Verlag Berlin Heidelberg 2010
Printed in Germany

Typesetting: Camera-ready by author, data conversion by Markus Richter, Heidelberg
Printed on acid-free paper   SPIN: 12823659   06/3180   5 4 3 2 1 0

Preface

This book is the result of the seminar "*A 30-Year Perspective on Replication*," which took place at Monte Verità, Ascona, Switzerland, in November 2007. As suggested by the title, the goal of the seminar was not to speculate about the future of replication, but rather to understand the present, by analyzing past successes and past failures, and to make an assessment of about 30 years of research on replication. Replication is a topic addressed by several communities: the distributed computing community, the distributed system community, and the database community. Each of these communities has looked at replication from different points of view and with different goals, e.g., performance vs. fault tolerance. Recently, these different goals have started to converge, and there has been work showing that efficiency and strong consistency can sometimes be reconciled.

During the seminar the observation was made that we had reached a point of understanding of the different issues of replication, and this knowledge should be materialized in a book covering the different aspects of replication. This book results from this observation. Its goal is to present a comprehensive view of the achievements of 30 years of research on replication. The book was written by most of the people who have contributed to developing the state-of-the-art replication techniques. It brings a comprehensive view of existing solutions, from a theoretical as well as from a practical point of view. It covers replication of processes/objects and of databases; replication for fault tolerance and replication for performance; benign faults and malicious (Byzantine) faults. By covering these different issues in an integrated way, we believe the book fills a gap, and as such it should find a place in the graduate teaching of distributed computing, distributed systems, and databases.

The book is organized in thirteen chapters. Chapter 1 introduces consistency models for replicated data, both in the context of process/object and database replication. Chapter 2 discusses replication techniques commonly used in process replication, focusing on primary back-up and related techniques; it considers both the fail-stop and the crash failure models. Chapter 3 considers modular approaches to process replication; it starts with state-machine replication based on atomic broadcast and shows how this can be built on top of consensus. Although the literature on consensus is vast, there are many misunderstandings, often involving different communities. Chapter 4 discusses these misunderstandings. Chapter 5 covers replication for performance; it contains different strategies and examples, and discusses trade-offs. Chapters 6 and 7 provide a historical account of the Virtual Synchrony Replication Model and Viewstamped Replication, two early replication systems and how they have evolved over the years. Chapters 8 and 9 are dedicated to state-machine replication with Byzantine faults; the first considers distributed trust systems, and the second introduces protocols for state-machine replication. Chapter 10 surveys Byzantine quorum systems, suitable for use when parts of the system cannot be trusted. Chapters 11 through 13 consider database replication. Chapter 11 bridges the gap between process/object replication and database replication, while Chap. 12 surveys database replication techniques; it discusses different replication approaches, consistency criteria for replicated databases and existing systems. Chapter 13 illustrates database replication with a case study: the details of an architecture for practical database replication.

Each one of the chapters in the book is self-contained, and can be read individually. Readers interested in certain specific aspects of replication, however, may prefer to focus on some of the chapters. Chapters 1 and 11 through 13 provide a detailed description of replication in the context of databases. Theoretical aspects of replication under benign failures are discussed in Chapters 1, 3 and 4. Chapters 5, 12 and 13 cover many issues involving practical replication issues. Chapters 8 through 10 address replication under malign failures (i.e., Byzantine failures). Readers mostly interested in historical aspects of replication should read Chaps. 6 and 7.

The Monte Verità seminar organizers are thankful to all the participants for accepting to take part in this unique seminar, and to all authors for taking their time to produce this book. We would also like to thank a number of institutions for the financial support to the seminar: the Monte Verità Foundation, the Hasler Foundation, Microsoft, Eidgenössische Technische Hochschule Zürich (ETHZ), École Polytechnique Fédérale de Lausanne (EPFL), Università della Svizzera italiana (USI), and the École polytechnique in Palaiseau.

October 2009

Bernadette Charron-Bost
Fernando Pedone
André Schiper

List of Authors

Marcos K. Aguilera	Microsoft Research Silicon Valley, USA
Gustavo Alonso	ETHZ, Switzerland
Ken Birman	Cornell University, USA
Christian Cachin	IBM Research - Zurich, Switzerland
Nuno Carvalho	Instituto Superior Técnico/INESC-ID, Portugal
Alfrânio Correia Jr.	Universidade do Minho, Portugal
Alan D. Fekete	University of Sydney, Australia
Rachid Guerraoui	EPFL, Switzerland
Ricardo Jiménez-Peris	Universidad Politécnica de Madrid, Spain
Bettina Kemme	McGill University, Canada
Barbara Liskov	MIT, USA
Michael G. Merideth	Carnegie Mellon University, USA
Rui Oliveira	Universidade do Minho, Portugal
Marta Patiño-Martínez	Universidad Politécnica de Madrid, Spain
Fernando Pedone	University of Lugano, Switzerland
José Pereira	Universidade do Minho, Portugal
Guillaume Pierre	VU University Amsterdam, The Netherlands
Krithi Ramamritham	I.I.T. Bombay, India
Michael K. Reiter	University of North Carolina, USA
Luís Rodrigues	Instituto Superior Técnico/INESC-ID, Portugal
André Schiper	EPFL, Switzerland
Fred B. Schneider	Cornell University, USA
Robbert van Renesse	Cornell University, USA
Maarten van Steen	VU University Amsterdam, The Netherlands
Lidong Zhou	Microsoft Research Asia, China

Contents

Chapter 1
Consistency Models for Replicated Data

Alan D. Fekete and Krithi Ramamritham

Abstract There are many different replica control techniques, used in different research communities. To understand when one replica management algorithm can
be replaced by another, we need to describe more abstractly the consistency model,
which captures the set of properties that an algorithm provides, and on which the
clients rely (whether the clients are people or other programs). In this chapter we
describe a few of the different consistency models that have been proposed, and we
sketch a framework for thinking about consistency models. In particular, we show
that there are several styles in which consistency models can be expressed, and we
also propose some axes of variation among the consistency models.

1.1 Introduction

The research of decades has produced many ideas for managing replicated data,
in contexts including distributed systems, databases, and multiprocessor computer
hardware. The chapters of this book present many system designs, which differ in
how replicas are updated, when they are updated, how failures are handled, and so
on. In this chapter, we try to abstract away from particular system designs, to think
about the functionality that a replicated system gives to its users.

Even systems that are widely different internally can be functionally interchange-
able. For example, users should not be aware of whether the replicas are communicating through a group communication infrastructure (described in Ch 3.2 and Ch
5), or running a consensus protocol (see Ch 3.3 and Ch 4); users shouldn't need
to care whether each replica stores a single version of the data, or multiple versions. Different system designs may have different characteristics for performance
or fault-tolerance, but the users should be able to take code that runs on one system,
and run it on another system without changing the behavior.

B. Charron-Bost, F. Pedone, and A. Schiper (Eds.): Replication, LNCS 5959, pp. 1–17, 2010.
© Springer-Verlag Berlin Heidelberg 2010

However, in some cases, the functionality itself changes between one system design and another. For example, a common theme in replication research is to seek improved performance by giving up some level of consistency between replicas (see Ch 6.4). For a user, it is very important to know exactly what functionality one can rely on, from each replicated data management system. A replication consistency model is a way to abstract away implementation details, and to identify the functionality of a given system. Like any other careful specification, a consistency model is a way for people to come to a common understanding of each others rights and responsibilities. For a consistency model, the people who must jointly understand the model are the users (who learn what they can rely on the system to provide, and what assumptions they might be inclined to make that are not guaranteed), and the system designers (who document the features of their design that will not change, as performance tuning, and other optimization is done).

A consistency model is a property of system designs, but a particular consistency model is usually presented in terms of a condition that can be true or false for individual executions. That is, we can determine whether or not the condition holds for a possible execution: one pattern of events that might occur at various places and times as the system runs (including information about the type and contents of messages, when and where these messages are sent and received, the state of each replica after each event, etc). If *every* possible execution that can occur for a system design makes the condition true, then we say that the system design itself satisfies the consistency model.

1.1.1 Contributions

The remainder of the chapter is structured as follows. In Section 1.2 we deal with the need to formalize the properties of the sequential data type which is being replicated. In Section 1.3 we explain the strongest consistency model, where the users can't ever discover that the data is replicated. We also introduce two styles for presenting consistency models: an operation-ordering style where there are logical conditions on how operations can be ordered into a sequence that is allowed by the sequential data type, and an ideal-system style where a abstracted state-machine model is given that generates executions which are indistinguishable to the clients from those in the real system. Section 1.4 looks at some weaker notions of consistency, that are provided by many systems as a tradeoff for better performance or better availability. In Section 1.5 we mention some of the ways in which consistency models can be defined for replicated databases; here we have a richer interface, where several operations can be grouped in a transaction. In Section 1.6 we comment on some general issues that are raised by the wide variety of different consistency models that have been proposed. Finally we conclude with a summary of the main ideas of this chapter.

1.2 Defining the Sequential Data Type

Before offering a definition of a particular consistency model, it is important to know what operations the clients will be submitting, and how these operations should be understood. This aspect of the model is captured by a sequential data type, which is a formalization of the semantics of the operations, or equivalently, of the unreplicated system that users understand or to which they relate the replicated system. Seminal early work on specification of a data type was done by Liskov and Zilles [12].

The simplest possible sequential data type is the read-write single-bit register. Here the operations are to read the value, or to write a new value (overwriting whatever is already present). Thus there would be three legal operations: read(), write(0), write(1). The return value from a read is either 0 or 1; the return value from a write is "OK". With a bit more realism, we can consider the read-write 32-bit register, whose operations are read(), and write(v) for each v from 0x00000000 to 0xFFFFFFFF.

The simple registers described above have read-only operations which do not affect the state, and update operations that modify the state but do not reveal anything about it. It is also possible to have more complicated operations that both modify state, and return a value based on the state. Many hardware platforms actually support operations like that. For example, a CAS-register offers compare-and-swap operations (as well as read and write). The effect of compare-and-swap($v1$, $v2$) depends on the previous value in the register. If the value present is equal to $v1$, the operation changes the value to be $v2$; otherwise the effect is to leave the register unchanged. The return value from this operation is always the value that was present in the register before the operation.

In distributed computing theory, there has also been consideration of traditional data types such as a queue or stack. Another direction for finding interesting sequential data types is to consider a type with many different locations. For example, a multi-location read-write memory has a set of locations (or addresses) A, and operations such as read(a) for $a \in A$, or write(a, w) for $a \in A$ and w in some finite domain of values. One can then also allow operations that deal with several locations at once. For example, a snapshot memory has an operation snapshot(), which doesn't modify the state but returns a collection of values, one value for each location.

We can formalize a sequential data type by a set of operations O, a set of states S, an initial state s_0, a set of return values R, and two functions[1]: next-state: $O \times S \rightarrow S$ and return-value: $O \times S \rightarrow R$. For example, a multi-location byte-valued snapshot memory is a sequential data type where $O = \{$read(a) for $a \in A$, write(a, w) for $a \in A$ and $w \in W$ (here W is the set of all 8-bit constants), and snapshot() $\}$; the set of states S consists of all functions $A \rightarrow W$, the initial state has all locations mapped to the zero word; the return values are elements of W (returned by read operations), the single string "OK" (returned by write operations) and the set of functions $A \rightarrow W$ (returned by snapshot operations; thus the return value from a snapshot is actually a state). The next-state function is defined by next-state(read(a),

---

[1] In this chapter we only deal with data types where the operations are total and deterministic, so an operation has a unique next-state and return value, when applied in a given state. This is implicit in having functions for next-state and return-value, and it sometimes requires adding error return-values and error states to the model, for cases such as performing a pop() on an empty stack. The theory becomes somewhat more complicated if we loosen the model to allow nondeterministic operations (which may move to one of several next-states) or partial operations (which may not be allowed in a particular state).

$s) = s$, next-state(write(a, w), s) = t where t is the function from A to W such that $t(l) = s(l)$ if $l \neq a$, and $t(a) = w$, and next-state(snapshot(), s) = s. The return-value function is return-value(read(a), s) = $s(a)$ [recall that a state is a function A to W], return-value(write(a, w) = "OK", return-value(snapshot(), s) = s.

Using these functions, or indeed as an alternative formalization, we can look at the possible legal histories of the data type: each history is a sequence of pairs (operation, return-value), where an operation is paired with the return value it receives, when performed in the state that results for all the operations before it in the sequence, done in order. Thus a legal history for a 4-location byte-valued snapshot memory might be the following:

$$\begin{aligned}
&(\text{write}(1, 5), \text{"OK"}) \\
&(\text{read}(1), 5) \\
&(\text{read}(2), 0) \\
&(\text{write}(2, 7), \text{"OK"}) \\
&(\text{snapshot}(), (0 \mapsto 0, 1 \mapsto 5, 2 \mapsto 7, 3 \mapsto 0) \\
&(\text{write}(3, 2), \text{"OK"})
\end{aligned} \tag{1.1}$$

One can use the sequential data type to carefully define concepts such as when an operation does not modify the state, or when operations commute with one another. Some techniques for implementing replication are specific to particular sequential types, while other algorithms work oblivious of the sequential type. Similarly, some consistency models rely on a particular sequential type, for example, by using the fact that each operation is on a single location, or by treating read operations differently from writes.

1.3 Strong Consistency

The principal goal of research on consistency models is to help application developers understand the behavior they will see when they interact with a replicated storage system, and especially so they can choose application logic that will function sensibly. The very easiest way a developer can understand the behavior of a replicated system, is to simply ignore the replication: if the application program gets the same behavior as with a single site, unreplicated system, then writing the application logic is no different to conventional programming. This transparency concept can be captured by saying that a system execution is *linearizable*; one similarly says that a system is *linearizable*, if every execution it produces has this property. The term "atomic" is often used instead of linearizable; we do not do so, to avoid confusing with the database meaning of atomic, described in Section 1.5 below. The idea of linearizability is very prominent in research in theory of distributed computing, having been introduced in [8]. Below we give an example to illustrate the concept, and then we discuss some ways to make this precise.

In Figure 1.1, we show one execution that is linearizable, for a system where the underlying serial data is the 4-location byte-valued snapshot memory mentioned

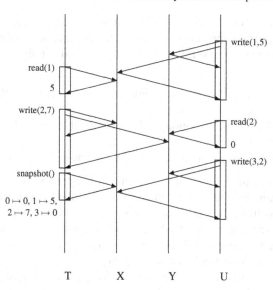

Fig. 1.1 Linearizable Execution.

above. This execution could arise in a system that has two replicas of the data (at sites X and Y), and clients located at T and U each follow a replica management algorithm: each read or snapshot is done on one replica, each write is done on both replicas, different writes are done in the same order at the replicas, and a write doesn't return to the client until all replicas are modified. A figure like this is called a space-time diagram; it shows time increasing down the page; the activity at each location (either a client or a replica) is shown as happening on a vertical line, and messages are shown as diagonal arrows, starting at a point on the vertical line representing the sender, and ending on the line representing the destination location. We use a rectangle around part of the client's vertical line, to indicate the duration of one operation, from its invocation till the operation returns and the next operation can begin. The details of the operation are written next to the top of the rectangle, and the return value is written next to the bottom of the rectangle (except that in this diagram we omit the uninformative return value "OK" from a write operation)

One approach to giving a precise definition of linearizable execution is based on the operations and their order. We take all the operations that occur in the execution, pairing the operation (name and arguments) with the return value produced in the execution, and then we must find a sequence (total order) of these pairs that is allowed by the sequential data type being replicated. An additional requirement is that the order of operations as they occur in the sequence must not contradict any order information visible to an observer of the system execution. Thus, we define a real-time partial order $<_{E,rt}$ between operations that occur in the execution E, where $p <_{E,rt} q$ means that the duration of operation p (from invocation till it returns) occurs entirely before the duration of operation q; in other words, the return from p

occurs at an earlier real time than the invocation of operation q. Notice that this is a partial order; if two operations overlap, they are unrelated in this order. We can then define that an execution E is *linearizable* provided that there exists a sequence H such that

[L1]   H contains exactly the same operations that occur in E, each paired with the return value received in E,

[L2]   the total order of operations in H is compatible[2] with the real-time partial order $<_{E,rt}$,

[L3]   H is a legal history of the sequential data type that is replicated.

We can apply this definition to the execution in Figure 1.1. For brevity in the discussion, we name an operation by mentioning only the location being written and not the value written; the execution involved has at most one write on each location, so there is no ambiguity introduced by eliding the value. In this execution, the read(1) operation occurs entirely before the operations write(2), read(2), snapshot() and write(3); however it overlaps with write(1). Similarly read(2) occurs entirely before snapshot() and write(3), but it overlaps write(2), and also write(3) overlaps both write(2) and snapshot(). A suitable H is the sequence given as (1.1) in Section 1.2 above. Notice that the order of operations in H is compatible with "occurs entirely before" , for example, read(1) is earlier in H than write(2), read(2), snapshot() and write(3). In this particular example, there is only one possible H that meets all the conditions [L1], [L2], and [L3]. In general, however, there may be several sequences H with these properties. The definition of linearizable merely asks that at least one such H exists.

A different style, based on an ideal system model, has also been used in the literature to define consistency properties. This style of definition involves providing an explicit system model for the unreplicated system that users can imagine they are dealing with. For linearizablity, we consider an ideal system, in which there is a single site where the data is stored, and this site also has a collection of pending requests, and a collection of pending responses. Whenever a client requests an operation, the operation is placed among the pending requests. At any time (nondeterministically) the system can (in one indivisible step) chose a pending request, perform it on the (unique) data, take the result into the collection of pending responses, and remove the chosen operation from the collection of pending requests. At any time, the system can non-deterministically chose a pending response, remove it from the collection, and return that value to the client which had originally requested the operation. This can be formalized as a state-transition machine. The definition of a linearizable execution E is that there exists an execution F of the unreplicated ideal system, such that E and F contain exactly the same steps at all the clients, in exactly the same real-time order.

---

[2] Two partial orders on the same set are called *compatible* provided that there exists a partial order containing their union. Equivalently, their union has no cycle. In this particular situation, the order in H is a total order, so compatibility is simply expressing that whenever $p <_{E,rt} q$ then p comes before q in H.

1.3.1 Relaxing Inter-Client Operation Ordering

The intuitive justification for the definition of linearizable, is that the replicated system gives the same functionality as the sequential data type. This is built on the idea that there is an "external observer" who is aware of all the activities of all the clients (but not internal activity within the replicas), and we require that what the observer sees in the real system is the same as what they would see in a system with a single copy of the sequential data. In particular, condition [L2] in the operation-order based definition, builds in the notion that the observer knows whether one operation occurs entirely before another, and similarly the ideal system model must have the same order of client steps (that is, the observer can see which client steps occur first, even when these are at different locations). For many issues in a distributed system, it is normal to disregard the order of activity at different locations, in cases where such order can't be determined by any observer within the system. This leads to various relaxations of the consistency model, which allow some operations to appear out of their real-time order. However, we do not usually allow arbitrary changes in the apparent order, and insist that some operations form a session, whose order must be respected in the apparent unreplicated system that users believe they are dealing with.

A consistency model of this kind is used in research on theory of distributed computing where it is called *sequential consistency*. An example of an execution that is sequentially consistent, but is not linearizable, is shown in Figure 1.2. This execution can be produced by an implementation in which each read or snapshot is done on one replica, each write is done on both replicas, different writes are done in the same order at the replicas, and a write returns to the client as soon as the messages have been sent out to the replicas (in this replica management approach, there is no need for the replica to reply to the client after a write, and indeed the write operation may return before the replicas are actually modified).

An operation ordering definition of sequential consistency uses a client partial order $<_{E,c}$ on the operations, in which $p <_{E,c} q$ means that the p and q occur at the same client and that p returns before q is invoked. We can then define that an execution E is *sequentially consistent* provided that there exists a sequence H such that

[SC1]   H contains exactly the same operations that occur in E, each paired with the return value received in E,

[SC2]   the total order of operations in H is compatible with the client partial order $<_{E,c}$,

[SC3]   H is a legal history of the sequential data type that is replicated.

We see that SC1 is the same as the earlier L1, and SC3 is the same as L3; thus the only difference between the definition of sequential consistency and that of linearizability, is in the change from L2 to SC2; for sequential consistency, H is required to be compatible with a weaker partial order. Thus any execution that is linearizable is also sequentially consistent, but the converse does not hold, as we show in an example.

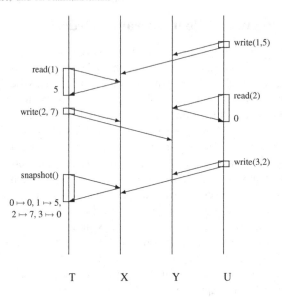

Fig. 1.2 Sequentially Consistent Execution.

The execution of Figure 1.2 is sequentially consistent; the sequence (1.1) above is a suitable choice for H to show this. Note that the operations write(3) and snapshot() are not related by the location partial order because they are at different clients (even though the duration of write(3) occurs entirely before the duration of snapshot()), and so it is acceptable for H to place snapshot() before write(3). The execution of Figure 1.2 is not linearizable, because for any sequence H in which snapshot() has the return value found in the execution, write(3) must be after snapshot(); such an order is not compatible with the real-time partial order on operations, where write(3,2) $<_{E,rt}$ snapshot().

The term sequential consistency is also used by researchers in computer architecture[3]. For this community, the client is envisioned as a CPU issuing instructions that operate on a shared memory (and also other instructions that are purely local to the client, such as those on registers); in contrast to the model we gave above, the client does not see the point at which an operation returns (merely, the return value must be available to the client when a later instruction makes use of it). Thus, in this community, the client order $p <_{E,c} q$ is defined by p and q are operations of the same client, and p is submitted before q is submitted. If each client does not submit any operation until it has the return value from the previous operation at that client, then the two definitions are the same. Sequential consistency is the strongest consistency model provided by common multiprocessor hardware.

---

[3] Indeed, while the concept was invented by Leslie Lamport who is most prominent as a distributed computing researcher, the paper[10] in which he defined the term is devoted to programming multiprocessor hardware.

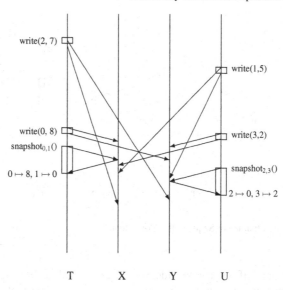

Fig. 1.3 Sequential Consistency Does Not Compose.

One significant aspect of the definition is that sequential consistency is not a compositional property; if we separately replicate two data items, and each is managed to be sequentially consistent, it may happen that the combined data is not sequentially consistent.

To illustrate this, consider a system with two separate two-location byte-valued snapshot data items. For clarity, we will give one data item locations called 0 and 1, and the other item's locations will be called 2 and 3. Thus the system has an operation (which we will call $\text{snapshot}_{0,1}()$) to observe the values in locations 0 and 1; another operation $\text{snapshot}_{2,3}()$ observes locations 2 and 3. We might have a system design based on read-any, write-all, with writes returning immediately, and we could use a separate communication infrastructure for the messages that deal with each data item; that is, the various replicas all see the same order for messages that deal with writes to locations 0 and 1, and they all see the same order for messages that deal with writes to locations 2 and 3; however, it can occur that the relative order in which replicas receive two messages is different, in the case where one message deals with locations 0 or 1, and the other message deals with the other data item. In Figure 1.3, we show a possible execution of this system.

The execution of Figure 1.3 is not sequentially consistent. The return value of $\text{snapshot}_{0,1}$ reports that write(0) appears to occur before the snapshot, and write(1) appears to occur after it; similarly the return value of $\text{snapshot}_{2,3}$ shows that write(3) appears to occur before write(2). The client partial order of T shows that write(2) must be before write(0), and the client partial order of U shows that write(1) must be before write(3). These relationships can't all hold at once.

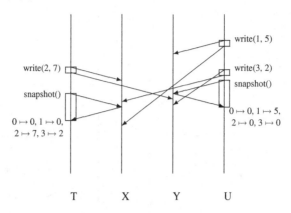

Fig. 1.4 Execution that is not Sequentially Consistent.

On the other hand, if we just consider the data item with locations 0 and 1, the operations on that item within Figure 1.3 are sequentially consistent. A suitable H to demonstrate this is the sequence with write(0) $snapshot_{0,1}()$ write(1). Similarly the sequence write(3) $snapshot_{2,3}$ write(2) shows that when we just look at the operations on locations 2 and 3, they are also sequentially consistent.

In contrast, two linearizable replicated items run next to one another forms a linearizable system for the combined data. We say that the property of being linearizable is a compositional property.

1.4 Weak Consistency

Strong consistency can be provided by appropriate hardware and/or software mechanisms, but these are typically found to incur considerable penalties, in latency, availability after faults, etc. In every research community where replication has been used, there have been proposals to offer the clients less guarantees than a transparent single-copy image, in order to deliver better performance. For example, strong consistency designs typically require all replicas to receive messages in the same order. A communication system that keeps messages in the same order typically sends all messages through a single sequencer node or on a common bus, and this becomes a bottleneck for the whole system. If instead we allow messages to be carried independently, and applied to each replica whenever they arrive, performance may be much better, but the clients can see inconsistencies that would never happen with unreplicated data [16]. Consider the execution in Figure 1.4.

In the execution shown in Figure 1.4, there is no possible history H that can meet both SC1 and SC2, to fit with the information returned in the two snapshot() operations. The snapshot() done by client T reveals the effects of the write(2) and write(3) operations, but not the effects of write(1); thus any history that contains this snapshot will have to place write(2) and write(3) before the snapshot(), and place write(1) after the snapshot(). In contrast, the snapshot() done by client U sees the effect of write(1) but not the effects of write(2) or write(3); so any history that contains it will have to place write(1) before both write(2) and write(3). These requirements are contradictory. Thus in this execution, each client sees information that is inconsistent with what the other sees. This execution also gives client U information which is internally inconsistent with the order in which the client itself submits operations: the snapshot() in client U returns information which does not show the previous write(3) operation. We can say that this execution has re-ordered the write(3) and the snapshot() within client U. Effects like these are characteristic of weak consistency models. Different weak models are separated from one another by the precise details of which reorderings are allowed, and which are not, within the activity of a client, and also by whether there are any constraints at all on the information provided to different clients.

We now propose a common framework, within the operation-ordering style, in which different weak consistency models can be defined. This is inspired by the framework for multiprocessor hardware consistency models [17]. We base our framework around each operation o in the execution E having a *justification* J_o, which is a sequence of other operations that occurred in E, such that the return value o received in E is that which the sequential data type would give to operation o when performed in the state which is produced by starting in the initial state and then applying each operation in J_o in turn. Note that we put a condition on the return value of o in relation to J_o, but we do not require (in the general framework) that the earlier operations have the same return values in J_o as they have in E, though this might be an added constraint in particular weak consistency models.

In a typical read-any-write-all design (such as in Ch 2) of a replicated system, we can take J_o to be the sequence of operations that had already been applied to the replica where the return value of o was calculated. For the execution shown in Figure 1.4, a justification for the snapshot() at client T could be the sequence write(2) write(3), and a justification for the snapshot() at U could be the sequence write(1). A given consistency definition then places some constraints on the relationships between the justifications of various operations. More precisely, a consistency model requires that justifications can be found for every operation, such that the set of justifications are related as the consistency model constrains them.

As one example of a weak consistency model, the computer architecture community describes some hardware as offering the *release consistency* model[4]. In release consistency, some of the operations are labelled as special: a special read operation is also called an acquire, and a special write operation is called a release. The requirements of an execution E to satisfy release consistency are that there exists a total order $<_{spec}$ on all the special operations, such that

[RC1]   for every operation o, the order of special operations in J_o is compatible with $<_{spec}$

[RC2]   for every operation o, J_o contains any acquire that occurs before o at the same client

---

[4] To be precise, the model we define here can be called RCsc; some authors instead give a slightly relaxed meaning which can be called RCpc, as described in [1].

[RC3]   for every operation o, if J_o contains a release operation r, and p is any operation that occurs before r at the same client as r, then J_o contains p before r,

[RC4]   for every operation o, J_o contains an operation q, and a is an acquire that occurs before q at the same client as q, then J_o contains a before q.

That is, the hardware makes sure that whatever order is seen anywhere in the system respects the order at a single client from an acquire to a subsequent operation at the same client, and from any operation to a subsequent release at the same client. A similar but more complicated memory model with synchronizing operations is that provided for Java programmers by the Java Virtual Machine [13].

To define a weak model within the ideal system style, one needs to come up with a state-transition system whose executions are exactly those where each operation has a justification. The ideal system typically can have a state which keeps all operations that have been requested and not yet dealt with, and also the state keeps a set of operations that have been dealt with, each with its associated justification (and an additional flag to show whether the return value has been given back to the client). A transition is given for a non-deterministic hidden event which deals with one request: it chooses a request that has not been dealt with, and a set of operations to justify it in accordance with all the requirements (such as RC1-RC4 above) on compatibility of justifications. Another transition is used for returning to the client, with the unique return value that is allowed by the sequential data type, if the requested operation were to be done immediately after all the justifying operations in turn.

In the distributed systems community, a model that has attracted a lot of attention is *eventual consistency*. This is the consistency model that allows the system to be highly-available, even in the face of network partition; it is often described as allowing "disconnected operation" [6]. The main implementation technique is to allow the client to update any replicas, and then the information about the change is propagated in the background[5] to other replicas through gossip messages. Because non-commuting updates can arrive at different replicas in different orders, a conflict-resolution mechanism is needed, in which some previously applied operations can be undone when a new message brings information about an operation which ought to have preceded the ones already done; the missing operation is applied, and after that, the replica re-applies the earlier messages that it had just undone. The recent focus on cloud computing services has made eventual consistency very well known[19]. Because eventual consistency is a liveness property rather than a safety property, it is harder to make precise, and any definition will need to deal with an infinitely long execution (representing one way the system can behave, observed without limit). In much of the research literature, eventual consistency is described using phrases similar to "replicas converge towards identical copies in the absence of further updates". This definition is less general than desirable, because it is expressed in terms of implementation detail (the values in the replicas), and because it involves a counter-factual (after all, updates never stop arriving in many executions). We offer here a new definition based on operation justifications; our

---

[5] This is also called anti-entropy.

definition does hold for a system built with gossip messages and conflict resolution, as described above. An infinitely long execution E of the replicated system satisfies *eventual consistency* if there exist justifications J_o and an sequence of operations F of the sequential data type, such that

[EC1]   F contains exactly the same operations that occur in E,

[EC2]   for every prefix P of F, there exists a time t in E such that for every operation o that occurs after t, the justification J_o has P as a prefix.

In this definition, we call a prefix P the "agreed past" for all the operations o mentioned in (EC2). The sequence F orders all the operations in the way that conflict resolution places them, and over time, longer and longer prefixes of F become fixed at all the replicas. In a gossip-based implementation, the agreed past for an operation is the beginning of the justification, which contains operations that will never be undone again, because all the previous operations have propagated to every replica.

To make an eventually consistent system more convenient for clients, it is common to place additional constraints on the contents of the justifications. These have been called "session properties" because they allow the client to do several operations one after another, and avoid some confusing situations[18]. One session property is *Read Your Writes*, which constrains the justifications so that for any read operation o submitted by a client, J_o contains all write operations that were submitted by the same client before o. The *Monotonic Reads* property constrains justifications so that if a client submits read operation $o1$ and later submits a read operation $o2$, then J_{o2} includes all of J_{o1}.

The *causal consistency* session model is a restriction of eventual consistency, based on the causal order between operations, defined by Lamport [11], where $o1 < o2$ means that information from o1 can flow to o2; formally, the Lamport causality partial order is the transitive closure of the order of operations at each client, and the partial order which relates a message send and the receipt of the same message. In causal consistency, the justification J_o must contain all operations that come before o in the causal partial order; also, whenever q occurs within J_o, and $p < q$ in the causal partial order, then p occurs in J_o before q. An interesting twist on causal consistency was proposed by Ladin et al [9], who allow the application code to choose, for each operation, a subset of the causal precedent operations, and then require only this subset to be in the justification for the operation, and always ordered before that operation in justifications.

Another style of additional constraint in replicated distributed systems is to bound the divergence between replicas, so clients see values that are reasonably "fresh". Several researchers introduced these ideas around the same time, one example was [3]. Again, this model is sometimes explained in terms of the implementation internals (limiting how far apart the values are at a given time, or limiting the time period between when an update is applied at different replicas). It can also be expressed as a constraint on the justifications: for example, we may require that every operation's justification should include all operations that were submitted more than Δ time units before the read (time bound) or that the total impact of the operations submitted before o but not in J_o justification, is to change the return value of o by less than Δ (value bound).

1.5 Transactions

Replication has been extensively studied in the database research community (see Ch 12). For this field, we need to consider not just separate operations, but also how these operations are combined into transactions. A transaction contains a set of the operations performed during an execution, and each operation belongs to exactly one transaction. Some systems require all operations of a transaction to be submitted by the same client; in other systems, a transaction may be distributed among several clients. Sometimes each operation, when it is submitted, carries with it the identifier of the transaction it is part of; in other systems, a client submits special operations that begin and complete a transaction; each operation is then part of the transaction whose begin operation most recently preceded the operation at that client.

There are two distinct outcomes for a transaction. The transaction may complete with a *commit*, or with an *abort*. The term *atomic* is used by the database community[6], to say that all the operations of a transaction are performed (if the transaction commits), or it is as if none of the operations are performed (if the transaction aborts). This can be achieved by the system implicitly undoing each operation of the transaction (in reverse chronological order) at the end of a transaction which aborts.

Strong consistency for a replicated database system means that the system looks like a single-site, unreplicated database. The sequential data type of a database has operations (usually given in the SQL language), these read and update sets of items, determined by predicates on the contents of those items, there are also operations to insert new items, and to delete items chosen by a predicate. This is a fairly sophisticated data type, compared to those usual in computer architecture or distributed computing. Many system optimizations depend on knowing when operations commute on the sequential type, but determining the commutativity between operations of a database takes care: for example, an insert may fail to commute with a read of a set of items, when the inserted item satisfies the predicate that selects the items being read.

Any database will have a mechanism for concurrency control, which provides *isolation* between the transactions. Isolation constrains the values observed in operations, and this is often done by delaying an operation of one transaction until other, conflicting, transactions have completed. The traditional criterion for correct concurrency control is serializability, so *one-copy serializability (1SR)* is a natural consistency model for replicated databases, first defined by Bernstein and Goodman [5]. A recent alternative isolation approach is called Snapshot Isolation (abbreviated as SI) [4]; this is provided by several widely-used platforms, and so *one-copy snapshot isolation (1SI)* is also considered by researchers, where a replicated system is indistinguishable from an unreplicated system with SI for concurrency control.

---

[6] Notice that this is a different meaning from atomic in the distributed systems community, where the term is used for a linearizable system or component.

In the 1SR model, for a given execution E of the replicated system, we can find a single history H, called a serial history: H is valid for the sequential data-type, H contains all the operations of the committed transactions of E (each paired with its return value), and in H, all the operations of a transaction occur together in the same order that these operations occurred in E. Typically one also demands *external consistency*: that the history H should respect the partial order between transactions that do not overlap in E. If we regard a transaction as a single super-operation, 1SR with external consistency is essentially the same as linearizability of the super-operations.

As for other systems, performance is greatly degraded by the requirements to keep strong consistency, and most commercial platforms provide weak consistency models when replicating data. A common approach is to designate a master copy of the data, where updates are done first; all the updates of a transaction then propagate lazily as a group from the master to other replicas. Thus any read that uses a replica may see an obsolete state of the data. The consistency model provided by a system design with master-copy and lazy propagation, can be expressed in the framework of justifications from Section 1.4: each read operation being justified by a sequence of transactions, with the additional restriction that between any two operations' justifications, one is a prefix of the other. However, different reads in a transaction may have different sets of transactions that justify them.

Many other sophisticated consistency models have been proposed for "extended transactions" which can share some data in managed ways, while being isolated on other ways. A powerful framework for presenting these definitions is ACTA [15].

1.6 Discussion

The operation-ordering style of definition is much more widely used than the ideal-system style. Operation ordering definitions are generally much more succinct, and they are good at suggesting many variant models by slight changes of the constraints. Ideal-system models, on the other hand, allow one to use the extensive theory of formal methods, when proving that a particular system design provides a given consistency model. Examples of such proofs are in [2, 7, 14].

For users of systems which offer weak consistency, a vital need is some way to know how to use the system without being inconvenienced by the lack of strong guarantees. For multiprocessor hardware, there are several results that assist with this; typically, each result says that if a program is written in a particular way, it can work correctly with hardware which provides a particular weak consistency model. For example, if the client programs are written to enclose any uses of common variable within acquire-release blocks, then an execution on release-consistent memory is equivalent to an execution on sequentially consistent memory. However, we do not yet have similar guidance for common weak models in distributed computing, such as eventual consistency with read your writes. As cloud computing platforms offer this type of consistency model, the lack of such guidance becomes a threat to sensible use of these platforms.

If we have an ideal-system style definition of a weak consistency model, this can support formal proof of results about correct use of a system. For example, one can give an abstracted model C of any client that is programmed in a certain way, and one can then consider the composition of such clients and the weak-consistency-ideal-system W. We need to prove that the composition of C and W refines the composition of C and a strong ideal-system S. Here, "refines" is a relationship between transition machines (often also called "satisfies"), where A refines B means that every execution of A is a possible execution of B.

Whichever style of consistency model one prefers, it is important for both users and system designers, to have a clear mutual understanding of the properties that are guaranteed for the clients, and those that are not.

1.7 Conclusion

We have shown how one can express the functionality provided by different replica management algorithms, in a way that hides internal detail and only depends on aspects that are observable by the clients. The same consistency model might be offered by a system using quorums, or by a system using a group communication infrastructure, and the clients will be portable from one system to the other. We have shown examples of strong consistency models (where there is a single history of the sequential data type that is compatible with all the observations made by clients in the replicated system's execution) and weaker models, where different clients, or even different operations of one client, have different justifications in terms of other operations which seem to have happened first. We have considered two styles for defining a consistency model, either using properties of the orderings of operations, or a state-transition model for an ideal system which can generate the required observations. In either style, however, we do not mention the actual implementation details of sites, replicas, and messages. Many of the consistency models include special operations that are used for synchronization between clients (some, such as transaction begin and commit operations, do nothing else and are treated as no-ops on the sequential data type, while in some models synchronization is an extra feature on some operations such as reads or writes that affect the sequential data type). Another axis on which models vary is the session properties, which enforce some amount of ordering between activities at a single client; an example is a requirement to keep the effect of all the clients' own earlier writes evident in any value seen by that client.

We hope that whenever another chapter of this book describes a replica management algorithm, the reader will find it useful to think about what functionality is being given, by identifying how the system fits into the framework of consistency models we have explained.

Acknowledgements We thank Shirley Goldrei for careful proofreading.

References

1. Adve, S.V., Gharachorloo, K.: Shared memory consistency models: A tutorial. Computer 29(12), 66–76 (1996)
2. Afek, Y., Brown, G., Merritt, M.: A lazy cache algorithm. In: SPAA '89: Proceedings of the first annual ACM symposium on Parallel algorithms and architectures, pp. 209–222. ACM Press, New York (1989)
3. Alonso, R., Barbará, D., Garcia-Molina, H., Abad, S.: Quasi-copies: Efficient data sharing for information retrieval systems. In: Schmidt, J.W., Missikoff, M., Ceri, S. (eds.) EDBT 1988. LNCS, vol. 303, pp. 443–468. Springer, Heidelberg (1988)
4. Berenson, H., Bernstein, P., Gray, J., Melton, J., O'Neil, E., O'Neil, P.: A critique of ansi sql isolation levels. In: SIGMOD '95: Proceedings of the 1995 ACM SIGMOD international conference on Management of Data, pp. 1–10. ACM Press, New York (1995)
5. Bernstein, P.A., Goodman, N.: Serializability theory for replicated databases. J. Comput. Syst. Sci. 31(3), 355–374 (1985)
6. Demers, A.J., Greene, D.H., Hauser, C., Irish, W., Larson, J., Shenker, S., Sturgis, H.E., Swinehart, D.C., Terry, D.B.: Epidemic algorithms for replicated database maintenance. In: Proc ACM Conference on Principles of Distributed Computing (PODC'87), pp. 1–12 (1987)
7. Gibbons, P.B., Merritt, M., Gharachorloo, K.: Proving sequential consistency of high-performance shared memories (extended abstract). In: SPAA '91: Proceedings of the third annual ACM symposium on Parallel algorithms and architectures, pp. 292–303. ACM Press, New York (1991)
8. Herlihy, M.P., Wing, J.M.: Linearizability: a correctness condition for concurrent objects. ACM Trans. Program. Lang. Syst. 12(3), 463–492 (1990)
9. Ladin, R., Liskov, B., Shrira, L., Ghemawat, S.: Providing high availability using lazy replication. ACM Trans. Comput. Syst. 10(4), 360–391 (1992)
10. Lamport, L.: How to make a multiprocessor computer that correctly executes multiprocess programm. IEEE Trans. Comput. 28(9), 690–691 (1979)
11. Lamport, L.: Time, clocks, and the ordering of events in a distributed system. Commun. ACM 21(7), 558–565 (1978)
12. Liskov, B., Zilles, S.: Specification techniques for data abstractions. SIGPLAN Not. 10(6), 72–87 (1975)
13. Manson, J., Pugh, W., Adve, S.V.: The java memory model. SIGPLAN Not. 40(1), 378–391 (2005)
14. Park, S., Dill, D.L.: An executable specification and verifier for relaxed memory order. IEEE Trans. Comput. 48(2), 227–235 (1999)
15. Ramamritham, K., Chrysanthis, P.K.: A taxonomy of correctness criteria in database applications. The VLDB Journal 5(1), 85–97 (1996)
16. Saito, Y., Shapiro, M.: Optimistic replication. Comput. Surveys 37(1), 42–81 (2005)
17. Steinke, R.C., Nutt, G.J.: A unified theory of shared memory consistency. J. ACM 51(5), 800–849 (2004)
18. Terry, D.B., Demers, A.J., Petersen, K., Spreitzer, M.J., Theimer, M.M., Welch, B.B.: Session guarantees for weakly consistent replicated data. In: PDIS '94: Proceedings of the third international conference on on Parallel and distributed information systems, pp. 140–150. IEEE Computer Society Press, Los Alamitos (1994)
19. Vogels, W.: Eventually consistent. Commun. ACM 52(1), 40–44 (2009)

Chapter 2
Replication Techniques for Availability

Robbert van Renesse and Rachid Guerraoui

Abstract The chapter studies how to provide clients with access to a replicated object that is logically indistinguishable from accessing a single yet highly available object. We study this problem under two different models. In the first, we assume that failures can be detected accurately. In the second we drop this assumption, making the model more realistic but also significantly more challenging. Under the first model, we present the primary-backup and chain replication techniques. Under the second model, we present techniques based on voting. We conclude with a discussion on reconfiguration.

2.1 Introduction

Replication is creating multiple copies of a possibly mutating object (file, file system, database, and so on) with the objective to provide high availability, high integrity, high performance, or any combination thereof. For high availability and integrity, the replicas need to be diverse, so failures are sufficiently independent. For high performance, there just needs to be a sufficient number of replicas in order to meet the load imposed on the replicated object.

In this chapter, we will focus on replication techniques that ensure high availability. In particular, we will study techniques that provide clients with access to a replicated object that is logically indistinguishable from accessing a single (non-replicated), yet highly available, object. This "indistinguishable from a single object" property is sometimes called linearizability, one-copy semantics, or simply consistency, and is ensured by enforcing a total order on client operations. Of course, such a strategy can only work under a restricted failure model. For example, if failed communication links partition the replicas, then it may be impossible to provide both availability and consistency for an object.

B. Charron-Bost, F. Pedone, and A. Schiper (Eds.): Replication, LNCS 5959, pp. 19–40, 2010.
© Springer-Verlag Berlin Heidelberg 2010

While a number of different replication techniques exists, two different approaches have become particularly well-known: *active replication* and *passive replication*. In active replication, also known as *state machine replication*, client operations are ordered by an ordering protocol and directly forwarded to a collection of replicas. Each replica individually executes the operation. Keeping the replicas consistent requires that processing be *deterministic*: given the same client operation and the same state, the same state update is produced by each replica.

In passive replication, also known as *primary-backup replication*, one of the replicas is designated *primary*. It executes the operations and sends the resulting state updates to each of the replicas (including itself), which, passively, apply the state updates in the order received. Note that in passive replication it is not necessary that operations be deterministic—typically, the primary will resolve non-determinism and produce state updates, which are deterministic.

These approaches have various advantages and drawbacks when compared with one another. If operations are compute intensive, then active replication can waste computational resources, but if state updates are large, passive replication can waste network bandwidth. Active replication cannot deal with non-deterministic processing but can mask failures without performance degradation, while passive replication may involve a detection and recovery delay in case the primary crashes.

Various hybrid solutions that combine both approaches are common. Some processing is executed on just one replica, while other processing is performed by all replicas. They are neither purely active nor passive approaches, and face different trade-offs.

This chapter avoids discussion of how operations are processed. Instead, it models an object's state by the sequence of operations. For example, if the object represents a bank account, we keep track of the history of deposit and withdraw operations, rather than of the running total. Doing so makes is easier to talk about consistency, as we can compare histories stored at different replicas and determine if one is a prefix of the other, or not. If all we had is a running total, then such a comparison would be impossible.

The chapter is organized as follows. In Section 2.2 we will present a convenient model of an unreplicated object. Then, using this model, we will describe two replication techniques that assume a simple failure model in Section 2.3. In Section 2.4 we will make the failure model more realistic (and more challenging) while discussing how to adapt the replication techniques accordingly. Section 2.5 discusses approaches for reconfiguring a replicated object. Finally, Section 2.6 concludes with a brief comparison of the techniques discussed in this chapter.

2.2 Model

For simplicity, we will assume that there is only one object. We find it convenient to model an object as a finite sequence of uniquely identified *deltas*, $H = \langle d_1, d_2, ..., d_b \rangle$, encoding a history of b updates applied to the object. A delta is a tuple $(update\ identifier, operation)$. A particular update identifier can only appear once in the history, although two different deltas may well contain the same operation. A client may add a delta by invoking updateHist (*operation*). The update identifier for the delta is automatically generated. An invocation of updateHist (*operation*) is expected to return a new history that can be used to compute the response of the operation.

While convenient for specification, in practice most services would not maintain the history of operations, but instead only the state resulting from applying the operations to a well-defined initial state, while updateHist () would normally return a simple result.

2.2.1 Environment

We also have to define a model of the distributed environment. Initially we will assume that processors are *fail-stop* [17]. More specifically:

- a processor follows its specification until it crashes (we say it is faulty);
- a crashed processor does not perform any action (*e.g.*, does not recover);
- a crash is detected eventually by every correct (non-crashed) processor;
- no process is suspected of having crashed until after it actually crashes.

The environment is assumed to be asynchronous: message delays and processing delays are arbitrarily long, and clocks on the processors are not synchronized.

We assume the processors are totally ordered: $p_1 < p_2 < \dots$. We also assume that the network is point-to-point and FIFO:

- messages from the same source are delivered in the order sent;
- messages between correct processors are eventually delivered.

2.2.2 Specification

In the unreplicated case, a single server stores the history of the object. Figure 2.1 depicts the specification (pseudo-code) for the client and the server. The specification distinguishes the function that can be invoked by the application (updateHist (*operation*)) and the events that can be invoked by the underlying system.

In the face of concurrency, functions and events act like monitors: on a processor only one thread of control can execute at a time. By invoking **wait until** *condition* the thread releases control until the condition is satisfied. Examples of events include failure notifications and receipt of messages.

Function updateHist (*op*) generates a unique identifier (typically consisting of a client identifier and a sequence number incremented for each request), and then sends a request message to the server. The response from the server contains the unique identifier, as well as the server's copy of the history, and is added to the set *responses*. The client waits until the request identifier appears among the *responses* or until the server is reported having failed. The server simply adds a delta to the history for each new update request and returns the resulting history.

(a) **Client code**

```
var server initially "server address";
var responses initially ∅;

event failure (p) :
    if p = server then  server := ⊥;

event receive ("response", r) from p :
    responses := responses ∪ {(p,r)};

function updateHist (op) :
    if server ≠ ⊥ then
        uid := genUID ();
        send ("updateHist", (uid,op)) to server;
        wait until (·,(uid,·)) ∈ responses ∨ server = ⊥ ;
        if ∃_H (·,(uid,H)) ∈ responses then  return H;
    end
    return ERROR("unavailable");
```

(b) **Server code**

```
var H initially ⊥;

event receive ("updateHist", (uid,op)) from client :
    H := H :: (uid,op);
    send ("response", (uid,H)) to client;
```

Fig. 2.1 Code for an unreplicated object.

The code for the unreplicated case serves as the specification of the semantics that we want to preserve when replicating the object onto multiple servers. From this specification one may derive that:

- Consider any two invocations updateHist (op_1) and updateHist (op_2) that return respectively histories H_1 and H_2. Either H_1 is a strict prefix of H_2 or vice versa.
- Furthermore, if updateHist (op_1) returns before updateHist (op_2) is invoked, then H_1 is a prefix of H_2.

Note that a client can also use updateHist () to query the state of the object by submitting a no-op update. We will look at optimizations for read-only operations in Section 2.3.3.

2.3 Fail-Stop Failure Model

The basic approach to replicating an object is as follows:

1. allocate a collection of processors (also called servers) $p_1, ..., p_n$;
2. place an empty history H_i on each p_i;
3. add updates in the same order to each H_i.

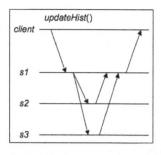

Primary-Backup

A client sends requests to the minimum server. The minimum server forwards the request to the other servers and awaits responses before responding to the client.

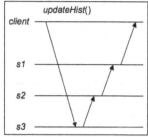

Chain Replication

A client sends update requests to the maximum server (*head*), which forwards the request to the next lower server until it reaches the minimum server (*tail*). The tail responds to the client.

Fig. 2.2 Normal case message patterns for Primary-Backup and Chain Replication.

In the following, we present two replication techniques, assuming a fail-stop model of the environment: *Primary-Backup* and *Chain Replication*, which are summarized in Figure 2.2.

2.3.1 Primary-Backup

In Primary-Backup (PB) [1, 3], perhaps the most common replication method in use today, the processor that has not crashed and that has the lowest identifier is designated *primary*. The remaining correct processors are called *backups*. During normal operation, a client sends an "updateHist" request to the primary and receives a response from the primary.

The client code (Figure 2.3) is similar to the unreplicated case, except that clients deal with the case of a failed primary. If the primary fails, the client determines the new primary to whom it retransmits its update. The client continues to do so until it receives a response or until there are no servers left.

Figure 2.4 shows the server code. We describe the underlying steps below.

1. Upon receipt of an "updateHist" request, the server may conclude correctly that it is the primary (because of accurate failure detection). If it had not yet detected the crash of a former primary itself, then it can do so now by removing all servers below itself from the list of servers that it maintains.
2. Next the server checks to see if the delta corresponding to the "updateHist" request is already in the history. This is possible because the primary may have

```
var servers initially {p₁,...,pₙ};
var responses initially ∅;

event failure (p) :
    servers := servers\{p}

event receive ("response", r) from p :
    responses := responses ∪ {(p,r)};

function updateHist (op) :
    uid := genUID ();
    repeat
        if servers = ∅ then return ERROR("unavailable");
        primary := min(servers);
        send ("updateHist", (uid,op)) to primary;
        wait until (·,(uid,·)) ∈ responses ∨ primary ∉ servers ;
        if ∃_H (·,(uid,H)) ∈ responses then
            return H;
    end
```

Fig. 2.3 Client code for an object replicated using Primary-Backup.

received the update when it was still a backup. In the normal case, however, the delta is not in the history.

3. In either case, the primary sends a "sync" request containing the primary's desired history to all backups.
4. A backup, upon receipt of a "sync" request, first updates its estimate of the list of correct servers by removing all servers that are below the source of the request, i.e., the current primary.
5. The backup verifies that indeed the request came from the primary (minimum server on its list), as the request might be a tardy message from a server that was primary but that has since crashed. If the request came from a current server (which must be the primary), then the backup updates its history and sends a response.
6. When the primary received responses from all current backups, it updates its own copy of the history and sends the result as a response to the client.

It is important that the server does not respond to the client until after the server received responses from all available backups. To see why, say a client submits an "updateHist" request to the primary, and the primary adds the corresponding delta to its history and responds. If the server crashes before sending a "sync" request to the backups, the update may be lost even though the client receives a response. A new client will contact a new primary and miss the previous update, violating one-copy semantics.

The primary is allowed to stream multiple updates to the backups, without waiting for responses between updates. This allows for higher throughput. An important invariant of PB replication, however, is that whenever the primary responds to the client, the history of the primary is a prefix of the histories held by the backups. By implication, a response received by the client reflects a history that is stored at all

```
const me = "my address";
var H initially ⊥;
var servers initially {p₁, ..., pₙ};
var responses initially ∅;

event failure (p) :
    servers := servers\{p}

event receive ("response", r) from p :
    responses := responses ∪ {(p, r)};

event receive ("sync", (H', uid)) from primary :
    ∀p ∈ servers : p < primary ⇒ servers := servers\{p};
    if primary ∈ servers then
        H := H';
        send ("response", uid) to primary;
    end

function sync (H') :
    uid₂ := genUID ();
    ∀p ∈ servers : send("sync", (uid₂, H')) to p;
    wait until ∀p ∈ servers : (p, uid₂) ∈ responses ;

event receive ("updateHist", (uid, op)) from client :
    ∀p ∈ servers : p < me ⇒ servers := servers\{p};
    H' := if (uid, ·) ∉ H then H :: (uid, op) else H ;
    sync (H') ;
    H := H';
    send ("response", (uid, H)) to client;
```

Fig. 2.4 Server code for an object replicated using Primary-Backup.

available replicas. Without this invariant, a future "sync" request by a new primary might remove the client's update, violating consistency guarantees.

For simplicity, a "sync" request sends the entire history from the primary to the backup. In practice it is usually sufficient to send the update along with a collision-resistant hash of the history prior to applying the update. On receipt, a server checks to make sure that the hash matches its history, and if so appends the update. In the rare case that there is no match (which is possible in certain failure scenarios), then the primary and the backup have to synchronize the entire history using additional messages.

Why It Works

Consider first liveness (*i.e.*, the property that each updateHist() operation eventually terminates) and assume there is at least one correct replica. Suppose by contradiction that a correct client submits an "updateHist" request and never receives any response. Consider now the time after which all faulty replicas have crashed. By the fail-stop model, there is a time after which a correct primary is elected and known as such to the client. (Such a primary exists for we assume at least one correct replica). The client eventually submits its request to this correct primary. This primary sends its "sync" message to all correct backups, which eventually respond. The primary responds back to the client: a contradiction.

For safety (*i.e.*, linearizability), suppose two invocations updateHist (op_1) and updateHist (op_2) return respectively histories H_1 and H_2. If both return results from the same primary, then clearly one is a prefix of the other. Moreover, H_1 is a prefix of H_2 if updateHist (op_2) is invoked after updateHist (op_1) has returned. Now assume they came from two primaries, p_1 returning H_1, and then p_2 returning H_2, such that $p_1 < p_2$. This means p_2 became primary only after p_1 crashed. For p_1 to return H_1, p_1 had to make sure all backups have acknowledged, and thus stored, H_1. No matter which processes become primary subsequently, all histories of p_2 must have H_1 as a prefix, including H_2.

For a complete treatment of the Primary-Backup technique and its correctness under various failure models, see [3].

2.3.2 Chain Replication

In Chain Replication (CR) [16], the servers are organized in a chain with a *head* (the maximum server) and a *tail* (the minimum server). A client sends update requests to the head, which forwards the request along the chain towards the tail. The tail responds to the client.

Figures 2.5 and 2.6 show the pseudo-code. Function predecessor (*servers*, p), returns the smallest $p' \in$ *servers* larger than p, or $\perp$ if p is the largest element in *servers*. Similarly, function successor (*servers*, p) returns the largest $p' \in$ *servers* smaller than p, or $\perp$ if p is the smallest element. As in PB replication, we have simplified the presentation by sending the entire history along the chain instead of only a collision-resistant hash and the update.

The CR technique simplifies the server code compared to PB replication. In particular, it is never necessary for a server to wait for other servers. An "updateHist" request received by the head can be applied immediately to the local history, forwarded (as a "sync" request) to the next server, and then forgotten. The head is responsible for ordering requests as they arrive from clients, but otherwise just serves as a backup. When a "sync" request arrives at the tail, the tail applies the update just like the other servers on the chain. Knowing that the update is now applied to all non-crashed replicas, the tail can respond to the client, finishing the entire update request.

No complicated recovery is necessary after a server fails. All that is necessary is for servers to keep track of who their successor and predecessor are. For this, the servers use two techniques. First, failure notification allow servers to update their estimate of the list of correct servers. Second, a server can make deductions based on the messages that it receives. For example, if a replica receives an update request from a client, the replica knows that any predecessors on the chain must have failed and that it is now the head of the chain.

In the face of failures, a client may have to retransmit an outstanding update request. Because an update can get lost anywhere in the chain, the client code of Figure 2.5 implements this by periodically retransmitting until a response is received.

```
const T = retransmission delay;
var servers initially {p₁,...,pₙ};
var responses initially ∅;

event failure (p) :
    servers := servers\{p}

event receive ("response", r) from p :
    responses := responses ∪ {(p,r)};

function updateHist (op) :
    uid := genUID ();
    repeat
        if servers = ∅ then return ERROR("unavailable");
        head := max(servers);
        send ("updateHist", (uid,op)) to head;
        wait up to T seconds until (·,(uid,·)) ∈ responses;
        if ∃_H (·,(uid,H)) ∈ responses then
            return H;
    end
```

Fig. 2.5 Client code for an object replicated using Chain Replication.

The time between retransmissions is defined by a constant T, which in practice should be set to a value so that most responses are expected to be received within that amount of time. There is a trade-off: if T is set too short, unnecessary retransmissions would create additional load. On the other hand, the larger T, the longer it takes to recover from a failure. However, the actual value of T does not affect correctness.

As in PB replication, multiple update requests can be streamed for increased throughput. The important invariant maintained by the chain is that for any two servers, the history of the server with the lower identifier is a prefix of the server with the higher identifier. This is true at any point in time, even in the face of crashes, and thus simplifies recovery with respect to Primary-Backup.

Why It Works

The liveness and safety arguments are similar to those of PB replication. Assume there is at least one correct replica and consider a correct client that submits an "updateHist" request and never receives any response. Consider the time after which all faulty replicas have crashed and the chain is stable. The client eventually submits its request to the head and eventually gets a response from the tail (possibly the head and the tail are the same replica if only one server is correct): a contradiction.

For safety, suppose invocations updateHist (op_1) and updateHist (op_2) return histories H_1 and H_2 resp. If both return results from the same tail, then clearly one is a prefix of the other. Moreover, H_1 is a prefix of H_2 if updateHist (op_2) is invoked after updateHist (op_1) has returned. Now assume they came from two tails, p_1 returning H_1 and p_2 returning H_2, such that $p_1 < p_2$. This means p_2

```
const me = "my address";
var H initially ⊥;
var servers initially {p₁,...,pₙ};

event failure (p) :
    servers := servers\{p}

event receive ("sync", (H′,client,uid)) from prev :
    ∀p ∈ servers : me < p < prev ⇒ servers := servers\{p};
    if prev = predecessor (servers, me) then
        H := H′;
        sync (H,client,uid);
    end

function sync (H′,client,uid) :
    next = successor (servers, me);
    if next ≠ ⊥ then
        send ("sync", (H′,client,uid)) to next;
    else
        send ("response", (uid,H)) to client;
    end

event receive ("updateHist", (uid,op)) from client :
    ∀p ∈ servers : p > me ⇒ servers := servers\{p};
    if (uid,·) ∉ H then H := H :: (uid,op);
    sync (H,client,uid);
```

Fig. 2.6 Server code for an object replicated using Chain Replication.

became tail only after p_1 crashed. Because of the invariant discussed above, at the time p_1 crashed p_2's history must have H_1 as a prefix. From there on, all histories of p_2 must have had H_1 as a prefix, including H_2.

For a complete treatment of Chain Replication and its correctness under the fail-stop model, see [16].

2.3.3 Queries

In many cases, one would like to distinguish *query operations*, operations that do not modify the state of the object, and optimize their performance. We explain below how this can be achieved in both PB and CR.

We provide a function queryHist() through which a client can consult a history without modifying it. The pseudo-code for the unreplicated case is depicted in Figure 2.7.

The queryHist() function also generates a unique identifier and sends a message to the server. The server simply returns the history for query operations. The following properties are now also ensured:

- Consider any two invocations (updateHist (op) or queryHist ()) that return respectively histories H_1 and H_2. Either H_1 is a strict prefix of H_2 or vice et versa. Furthermore, if the first invocation returns before the second is invoked, then H_1 is a prefix of H_2.

(a) **Client code**

```
function queryHist () :
    if server ≠ ⊥ then
        uid := genUID ();
        send ("queryHist", uid) to server;
        wait until (·, (uid, ·)) ∈ responses ∨ server = ⊥ ;
        if ∃_H (·, (uid, H)) ∈ responses then return H;
    end
    return ERROR("unavailable");
```

(b) **Server code**

```
event receive ("queryHist", uid) from client :
    send ("response", (uid, H)) to client;
```

Fig. 2.7 Code for the query function of an unreplicated object.

(a) **Client code**

```
function queryHist () :
    uid := genUID ();
    repeat
        if servers = ∅ then return ERROR("unavailable");
        primary := min(servers);
        send ("queryHist", uid) to primary;
        wait until (·, (uid, H)) ∈ responses ∨ primary ∉ servers ;
        if ∃_H (·, (uid, H)) ∈ responses then
            return H;
    end
```

(b) **Server code**

```
var first initially true;

event receive ("queryHist", uid) from client :
    ∀p ∈ servers : p < me ⇒ servers := servers\{p};
    if first then
        sync(H);
        first := false;
    end
    send ("response", (uid, H)) to client;
```

Fig. 2.8 Code for the query function of a replicated object using Primary-Backup.

In PB, during normal operation, a client c sends requests ("updateHist" or "query-Hist") to the primary and receives responses from the primary. The client code for PB's queryHist function is given in Figure 2.8(a). Figure 2.8(b) shows the server code. Both are almost the same as in the unreplicated case. Normally the primary can respond immediately. There is, however, a special case. If a server that used to be a backup but is now a primary receives a request for the first time, it must synchronize its state with that of the other backups. The reason for this is that the current

(a) **Client code**

```
function queryHist() :
    uid := genUID();
    repeat
        if servers = ∅ then return ERROR("unavailable");
        tail := min(servers);
        send("queryHist", uid) to tail;
        wait until (·,(uid,·)) ∈ responses ∨ tail ∉ servers ;
        if ∃_H (·,(uid,H)) ∈ responses then
            return H;
    end
```

(b) **Server code**

```
event receive("queryHist", uid) from client :
    ∀p ∈ servers : p < me ⇒ servers := servers\{p};
    send("response", (uid,H)) to client;
```

Fig. 2.9 Code for the query function of an object replicated using Chain Replication.

primary may have received deltas from the former primary that are not included in some of the backup servers. If they would be reflected in the response to the client, a crash of this new primary could lose deltas that a client has seen. Synchronizing state on the first query operation ensures that the backups have the same state as the primary.

Figure 2.9 shows the client and server code for the queryHist function in the context of Chain Replication. It is the tail that responds to the client. The tail handles a query request in much the same way as in the unreplicated case, responding immediately to the client. Unlike update requests, the client need only interact with the tail of the chain for queries.

2.4 Crash Failure Model

So far we assumed a fail-stop model. In particular, (1) if a server fails, all processes (clients and servers) eventually detect the failure, and (2) no process detects the failure of a server unless that server has actually failed. It is common to call this *perfect failure detection* [4]. In practice, failure detection is achieved using timeouts: Every server is periodically pinged and if it does not respond within a predetermined time period, the failure of the server is suspected. Unfortunately, unless there is a known bound on message latency, such a mechanism does not implement perfect failure detection. While crashes are correctly detected eventually, correct servers may be falsely suspected.

False failure detections might partition the distributed system into two disjoint subsets each containing clients and servers, that is, the processes in each of the subsets might wrongly consider those in the other subset as having failed. In each partition, the processes might elect a primary under PB replication (resp. construct a chain in CR) and clients in different partitions might see divergent histories as a result. For instance, one client might deposit an amount of money in an account after accessing the first partition, and, later, another client, which accesses the same account but within the other partition, might not see the deposited amount.

To avoid such inconsistencies, implementations of Primary-Backup and Chain Replication have to use large timeouts to make the probability of false detection low. The larger the timeout period, the larger the response time of a request directly following a failure. Setting the timeout period low increases the probability of false detections. This is not a good trade-off, and thus it would be better if we devised a replication technique that can tolerate false detections.

In this section, we present replication techniques that do not attempt to detect failures; instead the techniques seamlessly mask failures altogether. The first such technique is Stake Replication. The second technique, Broker Replication, builds on the first. Both techniques are summarized in Figure 2.10. Before describing the techniques in more detail, we will briefly review the quorum concept.

2.4.1 Quorums

Consistency and availability of a replicated object can be preserved in the face of false failure detections using a mathematical abstraction called *quorums* [18, 9, 19]. A quorum system is a set of subsets of processes, each called a quorum, such that the following properties are satisfied (see [8, 14] for more formal treatments):

Consistency: any two quorums intersect in at least one process;
Availability: at least one of the quorums (which ones is unknown) contains processes that never crash.

A simple instantiation of quorums is the following. There are n processes, of which fewer than $n/2$ are allowed to crash. Quorums then are all sets that have $\lceil \frac{n+1}{2} \rceil$ processes. It is easy to verify that this construction satisfies Consistency and Availability.

2.4.2 Stake Replication

In Stake Replication (SR), the division of labor between clients and servers is much different from before. The servers are still responsible for ordering client operations and making sure that there is a persistent history of deltas. They do so, for each position in the history, by voting on what the next delta should be. Once a quorum of servers voted for the same delta, then the delta is decided and permanent. However, servers not in that quorum may have voted differently or not at all. This is the case for every individual delta, and thus none of the servers knows what the history is. They only know how they voted for each delta.

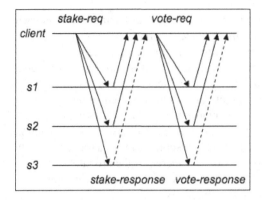

Stake Replication

A client broadcasts first a "stake-request" to all servers. Upon successful completing, the client requests all servers to vote.

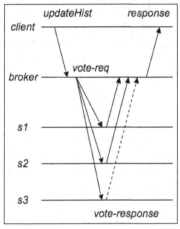

Broker Replication

A client sends an update request to a broker. Brokers use an optimized version of Stake Replication (eliminating "stake-request" messages in the common case) before responding to clients.

Fig. 2.10 Normal case message patterns for Stake Replication and Broker Replication.

In the SR implementation that we will present, the clients reconstruct the history from examining the votes rather than by obtaining the history directly from the servers as before. The servers do not communicate with one another; they only respond to requests from clients. Because the technique uses quorums, the technique can tolerate at most $\lfloor (n-1)/2 \rfloor$ failures given n servers.

Figures 2.11 to 2.13 show the code for Stake Replication. The updateHist() function, in Figure 2.11, simply invokes another function consensus() for each delta in the history. The client passes the desired delta to consensus(), but because of concurrent updates introduced by other clients, the actual delta added to the history may be different from the desired one. The client repeats until the desired delta has been successfully added to the history, and then the function can return the history.

The secret sauce is in the client's consensus() function of Figure 2.12 and the server code of Figure 2.13. Define *version* to be the length of the history, $|H|$. The consensus protocol only deals with one version at a time. Within a version,

```
var H initially ⊥;
function updateHist (op) :
    uid := genUID();
    repeat
        delta := consensus (|H|, uid, op) ;
        H := H :: delta;
        if delta = (uid, op) then
            return H;
    end
```

Fig. 2.11 Client code for Stake Replication, part 1.

there is a notion of logical time that we call *stakes*. A stake is a tuple consisting of a round number and the identifier of the client that owns the stake, so that two different clients cannot own the same stake. Stakes are lexicographically ordered, first by round, and then by client identifier.

A *vote* is a tuple consisting of a stake and a delta. In the implementation that we are describing, the client that owns the stake picks the delta, and therefore guarantees that two votes with the same stake will also have the same delta. The objective of a client is to get a quorum of servers to vote on the same stake and delta. We say that a vote is *decided* when this objective is reached. The consensus protocol runs in a loop, trying monotonically increasing stakes, until its corresponding vote is decided.

Each server maintains a stake and a vote for each version. In each iteration of the client's loop, the client first creates a new stake and tries to get a quorum of servers to progress to that particular stake. For this, the client broadcasts a "stake-request" message to all servers, containing the current version and the stake. Upon receipt, the server checks to see what stake it is at for that particular version. If the client's stake is further along, then the server advances its stake accordingly. In any case, it returns the stake that it now holds, as well as its last vote for that version. The client waits until it has received more than $n/2$ responses to ensure that it has responses from a quorum of servers.. Because fewer than $n/2$ are faulty, it will eventually receive a sufficient number of responses. Also, all servers that respond have advanced their stake to at least the client's stake.

The client now determines the maximum stake among the responses. If this maximum is further along than the client's, then the client declares failure, and tries again with a new stake. However, if all servers are at the client's stake, then the client tries to get all servers to vote using its current stake. However, for reasons explained below, it cannot just use the delta that it is trying to add to the history. Instead, it determines among the responses from the servers the maximum vote (that is, the vote with the maximum stake). If that maximum vote is $((0,0), \perp)$, meaning that no server has voted as of yet, then the client can use its own delta. But if not, the client uses the delta with the maximum stake.

Subsequently, the client tries to get all servers to vote on its selected delta for the given stake by broadcasting a "vote-request" message. Each server, upon re-

```
const servers = {p₁,...,pₙ};
const me = genUID();
var sResponses initially ∅;
var vResponses initially ∅;

event receive ("stake-response", r) from p :
    sResponses := sResponses ∪ {(p,r)};

event receive ("vote-response", r) from p :
    vResponses := vResponses ∪ {(p,r)};

function staked (version, stake) :
    return {(p,(vn,s,s',vote)) ∈ sResponses | vn = version ∧ s = stake};

function voted (version, stake) :
    return {(p,(vn,s,c)) ∈ vResponses | vn = version ∧ s = stake};

function consensus (version, uid, op) :
    round := 0;
    repeat
        stake := (round, me);
        broadcast ("stake-request", (version, stake)) to servers;
        wait until |staked (stake)| > n/2 ;
        S := staked (stake);
        maxStake := max{s' | (p,(vn,s,s',vote)) ∈ S};
        if stake = maxStake then
            maxVote := max{vote | (p,(vn,s,s',vote)) ∈ S};
            if maxVote = ((0,0),⊥) then
                delta := (uid,op);
            else
                delta := maxVote.delta;
            broadcast ("vote-request", (version, stake, delta)) to servers;
            wait until |voted (stake)| > n/2 ;
            V := {(p,(vn,s,c)) ∈ voted (stake) | c = ACCEPTED};
            if |V| > n/2 then
                return delta;
        end
        round := maxStake.round + 1;
    end
```

Fig. 2.12 Client code for Stake Replication, part 2.

ceipt, checks to see if it has not advanced its stake (because of a concurrent "stake-request" by another client). If so, the server votes as requested and responds with an ACCEPTED message. If the server did advance its stake, the server abstains from voting and responds DENIED. The client again waits for more than $n/2$ responses. If more than $n/2$ servers accepted the vote, then the vote is decided and consensus() returns the corresponding delta. If not, the client tries again with a new stake.

Why It Works

Again, we consider both liveness and safety. This technique, in fact, cannot guarantee termination of updateHist(), because two clients can alternate advancing

```
var stakes[] initially (0,0);
var votes[] initially ((0,0),⊥);

event receive ("stake-request", (vn,s)) from client :
    if s > stakes[vn] then
        stakes[vn] := s;
    send ("stake-response", (vn,s,stakes[vn],votes[vn])) to client;

event receive ("vote-request", (vn,s,vote)) from client :
    if s = stakes[vn] then
        votes[vn] := vote;
        send ("vote-response", (vn,s,ACCEPTED)) to client;
    else
        send ("vote-response", (vn,s,DENIED)) to client;
```

Fig. 2.13 Server code for Stake Replication.

stakes for a version without ever getting the servers to vote for one of their stakes. Indeed, no replication protocol can be designed that is guaranteed to terminate (a consequence of [7]). However, we can show that in the absence of contention, the protocol that we described is guaranteed to terminate.

To wit, consider any particular version, and assume only one client is active. It will send a "stake-request" to all servers, and wait for a response from more than $n/2$ servers. Because fewer than $n/2$ servers are faulty, eventually it will receive the required responses. If some of the servers have advanced further than the client, the client chooses a new stake that is further than any in the responses. Because there are no other clients active by assumption, eventually the client will be able to advance its stake sufficiently far along so that more than $n/2$ of the servers will advance to the client's stake and no further. At this point the subsequent "vote-request" is also guaranteed to succeed, with all servers accepting the stake and delta selected by the client.

For safety, we have to make sure that no two votes, with different deltas, can be decided for the same version. Stake Replication guarantees safety through the following invariant: if a vote (s,v) is decided, then any vote (s',v') (decided or not) with $s' > s$ has $v' = v$. This invariant depends on two important features of the protocol. First, when a client receives responses to its "stake-request" from a quorum of servers, it knows that the servers that responded can no longer vote using lower stakes than the one it requested. Second, it also collected for those servers the maximum stake that they voted on thus far. If any vote has decided, then, by quorum intersection, the responses must include a response from one of those servers. By clients always selecting the maximum vote, the invariant is guaranteed. If the maximum vote is $((0,0),⊥)$, it is guaranteed that no stake lower than the client's can have decided, and thus the client is free to choose any delta in that case, without fear of violating the invariant.

For good examples and treatments of Stake Replication techniques, see [6, 11].

```
var H initially ⊥;
var requests initially ∅;

event receive ("updateHist", delta) from client :
    requests := requests ∪ {(client, delta)};

function mainLoop () :
    repeat
        wait until requests ≠ ∅ ;
        r := selectOne(requests);
        requests := requests\{r};
        while r.delta ∉ H do
            delta := consensus (|H|, r.delta.uid, r.delta.op) ;
            H := H :: delta;
        end
        send ("response", (r.delta.uid, H)) to r.client;
    end
```

Fig. 2.14 Broker code for Broker Replication, which is an extension of the client code of Stake Replication.

2.4.3 Broker Replication

A disadvantage of Stake Replication is that clients need to reconstruct the history. This is inconvenient, and can involve considerable overhead. To remedy this, most SR implementations only support an "overwrite" delta, such that the last delta in a history completely determines the state of the replicated object. Then it is unnecessary to reconstruct the entire history, but only the last delta.

Broker Replication (BR) is an extension of Stake Replication that overcomes this disadvantage of SR in a different way. Unlike SR, BR does incorporate a collection of servers that maintain the state. BR is a three-tiered solution. One tier contains servers just like in Stake Replication. The middle-tier contains a set of processes that we shall call *brokers*. They run essentially the client code of SR in an infinite loop, deciding deltas and maintaining the resulting history (see Figure 2.14). The remaining tier are the ultimate clients that send requests to, and receive responses from, brokers. To tolerate f failures, the middle-tier must include $f + 1$ brokers. (To save on hardware and messages, the broker processes usually run on the same machines that are used for running server processes.)

Clients can go through any broker in order to update and access history. However, contention between brokers is avoided, and performance thus improved, if all clients used the same broker. To accomplish this, BR implementations use a weak leader election protocol to elect a leader among available brokers. The election is weak in the sense that the protocol may accidentally elect more than one leader at a time. This does not affect safety, but does affect performance and liveness.

Figure 2.15 shows a simple example of client code that uses weak leader election. The event $up(p)$ signifies that broker p is now believed to be reachable by the client, while $down(p)$ signifies that the connection between the client and p is suspicious. These events may provide mistaken information, but we assume that if a broker has

```
var brokers initially ∅;
var responses initially ∅;

event up (p) :
    brokers := brokers ∪ {p};

event down (p) :
    brokers := brokers\{p};

event receive ("response", r) from p :
    responses := responses ∪ {(p,r)};

function updateHist (op) :
    uid := genUID ();
    repeat
        wait until brokers ≠ ∅ ;
        leader := min(brokers);
        send ("updateHist", (uid,op)) to leader;
        wait until (·,(uid,·)) ∈ responses ∨ leader ∉ brokers ;
        if ∃_H (·,(uid,H)) ∈ responses then
            return H;
    end
```

Fig. 2.15 Client code for Broker Replication.

in fact crashed, then it will eventually be marked down and never up again. The client uses the broker with the minimum identifier among the brokers that it thinks are reachable.

An important optimization of the BR technique is to use a single stake for multiple operations. That is, when a broker receives an "updateHist" request, it first tries to re-use its last stake. It broadcasts a "vote-request" message to all servers. If it receives ACCEPTED responses from a quorum of servers, then the request completes and the broker can respond to the client. If not, then the broker has to establish a new stake. Assuming the weak leader election mechanism works reasonably well, establishing a stake will be a rare event.

Why It Works

Consider liveness of updateHist (). If there is a broker that never crashes, there is a lowest broker b that never crashes. If no broker lower than b completes the client's request, then b will eventually receive and execute the request. The liveness thus depends on the liveness of SR. As updates are performed by brokers, safety is inherited from the brokers as well.

Good examples of the BR technique are Viewstamped Replication [15] and Paxos [13].

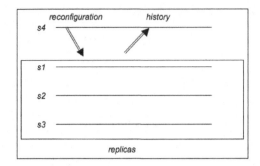

New server as a client

To join (again), a server acts as a client of the replicated system and issues a reconfiguration request.

New server is now in

Another client can now make use of the new server.

Fig. 2.16 Reconfiguration.

2.5 Recovery and Reconfiguration

So far, we assumed that a process that fails does not recover. From a practical perspective, this is too strict a limitation, especially for long lived services that need to be permanently available. One would typically seek for techniques where a replica that recovers after crashing is integrated again into the system.

In the PB and CR techniques, a failed server is removed from the configuration altogether. On the other hand, in theory, the SR technique supports reconfiguration already. If a server stores its state on disk, then a crash followed by a recovery is not technically a crash, but appears as a transient network outage during which the server could not be reached. However, some servers may never be able to recover.

We want to be able to dynamically add servers to a replicated service. A new replica needs to obtain a unique identifier. Also, except for the SR technique, each server (or broker in the case of BR) needs to obtain a copy of the current version of the history. A general way of handling configuration changes is to make the configuration part of the replicated object, and add special update operations to change the configuration [12]. A server initially acts like a client, executing the operation updateHist (ADD_SERVER(*network address*)) . The operation returns the current history, which the new server adopts as its own current history. The identifier of the server is simply the number of ADD_SERVER operations in the history, guaranteeing uniqueness. At this point, the server is fully integrated into the system.

Treating configuration update requests the same as normal update requests precisely ensures that the joining of this replica is totally ordered with other requests and this is key to ensuring consistency without hampering availability [12]. When completed, clients are informed about the new configuration (Figure 2.16). The same technique can also be used to remove servers from a configuration.

Many *group communication systems* such as Isis [2] integrate replication and reconfiguration mechanisms into a single tool for simplifying development of highly available services. For a treatment of group communication systems, see [5, 10].

Table 2.1 Comparison between the replication techniques discussed in this chapter. The table shows (normal case) latency in number of rounds, overhead in number of messages per update operation, and the number of failures tolerated. Here n is the number of servers.

technique	# rounds	# messages	# failures tolerated
PB	4	$2n$	$n-1$
CR	$n+1$	$n+1$	$n-1$
SR	4	$4n$	$\lfloor (n-1)/2 \rfloor$
BR	4	$2n$	$\lfloor (n-1)/2 \rfloor$

2.6 Conclusion

In this chapter we discussed four techniques to replication: Primary-Backup, Chain Replication, Stake Replication, and Broker Replication. Table 2.1 compares the four techniques with respect to update operations. Latency and message overheads in this table are simplified, and the extensive literature on replication techniques discusses many variants of these basic techniques. The first two are appropriate only for environments in which crash failures can be accurately detected, and depend on recovery for continued availability. The latter two techniques are significantly more robust, masking crash failures without attempting to detect them, but tolerate about half as many failures for the same number of servers.

References

1. Alsberg, P., Day, J.: A principle for resilient sharing of distributed resources. In: Proc. of the 2nd Int. Conf. on Software Engineering, pp. 627–644 (Oct. 1976)
2. Birman, K.P., Joseph, T.A.: Exploiting virtual synchrony in distributed systems. In: Proc. of the 11th ACM Symp. on Operating Systems Principles, Austin, TX, pp. 123–138 (Nov. 1987)
3. Budhiraja, N., Marzullo, K., Schneider, F., Toueg, S.: The primary-backup approach. In: Mullender, S. (ed.) Distributed systems, 2nd edn., ACM Press, New York (1993)
4. Chandra, T., Toueg, S.: Unreliable failure detectors for asynchronous systems. In: Proc. of the 11th ACM Symp. on Principles of Distributed Computing, pp. 325–340. ACM SIGOPS-SIGACT, Montreal (Aug. 1991)

5. Chockler, G., Keidar, I., Vitenberg, R.: Group communication specifications: a comprehensive study. ACM Computing Surveys 33, 427–469 (1999)
6. El Abbadi, A., Skeen, D., Cristian, F.: An efficient, fault-tolerant protocol for replicated data management. In: Proc. of the 4th ACM Symp. on Principles of Database Systems, pp. 215–229. ACM SIGACT, Portland (Mar. 1985)
7. Fischer, M., Lynch, N., Patterson, M.: Impossibility of distributed consensus with one faulty process. J. ACM 32(2), 374–382 (1985)
8. Garcia-Molina, H., Barbara, D.: How to assign votes in a distributed system. J. ACM 32(4), 841–860 (1985)
9. Gifford, D.: Weighted voting for replicated data. In: Proc. of the 7th ACM Symp. on Operating Systems Principles, pp. 150–162. ACM SIGOPS, Pacific Grove (Dec. 1979)
10. Guerraoui, R., Schiper, A.: Software-based replication for fault tolerance. IEEE Computer 30(4) (1997)
11. Herlihy, M.: A quorum consensus replication method for abstract data types. Trans. on Computer Systems 4(1), 32–53 (1986)
12. Lamport, L.: Using time instead of timeout for fault-tolerant distributed systems. Trans. on Programming Languages and Systems 6(2), 254–280 (1984)
13. Lamport, L.: The part-time parliament. Trans. on Computer Systems 16(2), 133–169 (1998)
14. Naor, M., Wool, A.: The load, capacity, and availabiliity of quorum systems. SIAM Journal on Computing 27(2), 423–447 (1998)
15. Oki, B., Liskov, B.: Viewstamped replication: A general primary-copy method to support highly-available distributed systems. In: Proc. of the 7th ACM Symp. on Principles of Distributed Computing, pp. 8–17. ACM SIGOPS-SIGACT, Ontario (Aug. 1988)
16. van Renesse, R., Schneider, F.: Chain Replication for supporting high throughput and availability. In: Sixth Symposium on Operating Systems Design and Implementation (OSDI '04), San Francisco, CA (Dec. 2004)
17. Schlichting, R., Schneider, F.: Fail-stop processors: an approach to designing fault-tolerant computing systems. Trans. on Computer Systems 1(3), 222–238 (1983)
18. Thomas, R.: A solution to the concurrency control problem for multiple copy data bases. In: Proc. of COMPCON'78, pp. 88–93 (1978)
19. Thomas, R.: A majority consensus approach to concurrency control for multiple copy database. ACM Trans. Database Syst. 4(2), 180–209 (1979)

Chapter 3
Modular Approach to Replication for Availability

Fernando Pedone and André Schiper

Abstract In this chapter, we show a modular, layered way to implement replication. This will lead us to introduce notions such as group communication primitives (atomic broadcast, generic broadcast), the consensus problem, failure detectors, and the round based model, and will allow us to better understand the challenges that underly the implementation of replication techniques. The chapter considers only benign faults.

3.1 Introduction

The goal of this chapter is to show that replication techniques can be implemented in a modular way, by relying on adequate abstractions. We will present several abstractions, starting with *group communication primitives*. A group refers here to a set of processes. If g is a group of processes with members p_1, p_2, and p_3, then a message m can be multicast to p_1, p_2, and p_3 by referring simply to g: the sender does not need to know what processes are member of g. This is similar to IP-multicast groups in the context of the UDP internet protocol, where a process can multicast a message m to a group identified by a number: the message m is sent to all processes that are members of the group. However, IP-multicast groups are not adequate for managing replication because they provide only weak guarantees. Implementing replication with strong consistency requires strong communication guarantees: reliable and ordered message transmission, neither one provided by IP-multicast. The group communication primitives that we will introduce provide such strong guarantees. We will also discuss the implementation of group communication primitives, which will lead us to introduce additional abstractions. Note that the chapter is restricted to benign faults: malicious faults (also called Byzantine faults) are not considered here.

B. Charron-Bost, F. Pedone, and A. Schiper (Eds.): Replication, LNCS 5959, pp. 41–57, 2010.

3.2 Atomic Broadcast for State Machine Replication

Consider some service replicated on three servers p_1, p_2, and p_3. With state machine replication, all servers handle client requests in the same order. In other words, state machine replication can be implemented by ensuring that all servers receive client requests in the same order. This property is provided by a group communication primitive called *atomic broadcast*, or simply *abcast*.

Consider a group g and the primitive $abcast(g,m)$, which broadcasts m to the members of g. Specifying $abcast(g,m)$ can be more or less complex, depending on the assumptions relative (i) to the properties of g, (ii) to the properties of the members of g, and (iii) to the membership of the sender process. The simplest case is the following: (i) the membership of g never changes (g is a *static* group), (ii) processes in g do not recover after a crash (called *crash-stop* model), and (iii) processes are member of at most one group and the sender process (i.e., the process that executes $abcast(g,m)$) is a member of that group. Such a model is too restrictive from a practical point of view, but has the advantage to lead to a relative simple definition of atomic broadcast. For example, the crash-stop model allows us to refer to *correct* as processes that never crash and to *faulty* as processes that are not correct. Assumption (iii) allows us to ignore g and simply refer to $abcast(m)$.

With the assumptions (i), (ii) and (iii) we can define atomic broadcast by $abcast(m)$ and $adeliver(m)$ that satisfy the following properties [13] ([1] for the last property)[1]:

- *Validity*: If a correct process abcasts message m, then it eventually adelivers m.
- *Uniform agreement*: If a process adelivers message m, then all correct processes eventually adeliver m.
- *Uniform integrity*: For any message m, every process adelivers m at most once, and only if m was previously abcast.
- *Uniform total order*: If some process adelivers message m before message m', then every process p adelivers m' only after it has adelivered m.

Atomic broadcast is also called *total order broadcast*. Note that atomic broadcast does not ensure FIFO ordering of messages: if p executes $abcast(m)$ and then $abcast(m')$, message m' may be adelivered before m. The FIFO property can be added to the four properties above, which leads to *FIFO atomic broadcast*.

State machine replication is easy to implement with atomic broadcast: clients simply send their requests using abcast (see Figure 3.1(a)), and wait for the first reply (other replies are identical and can be ignored). The reader may observe that the use of atomic broadcast illustrated on Figure 3.1(a) violates assumption (iii), since the sender is not member of the group. Figure 3.1(b) shows a use of atomic broadcast that is consistent with (iii): the client sends its request to one of the server replicas, which invokes atomic broadcast.

---

[1] Actually, the primitive defined here is called *uniform* atomic broadcast. For simplicity, we call it atomic broadcast.

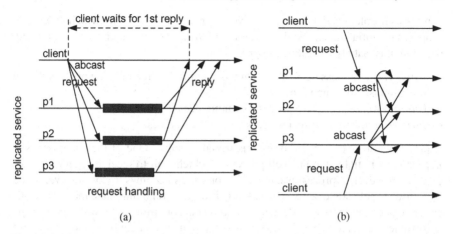

Fig. 3.1 (a) State machine replication using atomic broadcast. (b) Atomic broadcast invoked by the servers (request handling and replies not shown).

Atomic Broadcast *vs.* Atomic Multicast The difference between atomic "broadcast" and atomic "multicast" is related to the destination of a message. Strictly speaking, broadcast is used whenever a message is sent to "all" processes in the system, while multicast is used to denote a message sent to a specified subset of processes. According to this definition, we should use the term "atomic multicast" rather than "atomic broadcast" when referring to Figure 3.1. However, a slightly different usage of the terms broadcast/multicast has been adopted. Broadcast tends to be used whenever, given two messages, the destinations are either (i) identical or (ii) different and non-overlapping; multicast is used otherwise. For example, in the context of Figure 3.1, if any message sent to the group of three replicas is only sent to this group, the term "broadcast" is used. However, if a message sent to this group, may (or may not) sometimes also be sent to a different group of servers, destinations of messages may differ and overlap, and the term "multicast" is used.

3.3 The Consensus Problem, or How to Implement Atomic Broadcast in a Modular Way

3.3.1 Consensus

One dimension of modularity in the context of replication is the use of atomic broadcast. Another dimension of modularity is to identify an abstraction that simplifies the implementation of atomic broadcast. This abstraction is the *consensus* problem, which encapsulates the hard part of the implementation of atomic broadcast.

Informally, in the consensus problem we consider a set of n processes, each process p_i with an initial value v_i. These n processes have to agree on a common value v that is the initial value of one of the processes. For example if $n = 3$, $v_1 = 3$, $v_2 = 10$ and $v_3 = 1$, then p_1, p_2, and p_3 may agree on 10, but not on 2. Formally, the consensus problem is defined by the invocation of *propose*(v_i) by which process p_i proposes its initial value, and the execution of *decide*(v) by which p_i decides v. The decision must satisfy the following properties:

- *Validity*: If a process decides v, then v is the initial value of some process (i.e., v was proposed by some process).
- *Uniform Agreement*: Two processes cannot decide differently.
- *Termination*: Every correct process eventually decides.

If processes do not crash, consensus is trivial to solve: One of the processes, say p_1, sends its initial value v_1 to all processes, which wait to receive v_1 and then decide v_1. However, if processes can crash, consensus becomes tricky to solve. Since consensus is solvable exactly when atomic broadcast (and thus state machine replication) can be implemented [4], understanding the condition under which consensus is solvable is crucial. In Section 3.3.2 we discuss the use of consensus to implement atomic broadcast. Solutions to consensus will be discussed in Section 3.4.

3.3.2 Implementation of Atomic Broadcast

We describe two algorithms for atomic broadcast. The first one uses consensus as a black box and illustrates modularity. The second one does not use consensus, but is itself — in addition of being an atomic broadcast algorithm — also a consensus algorithm. Additional information, including algorithms for atomic multicast, can be found in [9, 22].

Modular Consensus-Based Algorithm

We show now an implementation of atomic broadcast that uses consensus: all the complexity of the solution is hidden in the consensus black box. The algorithm has been proposed in [4]. The principle of the algorithm is the following. Every process executes a sequence of consensus numbered 1, 2, ... The initial value for each consensus, for some process p, is the set of messages received by p but not yet adelivered. Let msg^k be the set of messages decided by consensus #k:

- Each process adelivers the messages in msg^k before the messages in msg^{k+1}.
- Each process adelivers the messages in msg^k in some *deterministic* order (e.g., according to their unique IDs).

The algorithm assumes quasi-reliable channels.[2] The details are given by Algorithm 3.1. Consensus is invoked at line 13 and the decision occurs at line 14. A new instance of consensus is launched whenever the condition of line 10 is true; the initial value for consensus is the set of messages received but not yet adelivered. Note that the algorithm does not launch one instance of consensus for every execution of abcast(m): more than one message may be adelivered by one instance of consensus.

---

[2] If p_i sends m to p_j, and the two processes are correct, then m is eventually received by p_j. With reliable channels, the reception of m is guaranteed if p_j is correct.

Algorithm 3.1 Atomic broadcast implemented by reduction to consensus (code of process p) [4].

1: **Initialization**
2:    $k_p := 0$ {*consensus number*}
3:    $adelivered_p := \emptyset$ {*set of messages adelivered by p*}
4:    $received_p := \emptyset$ {*set of messages received by p*}

5: **To abcast(m) :**
6:    send m to all

7: **upon** receive(m) **do**
8:    $received_p := received_p \cup \{m\}$
9:    **if** received m for the first time **then** send m to all

10: **upon** $received_p \setminus adelivered_p \neq \emptyset$ **do**
11:    $k_p \leftarrow k_p + 1$
12:    $a\_undelivered := received_p - adelivered_p$
13:    $propose(k_p, a\_undelivered)$ {*start consensus #k_p*}
14:    **wait until** $decide(k_p, msg^{k_p})$ {*msg^{k_p} is the decision of consensus #k_p*}
15:    $adeliver$ the messages in msg^{k_p} in some deterministic order
16:    $adelivered_p := adelivered_p \cup msgSet^{k_p}$

Non Modular Sequencer-Based Algorithm

For completeness, we sketch a largely referenced — although not modular — algorithm for atomic broadcast. It is basically the idea behind the multi-Paxos state machine replication algorithm [15], and the Viewstamped replication algorithm (see Chapter 7).

The algorithm is not modular in the sense that it does not use consensus as a black box. However, since every atomic broadcast algorithm can be used to solve consensus, the algorithm also solves consensus. The non modularity has the following consequence. In order to understand the conditions under which the algorithm implements atomic broadcast, it is necessary to understand the conditions under which consensus is solvable, which is only discussed later in Section 3.4. Some readers may find more convenient to read the following description after Section 3.4.

The algorithm is based on a sequencer process responsible for ordering messages. In a sequencer-based algorithm, one process s acts as the sequencer. When some process wants to broadcast message m, it sends m to s. Upon receiving m, the sequencer s assigns it a sequence number and relays m with its sequence number to the destinations. The latter deliver messages according to the sequence numbers.

This simple idea needs to be completed to handle the crash of the sequencer. To illustrate the issues to be addressed, consider the following scenario:

- The sequencer has received message m, assigned sequence number i to m, and has sent (m, i) to the destinations. One destination process p receives (m, i) and delivers m at rank i.
- The sequencer crashes, and no other destination process receives (m, i).

The crash of s requires to select a new sequencer s'. However, if the system is not synchronous, s' might not be able to learn that message m was delivered at rank i by p. Without this information, s' might assign the sequence number i to some other message m', leading to the violation of the properties of atomic broadcast.

To address this problem, a process p that (i) has delivered message m' with sequence number $i-1$, and (ii) receives (m, i), cannot deliver m immediately. Let n be the total number of destinations, and f the maximum number of faulty destinations. Process p can deliver m only once it knows that $f + 1$ processes (i.e., one correct process) have received (m, i). This can be implemented by having each destination process, once it has received (m, i), send an acknowledgement message (ack, m, i) to all destinations. Message m is delivered by p only once p has received $f + 1$ messages (ack, m, i).[3]

This mechanism allows the new sequencer s' to learn the existence of any message that could have been delivered thanks to the previous sequencer, but not yet delivered by all correct destinations. The idea is the following. When the sequencer changes to s', all destinations p send to s' the set $rcv_{p,s} = \{(m, i) \mid (m, i)$ received by p from $s\}$.[4] The sequencer s' waits to receive $rcv_{p,s}$ from $n - f$ processes p. If one single set $rcv_{p,s}$ received by s' contains some pair (m, i), then s' knows that, if some message has been delivered by a destination at rank i, it is message m. Moreover, if s' receives no $rcv_{p,s}$ with $(-, i') \in rcv_{p,s}$, then no process can have delivered any message at rank i'. This is easy to show. Assume that some message m' is delivered by some process at rank i'. Therefore, $f + 1$ processes p have sent $rcv_{p,s}$ with $(m', i') \in rcv_{p,s}$ to s'. The sequencer s' receives sets $rcv_{p,s}$ from $n - f$ processes. Since $(n - f) + (f + 1) > n$, at least one set $rcv_{p,s}$ received by s' contains (m', i').

Some other issues remain to be addressed. One issue is the selection of the sequencer. For this, we refer the reader to the discussion related to the choice of the coordinator for Algorithm 3.3 (page 50): selection of the sequencer here, or of the selection of the coordinator for Algorithm 3.3, is exactly the same problem. Another important issue is the system model, which specifies assumptions about processes and channels. This issue is discussed in the next section. Indeed, as we pointed out there, without adequate assumptions, consensus (and atomic broadcast) is simply not solvable.

We have only sketched the non-modular atomic broadcast algorithm. The complete algorithm requires to combine the ideas presented here with the consensus algorithm of Algorithm 3.3.

---

[3] Waiting for $f + 1$ messages will not block p if $f + 1 \leq n - f$, i.e., $n > 2f$.
[4] The information sent to s' can be optimized.

3.4 Solving Consensus

3.4.1 About System Models

As explained in the previous section, consensus is trivial to solve when processes do not crash. With crashes, solutions to consensus depend on the underlying system model. The two extreme models are the *synchronous* and the *asynchronous* system models. In a synchronous system there is (1) a bound Δ on the transmission delay of messages, and (2) a bound Φ on the relative speed of processes. This allows accurate failure detection. In an asynchronous system there is no bound on the transmission delay of messages and no bound on the relative speed of processes. This typically models a system with unpredictable load on the network and on the CPUs. The consequence is that in an asynchronous system, it is never possible to know whether a process has crashed or not.

Unfortunately, consensus is not solvable in an asynchronous system. This result has been established by Fischer-Lynch-Paterson, and is known as the FLP impossibility result [11] (see Chapter 4). The result states that there exists no deterministic algorithm that solves consensus in an asynchronous system with reliable channels if one single process may crash. Consensus is solvable in a synchronous system with process crashes. However, the synchronous system model has drawbacks from a practical point of view. Since the bounds on message transmission delays and process relative speeds must "never" be violated, worst case bounds must be considered. These worst case bounds have a negative impact on the performance of consensus algorithms in the case of process crashes: worst case bounds lead to a large black-out period that ends when the crash is detected. This explains why weaker models, strong enough to solve consensus, have been defined. We describe two such models: the partially synchronous system model and the asynchronous system augmented with failure detectors model.

3.4.2 Partially Synchronous Systems

Roughly speaking, a partially synchronous system is a system that is initially asynchronous and eventually becomes synchronous. The time at which the system becomes synchronous is called the *Global Stabilization Time* (or *GST*). Note that GST is not known to the processes (GST may be different in two different executions). This system model has been proposed by Dwork, Lynch and Stockmeyer [10]. In addition to the definition of the partially synchronous system model, the paper also proposes an abstraction on top of the system model, used to express consensus algorithms. This abstraction is called the *basic round model*.

The Basic Round Model Abstraction

In the basic round model, processing is divided into rounds of message exchange. Each round r consists of a *send step*, a *receive step*, and a *state transition step*. In a send step, each process sends a message to all. In a receive step of some round r, for each process, some subset of messages sent in round r is received (i.e., messages may be lost). In a state transition step each process updates its state based on the set of messages received.

In all rounds executed before GST messages may be lost. However, messages are not lost after GST. We can state this property in terms of rounds: there exists a round *GSR* such that no messages are lost in rounds $r \geq GSR$. This can also be expressed by the following predicate, where C denotes the set of correct processes, σ_p^r denotes the message sent by p in round r,[5] and $\mu_p^r[q]$ denotes the message received by p from q in round r, or $\perp$ if no message is received:

$$\forall r \geq GSR : \forall p, q \in C : \mu_p^r[q] = \sigma_q^r.$$

The basic round model can be implemented on top of a partially synchronous system [10].

Solving Consensus in the Basic Round Model

Let f be the maximum number of faulty processes. Dwork *et al.* [10] describe an algorithm that solves consensus in the basic round model with $f < n/2$ (see [6] for the pseudo-code). We give here a simpler consensus algorithm, namely Algorithm 3.2, which requires $f < n/3$ [7]. Line 5 is the send step, and lines 7 to 10 are the state transition step. The receive step is implicit (between lines 5 and 7).

Algorithm 3.2 OneThirdRule (OTR) algorithm: Solving consensus in the basic round model, $f < n/3$ (code of process p) [7].

```
1: Initialization:
2:     x_p ← v_p                                              { v_p is the initial value of p }

3: Round r:
4:     Send step:
5:         send ⟨x_p⟩ to all processes

6:     State transition step:
7:         if number of messages received ≥ n − f then
8:             x_p ← the smallest most often received value  {select the most frequent; if not unique, take the
                smallest}
9:         if (at least n − f values received are equal to v) and not decided_p then
10:             DECIDE(v)
```

The algorithm works as follows. Each process p manages a variable x_p that is initially set to v_p, the initial value of p. In each round r, every process sends x_p to all (line 5). If a process p receives $n - f$ values equal to some value v, then it decides v (line 10). Validity trivially holds. Uniform agreement holds because the algorithm ensures that once $n - f$ processes p have $x_p = v$, then by lines 7 and 8 variable x_p will be updated to v. This ensures that no process can decide on a value different from v. Termination holds after GSR for the following reason. Consider the smallest

---

[5] For simplicity, assume that p sends the same message to all.

round r_0 larger than GSR, such that all faulty processes have crashed before round r_0. By the property of the basic round model, in round r_0 all correct processes receive at least $n - f$ messages and the same set of messages, and so update x_p to the same value at line 8, say v. In round $r_0 + 1$ all correct processes receive at least $n - f$ messages with v and so decide at line 10.

A Consensus Algorithm "à la Paxos"

We give now a second consensus algorithm in the basic round model that requires only $f < n/2$, see Algorithm 3.3. The algorithm, called *LastVoting* [7], follows the basic line of Paxos [15], and can be seen as Paxos expressed in the basic round model.[6]

The rounds r in Algorithm 3.3 are grouped into phases ϕ, where one phase ϕ consists of four consecutive rounds $4\phi - 3$ to 4ϕ. The last round 4ϕ of phase ϕ is followed by the first round $4(\phi+1) - 3$ of phase $\phi + 1$. The algorithm relies on a coordinator $Coord(p, \phi)$, which is p's coordinator for phase ϕ. The algorithm is safe with multiple coordinators in the same phase, i.e., with $Coord(p, \phi) \neq Coord(q, \phi)$ for two different processes p and q. Termination requires one phase that starts after GSR in which all alive processes consider the same coordinator.

The algorithm uses variable x_p initially set to the initial value of p, and variable ts_p equal to the latest phase in which p has updated x_p. Each phase works as follows. Round $4\phi - 3$, thanks to the condition "number of $\langle ack \rangle$ received $> n/2$" (line 11), ensures that at most one coordinator sets $commit_p$ to $true$ at line 14. This coordinator also updates $vote_p$ based on the value received. We explain the update of $vote_p$ below.

In round $4\phi - 2$, at most one coordinator sends $vote_p$ to all. Process q, upon receiving this message, updates x_q and sets ts_q to the current phase number (line 21). After that, in the next round $4\phi - 1$, q sends $\langle ack \rangle$ to the coordinator. A coordinator p that receives a majority of $\langle ack \rangle$ (line 27) can decide on $vote_p$. This is done in round 4ϕ by sending $\langle vote_p \rangle$ at line 32. The reception of this messages leads a process to decide on the value received.

The decision after the reception of a majority of $\langle ack \rangle$ ensures the following property. If some process has decided v in phase ϕ, then a majority of processes have $x_p = v$ and $ts_p = \phi$ at the end of phase ϕ, and the other have $ts_p < \phi$. It follows that in the first round of phase $\phi + 1$, a coordinator p that receives a majority of messages, necessarily receives at least one message with $\langle v, \phi \rangle$; the messages received with $\langle v', \phi' \rangle$, $v' \neq v$ all have $\phi' < \phi$. Therefore, in phase $\phi + 1$ a coordinator can only set its vote to v, which ensures uniform agreement.

For termination, it is easy to show that if all processes agree on the same coordinator in some phase ϕ_0 that starts after GSR, then all correct processes decide in round $4\phi_0$.

One remaining issue is the selection of the coordinator. A simple solution is to rely on the *rotating* coordinator paradigm: if processes are denoted p_0 to p_{n-1}, and

---

[6] We refer here to the Paxos consensus algorithm. In Section 3.3.2 we were referring to the multi-Paxos atomic broadcast algorithm.

Algorithm 3.3 The LastVoting algorithm: consensus algorithm "à la Paxos" in the basic round model, $f < n/2$ (code of process p) [7].

```
1: Initialization:
2:    x_p ← v_p                                                    { v_p is the initial value of p }
3:    vote_p ←?
4:    commit_p ← false
5:    ready_p ← false
6:    ts_p ← 0                                                     {integer time-stamp}

7: Round r = 4φ − 3:
8:    Send step:
9:        send ⟨x_p, ts_p⟩ to Coord(p, φ)

10:    State transition step:
11:       if p = Coord(p, φ) and number of ⟨v, θ⟩ received > n/2 then
12:          let θ̄ be the largest θ from ⟨v, θ⟩ received
13:          vote_p ← one v such that ⟨v, θ̄⟩ is received
14:          commit_p ← true

15: Round r = 4φ − 2:
16:    Send step:
17:       if p = Coord(p, φ) and commit_p then
18:          send ⟨vote_p⟩ to all processes

19:    State transition step:
20:       if received ⟨v⟩ from Coord(p, φ) then
21:          x_p ← v ; ts_p ← φ

22: Round r = 4φ − 1:
23:    Send step:
24:       if ts_p = φ then
25:          send ⟨ack⟩ to Coord(p, φ)

26:    State transition step:
27:       if p = Coord(p, φ) and number of ⟨ack⟩ received > n/2 then
28:          ready_p ← true

29: Round r = 4φ:
30:    Send step:
31:       if p = Coord(p, φ) and ready_p then
32:          send ⟨vote_p⟩ to all processes

33:    State transition step:
34:       if received ⟨v⟩ from Coord(p, φ) then
35:          DECIDE(v)
36:       if p = Coord(p, φ) then
37:          ready_p ← false ; commit_p ← false
```

$\phi = 1$ is the first phase, then $p_{(\phi-1) \bmod n}$ is the coordinator of phase ϕ. Another option, used by Paxos, is to select the coordinator dynamically, using for example a leader election algorithm [2].

3.4.3 Asynchronous System Augmented with Failure Detectors

The Failure Detector Abstraction

The failure detector model has been proposed by Chandra and Toueg [4]. The idea is different from the partial synchrony model: the asynchronous system is "augmented" with devices that can be queried by processes. Each process p_i is equipped with such a device FD_i, the failure detector device of p_i. When queried by p_i, FD_i gives p_i a hint about the status crashed/alive of the other processes. The output of failure detectors may be incorrect, and failure detectors may change their mind. For example the failure detector FD_i may suspect p_j at time t, and no more suspect p_j at time $t' > t$. Moreover, it is important to note that, since the failure detectors FD_i is "queried" by p_i, even though FD_i has a state defined for all times t, not all these states are observed by p_i.

If we do not set any constraints on the output of the failure detectors, the model does not add anything with respect to an asynchronous system, and the FLP impossibility result still holds. To make consensus solvable, restrictions must be put on the output of the failure detectors. These restrictions are expressed in terms of two abstract properties, a *completeness* property and an *accuracy* property. Completeness defines constraints with respect to crashed processes, while accuracy defines constraints with respect to correct processes. We consider here only one example (see [4] for the complete failure detector hierarchy), namely the *eventual perfect failure detector* $\Diamond \mathcal{P}$, defined by the two following properties:

- *Strong completeness*: Eventually every process that crashes is permanently suspected by *every* correct process.
- *Eventual strong accuracy*: There is a time after which correct processes are not suspected by any correct process.

Solving Consensus with $\Diamond \mathcal{P}$

We adapt Algorithm 3.2 to solve consensus with the failure detector $\Diamond \mathcal{P}$ (see Algorithm 3.4). The algorithm requires quasi-reliable channels (see footnote 2), and consists of two parallel tasks, *Task 1* and *Task 2*. Task 1 of Algorithm 3.4, similarly to Algorithm 3.2, consists of a sequence of rounds, but rounds here are different: the handling of round numbers (line 4) and the receive step (line 8) are explicit. By Task 1, as in Algorithm 3.2, every process p in every round r_p sends x_p to all (line 7). The explicit reception of this message is handled as follows (see line 8): process p waits for messages, and from time to time queries its failure detector, denoted by $\Diamond \mathcal{P}_p$. Message reception ends when p has received a message from all processes that are not crashed according to the failure detector. Then p proceeds as in Algorithm 3.2 with one difference. When p is about to decide in Task 1, it sends the decision to all other processes (line 12), and Task 1 ends. A process q, upon receiving this message (line 17), decides if it has not yet done so, and forwards the message to all other processes (line 19). This mechanism ensures that if one correct process decides, then all correct processes also decide. Such a mechanism is not needed in Algorithm 3.2, since the algorithm is not quiescent—a quiescent algorithm eventually stops sending messages. This is related to the unreliable channel assumption of Algorithm 3.2.

The correctness arguments for validity and uniform agreement are the same for Algorithm 3.2 and Algorithm 3.4. The argument for termination is the following. First, the completeness property of $\Diamond \mathcal{P}$ together with the quasi-reliable channel assumption ensures that no correct process is blocked forever at line 8. Consider a

Algorithm 3.4 Solving consensus with $\Diamond \mathscr{P}$, $f < n/3$ (code of process p).

```
1: Initialization:
2:     x_p ← v_p                                              { v_p is the initial value of p }
3:     decide_p ← false                                       {true once p has decided}
4:     r_p ← 1                                                {round number}

5: Task 1:
6:     while not decided_p do
7:         send (r_p, x_p) to all processes
8:         wait until received (r_p, −) from all processes not in ◊𝒫_p
9:         if at least n − f values received then
10:            x_p ← most frequent value received (if more than one value satisfies the condition, take the smallest)
11:            if at least n − f value received are equal to some value v then
12:                send (decision, r_p, v) to all processes
13:                DECIDE(v)
14:                decided_p ← true
15:        r_p ← r_p + 1

16: Task 2:
17:    upon reception of (decision, −, v) for the first time do
18:        if not decided_p then
19:            send (decision, r_p, v) to all processes
20:            DECIDE(v)
21:            decided_p ← true
```

correct process p waiting at line 8 for a message from q: if q is correct, its message is eventually received; if q is not correct, q eventually crashes and is eventually suspected forever. Therefore, consider time t such that after t all faulty processes have crashed, and after t no correct process is suspected by any correct process (eventual strong accuracy). Let round r_0 be the smallest round such that no correct process has started round r_0 before t. In round r_0 all correct processes receive at least $n - f$ messages and the same set of messages, and so update x_p to the same value, say v. In round $r_0 + 1$ all correct processes receive at least $n - f$ messages with v and so decide.

3.4.4 Discussion

Although Algorithms 3.2 and 3.4 were designed for different system models, they are not very different. This may suggest that the two underlying system models are also similar. However, there are major differences between them. First, the notion of failure detector makes no sense if channels are not quasi-reliable. Consider for example line 8 of Algorithm 3.4 and the channel from q to p. If q is correct and the message sent by q to p is lost, then p waits forever. Second, message exchange is part of the round based model, while it is not part of the failure detector abstraction As a consequence, failure detectors do not have a simple extension from the crash-stop model to the crash-recovery model, contrary to the round based model [14]. Third, the fact that failure detectors extend the asynchronous model with an additional module imposes some restrictions on their output. In particular, to be useful, failure detectors properties must hold for an infinite period of time [5]. This is not the case with the partially synchronous model and its round abstraction, where the duration of a synchrony period sufficient for a given consensus algorithm can be expressed [10, 14].

It should be pointed out that the failure detector model, the partially synchronous model and its basic round model abstraction, as well as for example the *Round-by-Round Failure Detector* model proposed by Gafni [12], are all models in which the blame for not receiving messages is put on system components, namely links or processes. As pointed out by Santoro and Widmayer, these component failure models "do not fully capture the reality of systems subject to (possibly transient) ubiquitous failures" [19]. Influenced by [18], a model without component failure has been proposed by Charron-Bost and Schiper [7]. This model, called the *HO model* (*Heard Of*), is a round-based model that uses predicates as in [12], and allows a uniform handling of all benign faults.

3.5 Generic Broadcast

Although the state machine approach requires that all servers receive the client requests in the same order, this is not always necessary for the correctness of the applications. For example, consider a replicated *Account* object, defined by the operations *deposit*(x) and *withdraw*(x). While *deposit* operations commute with each other, *withdraw* operations do not, neither with each other nor with *deposit* operations, assuming that the account cannot overdraw. As a consequence, although totally ordering all account operations will produce a correct execution, it is not always required for the correctness of the replicated *Account* object. Since totally ordering requests has a cost (the atomic broadcast of Figure 3.1, for example, requires a consensus execution), better performance can be achieved if only non-commuting requests are ordered.

Generic broadcast is a group communication primitive that allows applications to specify their order requirements by means of a *conflict relation*. Two requests *conflict* if their order matters. In the previous example, if we let $\mathcal{M}_d$ and $\mathcal{M}_w$ be, respectively, the set of messages that carry a deposit and a withdraw operation, then the conflict relation $\sim_{Account}$ can be defined as $\sim_{Account} = \{(m, m') : m \in \mathcal{M}_w$ or $m' \in \mathcal{M}_w\}$. Generic broadcast guarantees that conflicting requests are delivered in the same order by all processes; non-conflicting requests, that is, those that commute, may be delivered in different orders by different processes.

However, the implementation of generic broadcast is more complex than the implementation of atomic broadcast. We illustrate its complexity with a run in which only two messages are broadcast, m and m'. A generalization of this idea for an unbounded number of messages can be found in [16]. To broadcast message m, a process sends it to all processes. Upon reception of m by some process p_i, there are three cases to consider:

1. p_i has not received message m',
2. p_i has received message m', and m' does not conflict with m, or
3. p_i has received message m', and m' conflicts with m.

In cases 1 and 2, p_i sends a message to all processes acknowledging the reception of m, denoted $ACK(m)$. If p_i receives $ACK(m)$ from some other process before m, it locally assumes the reception of m and acts as described above. A process that receives $ACK(m)$ from n_{ack} processes delivers m. If m and m' do not conflict, all correct processes eventually receive n_{ack} messages of type $ACK(m)$ and deliver m.

In case 3, p_i launches an instance of consensus to decide on the delivery order of m and m'. This should be done carefully though because some process may have already delivered m', in which case p_i should deliver m' before m—to avoid the case in which both m and m' could be delivered (by different processes), we require $n_{ack} \geq n/2$. Thus, before executing consensus, p_i should find out whether m' could have been possibly delivered by some other process. For this purpose, p_i sends to all processes a message, denoted CHK, containing the message it has acknowledged (i.e., m'), and waits for n_{chk} similar CHK messages before starting consensus. Provided that the condition $2n_{ack} + n_{chk} \geq 2n + 1$ holds, p_i will receive enough CHK messages to be able to determine if any message received enough ACKs and was possibly delivered.

This algorithm allows processes to deliver non-conflicting messages in two communication steps (i.e., the initial message propagation and the acknowledgments). To satisfy the constraints on n_{ack} and n_{chk} it assumes that fewer than one third of the processes are faulty. While this has been shown to be optimal [17], there are generic broadcast algorithms that require a majority of correct processes only, although non-conflicting messages need more than two communication steps to be delivered [1].

3.6 Dynamic Groups

In Section 3.2 we have explained the difference between static and dynamic groups, and have defined atomic broadcast in the context of static groups. From a practical point of view, static groups are too limitative. For example, if g is a group of three server replicas on three different machines, and replica p_3 crashes, it might be desirable to remove p_3 from g and to replace it with a new replica p_4. Consider another example. Assume that, in order to update the operating system on machine M_3, one may want to move replica p_3 from M_3 to some other machine M_4. This may be done by removing p_3 from g, and adding to g a new replica p_4 on M_4.

Dynamic groups lead to new problems. The first problem is to adequately model dynamic groups. The second problem is how to add and remove processes from a group. The third problem is how to extend the definition and implementation of group communication primitives from static groups to dynamic groups.

3.6.1 Group Membership Service

The group membership service allows to add and remove processes from a group. This is not very different from a set membership service, where a set of processes Π maintain and agree on the dynamically changing set of elements drawn from an arbitrary universe [21]. Processes can request the addition and removal of elements to/from the set, and the set changes accordingly. Each time the set changes, all processes are notified of the new value of the set. Each successive value of the set is called a *view*. The group membership service is a special case of the set membership, where the set maintained by processes in Π happens to be a subset of Π. A view of group g is a tuple (i,S), where S is a set of processes, and i an identifier. We refer below to the following terminology: if $p \in S$, then p is *member* of view $v = (i.S)$, and S is the *membership* of view v; the event by which a process adopts view v is called *view installation*; if view $v = (i,S)$ and view $v' = (i',S')$, then $v = v'$ holds if both $i = i'$ and $S = S'$. The basic requirement for a group membership service is an agreement among processes on the membership of the sequence of views. Examples of other possible requirements are given in [21].

In the literature, group membership is often defined and implemented as a service to maintain and agree on a particular set of processes, namely the set that is deemed to be *alive* [8]. To provide this service, one must solve two orthogonal problems [21]: (i) determining the set of processes that are alive, and (ii) agreeing on each successive view of this dynamically changing set. Both problems are unsolvable in an asynchronous system with failures. Nevertheless it is important to decouple the issue of *why* processes are added or removed from the group from *how* they are added or removed. The group membership service is only responsible for the latter.

3.6.2 Group Communication in Dynamic Groups

Historically, group communication in dynamic groups [8], were defined quite differently from group communication in static groups [13]. For example, when the group membership does not change, the dynamic definitions of atomic broadcast do not lead to the static definitions. This is rather confusing. New definitions for dynamic groups, which do lead to the static definitions when the group membership does not change, were proposed in [20]. We refer to these definitions here.

The definitions of static group communication distinguish correct processes from faulty processes. The obligation to adelivery messages is put on correct processes. This is not the case with dynamic groups, where a correct process can be removed from a group: a correct process p has no obligation with respect to messages abcast to g after p is removed from the group. Therefore, dynamic groups cannot be specified with respect to correct processes. Instead, the new notion of v-correct/v-faulty processes (where v is a view of g) is introduced. Given a view v of g, and a process p member of v, process p is v-correct if (i) p installs view v, (ii) p does not crash while its view is view v, and (iii) if v' follows immediately view v in the sequence of views of g, then p is a member of view v'. Specifically, if p installs v, but is not member of v' (p was removed from g), then p is v-faulty. We need also to refer to g-correct processes. Consider process p that installs v_p^{init} as its first view of group g. Process p is g-correct if p is v_p^{init}-correct, and is v'-correct for all views v' that follow view v_p^{init}. If group g is static, then v-correct and correct are equivalent. Similarly, g-correct and correct are equivalent.

With these notions, we can now adapt the static definition of atomic broadcast to dynamic groups with little changes:

- *Validity*: If a g-correct process abcasts message m, then it eventually adelivers m.
- *Uniform agreement*: If a process adelivers message m in view v, then all v-correct processes eventually adeliver m.
- *Uniform integrity*: For any message m, every process adelivers m at most once, and only if m was previously abcast.
- *Uniform same view delivery*: If two processes p and q adeliver a message in view v^p (for p) and v^q (for q), then $v^p = v^q$.
- *Uniform total order*: If some process adelivers message m in view v before it adelivers message m', then every process p in view v adelivers m' only after it has adelivered m.

Uniform same view delivery is the main change with respect to static groups. As the name suggests, it prevents p and q from adelivering m in different views. Without this property, uniform agreement could hold for p, but not for q [20].

If group g is static, then the same view property is trivially ensured. Moreover, since v-correct and g-correct are in this case equivalent to correct, it is easy to see that we are back to the static definitions.

The uniform "same" view delivery property can be strengthened into a "sending" view delivery property:

- *Uniform sending view delivery*: If two processes p and q adeliver a message in view v^p (for p) and v^q (for q), then $v^p = v^q$, where $v^p = v^q$ is the view in which abcast(m) was executed.

This property has been also called *virtual synchrony* and *view synchrony*, and has been popularized by the Isis system [3] (see also Chapter 6).

The implementation of atomic broadcast with dynamic groups can also be based on consensus [20]. Other implementations that rely on the membership change are described in [9].

3.7 Conclusion

We have shown that replication can be implemented in a modular, layered, way. In doing so, we have identified several layers, each defining a useful abstraction: atomic broadcast, consensus, failure detectors, and the round based model. In addition we have pointed out additional issues such as a dynamic set of servers, and using generic broadcast instead of atomic broadcast.

A modular implementation may be less efficient than a monolithic implementation. However, a modular description has other advantages: it allows us to understand the challenges that underly the implementation of replication. For example, the FLP impossibility result (Sect. 3.4.1), which applies to consensus, applies as well to replication. Positive results are also useful. For example, system models under which consensus is solvable are system models under which replication is implementable. Identifying such system models is of utmost importance.

Acknowledgements We would like to thank Bernadette Charron-Bost for her useful comments and suggestions.

References

1. Aguilera, M.K., Delporte-Gallet, C., Fauconnier, H., Toueg, S.: Thrifty generic broadcast. In: Herlihy, M.P. (ed.) DISC 2000. LNCS, vol. 1914, p. 268. Springer, Heidelberg (2000)
2. Aguilera, M.K., Delporte-Gallet, C., Fauconnier, H., Toueg, S.: On implementing Ω with weak reliability and synchrony assumptions. In: Proc. of the 22nd ACM Symp. on Principles of Distributed Computing, PODC (July 2003)
3. Birman, K.: The Process Group Approach to Reliable Distributed Computing. Comm. ACM 36(12), 37–53 (1993)
4. Chandra, T.D., Toueg, S.: Unreliable failure detectors for reliable distributed systems. Journal of ACM 43(2), 225–267 (1996)
5. Charron-Bost, B., Hutle, M., Widder, J. In Search of Lost Time. Tech. Rep. LSR-REPORT-2008-006, EPFL (October 2008)
6. Charron-Bost, B., Schiper, A.: Consensus with partial synchrony. In: Encyclopedia of Algorithms, pp. 198–202. Springer, Heidelberg (2008)
7. Charron-Bost, B., Schiper, A.: The Heard-Of model: computing in distributed systems with benign failures. Distributed Computing 22(1), 49–71 (2009)
8. Chockler, G.V., Keidar, I., Vitenberg, R.: Group Communication Specifications: A Comprehensive Study. ACM Computing Surveys 4(33), 1–43 (2001)
9. Défago, X., Schiper, A., Urban, P.: Totally Ordered Broadcast and Multicast Algorithms: Taxonomy and Survey. ACM Computing Surveys 4(36), 1–50 (2004)
10. Dwork, C., Lynch, N., Stockmeyer, L.: Consensus in the presence of partial synchrony. Journal of ACM 35(2), 288–323 (1988)
11. Fischer, M., Lynch, N., Paterson, M.: Impossibility of Distributed Consensus with One Faulty Process. Journal of ACM 32, 374–382 (1985)
12. Gafni, E.: Round-by-round fault detectors: Unifying synchrony and asynchrony. In: Proc. of the 17th ACM Symp. Principles of Distributed Computing, PODC (June-July 1998)
13. Hadzilacos, V., Toueg, S.: Fault-Tolerant Broadcasts and Related Problems. Tech. Rep. 94-1425, Department of Computer Science, Cornell University (May 1994)
14. Hutle, M., Schiper, A.: Communication Predicates: A High-Level Abstraction for Coping with Transient and Dynamic Faults. In: Proc. of the 37th IEEE Int. Conf. on Dependable Systems and Networks (DSN) (June 2007)
15. Lamport, L.: The Part-Time Parliament. ACM Trans. on Computer Systems 16(2), 133–169 (1998)
16. Pedone, F., Schiper, A.: Handling Message Semantics with Generic Broadcast Protocols. Distributed Computing 15(2), 97–107 (2002)
17. Pedone, F., Schiper, A.: Brief announcement: On the inherent cost of generic broadcast. In: Proc. of the 23rd ACM Symp. on Principles of Distributed Computing (PODC), pp. 401–401 (July 2004)
18. Santoro, N., Widmayer, P.: Time is not a healer. In: Proc. of the 6th Symp. on Theor. Aspects of Computer Science (STAC) (February 1989)
19. Santoro, N., Widmayer, P.: Agreement in synchronous networks with ubiquitous faults. Theoretical Computer Science 384, 232–249 (2007)
20. Schiper, A.: Dynamic Group Communication. Distributed Computing 18(5), 359–374 (2006)
21. Schiper, A., Toueg, S.: From Set Membership to Group Membership: A Separation of Concerns. IEEE Transactions on Dependable and Secure Computing (TDSC) 3(1), 2–12 (2006)
22. Schiper, N., Sutra, P., Pedone, F.: Genuine versus Non-Genuine Atomic Multicast Protocols for Wide Area Networks: An Empirical Study. In: Proc. of the 28th IEEE Symp. on Reliable Distributed Systems (SRDS) (September 2009)

Chapter 4
Stumbling over Consensus Research: Misunderstandings and Issues

Marcos K. Aguilera

Abstract The consensus problem has recently emerged as a major interest in systems conferences, yet the systems community tends to ignore most of the large body of theory on this subject. In this chapter, I examine why this might be so. I point out misunderstandings by the systems community of the theory. I also consider some issues in this work that remains to be addressed by the theory community.

4.1 Introduction

In the consensus problem, each process proposes some initial value, and processes that do not fail must reach an irrevocable decision on exactly one of the proposed values. The consensus problem captures an essential component of replication in distributed systems: the fact that replicas (processes) need to agree on the next request they handle, so that they can remain in identical states.

The consensus problem has been a fertile topic for theoretical study and it has recently become a major interest in systems conferences. Yet, theory and practice are divorced: the large body of theoretical work on this subject has had limited impact, and the systems community tends to ignore most of that theory. In this chapter, I examine why this may be so.

The chapter is divided into two main parts. In Section 4.2, I consider some misunderstandings by the systems community of the theoretical work on the consensus problem. In Section 4.3, I consider some issues in this body of work that remains to be addressed by the theory community. Section 4.4 concludes the chapter.

The chapter presents a somewhat personal point of view. Another perspective on consensus misunderstandings is provided in [8], while [3] describes an experience of applying consensus in practice.

B. Charron-Bost, F. Pedone, and A. Schiper (Eds.): Replication, LNCS 5959, pp. 59–72, 2010.

4.2 Misunderstandings

There are some deep misunderstandings by the systems community of a significant part of the theoretical research on the consensus problem. This section covers these misunderstandings. They have hindered the adoption of many interesting techniques, ideas, and algorithms, for incorrect reasons. My hope is that, once the misunderstandings are clarified, systems researchers can make better informed choices and benefit from work that they once thought to be inapplicable. At the same time, I hope that theory researchers can become sensitized to the misunderstandings so that they can present their research in a more effective manner.

4.2.1 Asynchronous Systems

An *asynchronous (distributed) system* is a system in which processes need not satisfy any timeliness properties. There are no bounds on the relative rate of execution of processes, so one process may execute at a much faster rate than another. Moreover, there are no bounds on message delays, so messages sent from one process to another may be delivered quickly or slowly. On the other hand, in a *synchronous system*, there *are* bounds on the rate of execution of non-faulty processes and on message delays.

Critics say that asynchronous systems are not realistic, because in reality one process cannot be 10^{999999} slower than another process, and a message never takes 10^{999999} seconds to be delivered. That is a fair criticism and, indeed, it is unlikely that asynchronous systems accurately model any real system. However, asynchronous systems have an important practical aspect: algorithms developed for them are very general, because they work irrespective of whether the system is fast or slow. In contrast, algorithms developed for *synchronous* systems explicitly rely on particular timing assumptions, and the algorithms can fail if those assumptions are violated. The problem is that it is hard for the system designer to decide what timing assumptions he should make, because the timing behavior of a real system tends to be imprecise and highly variable in practice. Specifically, the average message delay of a network could be 1 millisecond, but infrequently messages may take 1 second or much longer when there is congestion. In that case, what should the system designer assume as the maximum message delay? On one hand, if he chooses 1 millisecond then this choice will be incorrect sometimes, which can cause a premature timeout and lead to consistency problems (e.g., a premature timeout may cause a backup process to be promoted to the primary, while another primary is still active). On the other hand, if the system designer picks 1 second or more as the maximum message delay, then when a message is really missing (because, say, a server or a process crashes), it will take long to timeout on the message, causing the system to block in the meantime, leading to a loss of availability. Thus, the system designer is left with two bad choices: assuming a small maximum message delay affects consistency, while assuming a large conservative delay affects availability. With asynchronous systems, the system developer does not have to choose what timing assumptions to make: he simply develops an algorithm that works irrespective of whether the system is fast or slow. From this point of view, it is much harder to criticize asynchronous systems: they merely embody the fact that timing assumptions should be avoided. The fewer the assumptions needed by an algorithm, the smaller the likelihood that it will fail when used in practice. Thus, from a practical perspective, asynchronous systems can be highly desirable when it comes to designing algorithms.

However, asynchronous systems have some practical shortcomings. Impossibility results, which state that a problem cannot be solved in asynchronous systems, are particularly limited. These results rely on the fact that asynchronous systems admit executions where messages and processes are delayed arbitrarily, whereas these executions may be unlikely. Thus, these results are of limited interest in practice; even in theory, these results are weak because they do not carry over to a system with any form of synchrony. I will elaborate on this topic, focusing specifically on the consensus impossibility result, in Section 4.2.4.

4.2.2 Eventually-Forever Assumptions

In the consensus literature, it is common to find assumptions in the form of eventually-forever properties. An *eventually-forever* property is a property of the form "eventually X is true and continues to be true forever after". Common examples include the following:

- *Eventual leader election.* Eventually some correct process is elected as leader and it remains leader forever after [5, 4].
- *Eventual timeliness.* Eventually non-faulty processes are timely and messages are delivered and processed in a timely fashion, and this timeliness continues forever after [6].

These assumptions are made as a condition for the algorithms to solve consensus. Practitioners object that these assumptions are not realistic and therefore the algorithms that depend on them are not useful. However, it turns out that these assumptions are actually reasonable from a pragmatic perspective. Practitioners are right that these properties cannot hold in practice, but the misunderstanding is that they are not really *required* to hold; they are only *assumed* to hold for purely technical reasons. In reality, what is required to hold are somewhat weaker properties, such as "a process remains the leader for sufficiently long". These weaker properties, however, are cumbersome to formalize, and that is why eventually-forever properties are used instead.

To illustrate this point, consider the simple example of a washing machine. Its manufacturer would like to say that, after the machine is started, it eventually terminates the washing cycle. But it will not terminate if the machine is disconnected from the power supply during operation. Hence, to ensure termination one needs an assumption such as "eventually the machine is connected to the power supply and remains connected for 60 minutes". However, if the washing machine has a variable washing time that depends on its load, 60 minutes may not be enough and, in fact, it may be impossible to determine how long is enough without knowing the exact load.

An eventually-forever property comes handy in this case: the manufacturer simply assumes that "eventually the machine is connected to the power supply and it remains connected forever after". This assumption handles the case of every possible load. Note that, once the machine terminates, it is irrelevant whether or not the machine is connected to the power supply. Saying that the machine remains connected forever is just a simple way to say that the machine is connected for sufficiently long.

Similarly, consider a consensus algorithm that uses a leader election service. The algorithm designer assumes that some process eventually gets elected as leader and remains leader forever after. The algorithm does not really need the leader for eternity, but it can be hard or impossible to know in advance for how long the leader is needed, as this can depend on many factors, such as actual message delays and the load on processes.

The washing machine manufacturer could give a table that shows, for each load, how long the machine needs to be plugged in to terminate. Similarly, algorithm designers could state assumptions that depend on all factors that influence the behavior of their algorithm. Doing so, however, requires a more refined model than the asynchronous model—something that algorithm designers prefer to avoid to keep the model simple.

4.2.3 Eventual Guarantees

Many algorithms for consensus satisfy a progress guarantee described by *eventual* properties. An eventual property is a property of the form "eventually X holds". A common example is the termination property, which says that "eventually non-failed processes reach a decision". Such a property does not say exactly *when* processes reach a decision, only that sooner or later they do so.

Practitioners object that such a guarantee is not sufficient in practice, because it allows processes to terminate, say, only after 10^{99999} years. This is a valid objection, but there is a reason to do things in this way: to separate correctness from performance. As an analogy, the specification of the sorting problem requires that the algorithm eventually terminate. The exact running time of the algorithm, perhaps $O(n \log n)$, is a performance characteristic of the algorithm not a correctness guarantee, and it is good form to separate performance from correctness.

One way to address this objection is to include an analysis of the running time of the proposed algorithm, rather than just a termination proof. In an asynchronous system, this analysis can be done in terms of the maximum *observed* message delay (e.g., as in [1]), or in terms of the the largest causal chain of messages (e.g., as in [13]), or based on the time when the system starts "behaving well" (e.g., as in [6], using a partially synchronous system with a global stabilization time). This type of analysis should be done more often.

4.2.4 The Consensus Impossibility Result

The consensus impossibility result by Fischer, Lynch, and Paterson [7] is one of the most cited results in the consensus literature. It states that there does not exist a (deterministic) algorithm for the consensus problem in an asynchronous system subject to failures, even if messages can never be lost, at most one process may fail, and it can only fail by crashing (stopping executing).

This result is misunderstood because the exact nature of asynchronous systems is itself misunderstood. To get a better appreciation of what the result means exactly, let us examine its proof in some detail.

The proof considers a purported algorithm $\mathscr{A}$ that satisfies the safety properties of consensus[1], namely, that processes never decide differently and they never decide a value that is not proposed. It then shows that $\mathscr{A}$ violates the liveness property of consensus by constructing an execution of $\mathscr{A}$ in which processes never decide. The proof proceeds as follows. Consider the set of all possible global states of the system running algorithm $\mathscr{A}$. A state is said to be *bivalent* if the consensus decision has not been fixed yet: from that state, there are ways for processes to decide one value or another value. Note that I distinguish between the decision being known and it being fixed. For example, consider an initial state where all processes have proposed the same value v, but they have not yet communicated with each other. Then, the only possible decision is v, so the decision is certain to be v. However, the processes in the system have not yet learned that this is the case.

The proof is based on two key propositions. The first key proposition is that algorithm $\mathscr{A}$ has some initial state that is bivalent. This proposition is depicted in Figure 4.1, where the grey area represents the set of bivalent states and the leftmost disc represents a bivalent initial state. For example, in the $\Diamond S$-based algorithm of

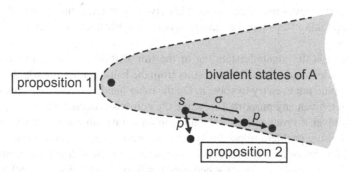

Fig. 4.1 Depiction of key propositions in the proof of impossibility of consensus.

---

[1] Roughly speaking, a safety property is a property that states that something bad does not happen, while a liveness property is a property that states that something good eventually happens. The safety properties of consensus are Agreement and Validity. Agreement says that no processes decide different values, and Validity says that a process can only decide on a value that is the initial value of some process. The liveness property of consensus is Termination. Termination says that eventually correct processes decide on a value.

Chandra-Toueg [5] or in the Paxos algorithm [11],[2] one bivalent initial state is the initial state in which half of the processes proposes some value and the other half proposes a different value. In fact, this initial state is bivalent in many of the known algorithms for consensus in partial synchrony models or in models with failure detectors.

The second key proposition is that if s is a bivalent state but after a step of some process p the state is no longer bivalent, there exists a sequence σ of steps such that if σ is inserted before the step of process p then p's step leads to a state that is still bivalent. This proposition is depicted in Figure 4.1, where the leftmost arrow labeled p is a step of process p after state s, which leads to a state that is not bivalent; the very same step by process p, if taken after the sequence σ, leads to a state that is still bivalent. For example, in the $\Diamond S$-based algorithm of Chandra and Toueg, a step that leaves the grey region occurs when the last process in a majority receives the new estimate proposed by the coordinator. However, if this receipt step is delayed until after the process sees that the coordinator is suspected and abandons the round, then this receipt no longer leaves the grey region. As another example, in the Paxos algorithm, a step that leaves the grey region occurs when the last process in a majority receives a high-numbered proposal. But if this step is delayed for long enough—until another higher-number proposal appears—then the proposal becomes stale and useless.

The first and second key propositions can be shown by contradiction with relatively simple arguments, whose details are not relevant here (they are given in [7]).

These two propositions allow us to find an execution of algorithm $\mathscr{A}$ in which processes never decide. Intuitively, in Figure 4.1, the execution starts in an initial state in the grey region and all processes keep taking steps, say in a round-robin fashion. If any step by some process leaves the grey region, then one inserts a sequence of steps by other processes such that, after those steps, the aforementioned step no longer leaves the grey region. This gives us an execution in which all processes keep taking steps but the state always remain bivalent. As a result, processes never decide.

So where is the misunderstanding of the impossibility result? Most computer scientists understand impossibility results from the halting problem, which suggests that one should not even try to solve it. On the other hand, the consensus impossibility says that, given any purported solution, the consensus decision may keep getting delayed forever if processes are scheduled in an unfavorable way. This is different from the halting problem impossibility in two ways. First, the consensus impossibility result is based on a model where processes can be scheduled according to the worst case, but in reality process scheduling tends to have a random aspect to it, and the probability of an unfavorable schedule could be small. Second, these unfavorable schedules produce a problem that is transient, not permanent: if processes fail to terminate because the schedule has been unfavorable, processes are still able to terminate subsequently if the schedule stops being unfavorable. A more enlighten-

---

[2] Technical remark: to illustrate the FLP proof, here I consider the behavior of these algorithms in an asynchronous model, where the failure detector or the leader election service output unreliable information.

ing formulation of the consensus impossibility result might be that any algorithm that ensures the safety properties of consensus could be delayed indefinitely during periods with no synchrony (the schedule is unfavorable). In fact, it can be shown that consensus is solvable when there is a very small amount of temporary synchrony in the system, namely, if there is a single link from one process to another such that this link is timely [2].

4.2.5 Uses of Replication

Most people realize that a consensus algorithm lies at the heart of a service replicated using the state machine approach [10, 14]. Fewer people realize that the replicated service need not be the entire system; it could be just a smaller component of the system. For example, each node in the system may need to know some set of system parameters, such as buffer sizes, resource limits, and/or a list that indicates what machines are responsible for what function. One could use a state machine to replicate just this information across nodes. This is illustrated in Figure 4.2.

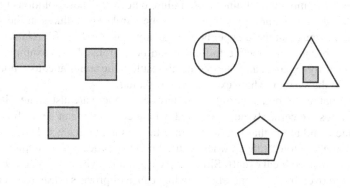

Fig. 4.2 Squares show what is replicated by consensus. On the left, the entire system is replicated. On the right, just some service within a larger (non-replicated) system is replicated.

There are some caveats in using consensus and state machines in that way. First, the number of replicas can be much larger than the minimum needed. (The minimum number of replicas needed is usually $2f+1$ or $3f+1$, depending on the failure model, where f is the maximum number of failures to be tolerated.) For example, if one replicates the set of system parameters as described above, then the number of replicas is the number of nodes in the system, which can be very large. In this case, it is important to use simple optimizations in which not all replicas actively participate in the consensus protocol, instead of, say, using all available replicas to increase the fault tolerance threshold f. Increasing f beyond the necessary is bad because consensus protocols scale poorly in f.

The second caveat is that only requests processed through the state machine are guaranteed to see the current state of the state machine, because some replicas may be missing some state machine updates. In the above example, suppose that a component of the system wants to know the current system parameters. If it tries to read the system parameters directly from the local replica, it may obtain stale information, because the local replica may be lagging behind. To ensure it obtains up-to-date information, the component must submit a read request to the state machine and wait for the request to execute through the consensus protocol. Note that, even if the read request executes through consensus, the returned information is guaranteed to be up-to-date only for a brief moment. By the time the component uses this information (perhaps immediately after obtaining it), the system parameters may have changed already. If this is a problem then the component needs to be placed as part of the state machine, so that the component's actions can be ordered using consensus. The bottom line is that, one needs to be very careful about how components outside the state machine interact with components inside the state machine.

4.2.6 Correlated Failures

The consensus problem has solutions in synchronous models, in models of partial synchrony, or in models with unreliable failure detectors. These solutions typically require that there exist an upper bound t on the number of failures in the system. Practitioners argue that these upper bounds are not realistic, even for relatively large values of t, because in practice failures could be correlated. For example, power failures, security exploits, and bugs could all result in the simultaneous failure of all processes in the system, which exceed the threshold t.

I argue that, even though correlated failures exist, there are also many situations where failures are certainly not correlated, where consensus can be useful. For instance, one could argue that tolerating crash failures is not always about tolerating crashes, but about tolerating slowness caused by busy processes, swapping to disk, or other unexpected local events. Slowness is less likely to be correlated across machines. Moreover, bugs are one of the leading cause of process crashes, and heisenbugs (bugs that are not deterministic) are probably the hardest ones to detect, and hence they are the bugs most likely to be left in a working system. Heisenbugs tend to produce failures that are not correlated.

One could argue that the techniques for handling correlated failures would automatically take care of uncorrelated failures, thus obviating the need for consensus. However, the costs of using those techniques are very different. For example, if there is a power failure, recovery may involve rebooting the machine and retrieving state from stable storage, which can take a long time, leading to a loss of availability. In contrast, one can use consensus-based replication to handle a single (uncorrelated) node crash without any downtime.

The jury is still out on whether most failures are correlated or not. But even if many failures are correlated, I believe there is still significant benefit in tolerating those cases when they are not.

4.3 Issues

Besides misunderstandings, there are also some issues in the consensus literature that have prevented a wider adoption of existing results, algorithms, and techniques. This section covers these issues. I do not adopt an absolute notion of what is an issue—this would amount to subscribing to moral dualism. Instead, my notion of an issue is *relative* to the point of view of a practitioner who would like to benefit from the research on consensus. It is worth noting that some of the issues that I describe, particularly in Sections 4.3.3–4.3.6, extend beyond just the consensus problem: they apply to research in theory of distributed computing in general.

4.3.1 The Application Interface

The notion of an *interface* to an abstraction is well-known to computer scientists. For example, the problem of sorting a list has a very simple, intuitive, and agreed-upon interface. If one needs to implement the interface, it is clear what must be done, and if one wants to use the interface, it is clear how to do that. Unfortunately, such is not the case for consensus, for the following reasons:

- *Multiple application interfaces.* In order for an abstraction to be well specified, it should have a single application interface that everyone adopts. Unfortunately, consensus has two commonly adopted interfaces. The first is the interface used by the Paxos algorithm, which I shall call the p-interface. The second is the interface used by all other consensus algorithms, including algorithms based on failure detection, randomization, or partial synchrony. I shall call the latter the r-interface. There are a number of differences between these interfaces, and practitioners do not understand why there are these differences and which interface they should use. The differences are the following:

  1. *Process roles.* In the p-interface, processes are divided into proposers, learners, and deciders[3] while in the r-interface there are just processes.
  2. *Termination condition.* With the r-interface, all correct processes are required to terminate, while with the p-interface, correct processes are required to terminate only if certain conditions are met (e.g., eventually a leader is elected for sufficiently long). With the r-interface, these conditions are assumptions made in the model.
  3. *Initial state of processes.* With the r-interface, *all* non-faulty processes initially propose a value, while with the p-interface, any positive number of non-faulty processes initially propose a value.

Of these differences, the first and second are cosmetic, but the third is more significant, so let us examine it more closely. The p-interface is more directly applicable to implementing a state machine, because only one replica may receive a request for the state machine to execute, and so only one replica may propose a value. However, the r-interface can also be used to implement a state machine:

---

[3] In the original Paxos paper, this division did not exist, but it appeared in a later description [12].

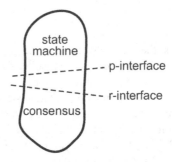

Fig. 4.3 The two different interfaces for the consensus problem.

when a replica receives a request v for the state machine, it sends this request to other replicas telling them to propose v if they have not proposed yet. In this way, all correct replicas will propose, as required by the r-interface. An inspection of the algorithms that implement the p-interface reveals that the first thing that a process does after proposing is to send a message to all other processes. Thus, intuitively, one can think that algorithms for the r-interface "leave out" this send-to-all step for the application to do before invoking consensus. This difference essentially corresponds to two different cuts in the boundary between a state machine and consensus, shown in Figure 4.3. The r-interface cuts at a lower level, requiring that the state machine perform a send-to-all before invoking consensus. With the p-interface, this send-to-all is effectively done by the consensus algorithm.

So this difference is not inherent. However, it is problematic because it makes it difficult for practitioners to understand the consensus literature. For example, there is an algorithm for the r-interface in which all non-faulty processes decide in one communication step if all processes propose the same value. At the same time, one can show that this is not possible for the p-interface. (Intuitively, this is because with the r-interface, all correct process can initially send their proposed value to all and then wait to receive $n-f$ messages, but this initial waiting is not possible with the p-interface since only a few processes may propose.) These two results look contradictory, but they are not.

The reason for having two interfaces is historic. The r-interface appeared as a variation of the interactive-consistency problem, in which every process starts with some initial value. The p-interface was later proposed as an interface more directly applicable to the state machine approach. Regardless of the historical development, it is about time to converge on a single interface for consensus.

- *Usability issues.* Another problem with the consensus interface is usability, and this problem has multiple facets.

First, consensus is a single-use service: after decision is reached, the consensus instance is stuck and must be eventually garbage collected. Garbage collection must be done manually by the application, and this can be tricky, because a process that crashes before the decision may subsequently recover and want to learn the decision, but it cannot do that if the consensus instance has been garbage collected. Another problem with a single-use service is that it needs to be instantiated repeatedly, which imposes overhead and impacts performance. This can be an issue for applications that must solve consensus repeatedly at a high rate.

Second, the consensus problem assumes that the set of processes that propose and decide (the participants) is fixed and known a priori. However, in practice, a machine may crash and remain crashed for long periods (even permanently), and this machine must be excluded from the set of participants and eventually be replaced. How to do that is explained in an extension of Paxos to multiple instances, called Multi-Paxos, but Multi-Paxos is an algorithm not an interface. This feature needs to be described by the interface, by specifying it independently of how it is implemented. Furthermore, Multi-Paxos has several important optimizations but these optimizations are not expressible through the consensus interface: they apply neither for a (one-instance) consensus algorithm nor for multiple instances of a consensus algorithm given as a black box.

The above problems perhaps indicate that consensus is the wrong abstraction to expose. In other words, the consensus problem does not have the same simple and universal appeal that the sorting problem has. Consensus may not be the most intuitive and applicable abstraction for practitioners. An alternative to consensus is the atomic multicast abstraction as defined in [9], which provides reliable and totally-ordered delivery to a variable subset of users which need not include the broadcaster. In my opinion, this abstraction should be studied and adopted more often in the theoretical literature.

4.3.2 Violation of Abstraction Boundaries

The consensus literature often states key properties and results by referring to the inside of a consensus algorithm, instead of referring to the interfaces exposed by the consensus algorithm. This is problematic for practitioners because often they do not want to know what is "inside the box"; they only care about how the box behaves externally.

A common example is to analyze the performance of a consensus algorithm in terms of the number of phases that it needs to decide, where a phase is an algorithm-specific notion. This metric looks inside the box and it is not useful to compare different algorithms, since each algorithm may have its own notion of what is a phase, or may not have phases at all.

Another common example is to state the timeliness requirements of an algorithm in terms of a communication primitive implemented by the algorithm itself. For example, some consensus algorithms in a partially synchronous system require that some non-faulty process be able to receive responses to its queries in a timely fashion. However, a query is an algorithm-specific notion.

To follow the principles of abstraction, results and properties about an algorithm should always be stated in terms of the algorithm's upper and lower interfaces. The upper interface is the consensus application interface, while the lower interface refers to the services on top of which the consensus algorithm runs, such as interprocess communication and leader election or failure detection. Rather than analyzing the performance of an algorithm in number of phases, it is more useful to do so in terms of the lower interface—say, based on the maximum observed message delay, in executions where the failure detector makes no mistakes (e.g., as in [1]). Rather than stating the synchrony requirements of an algorithm in terms of timeliness of a query-response mechanism implemented by the algorithm, it is more useful to do so in terms of properties in the lower interface—say, by indicating which links in the message-passing service are timely (e.g., as in [2]). If this is not possible, then the query-response mechanism needs to be placed in the lower interface so that it is exposed *outside* the algorithm.

4.3.3 Ambiguities and Errors

In distributed computing, it is easy to make mistakes in algorithms and results. This is because distributed systems are inherently non-sequential and failures create exceptional conditions, resulting in many corner cases that are easy to overlook. This, in turn, leads to technical glitches, ambiguous results, or even more serious mistakes in published results.[4] These problems are eventually detected (and perhaps corrected), but many times they are only publicized informally through word of mouth. This method may suffice for the researchers in the area, but may not reach practitioners and outsiders, making it very hard for them to understand the literature.

One proposal to address this issue is to publish the mistakes and possible corrections in the form of small notes. These notes could appear as short papers or brief announcements in one of the important theory conferences in distributed computing. This would create a public record of the problem for outsiders (and insiders) to be aware of.

4.3.4 Unfriendly Formalisms

As a reaction to ambiguous algorithms and incorrect results, the theoretical community has proposed the use of formal frameworks to present algorithms and results, and to prove their correctness. These formalisms certainly eliminate ambiguity and reduces errors, but they are difficult for practitioners to digest because they are too low-level or abstract.

A common practice is to explain results both intuitively and formally, in order to reap the benefits of both approaches. However, it is dangerously easy to provide intuitions that are much too superficial, using as justification a formal presentation "given later". It is also dangerous to provide formal presentations that are much too low-level, using as justification the intuition "given earlier". The result is that neither intuitive nor formal presentations end up being useful.

---

[4] Lest this discussion be interpreted as a remark about any particular paper, I note that there are many results about which this concern can be raised.

Researchers in the theoretical community must find the right balance between formalism and intuition for the particular result that they want to convey. A one-size-fits-all solution cannot adequately address every case, or even most cases.

4.3.5 Lack of Feedback from Practitioners

Practitioners provide very little feedback to theoretical algorithm designers on what needs to be improved, and algorithm designers rarely seek feedback from practitioners. As a result, one often finds algorithm designers optimizing for many different variations of cases and parameters, without knowing which are relevant. That is a somewhat inefficient way to proceed, because only a few cases and parameters require optimization in practice. It would be much better to get input on an actual system from practitioners on what is not working well, and thereby focus on improvements that are likely to be used. Perhaps part of the problem is that it is often difficult to understand a system and isolate which aspects are likely to benefit from better algorithms. Doing so requires close collaboration between theoreticians and practitioners.

4.3.6 Hidden Limitations in Algorithms

Sometimes algorithms proposed in the literature have hidden limitations that could be troublesome in practice. For example, there are many consensus algorithms that decide quickly if some fixed designated process is the leader ("process 1"), but these algorithms become much slower if this process crashes or is not the leader. Such limitations can often be circumvented, but only if practitioners are aware of them. For that to happen, algorithm designers need to be explicit about the weaknesses of their algorithms.

In some cases, the limitations of an algorithm are inherent and cannot be overcome, and whether they are tolerable in practice depends on factors that only practitioners can determine. In these cases, it is even more important for them to be disclosed. If limitations are hidden, a practitioner that implements the algorithm eventually finds out the limitation by herself, but only after much effort. At that point, the practitioner will conclude that either the algorithm designer could not see the problem or, perhaps worse, he was trying to hide it.

Limitations of an algorithm should be explained by the designer of the algorithm, when the algorithm is published. It is better if the designer tell readers of a limitation than if readers later tell the designer.

4.4 Conclusion

The consensus problem is at the heart of replicated distributed systems, which are increasingly becoming a vital part of our society in areas such as commerce, banking, finance, communication, critical infrastructure, and others. While consensus has recently attracted the attention of the systems community and practitioners, the theoretical work on this problem remains underutilized due to misunderstandings and issues. This situation is a loss for everyone: theoreticians are missing an opportunity to apply their work, while practitioners are overlooking an untapped resource. To address this problem, the theory and practical communities need to engage in a more open dialog. This step is sorely needed. The conceptual mechanisms and techniques underlying the consensus problem are very subtle and, without a firm theoretical foundation, it will be hard to go very far. At the same time, consensus is a problem initially motivated by practical concerns, and without interest and feedback from practitioners, the theory will have limited impact.

Acknowledgements I am grateful to Ken Birman, who provided many valuable comments that helped improve this chapter.

References

1. Aguilera, M.K., Chen, W., Toueg, S.: Failure detection and consensus in the crash-recovery model. Distributed Computing 13(2), 99–125 (2000)
2. Aguilera, M.K., Delporte-Gallet, C., Fauconnier, H., Toueg, S.: Communication-efficient leader election and consensus with limited link synchrony. In: ACM Symposium on Principles of Distributed Computing, pp. 328–337 (July 2004)
3. Chandra, T., Griesemer, R., Redstone, J.: Paxos made live—an engineering perspective. In: ACM symposium on Principles of distributed computing, pp. 398–407 (Aug. 2007)
4. Chandra, T.D., Hadzilacos, V., Toueg, S.: The weakest failure detector for solving consensus. J. ACM 43(4), 685–722 (1996)
5. Chandra, T.D., Toueg, S.: Unreliable failure detectors for reliable distributed systems. J. ACM 43(2), 225–267 (1996)
6. Dwork, C., Lynch, N.A., Stockmeyer, L.: Consensus in the presence of partial synchrony. J. ACM 35(2), 288–323 (1988)
7. Fischer, M.J., Lynch, N.A., Paterson, M.S.: Impossibility of distributed consensus with one faulty process. J. ACM 32(2), 374–382 (1985)
8. Guerraoui, R., Schiper, A.: Consensus: the big misunderstanding. In: IEEE Computer Society Workshop on Future Trends of Distributed Computing Systems, pp. 183–188 (Oct. 1997)
9. Hadzilacos, V., Toueg, S.: A modular approach to fault-tolerant broadcasts and related problems. Tech. Rep. TR 94-1425, Department of Computer Science, Cornelpublisl University, Dept. of Computer Science, Cornell University, Ithaca, NY (May 1994)
10. Lamport, L.: Time, clocks, and the ordering of events in a distributed system. Commun. ACM 21(7), 558–565 (1978)
11. Lamport, L.: The part-time parliament. ACM Transactions on Computer Systems 16(2), 133–169 (1998)
12. Lamport, L.: Paxos made simple. ACM SIGACT News (Distributed Computing Column) 32(4), 51–58 (2001)
13. Schiper, A.: Early consensus in an asynchronous system with a weak failure detector. Distributed Computing 10(3), 149–157 (1997)
14. Schneider, F.B.: Implementing fault-tolerant services using the state machine approach: A tutorial. ACM Computing Surveys 22(4), 299–319 (1990)

Chapter 5
Replicating for Performance: Case Studies

Maarten van Steen and Guillaume Pierre

Abstract In this chapter we take a look at the application of replication techniques for building scalable distributed systems. Unlike using replication for attaining dependability, replicating for scalability is generally characterized by higher replication degrees, and thus also weaker consistency. We discuss a number of cases illustrating that differentiation of replication strategies, for different levels of data granularity, is needed. This observation leads us to conclude that automated replication management is a key issue for future research if replication for scalability is to be successfully deployed.

5.1 Introduction

Building scalable distributed systems continues to be one of the more challenging tasks in systems design. There are three independent and equally important perspectives on scalability [20]:

- **Size scalability** is formulated in terms of the growth of number of users or data, such that there is no noticeable loss in performance or increase in administrative complexity.
- A system is said to be **geographically scalable** when components can be placed far apart without seriously affecting the perceived performance. This perspective on scalability is becoming increasingly important in the face of distributing a service across the Internet.
- **Administrative scalability** describes the extent to which a system can be put under the control of multiple administrative organizations without suffering from performance degradation or increase of complexity.

In this chapter, we will concentrate on size and geographical scalability, in particular in relation to the perceived performance of a system. More specifically, we are interested in scalability problems that manifest themselves through performance degradation. To keep matters simple, in the following we will refer to scalability in only this more narrow context.

B. Charron-Bost, F. Pedone, and A. Schiper (Eds.): Replication, LNCS 5959, pp. 73–89, 2010.

To address scalability problems, there are essentially only two techniques that we can apply. Following the terminology as proposed in [5], we can **partition** the set of processes and the collection of data those processes operate on, and spread those parts over different nodes of the distributed system. An excellent example of where this scaling technique has been successfully applied is the Web, which can be viewed as a huge, distributed information system. Each Web site is responsible for handling its own part of the entire data set, allowing hundreds of millions of users to access the system simultaneously. As we will discuss later, numerous sites need further partitioning as a single machine can not handle the stream of requests directed to them.

Another illustrative example of where partitioning has been successfully applied is in the Internet's Domain Name System. By October 2008, the entire name space had been partitioned across an estimated 11.9 million servers[1]. These servers collaborate in resolving names, and in such a way that many requests can be handled simultaneously. However, an important reason why DNS generally performs so well, is also because much of its data has been **cloned**, or more formally, **replicated**.

Cloning processes and associated data is useful for addressing geographical scalability problems. The principle is simple: by placing services close to where they are needed, we can reduce performance degradation caused by network latencies, and at the same time by placing a service everywhere it is needed, we address size scalability by dividing the load across multiple servers. In the following, we shall often use the term replication instead of cloning.

A main issue with replication is that it requires each update to be carried out at each replica. As a consequence, it may take a while before all replicas are the same again, especially when updates need to be carried out at many replicas spread across a large network such as the Internet. More problematic is when multiple updates need to be carried out concurrently, as this requires global synchronization if we wish to guarantee that in the end the replicas are indeed the same. Global synchronization requires the execution of an agreement protocol. Such an execution is generally not scalable: too many parties may need to communicate and wait for results before an update can be finally committed. An important consequence is that if we apply replication as a scaling technique, then we generally need to compromise on consistency: copies cannot be kept the same at all time.

This observation is not new. For example, it is well known among architects of very large Web-based systems such as Amazon, Google, and eBay that scalability can be attained only by "embracing inconsistency"[2]. A keyword here is **eventual consistency**: in the absence of further updates, replicas will converge to the same state (see also [34]). Accepting eventual consistency as the best possible option is needed when dealing with cloned services. The problem is that there is no way that one can guarantee the combination of strong consistency, availability, and coping with partitionable networks at the same time. This so-called CAP conjecture was postulated by Eric Brewer in 2000 and proved correct two years later [9]. For large-

---

[1] http://dns.measurement-factory.com/surveys/200810.html
[2] eBay's Randy Shoup at his presentation at Qcon, London, 2008.

scale distributed systems, it simply means that one cannot guarantee full systemwide consistency of update operations unless we avoid cloning services.

Unfortunately, there are no general, application-independent rules by which we can specify to what extent inconsistencies can be tolerated. In other words, replication for scalability is inherently coupled to the access, usage, and semantics of the data that are being replicated. For example, caching in DNS generally works because name-to-address bindings are relatively stable, allowing caches to be refreshed only once every few hours. Such dependencies, in turn, have led to a myriad of solutions regarding replication strategies. In addition, determining the appropriate granularity of the data to be replicated turns out to be crucial.

In this chapter, we will take a closer look at replication as a scaling technique, and in particular consider those situations in which scalability can be achieved only if the replication degree is relatively large. Such replication is necessarily coupled to applications, but also requires that we can tolerate inconsistencies between replicas. For these reasons, we follow an approach by discussing several cases, each dealing in its own with inconsistencies. In particular, we will argue that in order to achieve performance, we need to automatically decide on (1) which data needs to be replicated, (2) at which granularity, and (3) according to which replication strategy.

To keep matters simple, we assume that updates are coordinated such that write-write conflicts will not occur. In effect, this means that concurrent updates are serialized such that all replicas will process all updates in the same order. This assumption is realistic: in many practical settings we see that potential conflicts on some data set are avoided by having a coordinator for that data set. This coordinator sees all write requests and orders them accordingly, for example, by first timestamping requests before they are passed on to replicas. Furthermore, we focus on scalable Web-based distributed systems, which makes it easier to compare the various trade-offs regarding replication for scalability. Note that many issues we bring up are also applicable to other types of distributed systems, such as large-scale enterprise information systems. We ignore replication for wireless distributed systems, including large-scale systems based on sensor networks, mobile ad hoc networks, and so on. These type of distributed systems are becoming increasingly important, but often require specific solutions when it comes to applying scaling techniques.

In the remainder of this chapter, we start with discussing the large variety of possible replication strategies in Section 5.2. This is followed by a discussion on the data granularity at which these strategies must be applied in Section 5.3. Different forms of consistency guarantees are discussed in Section 5.4, followed by replication management (Section 5.5). We come to conclusions in Section 5.6.

5.2 Replication Strategies

A **replication strategy** describes **which** data or processes to replicate, as well as **how**, **when**, and **where** that replication should take place. In the case of replication for fault tolerance, the main distinguishing factor between strategies is arguably *how* replication takes place, as reflected in a specific algorithm and implementation (see also [35]). Replication for scalability also stresses the *what*, *where* and *when*.

Moreover, where algorithms for fault-tolerance replication strategies are compared in terms of complexity in time, memory, and perhaps messages, the costs of a replication strategy employed for performance should be expressed in terms of *usage* of resources, and the trade-off that is to be made concerning the level of consistency.

The costs of replication strategies are determined by many different factors. In particular, we need to consider replica placement, caching versus replication, and the way that replicated content is updated. Let us briefly consider these aspects in turn (see also [30]), in order to appreciate replica management when performance is at stake.

5.2.1 Replica Placement

Replica placement decisions fall into two different categories: decisions concerning the placement of *replica servers*, and those concerning the placement of *replicated data*. In some cases, the decisions on server placement are irrelevant, for example, when any node in a distributed system can be used for replica placement. This is, in principle, the case with data centers where the actual physical location of a replica server is less important. However, in any distributed system running on top of a large computer network such as an intranet or the Internet, where latencies to clients and between servers play a role, server placement may be an important issue and precedes decisions on data placement.

In principle, server placement involves identifying the K out of N best locations in the network underlying a distributed system [22, 25]. If we can assume that clients are uniformly distributed across the network, it turns out that server placement decisions are relatively insensitive to access patterns by those clients, and that one need only take the network topology into account when making a decision. An obvious strategy is to place servers close to the center of a network [3], that is, at locations to which most communication paths to clients are short. Unfortunately, the problem has been proven to be NP-hard, and finding good heuristics is far from trivial [12]. Also, matters become complicated when going to more realistic scenarios, such as when taking actual traffic between clients and servers into account [10].

Once replica servers are in place, we have the facilities to actually place replicated data. A distinction should be made between client-initiated and server-initiated replication [31]. With server-initiated replication, an **origin server** takes the decision to replicate or migrate data to replica servers. An origin server is the main server from which content is being served and where updates are coordinated. This technique is typically applied in Content Delivery Networks (CDNs) [23], and is based on observed access patterns by clients.

Client-initiated replication is also known as client-side caching. The most important difference with server-initiated replication is that clients can, independently of any replication strategy followed by an origin server, decide to keep a local copy of accessed data. Client-initiated replication is widely deployed in the Web for all kinds of content [11]. It has the advantage of simplicity, notably when dealing with mostly-read data, as there is no need for global coordination of data placement. Instead, clients copy data into local caches based completely on their own access patterns. Using shared caches or cooperative caches [1], highly effective data replication and placement can be deployed (although effectiveness cannot be guaranteed, see [36]).

As an aside, note that caching techniques can be deployed to establish server-initiated replication. In the protocol for the Akamai CDN, a client is directed to a nearby proxy server. The proxy server, configured as a traditional Web caching server, inspects its local cache for the referred content, and, if necessary, first fetches it from the origin server before returning the result to the client [19].

5.2.2 Content Distribution

Once replicas are in place, various techniques can be deployed for keeping them up-to-date. Three different aspects need to be considered:

State versus function shipping: A common approach for bringing a replica up-to-date is to simply transfer fresh data and overwrite old data, with variations based on data compression or transferring only differences between versions (i.e., delta shipping). As an alternative to this form of passive replication, a replica can also be brought up-to-date by locally executing the operation that led to the update, leading to active replication [28]. This form of update propagation is known as function or operation shipping, and has proven to be an alternative when communication links are slow [17].

Pull versus push protocols: Second, it is important to distinguish between protocols that *push* updates to replica servers, or the ones by which updates are *pulled in* from a server holding fresher updates. Pushing is often initiated by a server where an update has just taken place, and is therefore generally proactive. In contrast, pulling in updates is often triggered by client requests and can thus be classified as on-demand. Combinations of the two, motivated by performance requirements, is also possible through leases by which servers promise to push updates until the lease expires [6].

Dissemination strategies: Finally, we need to consider which type of channels to use when delivering updates. In many cases, unicasting is used in the form of TCP connections between two servers. Alternatively, multicasting techniques can be deployed, but due to lack of network-level support we generally see these being used only at application level in (peer-to-peer) content delivery networks [37]. Recently, probabilistic, epidemic-style protocols have been developed as an alternative for content delivery [14, 7].

Clearly, these different aspects together result in a myriad of alternatives for implementing replication strategies. Note also that although such implementations could also be used for replicating for fault tolerance, emphasis is invariably on efficiently delivering content to replica servers, independently of requirements regarding consistency.

5.2.3 Strategy Evaluation

With so many ways to maintain replicas, it becomes important to compare and evaluate strategies. Unfortunately, this is easier said than done. In fact, it can be argued that a blatant omission in the scientific approach to selecting replication strategies is a useful framework for comparing proposals (although such an attempt has been made [13]). The difficulty is partly caused by the fact that there are so many performance metrics that one could consider. Moreover, metrics are often difficult if not impossible to compare. For example, how does one compare a replication strategy that results in low perceived latencies but which consumes a lot of bandwidth, to one that saves network bandwidth at the cost of relatively poor response times?

An approach followed in the Globule system (and one we describe below), is to make use of a general cost function (which is similar to a payoff or utility function in economics). The model considers m performance metrics along with a (nondecreasing) cost $c_k(s)$ of the kth metric. The cost $c_k(s)$ is dependent on the deployed replication strategy s. Combined, this leads to a total replication cost expressed as

$$rep(s) = \sum_{k=1}^{m} w_k c_k(s)$$

where w_k is the (positive) weight associated with making costs $c_k(s)$. With this model, it becomes possible to evaluate and compare strategies, with the obvious goal to minimize the total costs of replication. Note that there may be no obvious interpretation in what the total costs actually stand for. Also, it is up to the designers or administrators of the system in which data are being replicated to decide on the weights. For example, in some cases it may be more important to ensure low latency at the cost of higher usage of bandwidth. Besides latency and network bandwidth, typical performance metrics include used storage, energy consumption, monetary costs, computational efforts, and the "cost" of delivering stale data.

5.3 Replication Granularity

We now take a closer look at a number of cases where replication is used to improve the scalability of a system. In all cases, the improvement comes from adapting the system in such a way that it can simultaneously support several replication strategies, and differentiate among these strategies for smaller units of data than before. Concretely, in our first example, we will demonstrate that supporting a replication strategy on a per-page basis for sites storing static Web pages leads to higher scalability and better performance. In our second example, this kind of differentiation and higher granularity will be shown to also benefit cloning of Web services. As a last example, we take a look at an extensive analysis of Wikipedia traces. The overall conclusion is that replicating for performance requires differentiating replication strategies for smaller data units than is presently common.

5.3.1 Example 1: Content Delivery Networks

An important class of large-scale distributed systems is formed by content delivery networks (CDNs) Internet. Specific content, such as a collection of Web pages,
is serviced by what is known as an origin server. As mentioned before, an origin
server is responsible for handling updates as well as client requests. Also, it provides replica servers with content to which client requests can then be redirected.
The size of a typical CDN may vary between a few tens of servers to tens of thousands of servers.

In order to guarantee availability and performance, replication of content plays a
key role in any CDN. Besides the general issues discussed above concerning where
to place replicas and how to keep them up-to-date, it turns out that the granularity of
the data to consider for replication is equally important. For example, applying a single replication strategy to an entire Web site leads to much worse performance than
replicating each Web page separately according to a page-specific strategy. Furthermore, even for seemingly stable Web sites, we have found that access patterns originating from a site's clients, change enough to warrant continuous monitoring and
adaptation of per-page replication strategies. We briefly report on one such study.

Pierre et al. [21] conducted experiments to examine to what extent differentiating
replication strategies could make a difference in the overall performance of a Web
site. To that end, they considered several sites consisting of only static Web pages.
Experiments were conducted by choosing a single replication strategy for an entire
site, as well as experiments in which each document, i.e. Web page, would be subject to its own replication strategy. In the experiments, clients were traced to their
autonomous system (AS), measuring latency as well as bandwidth. In addition, they
kept an accurate account of updates on documents. Using these data, a *what-if* analysis was performed using a situation in which so-called **edge servers** were assumed
to be placed in the various ASes as sketched in Figure 5.1.

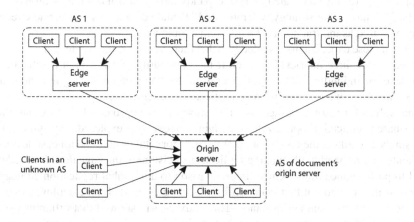

Fig. 5.1 Set-up of the CDN experiment with Web sites having static Web pages.

Table 5.1 Evaluated caching and replication strategies.

Abbr.	Name	Description
NR	No replication	No replication or caching takes place. All clients forward their requests directly to the origin server.
CV	Verification	Edge servers cache documents. At each subsequent request, the origin server is contacted for revalidation.
CLV	Limited validity	Edge servers cache documents. A cached document has an associated expiration time before it becomes invalid and is removed from the cache.
CDV	Delayed verification	Edge servers cache documents. A cached document has an associated expiration time after which the primary is contacted for revalidation.
SI	Server invalidation	Edge servers cache documents, but the origin server invalidates cached copies when the document is updated.
SUx	Server updates	The origin server maintains copies at the x most relevant edge servers; $x = 10$, 25 or 50
SU50+CLV	Hybrid SU50 & CLV	The origin server maintains copies at the 50 most relevant edge servers; the other edge servers follow the CLV strategy.
SU50+CDV	Hybrid SU50 & CDV	The edge server maintains copies at the 50 most relevant edge servers; the other edge servers follow the CDV strategy.

Clients for whom the AS could not be determined were assumed to directly contact the origin server when requesting a Web page. In all other cases, client requests would be assumed to pass through the associated AS's edge server. With this setup, the caching and replication strategies listed in Table 5.1 were considered.

The traces were used to drive simulations in which different strategies were explored, leading to what is generally known as a *what-if analysis*. As a first experiment, a simple approach was followed by replicating an entire Web site according to a single strategy. The normalized results are shown in Table 5.2. Normalized means that the best results were rated as 100. If bandwidth for a worse strategy turned out to be 21% more, that strategy was rated as 121. Stale documents returned to clients are measured as the fraction of the different documents requested.

What these experiments revealed was that there was no single strategy that would be best in all three metrics. However, if the granularity of replication is refined to the level of individual Web pages, overall performance increases significantly. In other words, if we can differentiate replication strategies on a per-page basis, optimal values for resource usage are much more easily approached. To this end, the cost-based replication optimization explained above was explored. Not quite surprisingly, regardless the combination of weights for total turnaround time, stale documents, and or bandwidth, making replication decisions at the page level *invariably* led to performance improvement in comparison to any global replication strategy. Moreover, it turned out that many different strategies needed to be deployed in order to achieve optimal performance. The study clearly showed that differentiating replication strategies at a sufficient level of granularity will lead to significant performance improvements. The interested reader is referred to [21] for further details.

Table 5.2 Normalized performance results using the same strategy for all documents, measuring the total turnaround time, the fraction of stale documents that were returned, and the total consumed bandwidth. Optimal values are highlighted for each metric.

Strategy	Site 1			Site 2		
	Turnaround	Stale docs	Bandwidth	Turnaround	Stale docs	Bandwidth
NR	203	0	118	183	0	115
CV	227	0	113	190	0	**100**
CLV	182	0.61%	113	142	0.60%	**100**
CDV	182	0.59%	113	142	0.57%	**100**
SI	182	0	113	141	0	**100**
SU10	128	0	**100**	160	0	114
SU25	114	0	123	132	0	119
SU50	102	0	165	114	0	132
SU50+CLV	**100**	0.11%	165	**100**	0.19%	125
SU50+CDV	**100**	0.11%	165	**100**	0.17%	125

5.3.2 Example 2: Edge-Server Computing

The previous example dealt only with static Web pages. However, modern CDNs require replication of dynamic pages and even programs [23, 24]. In general, this means that the architecture needs to be extended to what is known as an edge-server system. In such a system, the origin server is supported by several servers situated at the "edge" of the network, capable of running a (partial) replica of the origin server's database, along with programs accessing those data. There are essentially four different organizations possible, as shown in Figure 5.2.

The simplest organization is to clone only the application logic to the edge servers, along with perhaps some data. In this case, requests are processed locally, but if necessary, data are still fetched from the origin server. This scheme is typically used to address size scalability by reducing the computational load of the origin server. However, it will not be sufficient if performance costs are dominated by accesses to the database. If data has been copied to the edge server, it is assumed to be mostly read-only and any updates can be easily dealt with offline [24].

With full replication, the database at the origin server is cloned to the edge servers along with the logic by which data are accessed and processed. Instead of fully cloning the database, it is also possible to clone only those parts that are accessed by the clients contacting the particular edge server. In practice, this means that the origin server needs to keep track of access traces and actively decide which parts of the database require replication.

An alternative scheme is to deploy content-aware caching. In this case, the queries that are normally processed at the origin server are assumed to fit specific templates, comparable to function prototypes in programming languages. In effect, templates implicitly define a simple data model that is subsequently used to store results from queries issues to the origin server. Whenever a query addresses data

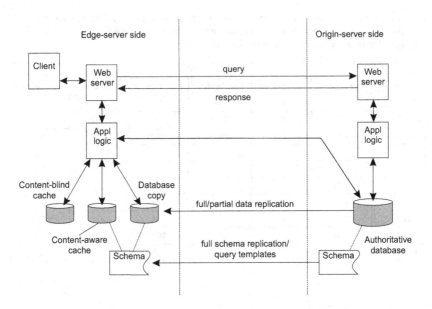

Fig. 5.2 Different ways to organize edge-server computing.

that has already been cached, the result can be retrieved locally. To illustrate, consider a query for listing all books by a given author of which the result is cached at the edge server from which the query originated. Then, when a subsequent query is issued for listing all books by that same author, but for a specific time frame, the edge server need, in principle, only inspect its local cache. This approach is feasible only if the edge server is aware of the templates associated with the queries.

Finally, edge servers can follow a content-blind caching scheme by which a query is first assigned a unique key (e.g., through hashing the query including its parameter values), after which the results are cached under that key. Whenever the exact same query is later issued again, the edge server can look up the previous result from its cache.

All these schemes require that edge servers register for updates at the origin server. In principle, this means that the cloned data at an edge server can be kept identical with that stored at the origin server. For scalability purposes, updates may not be propagated simultaneously to all edge servers, but instead an update is delivered only when there is a need to do so. This may happen, for example, because cloned data are requested by an edge server's client.

For scalability purposes, it is often convenient to let the edge server decide when updates are actually fetched from the origin server. In effect, an edge server will allow its clients to operate on stale data for some time. As long as clients are unaware that some updates have taken place, they will rightfully perceive the cloned data to be consistent. This approach toward delaying update propagation has been used in the file sharing semantics of the Coda distributed file system [15]. Problems

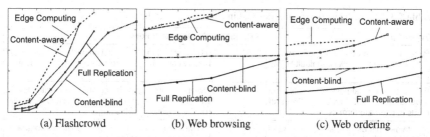

Fig. 5.3 Performance of edge-server systems for different workloads. The x-axis shows increased client-side browsing activity, whereas the y-axis shows response times.

with such schemes occur when clients are allowed to switch between edge servers. In that case, it may happen that a client observes a version D_t of same data at one edge server, and later a *previous* version D_{t-1} of that data at another edge server. Of course, this is not supposed to happen. One solution that has been extensively explored in the Bayou system, is to support client-centric consistency models [32]. Simplifying matters somewhat, these models guarantee that data are kept consistent on a per-client basis. In other words, an individual client will always see the same or fresher data when issuing requests, regardless through which edge server it is accessing that data. However, guaranteeing client-centric consistency requires keeping track of what clients have accessed, which imposes an extra burden on edge servers.

Having a choice from different replication and caching strategies immediately brings up the question which strategy is the best one. Again, in line with the results discussed for simple CDNs, there is no single best solution. Sivasubramanian et al. conducted a series of trace-driven simulations using different workloads for accessing Web services. The results of these experiments are shown in Figure 5.3, of which a detailed report can be found in [29]. Again, what these studies show is that differentiating strategies is important in order to achieve higher performance. In addition, edge-server computing also puts demands on which edge servers clients are allowed to access in order to circumvent difficult consistency problems. Similar results have been reported by Leff et al. [18] in the case of Java-based systems, and distributed objects [8].

5.3.3 Example 3: Decentralized Wikipedia

As a final example, consider the increasingly popular Wikipedia system. This system is currently organized in a near-centralized fashion by which traffic is mostly directed to one of two major sites. Each site maintains a database of so-called wikis: a collection of (hypertext) pages marked up in the *wikitext* markup language. The Wikipedia system provides a Web-based interface by which a Wiki document is returned in HTML form for display in standard Web browsers.

A serious problem for the Wikimedia organization hosting the various wiki's is that the increase in traffic is putting a significant burden on their infrastructure. Being a noncommercial and independent organization means that financial support is

Table 5.3 Wikipedia workload analysis and impact for decentralization.

Type of page	% Requests	Strategy to follow
Pages that are read-only in practice and are mostly read (>75%) in default HTML format.	27.5%	HTML caching or replication with the degree of replication depending on the popularity of the page.
Pages that are almost read-only and have a significant fraction (>25%) of reads in alternate formats.	10.9%	Wikitext replication in combination with HTML caching. The degree of replication should depend on the popularity of the page.
Maintained pages that are mostly read (>75%) in default HTML format.	46.7%	HTML replication with a replication factor controlled by the popularity of the page.
Maintained pages that have a significant fraction (>25%) of reads in alternate formats.	8.3%	Wikitext replication with a replication factor controlled by the popularity of the page. HTML caching can be considered if the read/save ratio is considerably high.
Nonexisting pages.	8.3%	Negative caching combined with attack detection techniques.

always limited. Therefore, turning over to a truly collaborative, decentralized organization in which resources are provided and shared by the community would most likely significantly relieve the current infrastructure allowing further growth.

To test this hypothesis, Urdaneta et al. conducted an extensive analysis of Wikipedia's workload, as reported in [33]. The main purpose of that study was to see whether and how extensive distributed caching and replication could be applied to increase scalability. Table 5.3 shows the main conclusions.

Although most requests to Wikipedia are for reading documents, we should distinguish between their rendered HTML forms and data that is read from the lower-level wikitext databases. However, it is clear that there are still many updates to consider, making it necessary to incorporate popularity when deciding on the replication strategy for a page. Surprisingly is the fact that so many nonexisting pages are referenced. Performance can most likely be boosted if we keep track of those pages through negative caching, i.e. storing the fact that the page does *not* exist, and thus avoiding the need to forward a request.

5.4 Replicating for Performance versus Consistency

From the examples discussed so far, it is clear that differentiating replication strategies and considering finer levels of replication granularity in order to improve performance will help. However, we have still more or less assumed that consistency need not be changed: informally, clients will always be able to obtain a "fresh" copy of the data they are accessing at a replica server. Note that in the case of content delivery networks as well as edge-server computing, we made the assumption that clients will always access *the same server*. Without this assumption, maintaining client-perceived strong consistency becomes more difficult.

Of course, there may be no need to sustain relatively strong consistency. In their work on consistency, Yu and Vahdat [38] noted that consistency can be defined along multiple dimensions:

Numerical deviation: If the content of a replicated data object can be expressed as a numerical value, it becomes possible to express the level of consistency in terms of tolerable deviations in values. For example, in the case of a stock market process, it may be allowed to let replicas deviate to a maximum of 1% before update propagation is required, or likewise, that values are not allowed to differ by more than $0.02.

Numerical deviations can also be used to express the number of outstanding update operations that have not yet been seen by other replica servers. This form of consistency is analogous to allowing transactions to proceed while being ignorant of the result of N preceding transactions [16]. However, this type of consistency is generally difficult to interpret in terms of application semantics, rendering them practically useless.

Ordering of updates: Related to the number of outstanding update operations, is the extent to which updates need to be carried out in the same order everywhere. Tolerating deviations in these orders may lead to conflicts in the sense that two replicas cannot be brought into the same state unless specific reconciliation algorithms are executed. Consistency in terms of the extent that out-of-order execution of operations can be tolerated is highly application specific and may be difficult to interpret in terms of application semantics.

Staleness: Consistency can also be defined in terms of how old a replica is allowed to be in comparison to the most recent update. Staleness consistency is naturally associated with real-time data. A typical example of tolerable staleness is formed by weather reports, of which replicas are generally allowed to be up to a few hours old.

This so-called **continuous consistency** is intuitively simple when dealing with deviations in the value of content, as well as in the staleness of data. However, practice has shown that as soon as ordering of operations come into play, application developers generally find it difficult to cope with the whole concept of data (in)consistency. As mentioned by Saito and Shapiro [27], we would need to deal with a notion of *bounded divergence* between replicas that is properly understood by application developers. Certainly when concurrent updates need to be supported, understanding how conflict resolution can be executed is essential.

Researchers and practitioners who have been working on replication for performance seem to agree that, in the end, what needs to be offered to end users and application developers is a perception of strong consistency: what they see is always perceived as what they saw before, or perhaps fresher. In addition, if they are aware of the fact that what they are offered deviates from the most recent value, then at the very least the system should guarantee eventual consistency. This observation had already led researchers in the field of distributed shared memory (DSM) to simplify the weaker consistency models by providing, for example, software patterns [4]. In other cases, only simple primitives were offered, or weaker consistency was supported at the language level, for example in object-based DSM systems, which provided an workable notion of weak consistency (called *entry consistency* [2]).

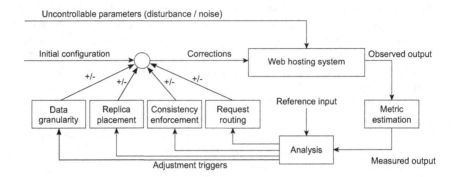

Fig. 5.4 The feedback control loop for automated replica management.

5.5 Replication Management

What all these examples illustrate is that when applying replication for performance, there is no single best solution. We will need to take application semantics into account, and in general also stick to relatively simple consistency models: well-ordered updates and eventual consistency (be it in time or space).

This brings us immediately to one of the major issues in replication for performance: because acceptable weak consistency is dependent on application semantics, we are confronted with a serious replication management problem, which is now also application dependent. By replication management we mean deciding on a replication strategy and ensuring that the selected strategy can be implemented (e.g., by ensuring that appropriate replica servers are in place). As we have discussed above, not only do we need to choose from multiple strategies, we also need to figure out at which level of data granularity we should differentiate strategies.

Manually managing replication for performance in large-scale systems is a daunting task. What is needed is a high degree of automated management, effectively meaning that we are required to implement a feedback loop as shown in Figure 5.4. The control loop shows four different adjustment measures: replica placement (*where to replicate*), consistency enforcement (*how and when to replicate*), request routing (*how to route requests to replicas*), and deciding on data granularity (*what to replicate*).

Notably the deciding on the granularity of data is important for efficient analysis and selection of strategies. For example, by grouping data items into the largest possible group to which the same strategy can be applied, fewer comparisons to reference input is needed thus improving the throughput of feedback.

However, the real problem that needs to be addressed in this scheme is the realization of the analysis component. In content delivery networks such as Globule where data items have an associated origin server, this server is an obvious candidate to carry out the analysis. Doing so will lead to a natural distribution of the load across the system. In this case, an origin server simply logs requests, or collects access traces from replica servers that host content it is responsible for.

Such a scheme cannot be universally applied. Consider, for example, the case of a collaborative, decentralized Wikipedia system. Unlike content delivery networks, there is no natural owner of a Wikipedia document: most pages are actively maintained by a (potentially large) group of volunteers. Moreover, considering that extensive replication is a viable option for many pages, many requests for the same page may follow completely independent paths, as is often also the case in unstructured peer-to-peer networks [26]. As a consequence, knowledge on access patterns is also completely distributed, making analysis for replication management more difficult in comparison to that in content delivery networks.

There seems to be no obvious solution to this problem. What we are thus witnessing is the fact that replication for performance requires differentiating replication strategies at various levels of data granularity and taking application semantics into account when weak consistency can be afforded. However, this replication management requires the instantiation of feedback control loops of which it is not obvious how to distribute their components. Such a distribution is needed for scalability purposes.

5.6 Conclusions

Replicating for performance differs significantly from replicating for availability or fault tolerance. The distinction between the two is reflected by the naturally higher degree of replication, and as a consequence the need for supporting weak consistency when scalability is the motivating factor for replication. In this chapter, we have argued that replication for performance requires automated differentiation of replication strategies and at different levels of data granularity.

In many cases, this automated differentiation implies the instantiation of decentralized feedback control loops, an area of systems management that still requires much attention. If there is one conclusion to be drawn from this chapter, it is that research should focus more on decentralized replication management if replication is to be a viable technique for building scalable systems.

Acknowledgements This chapter could not have been written without the hard research work conducted by a number of people at (one time working at) VU University. We thank Michal Szymaniak, Swaminathan Sivasubramanian, and Guido Urdaneta for their contributions.

References

1. Annapureddy, S., Freedman, M., Mazieres, D.: Shark: Scaling File Servers via Cooperative Caching. In: Second Symp. Networked Systems Design and Impl. USENIX, USENIX, Berkeley, CA (May 2005)
2. Bershad, B., Zekauskas, M., Sawdon, W.: The Midway Distributed Shared Memory System. In: COMPCON, pp. 528–537. IEEE Computer Society Press, Los Alamitos (1993)
3. Bondy, J., Murty, U.: Graph Theory. Springer, Berlin (2008)

4. Carter, J., Bennett, J., Zwaenepoel, W.: Techniques for Reducing Consistency-Related Communication in Distributed Shared Memory Systems. ACM Trans. Comp. Syst. 13(3), 205–244 (1995)
5. Devlin, B., Gray, J., Laing, B., Spix, G.: Scalability Terminology: Farms, Clones, Partitions, Packs, RACS and RAPS. Tech. Rep. MS-TR-99-85, Microsoft Research (Dec. 1999)
6. Duvvuri, V., Shenoy, P., Tewari, R.: Adaptive Leases: A Strong Consistency Mechanism for the World Wide Web. In: 19th INFOCOM Conf., pp. 834–843. IEEE Computer Society Press, Los Alamitos (Mar. 2000)
7. Eugster, P., Guerraoui, R., Kermarrec, A.M., Massoulié, L.: Epidemic Information Dissemination in Distributed Systems. IEEE Computer 37(5), 60–67 (2004)
8. Gao, L., Dahlin, M., Nayate, A., Zheng, J., Iyengar, A.: Application Specific Data Replication for Edge Services. In: 12th Int'l WWW Conf., ACM Press, New York (2003)
9. Gilbert, S., Lynch, N.: Brewer's Conjecture and the Feasibility of Consistent, Available, Partition-tolerant Web Services. ACM SIGACT News 33(2), 51–59 (2002)
10. Ho, K.-H., Georgoulas, S., Amin, M., Pavlou, G.: Managing Traffic Demand Uncertainty in Replica Server Placement with Robust Optimization. In: Boavida, F., Plagemann, T., Stiller, B., Westphal, C., Monteiro, E. (eds.) NETWORKING 2006. LNCS, vol. 3976, pp. 727–739. Springer, Heidelberg (2006)
11. Hofmann, M., Beaumont, L.: Content Networking: Architecture, Protocols, and Practice. Morgan Kaufman, San Mateo (2005)
12. Karlsson, M., Karamanolis, C.: Choosing Replica Placement Heuristics for Wide-Area Systems. In: 24th Int'l Conf. on Distributed Computing Systems, Mar. 2004, pp. 350–359. IEEE Computer Society Press, Los Alamitos (2004)
13. Karlsson, M., Karamanolis, C., Mahalingam, M.: A Framework for Evaluating Replica Placement Algorithms. Tech. rep., HP Laboratories, Palo Alto, CA (2002)
14. Kermarrec, A.M., Massoulié, L., Ganesh, A.: Probabilistic Reliable Dissemination in Large-Scale Systems. IEEE Trans. Par. Distr. Syst. 14(3), 248–258 (2003)
15. Kistler, J., Satyanaryanan, M.: Disconnected Operation in the Coda File System. ACM Trans. Comp. Syst. 10(1), 3–25 (1992)
16. Krishnakumar, N., Bernstein, A.J.: Bounded Ignorance: A Technique for Increasing Concurrency in a Replicated System. ACM Trans. Database Syst. 4(19), 586–625 (1994)
17. Lee, Y.W., Leung, K.S., Satyanarayanan, M.: Operation Shipping for Mobile File Systems. IEEE Trans. Comp. 51(12), 1410–1422 (2002)
18. Leff, A., Rayfield, J.T.: Alternative Edge-Server Architectures for Enterprise JavaBeans Applications. In: Jacobsen, H.-A. (ed.) Middleware 2004. LNCS, vol. 3231, pp. 195–211. Springer, Heidelberg (2004)
19. Leighton, F., Lewin, D.: Global Hosting System. United States Patent, Number 6,108,703 (Aug. 2000)
20. Neuman, B.: Scale in Distributed Systems. In: Casavant, T., Singhal, M. (eds.) Readings in Distributed Computing Systems, pp. 463–489. IEEE Computer Society Press, Los Alamitos (1994)
21. Pierre, G., van Steen, M., Tanenbaum, A.: Dynamically Selecting Optimal Distribution Strategies for Web Documents. IEEE Trans. Comp. 51(6), 637–651 (2002)
22. Qiu, L., Padmanabhan, V., Voelker, G.: On the Placement of Web Server Replicas. In: 20th INFOCOM Conf., Apr. 2001, pp. 1587–1596. IEEE Computer Society Press, Los Alamitos (2001)
23. Rabinovich, M., Spastscheck, O.: Web Caching and Replication. Addison-Wesley, Reading (2002)
24. Rabinovich, M., Xiao, Z., Aggarwal, A.: Computing on the Edge: A Platform for Replicating Internet Applications. In: Eighth Web Caching Workshop (Sep. 2003)
25. Radoslavov, P., Govindan, R., Estrin, D.: Topology-Informed Internet Replica Placement. In: Sixth Web Caching Workshop, Jun. 2001, North-Holland, Amsterdam (2001)
26. Risson, J., Moors, T.: Survey of Research towards Robust Peer-to-Peer Networks: Search Methods. Comp. Netw. 50(17), 3485–3521 (2006)

27. Saito, Y., Shapiro, M.: Optimistic Replication. ACM Comput. Surv. 37(1), 42–81 (2005)
28. Schneider, F.: Implementing Fault-Tolerant Services Using the State Machine Approach: A Tutorial. ACM Comput. Surv. 22(4), 299–320 (1990)
29. Sivasubramanian, S., Pierre, G., van Steen, M., Alonso, G.: Analysis of Caching and Replication Strategies for Web Applications. IEEE Internet Comput. 11(1), 60–66 (2007)
30. Sivasubramanian, S., Szymaniak, M., Pierre, G., van Steen, M.: Replication for Web Hosting Systems. ACM Comput. Surv. 36(3), 1–44 (2004)
31. Tanenbaum, A., van Steen, M.: Distributed Systems, Principles and Paradigms, 2nd edn. (translations: German, Portugese, Italian). Prentice-Hall, Upper Saddle River (2007)
32. Terry, D., Demers, A., Petersen, K., Spreitzer, M., Theimer, M., Welsh, B.: Session Guarantees for Weakly Consistent Replicated Data. In: Third Int'l Conf. on Parallel and Distributed Information Systems, Sep. 1994, pp. 140–149. IEEE Computer Society Press, Los Alamitos (1994)
33. Urdaneta, G., Pierre, G., van Steen, M.: Wikipedia Workload Analysis for Decentralized Hosting. Comp. Netw. (to be published 2009)
34. Vogels, W.: Eventually Consistent. ACM Queue, pp. 15–18 (Oct. 2008)
35. Wiesmann, M., Pedone, F., Schiper, A., Kemme, B., Alonso, G.: Understanding Replication in Databases and Distributed Systems. In: 20th Int'l Conf. on Distributed Computing Systems, Taipei, Taiwan, Apr. 2000, pp. 264–274. IEEE (2000)
36. Wolman, A., Voelker, G., Sharma, N., Cardwell, N., Karlin, A., Levy, H.: On the Scale and Performance of Cooperative Web Proxy Caching. In: 17th Symp. Operating System Principles, Kiawah Island, SC, Dec. 1999, pp. 16–31. ACM (1999)
37. Yeo, C., Lee, B., Er, M.: A Survey of Application Level Multicast Techniques. Comp. Comm. 27(15), 1547–1568 (2004)
38. Yu, H., Vahdat, A.: Design and Evaluation of a Conit-Based Continuous Consistency Model for Replicated Services. ACM Trans. Comp. Syst. 20(3), 239–282 (2002)

Chapter 6
A History of the Virtual Synchrony Replication Model

Ken Birman

Abstract In this chapter, we discuss a widely used fault-tolerant data replication model called *virtual synchrony*. The model responds to two kinds of needs. First, there is the practical question of how best to embed replication into distributed systems. Virtual synchrony defines dynamic *process groups* that have self-managed membership. Applications can join or leave groups at will: a process group is almost like a replicated variable that lives in the network. The second need relates to performance. Although state machine replication is relatively easy to understand, protocols that implement state machine replication in the standard manner are too slow to be useful in demanding settings, and are hard to deploy in very large data centers of the sort seen in today's cloud-computing environments. Virtual synchrony implementations, in contrast, are able to deliver updates at the same data rates (and with the same low latencies) as IP multicast: the fast (but unreliable) Internet multicast protocol, often supported directly by hardware. The trick that makes it possible to achieve these very high levels of performance is to hide overheads by piggybacking extra information on regular messages that carry updates. The virtual synchrony replication model has been very widely adopted, and was used in everything from air traffic control and stock market systems to data center management platforms marketed by companies like IBM and Microsoft. Moreover, in recent years, state machine protocols such as those used in support of Paxos have begun to include elements of the virtual synchrony model, such as self-managed and very dynamic membership. Our exploration of the model takes the form of a history. We start by exploring the background, and then follow evolution of the model over time.

6.1 Introduction

A "Cloud Computing" revolution is underway, supported by massive data centers that often contain thousands (if not hundreds of thousands) of servers. In such systems, scalability is the mantra and this, in turn, compels application developers to replicate various forms of information. By replicating the data needed to handle client requests, many services can be spread over a cluster to exploit parallelism.

B. Charron-Bost, F. Pedone, and A. Schiper (Eds.): Replication, LNCS 5959, pp. 91–120, 2010.

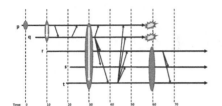

Fig. 6.1 Synchronous run.

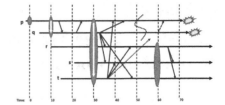

Fig. 6.2 Virtually synchronous run.

Servers also use replication to implement high availability and fault-tolerance mechanisms, ensure low latency, implement caching, and provide distributed management and control. On the other hand, replication is hard to implement, hence developers typically turn to standard replication solutions, packaged as sharable libraries.

Virtual synchrony, the technology on which this article will focus, was created by the author and his colleagues in the early 1980's to support these sorts of applications, and was the first widely adopted solution in the area. Viewed purely as a model, virtual synchrony defines rules for replicating data or a service that will behave in a manner indistinguishable from the behavior of some non-replicated reference system running on a single non-faulty node. The model is defined in the standard asynchronous network model for crash failures. This turns out to be ideal for the uses listed above.

The Isis Toolkit, which implemented virtual synchrony and was released to the public in 1987, quickly became popular [40, 14, 65, 10]. In part this was because the virtual synchrony model made it easy for developers to use replication in their applications, and in part it reflected the surprisingly good performance of the Isis protocols. For example, Isis could do replicated virtually synchronous updates at almost the same speed as one could send raw, unreliable, UDP multicast messages: a level of performance many would have assumed to be out of reach for systems providing strong guarantees. At its peak Isis was used in all sorts of critical settings (we'll talk about a few later). The virtual synchrony model was ultimately adopted by at least a dozen other systems and standardized as part of the CORBA fault-tolerance architecture.

Before delving into the history of the area and the implementation details and tradeoffs that arise, it may be useful to summarize the key features of the approach. Figures 6.1 and 6.2 illustrate the model using time-space diagrams. Let's focus initially on Figure 6.1, which shows a nearly synchronous execution; we'll talk about Figure 6.2 in a moment. First, notation. Time advances from left to right, and we see timelines for processes p, q, r, s and t: active applications hosted in a network (some might run on the same machine, but probably each is on a machine by itself). Notice the shaded oval: the virtual synchrony model is focused on the creation, management and use of *process groups*. In the figures, process p creates a process group, which is subsequently joined by process q, and then by r, s and t. Eventually p and q are suspected of having crashed, and at time 60 the group adjusts itself to drop them. Multicasts are denoted by arrows from process to process: for example, at time 32, process q sends a multicast to the group, which is delivered to p, r, s and t: the current members during that period of the execution.

Process groups are a powerful tool for the developer. They can have names, much like files, and this allows them to be treated like topics in a publish-subscribe system. Indeed, the Isis "news" service was the first widely used publish-subscribe solution [8]. One thinks of a process group as a kind of object (abstract data type), and the processes that join the group as importing a replica of that object.

Virtual synchrony standardizes the handling of group membership: the system tracks group members, and informs members each time the membership changes, an event called a *view change*. In Figure 6.1, new group views are reported at time 0, 10, 30 and 60. All members are guaranteed to see the same view contents, which includes the ranking of members, the event that triggered the new view, and an indication of whether the view is a "primary" one, in a sense we'll define just below. Moreover, virtually synchronous groups can't suffer "split brain" problems. We'll say more about this topic later, but the guarantee is as follows: even if p and q didn't actually fail at time 60, but simply lost connectivity to the network, we can be sure that they don't have some divergent opinion about group membership.

When a new member joins a group, it will often need to learn the current state of the group — the current values of data replicated within it. This is supported through *a state transfer*: when installing a new view that adds one or more members to a group, the platform executes an upcall in some existing member (say, q) to request a state checkpoint for the group. This checkpoint is then sent to the joining member or members, which initialize their group replica from it. Notice that state transfer can be thought of as an instantaneous event: even if a multicast is initiated concurrently with a membership change, a platform implementing virtual synchrony must serialize the events so that the membership change seems atomic and the multicast occurs in a well-defined view.

The next important property of the model concerns support for group multicast. Subject to permissions, any process can multicast to any group, without knowing its current membership (indeed, without even being a member). Multicast events are ordered with respect to one-another and also with respect to group view events, and this ensures that a multicast will be delivered to the "correct" set of receivers. Every process sees the same events in the same order, and hence can maintain a consistent perspective on the data managed by the group.

Now, consider Figure 6.2. We referred to the run shown in Figure 6.1 as *nearly synchronous*: basically, one event happens at a time. *Virtual synchrony* (Figure 6.2) guarantees an execution that looks synchronous to users, but event orderings sometimes deviate from synchrony in situations where the processes in the system won't notice. These departures from synchrony are in situations where two or more events commute. For example, perhaps the platform has a way to know that delivering event a followed by b leaves q in the same state as if b was delivered first, and a subsequently. In such situations the implementation might take advantage of the extra freedom (the relaxed ordering) to gain higher performance.

We mentioned that protocols implementing virtual synchrony can achieve high update and group membership event rates — at the time this chapter was written, in

2009, one could certainly implement virtual synchrony protocols that could reach hundreds of thousands of events per second in individual groups, using standard commodity hardware typical of cloud computing platforms.[1] We'll say more about performance and scale later, but it should be obvious that these rates can support some very demanding uses.

In summary: virtual synchrony is a distributed execution model that guarantees a very strong notion of consistency. Applications can create and join groups (potentially, large numbers of them), associate information with groups (the state transferred during a join), send multicasts to groups (without knowing the current membership), and will see the same events in equivalent orders, permitting group members to update the group state in a consistent, fault-tolerant manner. Moreover, although we've described the virtual synchrony model in pictures, it can also be expressed as a set of temporal logic equations. For our purposes in this chapter,[2] we won't need that sort of formalism, but readers can find temporal logic specifications of the model in [72, 25].

6.2 Distributed Consistency: Who Needs It?

Virtual synchrony guarantees a very powerful form of distributed, fault-tolerant consistency. With a model such as this, applications can replicate objects (individual variables, large collections of data items, or even files or databases), track their evolving state and cooperate to perform such actions as searching in parallel for items within the collection. The model can also easily support synchronization by locking, and can even provide distributed versions of counting semaphores, monitor-like behavior, etc. But not every replicated service requires the sorts of strong guarantees that will be our focus here, and virtual synchrony isn't the only way to provide them.

Microsoft's scalable cluster service uses a virtual synchrony service at its core [54], as does IBM's DCS system, which provides fault-tolerant management and communication technology for WebSphere and server farms [30, 29]. Yahoo's Zookeeper service [64] adopts a closely related approach. Google's datacenters are structured around the Google File System which, at its core, depends on a replicated "chunk master" service (it uses a simple primary/backup scheme), and a locking service called Chubby [19, 21]. The Chubby protocols were derived from Lamport's Paxos algorithm [48]. Most Google applications depend on Chubby in some way: some share a Chubby service, others instantiate their very own separate Chubby service and use it privately, while others depend on services like Big Table or MapReduce, and thus (indirectly) on Chubby. But not all roads lead to state machines. HP's

---

[1] The highest event rates are reached when events are very small and sent asynchronously (without waiting for recipients to reply). In such cases an implementation can pack many events into each message it sends. Peak performance also requires network support for UDP multicast, or an efficient overlay multicast.

[2] We should note that [72] is a broad collection of Isis-related papers and hence probably the best reference for readers interested in more detail. A more recent text [11] covers the material reviewed in this chapter in a more structured way, aimed at advanced undergraduates or graduate students.

Sinfonia service implements a distributed shared memory abstraction with transactional consistency guarantees [1].

The need for consistent replication also arises in settings outside of data centers that support cloud computing. *Edge Computing* may be the next really big thing: this involves peer-to-peer technologies that allow applications such as the widely popular Second Life game to run directly between client systems, with data generated on client machines or captured from sensors transmitted directly to applications that consume or render it [60]. Although highly decentralized, when edge computing systems need consistency guarantees, they require exactly the same sorts of mechanisms as in the datacenter services mentioned above. On the other hand, many peer-to-peer applications manage quite well without the forms of consistency of interest here: Napster, Gnutella, PPLive and BitTorrent all employ stochastic protocols.

6.3 Goals in This Chapter

Whether one's interest is focused on the cloud, looks beyond it to the edge, or is purely historical, it makes sense to ask some basic questions. What sorts of mechanisms, fundamentally, are needed, and when? How were these problems first identified and solved? What role does the classic consensus problem play? What are the arguments for and against specific protocol suites, such as virtual synchrony or Paxos? How do those protocol families relate to one-another?

This article won't attempt to answer all of those questions; to do so would require a much longer exposition than is feasible here, and would also overlap other articles in this collection. As the reader will already have gathered, we'll limit ourselves to virtual synchrony, and even within this scope, will restrict our treatment. We'll try to shed light on some of the questions just mentioned, and to record a little snapshot of the timeline in this part of the field. For reasons of brevity, we won't get overly detailed, and have opted for a narrative style rather light on theoretical formalism. Moreover, although there were some heated arguments along the way, we won't spend much time on them here. As the old saying goes, academic arguments are especially passionate because the underlying issues are so unimportant!

6.4 Historical Context

Virtual synchrony arose in a context shaped by prior research on distributed computing, some of which was especially influential to the model, or to the Isis Toolkit architecture:

1. Leslie Lamport's seminal papers had introduced theoretical tools for dealing with time in distributed systems — and in the process, suggested what came to be known as the "replicated state machine" approach to fault-tolerance, in which a deterministic event-driven application is replicated, and an atomic broadcast primitive used to drive its execution. Especially relevant were his 1978 paper, which was mostly about tracking causality with logical clocks but introduced

state machine replication in an example [45], and his 1984 paper, which explored the approach in greater detail [46]. Fred Schneider expanded on Lamport's results, showing that state machine replication could be generalized to solve other problems [68].

2. The Fischer, Lynch and Patterson result proved the impossibility of asynchronous fault-tolerant consensus [35]. One implication is that no real-world system can implement a state machine that would be guaranteed to make progress; another is that no real system can implement an accurate failure detector. Today, we know that most forms of "consistency" for replicated data involve solving either the consensus problem as originally posed in the FLP paper, or related problems for which the impossibility result also holds [20, 25].

3. On the more practical side of the fence, Cheriton, Deering and Zwaenepoel proposed network-level group communication primitives, arguing that whatever the end-to-end abstraction used by applications, some sort of least-common denominator would be needed in the Internet itself (this evolved into IP multicast, which in turn supports UDP multicast, much as IP supports UDP). Zwaenepoel's work was especially relevant; in [24] he introduced an operating-system construct called a "process group", and suggested that groups could support data replication, although without addressing the issue of replication models or fault-tolerance.

4. Database transactions and the associated theory of transactional serializability were hot topics. This community was the first to suggest that replication platforms might offer strong consistency models, and to struggle with fundamental limits. They had their own version of the FLP result: on the one hand, the fault-tolerant "available copies" replication algorithm, in which applications updated replicas using simple timeout mechanisms for fault-tolerance, was shown to result in non-serializable executions [5]. On the other, while quorum mechanisms were known to achieve 1-copy serializability [4], they required two-phase commit (2PC) protocols that could block if a failure occurred. Skeen proposed a three-phase commit (3PC) [70]: with a perfect failure detector, it was non-blocking. (The value of 3PC will become clear later, when we talk about group membership services.)

5. Systems such as Argus and, later, Clouds were proposed [49, 55]. The basic premise of this work was that the transactional model could bring a powerful form of fault-tolerance to the world of object-oriented programming languages and systems. A criticism of the approach was that it could be slow: the methodology brings a number of overheads, including locking and the need to run 2PC (or 3PC) at the end of each transaction.

All of this work influenced the virtual synchrony model, but the state machine model [45, 46, 68] was especially important. These papers argued that one should think of distributed systems in terms of event orderings and that doing so would help the developer arrive at useful abstractions for fault-tolerance and replication. The idea made sense to us, and we set out to show that it could have practical value in real systems.

To appreciate the sense of this last remark, it is important to realize that in 1983, state machine replication meant something different than it does today. Today, as many readers are probably aware, the term is used in almost any setting where a system delivers events in the same order to identical components, and they process them deterministically, remaining in consistent states. In 1983, however, the state machine model was really offered as an illustration of how a Byzantine atomic broadcast primitive could be used in real applications. It came with all sorts of assumptions: the applications using state machine replication were required to be deterministic (ruling out things like threads and exploitation of multicore parallelism), and the network was assumed to be synchronous (with bounded message delays, perfectly synchronized clocks, and a way to use timeout to sense failures). Thus, state machine replication was really a conceptual tool of theoretical, but not practical, value at the time the virtual synchrony work began. This didn't change until drafts of the first Paxos paper began to circulate in 1990 [48], and then Paxos was used as a component of the Frangiapani file server in 1997.

In our early work on virtual synchrony, we wanted to adapt the state machine concept of "ordered events" to practical settings. Partly, this involved reformulating the state machine ideas in a more object oriented manner, and under assumptions typical of real systems. But there was also the issue of the Byzantine atomic broadcast protocol: a very slow protocol, at least as the community understood such protocols at the time (faster versions are common today). Our thinking led us to ask what other sorts of fault-tolerant multicast protocols might be options.

This line of reasoning ultimately took us so far from the state machine model that we gave our model its own name. In particular, virtual synchrony weakened the determinism assumptions, targeted asynchronous networks, added process groups with completely dynamic membership, and addressed network partitioning faults. All were innovations at that time. By treating process groups as replicated objects, we separated the thing being replicated (the object) from the applications using it (which didn't need to even be identical: a process group could be shared among an application coded in C, a second one coded in Ada, and a few others coded in C++). Groups could be used to replicate a computation, but also to replicate data, or even for purposes such as synchronization.

Today, as readers will see from other chapters in this collection, the distinctions just listed have been eroded because the two models both evolved over time (and continue to do so). The contemporary state machine approach uses dynamic process group membership mechanisms very similar to those used in virtual synchrony. These mechanisms, however, were introduced around 1995, almost a decade after the first virtual synchrony papers were published. Virtual synchrony evolved too, for example by adding support for partitionable groups (work done by the Transis group; we'll say more about it later). Thus, today, it isn't easy to identify clear differences between the best replicated state machine implementations and the most sophisticated virtual synchrony ones: the approaches have evolved towards one-another over the decades. But in 1983, the virtual synchrony work was a real departure from anything else on the table.

6.4.1 Resilient Objects in Isis V1.0

We've summarized the background against which our group at Cornell first decided to develop a new system. Staying with the historical time-line, it makes sense to discuss this first system briefly: it had some good ideas that lived on, although it also embodied a number of questionable decisions. This first system was called Isis (but not the Isis "Toolkit"), and was designed to support something we called *resilient objects*. The goal was to help developers build really fast, fault-tolerant services.

Adopting what was then a prevailing paradigm, Isis V1.0 was a translator: it took simple object-oriented applications, expressed in a language similar to that of Argus or Clouds, and then translated them into programs that could run on multiple machines in a network, and would cooperate to implement the original object in a fault-tolerant, replicated manner. When an application issued a request to a resilient object, Isis would intercept the call, then distribute incoming queries in a way that simultaneously achieved high availability and scalable performance [16, 8]. The name Isis was suggested by Amr El Abbadi, and refers to an Egyptian resurrection myth in which Isis revived Osiris after he had been torn apart by his enemy, Seth. Our version of Isis revived resilient objects damaged by failure.

In retrospect, the initial version of Isis reflected a number of misconceptions on our part. Fortunately, it wasn't a complete wash: in building the system, we got one thing right, and it had a huge impact on the virtual synchrony model. Isis dealt with failure detection in an unusual way, for the time. In most network applications, failures are detected by timeout at the network layer, and throw exceptions that are handled "end to end" by higher layer logic. No failure detector can achieve perfect accuracy, hence situations can arise in which processes p, q, and r are communicating, and p believes that q has failed — but r might still believe both are healthy. Interestingly, this is almost exactly the scenario that lies at the core of the problem with the transactional available copies replication scheme. Moreover, one can provoke such a problem easily. Just disrupt your local area network. Depending on the value of the TCP_KEEPALIVE parameter, connections will begin to break, but if the network outage is reasonably short, some connections will survive the outage, purely as a random function of when the two endpoints happen to have last exchanged messages or acknowledgements. This illustrates a pervasive issue: timeouts introduce inconsistency. FLP teaches us that the problem is fundamental.

Transactional systems generally overcome such problems using quorum methods, but Isis adopted a different approach: it included a separate *failure detection service*. When an Isis component detected a timeout, rather than severing the associated connection, it would complain to the failure detection service (which was itself replicated using a fault-tolerant protocol [15]). This group membership service (GMS) virtualized the notion of failure, transforming potentially inaccurate failure suspicions into what the system as a whole treated as bedrock truth. Returning to our example above, p would report q as faulty, and the service would dutifully echo this back out to every process with a connection to q. The word of this detection service was authoritative: once it declared a component faulty, the remainder of our system believed the declaration and severed connections to q. If a mistake occurred and process q was still alive, q would be forced to rejoin the system much like a freshly-launched process. In particular, this entails rejoining the process groups to which it previously belonged, and reinitializing them.

Today, it would be common to say that Isis implemented a *fail-stop* model [69]: one in which processes fail by halting, and where those failures are detectable. In effect, the Isis GMS creates a virtual network abstraction, translating imprecise timeouts into authoritative failure events, and then notifying all components of the system so that they can react in a coordinated way. This simplifies the design of fault-tolerant protocols, although they remain challenging to prove correct.

The reader may be puzzled by one issue raised by this approach. Recall from the introduction that we need to avoid split-brain behavior, in which a system becomes logically partitioned into two or more subsystems that each think the other has failed, and each think themselves to be running the show. We mentioned that the GMS itself was replicated for high availability. How can the GMS itself avoid split-brain failures?

Isis addressed this by requiring a form of rolling majority consent within the GMS. Membership in the service was defined as a series of membership epochs — later, we began to use the term "view."[3] To move from view i to view $i+1$, a majority of the GMS processes in view i were required to explicitly acknowledge view $i+1$. The protocol was initiated by the oldest GMS process still operational, and requires a 2PC as long as the leader is healthy. If any process suspects the current leader of being faulty, it can trigger a 3PC whereby the next oldest process replaces the apparently faulty one as leader. Our 1985 SOSP paper focused on the system issues and performance [8]; a technical report gave the detailed protocols [13], and later those appeared as [15]. In a departure from both the Byzantine Agreement work and the Consensus model used in FLP, Isis made no effort to respect any sort of ground-truth about failures. Instead, it simply tried to detect real crash failures quickly, without making too many mistakes.[4]

In adopting this model, Isis broke new ground. Obviously, many systems developed in that period had some form of failure detection module. However, Isis used

---

[3] Isis was the first to use this term, which was intended as an allusion to "dynamically materialized views", a virtualization mechanism common in relational database systems: the user poses a standing query, and as the database is updated, the result of the query is continuously recomputed. Queries treat the resulting relation as if it were a real one. At the time, we were thinking of the membership of a group as a sequence of records: membership updates extend the sequence, and multicast operations read the current membership and deliver messages to the operational processes within it. In effect, a multicast is delivered to a "dynamically materialized view of the membership sequence" containing the target processes. The term was ultimately adopted by many other systems.

[4] Obviously, this approach isn't tolerant of malicious behavior: any mistaken failure detection could force an Isis process to drop out of the system and then rejoin. Our reasoning was pragmatic: Isis was a complex system and early versions were prone to deadlock and thrashing. We included mechanisms whereby a process would self-check and terminate itself if evidence of problems arose, but these didn't always suffice. By allowing any process to eject any other process suspected as faulty, Isis was able to recover from many such problems. The obvious worry would be that a faulty process might start to suspect everyone else, but in practice, this sort of thing was never observed.

its membership module throughout, and the membership protocol can be recognized as a fault-tolerant agreement (consensus) solution.

Today, this mechanism may seem much less novel. For example, contemporary implementations of the state machine approach, such as the modern Paxos protocols, have a dynamically tracked notion of membership (also called a view), and use a leader to change membership. However, as noted earlier, when Paxos was introduced in 1990, the protocol wasn't leader-based: it assumed a fixed set of members, and all of them had perfectly symmetric roles. Leaders were introduced into Paxos much later, with a number of performance-enhancing optimizations. Thus when Isis introduced the approach in 1983, it was the first system to use this kind of dynamic membership tracking.

In adopting this approach, we rejected a tenet of the standard Internet TCP protocol: in keeping with the end-to-end philosophy, TCP (and later, early RPC protocols) used timeouts to detect failures in an uncoordinated manner. We also departed from the style of quorum-based update used in database systems, where the underlying set of nodes is fixed in advance (typically as a set of possible participants, some of which might be unavailable from time to time), and where each update must run as a 2PC: a first phase in which an attempt is made to reach a write-quorum of participants, and a second phase in which the participants are told if the first phase succeeded. As we'll see momentarily, the cheapest virtually synchronous multicast avoids this 2PC pattern and yet still ensures that delivery will occur within the primary partition of the system: not the identical guarantee, but nonetheless, very useful.

With the benefit of hindsight, one can look back and see that the convergence of the field around uncoordinated end-system based failure detection enshrined a form of inconsistency into the core layers of almost all systems of that period. This, in turn, drove developers towards quorum-based protocols, which don't depend on accurate failure detection — they obtain fault-tolerance guarantees by reading and writing to quorums of processes, which are large enough to overlap. Yet as we just saw, such protocols also require a two phase structure, because participants contacted in the first phase don't know yet whether a write quorum will actually be achieved. Thus, one can trace a line of thought that started with the end-to-end philosophy, became standardized in TCP and RPC protocols, and ultimately compelled most systems to adopt quorum-based replication. Unfortunately, quorum-based replication is very slow when compared with unreliable UDP multicast, and this gave fault-tolerance a bad reputation. The Isis protocols, as we've already mentioned, turned out to do well in that same comparison.

We've commented that a GMS greatly simplifies protocol design, but how? The key insight is that in a failstop setting, protocols benefit from a virtualized environment where processes appear to fail by halting, and where failures are reported as an event, much like the delivery of a "final message" from the failed process (in fact, Isis ignored messages from processes reported as faulty, to ensure that if a failure was transient, confusion couldn't arise). For example, it became safe to use the available copies replication scheme, an approach that risks non-serializable executions when timeouts are used to detect failures. Internally, we were able to use protocols similar in style to Skeen's 3PC, which is non-blocking with "accurate" failure detections.

Above, we indicated that this article won't say very much about the various academic arguments that erupted around our work. It is interesting, however, to realize that while Isis drew on ideas from many research communities, it also had elements that were troubling to just about every research community of that period. We used a technology reminiscent of state machines, but in a non-Byzantine setting. We use terminology close to that of the consensus literature, but proposed a solution in which a healthy process might be treated as faulty and forced to restart, something that a normal consensus definition wouldn't allow. Our GMS service violated the end-to-end approach (network-level services that standardize failure detection are the antithesis of end-to-end design). Finally, we claimed that our design was intended to maximize performance, and yet we formalized the model and offered protocols with (partial) correctness proofs. Not surprisingly, all of this resulted in a mixed reception.

6.4.2 Beyond Resilient Objects

As it turned out, resilient objects in Isis V1.0 weren't much of a success even relative to our own goals. Beyond its departures from the orthodoxies of the period, the system itself had all sorts of problems. First, resilient objects used a transactional programming language similar to the ones used by Argus and Clouds. However, whereas those systems can now be understood as forerunners of today's transactional distributed computing environments and software transactional memories, Isis was aimed at what we would now call the cloud computing community. To convince users that this language was useful, we needed to apply it to network services such as load balancers, DNS resolvers, etc. But most such services are implemented in C or C++, hence our home-brew language seemed unnatural. Moreover, it turned out to be difficult to adapt the transactional model for such uses.

The hardest problems relate to transactional isolation (the "I" in the ACID model). In a nutshell, transactional systems demand that uncommitted actions be prevented from interacting. For example, if an uncommitted transaction does a DNS update, that DNS record must be viewed as provisional. Until the transaction commits or aborts, other applications either can't be allowed to look at it or, if they "optimistically" read the record, the readers become dependent upon the writer.

This may seem straightforward, but creates a conundrum. Locking records in a heavily-used service such as the DNS isn't practical. But if such records aren't locked, long dependency chains arise. Should an abort occur, it may cascade through the system. Moreover, no matter how one implements concurrency control, it is hard to achieve high performance unless transactions are very short-lived. This forces applications to use lots of very short atomic actions, and to employ top-level actions whenever possible. But such steps "break" the transactional model. There was a great deal of work on this issue at the time (the Argus team had one approach, but it was just one among many: others included Recovery Blocks [63] and Sagas

[26]). None of these solutions, however, appeared to be well matched with our target environment.

Faced with these issues, it occurred to us that perhaps the core Isis infrastructure might be more effective if we unbundled it and offered it as a non-transactional library that could be called directly from C or C++. Of course, the system had been built to support transactions, and our papers had stressed transactional consistency models. This led us to think about what it would mean to offer a "transactional process group" in which we could retain strong consistency and fault-tolerance properties, but free applications from the problematic consequences of the transactional model.

The key idea was to think of the membership of each group as a kind of shared database that would be updated when processes joined and left the group, and "read" by multicast protocols, resulting in a form of transactional serializability at the level of the multicasts used to send updates to replicated data. This perspective led us to the virtual synchrony model. Stripped down versions of the model were later proposed, notably "view-atomic multicast" as used by Schiper and Sandoz [66] and "view synchrony", proposed by Guerraoui and Schiper in [36] (the Isis literature used the term "virtually synchronous addressing" for this property). In [3], Babaoglu argued that view synchrony should be treated as the more fundamental model, and developments have tended to reinforce this perspective.

6.4.3 The Isis Toolkit and the Virtual Synchrony Model

Accordingly, we set out to re-implement the Isis system as a bare-bones infrastructure that would present a "toolkit" API focused on processes that form groups to replicate data, back one-another up for fault-tolerance, coordinate and synchronize their actions, and perform parallel operations such as concurrent search of large databases.[5] Other tools within the toolkit offered access to the group membership data structure, delivered event upcalls when membership changed, and supported state transfer. A "news" service developed by Frank Schmuck provided topic-oriented publish/subscribe. None of these services was itself transactional, but all gained consistency and fault-tolerance from the underlying model. Isis even included a conventional transactional subsystem (nobody used it).

Of course, our goal wasn't just to make our own tools fault-tolerant: we wanted to make the life the application developer simpler, and for this reason, the virtual synchrony model was as much a "tool" as the ones just listed: those were library tools, while the model was more of a conceptual tool. As we saw in the introduction, a virtually synchronous system is one indistinguishable from a synchronous one. This is true of applications built using virtual synchrony too: the developer starts with a very synchronous design, and is assisted in developing a highly con-

---

[5] The system also included a home-brew threads package, and a standard library for serializing data into messages and extracting data from them. Cthreads weren't yet available, and we learned later that quite a few of the early Isis users were actually looking for a threads package when they downloaded the toolkit!

current, performance-efficient solution that retains the simplicity and correctness characteristics of the original synchronous version.

The key to this methodology is to find systematic ways that event ordering can be relaxed, leaving the platform the freedom to deliver some messages in different orders at different group members. We'll discuss the conditions under which this can happen below, but the essential idea is to allow weaker delivery orderings when the delivery events commute, so that the states of the members turn out to be identical despite the different event orderings. One benefit of this approach is to reduce the risk of a "poison pill" scenario, in which a state-sensitive bug might cause all members of a traditional state-machine replicated service to crash simultaneously. In virtual synchrony, the members of a group are in equivalent states, but recall that a group is usually a replicated object: Isis rarely replicated entire processes. Thus the processes joining a group might actually differ widely: they could be coded in different languages, may have joined different sets of additional groups, and their executions could be quite non-deterministic. In contrast the code implementing a typical object replica might be very small: often, just a few lines of simple logic. All of this makes it much less likely that a single event will cause many members to crash simultaneously.

Another difference is visible at the "end" of the execution, on the right: two processes become partitioned from the others, and continue to exchange some messages for a short while before finally detecting their isolated condition and halting. Although the application developer can ask Isis not to allow such runs (they use the *gbcast* primitive to send messages, or invoke the *flush* primitive before delivering messages), the default allows them to arise for bounded periods of time.[6] These messages may never be delivered at all in the other processes, and if they are, may not be delivered in the order seen by the processes that failed. Given an application that can tolerate these kinds of minor inconsistencies, Isis gained substantial performance improvements by permitting them. Moreover, by working with application developers, we discovered that stronger guarantees are rarely required. Often, an application that seems to need strong guarantees can easily be modified into one for which weaker guarantees suffice.[7]

One proves that a system implements virtual synchrony by looking at the runs it can generate. Given a run, the first step is to erase any invisible events — events that occurred at processes that later failed, and that didn't have a subsequent causal

---

[6] The internal timeout mechanisms mentioned earlier ensure that an isolated process would quickly discover the problem and terminate itself; developers could fine-tune this delay.

[7] Few Isis applications maintained on-disk state that couldn't be discarded after a restart. For example, consider a load-balancing service, in which nodes report their loads through periodic multicasts, and assign new tasks to lightly-loaded nodes. Now suppose that a node running the service crashes and later restarts. It won't need any state from prior to the crash: a state-transfer can be used to bring it up to date. The example illustrates a kind of multicast that reports a transient state change: one that becomes stale and is eventually forgotten as the system evolves over time. Experience with Isis suggested that these kinds of multicasts are not merely common, but constitute the overwhelming majority of messages transmitted within applications. The insight here is that even if a transient multicast is delivered non-atomically, the service using the multicast might not be at risk of user-visible inconsistencies.

path to the processes that survived. Next, where events are known to commute, we sort them. If we can untangle Figure 6.2 and end up with Figure 6.1, our run was "indistinguishable" from a synchronous run; if *all* runs that a protocols permits are indistinguishable from synchronous runs, it is virtually synchronous.

As discussed earlier, network partitioning is avoided by requiring that there can only be one "primary" partition active in the network. In Figure 6.2, the majority of the processes are on the side of the system that remains active. The isolated processes are too few in number to form a primary partition, and will quickly discover this problem and then shut down (or, in fancier applications, shift to a "disconnected" mode of operation).[8] A special mechanism was used to handle "total" failure, in which the primary partition is lost. Basically, the last processes to fail are able to restart the group, resuming execution using whichever state reflects the most updates. Although the problem is difficult in general settings [71], in a virtual synchrony environment identifying these last failed processes becomes easy if we simply log each group view.

6.4.4 A Design Feature Motivated by Performance Considerations

The most controversial aspect of virtual synchrony centers on the willingness of the system to deliver unstable events to applications, despite the risk that a failure might "erase" all evidence that this occurred. Doing so violates one of the tenants of the Consensus model as articulated by the FLP paper: the *uniform agreement property*, which requires that if one process *decides* $v \in \{0, 1\}$, then every non-faulty process that decides, decides v. As stated, this implies that even if a process decides and then crashes immediately, the rest of the system will make the identical decision value. Paxos, for example, provides this guarantee for message delivery, as does the uniform reliable multicast [65]. Moreover, virtual synchrony sometimes does so as well: this is the case for process group views, uniform multicast protocols, and for events delivered using *gbcast*. Why then did we offer a "broken" multicast primitive as our default mode of operation?

To understand our reasoning, the reader will need to appreciate the emphasis on performance that dominated the systems community during that period, and continues to dominate today. For the networking community, there will never be a point at which the network is "too fast" to be seen as a bottleneck. Even our earliest papers came under criticism because reviewers argued that in the real world, no protocol slower than UDP multicast would be tolerated. Yet UDP multicast is a hardware-supported unreliable protocol in which the sender sends a message, and "one hop downstream", the receivers deliver it! Competing with such a short critical path creates all sorts of pressures. The features of the virtual synchrony model,

---

[8] The developer controlled the maximum delay before such a problem would be detected. By manipulating timeout parameters, the limit could be pushed to as little as three to five seconds. Modern machines are faster, and today the limit would be a small fraction of a second. By using *gbcast* or *flush*, "lost events" such as the ones shown in Figure 6.2 are eliminated, but performance is sharply reduced.

taken as a whole, represent a story that turned out to be competitive with this sort of raw communication primitive: most virtually synchronous multicasts could be sent asynchronously, and delivered immediately upon receipt, just as would be the case if one were using raw UDP multicast. This allowed us to argue that users could have the full performance of the hardware, and yet would also gain much stronger fault-tolerance and consistency semantics.

As we've emphasized, an application can be designed so that if a multicast needs the stronger form of safety, in which any multicast is delivered to all operational processes, or to none, the developer simply sends it with a uniform multicast primitive, or with *gbcast*, or invokes *flush* prior to delivery. But our experience with Isis revealed that this is a surprisingly rare need. The common case was simply to send the multicast unsafely. Doing so works because the great majority of multicasts either don't change the application state at all, or update what can be understood as "transient" state, relevant to the system for a short period of time, but where persistency isn't needed. In such cases, it may not matter if a failed process received a multicast that nobody else will receive, or so an unusual event ordering: if it ever recovers, nobody will notice that immediately before crashing, it experienced a strange sequence of events.

For example, a query might be multicast to a group in order to request some form of parallel search by its members. Queries don't change application state at all, so this kind of multicast can certainly be delivered without worrying about obscure failure cases.

Many kinds of updates can be sent with a non-uniform multicast primitive, too. Probably the best example is an update to a cache. If a process restarts from a crash, it certainly won't assume that cached data is currently accurate; either it will validate cached items or it will clear the cache. Thus a really fast, reliable, ordered multicast is exactly what one wants for cache updates; uniform delivery simply isn't needed. Other examples include updates that only touch transient state such as load-balancing data, and internal chit-chat about the contents of transient data structures such as a cache, a lock queue or a pending-task queue (a "work queue"). On recovery from failure, a process using such a data structure will reinitialize itself using a state transfer from an operational process. If the whole group fails, we either restart in a default state, or have one of the last processes to fail restart from a checkpoint.

The application that really needs uniform delivery guarantees, because it maintains persistent state, would be a big on-disk database. Obviously, databases are important, but there aren't many more such examples. Our point, then, is that this category is relatively small and the stronger guarantees they need are costly. In Isis, we simply made the faster, more common multicast the default, and left it to the developer to request a stronger guarantee if he or she needed it. In contrast, the Paxos protocols offer the stronger but more costly protocol by default, whether needed or not.

6.5 Dynamic Membership

Let's revisit the features of the model somewhat more carefully. As we've seen, the basic idea of replicating data within a group of processes traces to Lamport's state machine concept. In addition to removing state machines from the Byzantine world where they were first proposed, Isis departed from Lamport's work in several ways.

We've already seen one departure, namely our use of a dynamic membership model. At the time we built Isis, one might think that a static model of the sort used in databases (and later in Paxos) would have seemed more natural, but in fact our model of how process groups would be used made dynamic membership seem much more obvious. After all: we assumed that applications might use large numbers of groups, because for us, the granularity of a group was a single object, not an entire application. Like files that applications open, access, then close, we saw groups as shared structures that applications would join, participate in for a while, and then depart from. With completely dynamic membership, a group becomes an organic abstraction that can, in effect, wander around the system, residing at processes that are currently using it, but over time, moving arbitrarily far from the initial membership.

Of course, we realized that some systems have groups of server platforms and need to know that groups will always contain a majority of the servers (databases often require this). In fact, Isis supported both models. Implicit in the normal behavior was a *weighting function* and a *minimum group commit weight*. By default, the weighting function weighted all processes 1.0, and used a minimum commit weight of 0.0, but it was possible to override these values, in which case no new view could be committed unless a majority of the members of the previous view had consented to it *and* the sum of weights of the new group view exceeded the minimum. Thus, to ensure that the majority of some set of k servers would always be present in each new group view, one simply told Isis to weight the servers 1.0 and all non-servers 0.0, and then specified that new views have a weight greater than $k/2$.

6.5.1 Local Reads and Fast Updates

Dynamic membership is the key to an important performance opportunity: many of the protocols we were competing with at the time assumed that their role was to replicate some service at a statically defined set of replicas, and used quorum methods to do both reads and updates. To tolerate failures, even reads needed to access at least two members, since any single member might have been down when an update was done and hence have a stale state. By tracking membership dynamically, in a setting where a trusted primary-partition GMS reports liveness, we could be sure that every member of a group was also up to date, and reads could then be done entirely locally. In [38] we showed this, and also gave a locking protocol in which read-locks are performed locally. Thus, reads never require sending messages, although updates obviously do — for locking, to communicate the changes to data, and for the commit protocol when the transaction completes. The resulting protocol far outperforms quorum-based algorithms in any setting where reads are common, or where updates are bursty. In the worst case, when updates are common and each transaction performs just one, performance is the same as for a quorum scheme.

The key insight here is that within a virtual synchrony system, the group view represents a virtual world that can be "trusted". In the event of a partitioning of the group, processes cut off from the majority might succeed in initiating updates (for example if they were holding a lock at the time the network failed), but would be unable to commit them — the 2-phase protocol would need to access group members that aren't accessible, triggering a view change protocol that would fail to gain majority consent. Thus any successful read will reflect all prior updates: committed ones by transactions serialized prior to the one doing the read, plus pending updates by the reader's own transaction. From this we can prove that our protocol achieves one-copy serializability when running in the virtual synchrony model. And, as noted, it will be dramatically faster than a quorum algorithm achieving the identical property.

This may seem like an unfair comparison: databases use quorums to achieve serializability. But in fact Isis groups, combined with locking, also achieve serializability. Because the group membership has become a part of the model, virtually synchronous locking and data access protocols guarantee that any update would be applied to all replicas and that any read-locked replica reflects all prior updates. In contrast, because quorum-based database systems lack an agreed-upon notion of membership, to get the same guarantees in the presence of faults, a read must access two or more copies: a read quorum. Doing so is the only way to be sure that any read will witness all prior updates.

Enabling applications to read a single local replica as opposed to needing to read data from two or more replicas, may seem like a minor thing. But an application that can trust the data on any of its group members can potentially run any sort of arbitrary read-oriented computation at any of its members. A group of three members can parallelize the search of a database with each member doing 1/3 of the work, or distribute the computation of a costly formula, and the code looks quite normal: the developer builds any data structures that he or she likes, and accesses them in a conventional, non-distributed manner. In contrast, application programmers have long complained about the costs and complexity of coding such algorithms with quorum reads. Each time the application touches a data structure, it needs to pause and do a network operation, fetching the same data locally and from other nodes and then combining the values to extract the current version. Even *representing* data becomes tricky, since no group member can trust its own replicas. Moreover, whereas virtually synchronous code can execute in straight-line fashion without pausing, a quorum-read algorithm will be subjected to repeated pauses while waiting for data from remote copies.

Updates become faster, too. In systems where an update initiator doesn't know which replicas to "talk to" at a given point in time, there isn't much choice but to use some kind of scatter-shot approach, sending the update to lots of replicas but waiting until a quorum acknowledged the update before it can be safely applied. Necessarily, such an update will involve a 2PC (to address the case in which a quorum just can't be reached). In virtual synchrony, an update initiated by a group member can be sent to the "current members", and this is a well-defined notion.

6.5.2 Partitionable Views

This discussion raises questions about the conditions under which progress can be guaranteed during partitioning failures. Danny Dolev's research group became fascinated with the topic and went much further with it than we ever did at Cornell. Dahlia Malkhi, visiting with us in 1992, helped formalize the Isis model; the model in Chapter 6 of the book we published on the Isis system was due to her [72]. Upon returning to Hebrew University, she was the lead developer for the Transis [31] system, sharing some code with our Horus system, but using her own GMS protocols redesigned to maximize availability during partitioning failures, and including multicast protocols that can be traced back to the UCSB Totem project. The Transis protocol achieves the highest possible availability during partitioning failures [42]. However, this author always found the resulting model tricky to work with, and it was not widely adopted by application developers. Subsequent work slightly simplified the model, which became known as *extended view synchrony* [57], but it remains hard to develop non-trivial applications that maximize availability during partitioning failures.

6.6 Causally Ordered Multicast: *cbcast*

Dynamic membership only addresses some costs associated with multicasts that carry updates. In the timeframe when we developed our update protocols, the topic was very much in the air. Lamport's papers had been followed by a succession of theoretical papers proposing all sorts of protocols solving such problems as Byzantine Agreement, totally ordered atomic broadcast, and so forth — again, within static groups. For example, one widely cited paper was the Chang and Maxemchuck protocol [22], which implemented a totally ordered atomic multicast that used a circulating token to order messages. To deliver an update, one might have to wait for the token to do a full circuit of a virtual ring linking the group members. Latency increased linearly in the size of the group: a significant cost for large groups, but tolerable for a group with just two or three members.

Our initial work with Isis used a totally ordered protocol proposed by Dale Skeen and based on a similar, earlier, protocol by Leslie Lamport: it involved a 2PC in which logical timestamps were exploited to order multicasts [15, 45]. This was faster than most other total ordering protocols, but still was potentially as slow as the slowest group member. We wanted to avoid the two-phase flavor that pervade such protocols, and became interested in protocols that exploited what might be called application-specific optimizations. For example, knowing that the sender of a multicast holds a mutually exclusive lock within a group, a totally ordered multicast can be built using a protocol with the "cost" of a sender-ordered (FIFO) multicast. Frans Kaashoek, who ultimately wrote his PhD thesis on this topic [41], showed that token-based protocols of this sort have all sorts of other advantages too, including better opportunities to aggregate small messages into big ones, the possibility of asynchronous garbage collection, and also match well with applications that produce updates in a bursty pattern.

In our work, we realized that FIFO order has a generalization that can extend the power of the multicast primitive at surprisingly low cost — just a few bytes per message. The trick is to put a little extra ordering information onto the message (the solution we ultimately favored used a small *vector timestamp* with a single counter per member of the current group view [17]). The rule for delivering a message generalizes the rule used for FIFO ordering: "if message x arrives and its header indicates that there is a prior message y, delay x until y has been delivered". But now, "prior" is interpreted using the vector timestamp ordering rule, rather than the usual comparison of sender sequence numbers.

Isis used this approach to support a protocol we called *cbcast*: a reliable, view-synchronous multicast that respected the potential causality ordering (the transitive closure of the FIFO ordering). One way to visualize this ordering property is to think about a system in which process p does some work, and then sends an RPC to process q asking it to do a subtask, and so forth. When the RPC returns, p resumes working. Now suppose that "work" involves sending multicasts. A FIFO ordering would deliver messages from x in the order it sent them, and similar for y, but a node receiving messages from both p and q could see them in an arbitrary order. We see this in the figure below; the heavy lines denote the "thread of execution".

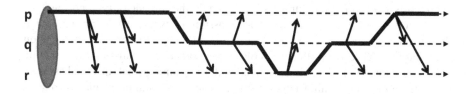

Fig. 6.3 Causally ordered multicasts.

One way to think about Figure 6.3 is to imagine that process p "asked" q to do that work, and q in turn issued a request to r. In some sense, q is a continuation of a thread of execution running in p. The figure highlights this visually: the single thread of control is the one shown in dark black, first running at p, then q, then r, and then finally returns back to p. The *cbcast* primitive respects ordering along this kind of thread of control. If multicast b (perhaps sent by q) could be causally ordered after multicast a (perhaps sent by p), a FIFO ordering won't necessarily deliver the messages in the order they were sent because they had different senders. In contrast, *cbcast* will deliver a before b at any destinations they share. The idea is very intuitive if one visualizes it this way.

Performance for *cbcast* can be astonishingly good: running over UDP multicast, this primitive is almost as fast as unreliable UDP multicast [17]. By using *cbcast* to carry updates (and even for locking, as discussed in [39]), we accomplished our goal, which was to show that one could guarantee strong reliability semantics in a system that achieved performance fully comparable to that of Zwaenepoel's process groups running in the V system.

6.7 Time-Critical Applications

With its focus on speed, one major class of Isis applications turned out to involve systems that would traditionally have been viewed as "real-time" by the research community. As a result, Isis was often contrasted with the best known protocols in the fault-tolerant real-time community, notably the so-called Δ-T fault-tolerant broadcast protocols developed by Flaviu Cristian and his colleagues [27].

These protocols work in the following manner. The designer starts by specifying bounds on the numbers and types of failures that can occur (process failures, packet loss, clock failures). They also bound delays for packet delivery and clock skew by correct processes. Then, through multiple all-to-all broadcast stages, each multicast is echoed by its receivers until one can prove that at least one round included a correct sender and experienced no network faults (in effect: there must be enough rounds to use up the quota of possible failures). Finally, received multicasts are delayed for long enough to ensure that even if correct processes have worst-case clock skew and drift, they will still deliver messages in the same order and at roughly the same time as all other correct processes.

All of this takes time: at one workshop in the early 1990's, a speaker concerned about costs worked out the numbers for this and other broadcast protocols and argued that with as few as 10 processes under assumptions reasonable for that time, a Δ-T broadcast could take between 5 and 20 seconds to be delivered, depending upon the failure model selected (the protocols cover a range from fail-stop to Byzantine behavior). Most of the delay is associated with overcoming clock-drift and skew so as to deliver messages within a tight temporal window: the multicast relaying phases would normally run very quickly.

The strength of the Δ-T suite was its guarantee that messages will be delivered fault-tolerantly, in total order, *and within a bounded temporal delay* despite failures. On the other hand, these protocols lack the consistency property of virtual synchrony. For example, a "faulty" group member using the Δ-T protocols could miss a message, or deliver one out of order. This may not seem like a big deal until one realizes that a process can be temporarily faulty by simply running a bit slower than the bounds built into the system, or temporarily having a higher-than-tolerable clock skew. Since the Δ-T protocols have no explicit notion of group view, the protocols work around faults, rather than excluding faulty members. A discussion of the issue, with diagrams showing precisely how it can arise, can be found in [11].

Since no process can be sure it hasn't ever been faulty, no group member can ever be sure that its own data is current, because the protocol isn't actually required to operate correctly at faulty participants. This is a bit like obeying the speed limit without a reliable speedometer. One does the best one can, but short of driving absurdly slowly, there is a definite risk of briefly breaking the law. And indeed, driving slowly is the remedy Δ-T protocol designers recommended: with these protocols, it was critical to set the parameters to very conservative values. One really doesn't want a correct process to be transiently classified as faulty; if that happens, all guarantees are lost.

Thus, builders of real-time systems who needed *provable* temporal guarantees, but could sacrifice speed and consistency, would find what they wanted in the Δ-T protocols. Isis, in contrast, offered much better performance and strong consistency, but without hard temporal delivery guarantees. The real-time community found itself immersed in a philosophical debate that continues to this day: Is real-time about predictable speed, or provable worst-case deadlines? The question remains unanswered, but Isis was used successfully in many sensitive settings, including air traffic control and process control in chemical refineries.

6.8 A Series of Commercial Successes, but Ultimately, a Market Failure

The combination of the virtual synchrony consistency model with an easily used toolkit turned out to be quite popular. Isis soon had large numbers of real users, who downloaded the free release from a Cornell web site. Eventually, the user base became so demanding that it made sense to launch a company that would do support, integration work and enhance the platform. Thus, the same protocols we designed and implemented at Cornell found their way into all sorts of real systems (details on a few can be found in [15] and [72]). These included the New York and Swiss Stock Exchange, the French Air Traffic Control System, the US Navy AEGIS, dozens of telecommunications provisioning systems, the control system of some of the world's largest electric and gas grid managers, and all sorts of financial applications. Many of these live on: today, the French ATC solution has expanded into many other parts of Europe and, to this author's knowledge, has never experienced a single problem. The New York Stock Exchange system operated without problems for more than a decade (they phased the Isis solution out in early 2007), running the fault-tolerant system that delivers data to the overhead displays and to external "feeds" like Reuters, Bloomberg and the SEC. During that decade, there were plenty of component crashes, but not a single disruption of actual trading.

Virtual synchrony was also adopted by a number of other research groups, including the Totem project developed by Moser and Melliar Smith [58], Dolev's Transis project [31], the European Phoenix project [52], Babaoglu's early e-Grid project, Amir's Spread system [2] (which continues to be widely used), and others. The UCSB team led a successful effort to create a CORBA fault-tolerance standard based on virtual synchrony. It offers lock-step state-machine replication of deterministic CORBA objects, and there were a number of products in the area, including Eternal [59], and Orbix+Isis, offered by IONA.

Unfortunately, despite these technical successes, virtual synchrony never became a huge market success [12]. The main commercial applications tended to be for replication of services, and in the pre-cloud computing data, revenue was mostly generated on the "client side". The model continues to play an important role in many settings, but at the time of this writing there are only three commercial products using the model: JGroups, Spread and C-Ensemble. Of these, JGroups and Spread are the most widely used.

At Cornell, after completing Isis, we developed two Isis successors: first Horus [73], in which Van Renesse showed that a virtual synchrony protocol stack could be constructed as a composition of microprotocols (and set performance records along the way), and then Ensemble [37], a rewrite of Horus into O'CaML (a dialect of ML) by Mark Hayden. Ensemble was the basis of an interesting dialog with the formal type theory community. In a collaboration that drew upon an I/O Automata specification developed jointly by the Cornell team and Lynch's group at MIT, and used the Cornell NuPRL automated theorem proving system developed by Constable's group[50], a specification of many of the Ensemble protocols was created. NuPRL was then used to prove protocol properties and (through a form of partial evaluation) to generate optimized versions of the Ensemble protocols. Although the protocol stack as a whole was never "proved correct", the resulting formal structure was still one of the largest ever treated this way: the Ensemble protocol stacks that implement virtual synchrony included nearly 25,000 lines of code!

Virtual synchrony continues to play some important roles hidden within products that don't expose any form of directly usable group communication API. IBM has described patterning its DCS product on Ensemble [30, 29]. As mentioned early in this article, DCS is used for fault-tolerance and management layer in Websphere and in other kinds of services deployed within datacenters. We also worked with Microsoft to develop a scalable cluster management solution that ultimately shipped with the recent Longhorn enterprise server product; it runs large clusters and provides core locking and state replication services [54]. Again, a virtual synchrony protocol is used where strong consistency matters. Moreover, Google's Chubby and Yahoo's Zookeeper services both have structures strongly reminiscent of virtually synchronous process groups.

6.8.1 How Replication Was Used

In light of the focus on this volume on replication, it makes sense to review some of the uses to which these applications put the technology. Details can be found in [15] and [72].

- One popular option was to simply replicate some sort of abstract data type, in effect associating the object with the process group. In Isis, we saw two "styles" of data replication. For non performance-intensive uses, applications simply used the totally ordered multicast protocol, *abcast*, to propagate updates, and performed reads against any local copy. For performance-critical purposes, developers typically started with *abcast* but then optimized their applications by introducing some form of locking and then replacing the *abcast* calls with asynchronous[9] *fbcast* (the FIFO multicast) or its cousin *cbcast*. One common pattern used *cbcast* for both purposes: to request and grant locks, and to replicate updates [39]. With the Isis implementation of *cbcast* this implements the Herlihy-Wing *linearizability* model [38].

- Replication was also applied to entire services. We expected that state-machine replication would be common among Isis users, but in fact saw relatively little use of this model until the CORBA "Orbix+Isis" product came out. Users objected to the requirement that applications be deterministic. The problem is that on modern platforms, concurrency through multithreading, timer interrupts, and non-deterministic I/O is so common that most developers couldn't develop a deterministic application even if they wanted to do so.

- Some applications used request replication for parallelism. Most servers are I/O bound, hence response time for many applications is limited by the speed with which a file or database can be searched. Many virtual synchrony applications replicate requests by multicasting them to a process group consisting of identical servers, which subdivided the work. For example, perhaps one server could search the first half of a database, and another the second half. This was a popular model, and is a very good match with search in datacenters, which often work with enormous files and databases. One can think of it as a very simple form of "map-reduce".

- Variations on primary-backup fault-tolerance were common. Isis users were loath to dedicate one machine to simply backing up another machine. However, the system also supported a generalization of primary-backup that we called "coordinator-cohort" that could be combined with a transparent TCP fail-over mechanism. In this model, each request was assigned to a different process group member, with another group member functioning as a backup, stepping in only if the primary crashed. The coordinator role was spread evenly within the group. Since the cost of replicating the request itself is negligible, with k members available to play the coordinator role for distinct requests, users obtained a k-fold speedup. Moreover, because the client's connection to the group wouldn't break even if a fault did occur, the client was completely insulated from failures. The mechanism was very popular.

- Many applications adopted a publish-subscribe communication pattern. As mentioned above, Isis offered a "news" interface that supported what later became known as topic-based publish-subscribe. In the simplest model, each topic maps one-to-one to a process group, but this creates huge numbers of groups. Accordingly, the tool used a form of channelization, mapping each topic to one of a small set of groups and then filtering incoming messages to deal with the resulting inaccuracy. This approach remains common in modern publish-subscribe products.

With the exception of publish-subscribe applications, it is interesting to realize that most uses of Isis involved servers running on small clusters. For example, the French Air Traffic Control System runs Isis in datacenters with hundreds of machines, but

---

[9] In Isis, a multicast could be invoked asynchronously (no replies), or could wait for replies from one, several, or all group members.

organized as clusters of 3 to 5 consoles. Isis was configured to run in disjoint configurations, keeping loads light and providing fault isolation.

Publish-subscribe, however, is a very different world: data rates can be very high,
groups can be big, and enterprises may have other desires too, such as security or
management interfaces. Group communication of all kinds, not merely virtual synchrony, is challenged by such goals — indeed, operators of today's largest datacenter platforms report that instability of large-scale publish-subscribe deployments
represents a very serious problem, and we know of a number of very high-profile
settings in which publish-subscribe has effectively been banned because the technology proved to be unreliable at high data rates in large-scale uses. Such stories
make it clear that the French Air Traffic Control project made a very wise decision.
Later, we'll comment on our recent work to overcome these issues, but they clearly
point to important research challenges.

6.8.2 Causal and Other Controversies

Although virtual synchrony has certainly been successful and entered the main-
stream computing world, this history wouldn't be complete without at least allusion
to some of the controversies mentioned earlier. There were many of them:

- The causally ordered multicast primitive used in Isis was debated with enormous
  enthusiasm (and much confusion) [23, 9].
- There was a period of debate about the applicability of the FLP result. The question was resolved emphatically with the not-surprising finding that indeed, consensus and virtual synchrony are related [25, 53, 67].
- We noted that the formal definition of consensus includes an agreement property
  that Isis violates by default. Is virtual synchrony therefore incorrect by default?
- Because Paxos can be used to build multicast infrastructures, and virtual synchrony communication systems can be used to solve consensus, one can ask
  which is "better". Earlier, we noted that virtual synchrony can implement guarantees identical to Paxos if the user limits himself to uniform multicast or *gbcast*,
  or uses *flush*. As noted earlier, systems like Chubby do use Paxos, but tend to be
  engineered with all sorts of optimizations and additional mechanisms: Paxos is
  just one of several protocols, just as the virtual synchrony view update protocol
  is just one of many Isis protocols. Thus, it makes little sense to talk about choosing "between" Paxos and virtual synchrony. The protocol suites we end up using
  incorporate elements of both.
- There was much interest in using groups to securely replicate keys for purposes
  of end-to-end cryptographic security. Interestingly, this model runs afoul of the
  cloud-computing trend towards hosting everything: these days, companies like
  Google want to manage our medical records, provide transcripts of telephone calls,
  and track our digital lives. Clearly, one is supposed to trust one's cloud provider,
  and perhaps for this reason, the major security standards are all client-server infrastructures; true end-to-end security keys that might deny the cloud platform a
  chance to see the data exchanged among clients have no obvious role. But this
  could change, and if so, secure group keys could be just what the doctor ordered.

6.8.3 What Next? Live Objects and Quicksilver Scalable Multicast!

The story hasn't ended. Today's challenges relate to scale and embeddings. With respect to scalability, the push towards cloud computing has created a new interest on infrastructure for datacenter developers. The tools used in such settings must scale to accommodate deployments on tens or hundreds of thousands of machines and correspondingly high data rates. Meanwhile, out at the edge, replication and multicast patterns are increasingly interesting in support of new forms of collaboration and new kinds of social networking technologies.

At Cornell, our current focus is on solving these next generation scalability challenges, while also integrating reliable multicast mechanisms with the modern generation of componentized platforms that support web services standards — for example, the Microsoft .net platform and the J2EE platform favored by Java developers. We've created a system that implements what we are calling "Live Distributed Objects[10]" [60, 62]. The basic idea is to enable end-users, who may not be programmers, to build applications by drag-and-drop, much as one pulls a figure or a table into a text document.

From the perspective of the application designer, live objects are edge-mashups, created on the client platform much in the same sense as a Google mashup that superimposes push-pin locations on maps: the user drags and drops objects, constructing a graph of components that interact by event passing. The main difference is that the Google mashup is created on Google's platform and exported through a fairly sophisticated minibrowser with zoom, pan and layer controls; a live object is a simpler component designed to connect with other live objects within the client machine to form a graph that might have similar functionality to the Google version, but could import content from multiple hosted platforms (for example, we routinely combine Google maps with Yahoo! weather and population data from the National Census), and with peer-to-peer protocols that can achieve very low latency and jitter when clients communicate with one-another. Once created, a Live Object-based application can be shared by making copies — it can even be emailed — and each node that activates it will effectively become an endpoint of a group associated with that object.

We've packaged a number of multicast protocols as Live Objects, and this creates a connection to the theme of the present article: one of the protocols supports virtually synchronous replication at high data rates and large scale. However, not all objects have complex distributed behaviors. Live objects can also be connected to sensors, actuators, applications that generate events, and even databases or spreadsheets.

With Live Objects, we're finding that even an unskilled user can build non-trivial distributed collaboration applications, workflow systems, or even games. The experience is very similar to building scenarios in games like Second Life, but whereas Second Life "runs" on a data center, Live Objects run directly on and between the client platforms where the live application is replicated. Although doing so poses

---

[10] A video of a demo can be seen at http://liveobjects.cs.cornell.edu

many challenges, one of our research goals is to support a version of Second Life built entirely with Live Objects.

In support of Live Objects, we've had to revisit reliable multicast and replication protocols [61]. As noted, existing solutions can scale a single group to perhaps 100 members, but larger groups tend to destabilize at high data rates. None of the systems we've evaluated can handle huge numbers of groups with irregular overlap. Yet, even simple Live Object applications can create patterns of object use in which a single machine might end up joining thousands of replication groups, and extremely high data rates. In [60] we discuss some of the mechanisms we're exploring in support of these new dimensions of scalability. With these, we believe that groups providing a slightly weaker reliability model than virtual synchrony can scale to at least hundreds of members, can sustain data rates as high as 10,000 1-kbyte messages per second, and individual nodes can join thousands of groups that overlap in irregular ways.

We're also revisiting the way that virtual synchrony, consensus and transactional guarantees are implemented. The standard way to build such protocols is to do so as a library constructed directly over UDP message passing. We're currently working on a scripting language (we call it the *properties framework*) in which higher level reliability properties can be described. An interpretive runtime executes these scripts in a scalable, asynchronous, dataflow manner. Preliminary results suggest that strong reliability properties can scale better than had previously been believed, but we'll need to complete the work to know for sure.

Live objects include a simple type system, matched to the limited interface model favored in modern web services platforms, but far from the state of the art. Readers interested in connections between replication and type theory may want to look at papers such as [43, 44, 47, 51]. Research on componentized protocols includes [6, 7, 37, 39, 56, 73]. These lines of study come together in work on typed endpoints in object oriented systems, such as [18, 28, 32, 34, 33].

6.9 Closing Thoughts

It seems appropriate to end by sharing an observation made by Jim Gray, who (over dinner at a Microsoft workshop) commented on a parallel between the early database community, and what he believed has happened with virtual synchrony and other strong replication models. In its early days, the transactional community aggressively embraced diversity. Researchers published on all sorts of niche applications and papers commonly argued for specialized variations on the transactional model. The field was awash in specialized database systems. Yet real success only came with consolidation around transactions on relational databases: so much investment was focused on the model that the associated technology advanced enormously.

With this success, some researchers probably felt that the field was taking a step "backwards", abandoning superior solutions in favor of less elegant or less efficient ones. Yet success also brought research opportunities: research was needed to overcome a new set of challenges of scale, and performance. The science that emerged was no less profound than the science that had been "displaced."

In this, Jim saw a general principle. If a technology tries too hard to make every user happy, so much effort is needed to satisfy the 20% with the hardest problems that the system ends up being clumsy and slow. The typical user won't need most of its features, and many will opt for a simpler, cheaper solution that's easier to use. The irony is that in striving to make every user happy, a technology can actually leave the majority *unhappy*. In the end, an overly ambitious technology merely marginalizes itself.

Did the Isis system actually "need" four flavors of ordered multicast? Probably not: we got carried away, and it made the system difficult for the community to understand.

Today, the opportunity exists to create consistency-preserving replication tools that might be widely adopted, provided that we focus on making replication as easy as possible to use in widely standard platforms. In some ways this may force us to focus on a least common denominator approach to our past work. Yet making replication with strong semantics work for real users, on the scale of the Internet, also reveals profound new challenges, and as we solve them, we may well discover that the underlying science is every bit as interesting and deep as anything we discovered in the past.

Acknowledgements The author is grateful to André Schiper, Robbert van Renesse and Fred Schneider. Not only would virtual synchrony not exist in its current form without the efforts of all three, but they were generous enough to agree to read an early draft of this paper. This revision is certainly greatly improved as a result.

References

1. Aguilera, M., Merchant, A., Shah, M., Veitch, A., Karamanolis, C.: Sinfonia: a new paradigm for building scalable distributed systems. In: 21st ACM SOSP, Nov. 2007, pp. 159–174 (2007)
2. Amir, Y., Nita-Rotaru, C., Stanton, J., Tsudik, G.: Secure Spread: An Integrated Architecture for Secure Group Communication. IEEE TDSC 2(3) (2005)
3. Babaoglu, Ö., Bartoli, A., Dini, G.: Enriched view synchrony: A programming paradigm for partitionable asynchronous distributed systems. IEEE Transactions on Computers 46(6), 642–658 (1997)
4. Bernstein, P., Goodman, N.: Concurrency Control in Distributed Database Systems. ACM Computing Surveys 13(2) (1981)
5. Bernstein, P., Goodman, N.: An algorithm for concurrency control and recovery in replicated distributed databases. ACM Transactions on Database Systems 9(4), 596–615 (1984)
6. Bhatti, N., Hiltunen, M., Schlichting, R., Chiu, W.: Coyote: A System for Constructing Fine-Grain Configurable Communication Services. ACM Transactions on Computer Systems 16(4), 321–366 (1998)
7. Biagioni, E., Harper, R., Lee, P.: A Network Protocol Stack in Standard ML. Journal of Higher-Order and Symbolic Computation 14(4) (2001)
8. Birman, K.: Replication and Fault-Tolerance in the ISIS System. In: 10th ACM Symposium on Operating Systems Principles, Dec. 1985, pp. 79–86 (1985)
9. Birman, K.: Responses to Cheriton and Skeen's SOSP paper on Understanding the Limitations of Causal and Total Event Ordering. SIGOPS Operating Systems Review 28(1) (1994)

10. Birman, K.: A review of experiences with reliable multicast. Software Practice and Experience 29(9) (1999)
11. Birman, K.: Reliable Distributed Systems. Springer, New York (2004)
12. Birman, K., Chandersekaran, C., Dolev, D., Van Renesse, R.: How the Hidden Hand Shapes the Market for Software Reliability. In: Proceedings IEEE Workshop on Applied Software Reliability, Philadelphia, PA (June 2006)
13. Birman, K., Joseph, T.: Reliable communication in the presence of failures. Tech. Rep. TR85-694 (August 1985)
14. Birman, K., Joseph, T.: Exploiting Virtual Synchrony in Distributed Systems. In: 11th ACM Symposium on Operating Systems Principles (Dec. 1987)
15. Birman, K., Joseph, T.: Reliable communication in the presence of failures. ACM Transactions on Computer Systems 5(1) (1987)
16. Birman, K., Joseph, T., Raeuchle, T., El Abbadi, A.: Implementing Fault-Tolerant Distributed Objects. IEEE Transactions on Software Engineering 11(6) (1985)
17. Birman, K., Schiper, A., Stephenson, P.: Lightweight causal and atomic group multicast. ACM Transactions on Computer Systems 9(3), 272–314 (1991)
18. Briot, J., Guerraoui, R., Lohr, K.: Concurrency and Distribution in Object-Oriented Programming. ACM Comput. Surv. 30(3), 291–329 (1998)
19. Burrows, M.: The Chubby Lock Service for Loosely-Coupled Distributed Systems. In: OSDI, pp. 335–350 (2006)
20. Chandra, T., Hadzilacos, V., Toueg, S., Charron-Bost, B.: On the impossibility of group membership. In: Proc. 15th PODC, May 23-26, 1996, pp. 322–330 (1996)
21. Chandra, T.D., Griesemer, R., Redstone, J.: Paxos Made Live — An Engineering Perspective (based on Chandra's 2006 invited talk). In: Proc. 26th PODC, Aug. 2007, pp. 398–407 (2007)
22. Chang, J., Maxemchuk, N.: Reliable broadcast protocols. ACM Trans. on. Computer Systems 2(3), 251–273 (1984)
23. Cheriton, D., Skeen, D.: Understanding the Limitations of Causally and Totally Ordered Communication. In: SOSP, pp. 44–57 (1993)
24. Cheriton, D., Zwaenepoel, W.: Distributed process groups in the V Kernel. ACM Transactions on Computer Systems (TOCS) 3(2), 77–107 (1985)
25. Chockler, G., Keidar, I., Vitenberg, R.: Group Communication Specifications: A Comprehensive Study. ACM Computing Surveys 33(4) (2001)
26. Chrysanthis, P.K., Ramamritham, K.: ACTA: the SAGA Continues. In: Elmagarmid, A. (ed.) Database transaction models for advanced applications, Morgan Kaufmann, San Francisco (1992)
27. Cristian, F., Aghili, H., Strong, R., Volev, D.: Atomic Broadcast: From Simple Message Diffusion to Byzantine Agreement. In: Proc. 15th Int. Symp. on Fault-Tolerant Computing (FTCS-15), Ann Arbor, MI, USA, June 1985, pp. 200–206. IEEE Computer Society Press, Los Alamitos (1985)
28. Damm, C., Eugster, P., Guerraoui, R.: Linguistic Support for Distributed Programming Abstractions. In: CDCS, pp. 244–251 (2004)
29. Dekel, E., et al.: Distribution and Consistency Services (DCS), http://www.haifa.ibm.com/projects/systems/dcs/index.html
30. Dekel, E., Frenkel, O., Goft, G., Moatti, Y.: Easy: engineering high availability QoS in wservices. In: Proc. 22nd Reliable Distributed Systems, pp. 157–166 (2003)
31. Dolev, D., Malkhi, D.: The Transis Approach to High Availability Cluster Communication. Comm. ACM 39(4), 87–92 (1996)
32. Eugster, P.: Type-based Publish/Subscribe: Concepts and Experiences. ACM Transactions on Programming Languages and Systems (TOPLAS) 29(1) (2007)
33. Eugster, P., Damm, C., Guerraoui, R.: Towards Safe Distributed Application Development. In: ICSE, pp. 347–356 (2004)
34. Eugster, P., Guerraoui, R., Damm, C.: On Objects and Events. In: OOPSLA, pp. 254–269 (2001)

35. Fischer, M., Lynch, N.A., Paterson, M.: Impossibility of distributed consensus with one faulty process (initially published in ACM PODS, August 1983). Journal of the ACM (JACM) 32(2) (1985)
36. Guerraoui, R., Schiper, A.: Consensus Service: A Modular Approach for Building Agreement Protocols in Distributed Systems. In: Proc. 26th FTCS, Japan, June 1996, pp. 168–177 (1996)
37. Hayden, M.: The Ensemble System. Ph.D. thesis, Cornell University, available as TR 98-1662 (May 1998)
38. Herlihy, M., Wing, J.: Linearizability: A Correctness Condition for Concurrent Objects. ACM TOPLAS 12(3), 463–492 (1990)
39. Hutchinson, N.C., Peterson, L.L.: The x-Kernel: An architecture for implementing network protocols. IEEE Trans. Software Eng. 17(1) (1991)
40. Joseph, T.A., Birman, K.: Low Cost Management of Replicated Data in Fault-Tolerant Distributed Systems. ACM Trans. Comput. Syst. 4(1), 54–70 (1986)
41. Kaashoek, M.F., Tanenbaum, A.S., Verstoep, K.: Group Communication in Amoeba and its Applications. Distributed Systems Engineering 1(1), 48–58 (1993)
42. Keidar, I., Dolev, D.: Increasing the Resilience of Atomic Commit at no Additional Cost. In: ACM PODS, May 1995, pp. 245–254 (1995)
43. Keidar, I., Khazan, R., Lynch, N., Shvartsman, A.: An Inheritance-Based Technique for Building Simulation Proofs Incrementally. ACM TOSEM 11(1) (2002)
44. Krumvieda, C.: Distributed ML: Abstractions for Efficient and Fault-Tolerant Programming. Ph.D. thesis, Cornell University, available as TR 93-1376 (1993)
45. Lamport, L.: Time, Clocks, and the Ordering of Events in a Distributed System. Comm. ACM 21(7) (1978)
46. Lamport, L.: Using Time Instead of Timeout for Fault-Tolerant Distributed Systems. ACM TOPLAS 6(2) (1984)
47. Lamport, L.: The temporal logic of actions. ACM TOPLAS 16(3), 872–923 (1994)
48. Lamport, L.: The Part-Time Parliament (technical report version: 1990). ACM Transactions on Computer Systems 16(2), 133–169 (1998)
49. Liskov, B., Scheifler, R.: Guardians and Actions: Linguistic Support for Robust, Distributed Programs. ACM TOPLAS 5(3) (1983)
50. Liu, X., Kreitz, C., van Renesse, R., Hickey, J., Hayden, M., Birman, K., Constable, R.: Building reliable, high-performance communication systems from components. In: 17th ACM SOSP (Dec. 1999)
51. Lynch, N., Tuttle, M.: An Introduction to Input/Output automata (also Technical Memo MIT/LCS/TM-373, Laboratory for Computer Science, Massachusetts Institute of Technology). CWI Quarterly 2(3), 219–246 (1989)
52. Malloth, C.P., Felber, P., Schiper, A., Wilhelm, U.: Phoenix: A Toolkit for Building Fault-Tolerant Distributed Applications in Large Scale. In: Proc. of IEEE Workshop on Parallel and Distributed Platforms in Industrial Products, San Antonio, TX (Oct. 1995)
53. Malloth, C.P., Schiper, A.: View Synchronous Communication in the Internet. Tech. Rep. 94/84, EPFL (Oct. 1994)
54. Manferdelli, J.: Microsoft Corporation. Unpublished correspondence (Oct. 2007)
55. McKendry, M.S.: Clouds: A fault-tolerant distributed operating system. IEEE Tech. Com. Distributed Processing Newsletter 2(6) (1984)
56. Mishra, S., Peterson, L.L., Schlichting, R.D.: Experience with modularity in Consul. Software—Practice and Experience 23(10) (1993)
57. Moser, L.E., Amir, Y., Melliar-Smith, P.M., Agarwal, D.A.: Extended virtual synchrony. In: Proceedings of the 14th IEEE International Conference on Distributed Computing Systems, Poznan, Poland, June 1994, pp. 56–65 (1994)
58. Moser, L.E., Melliar-Smith, P.M., Agarwal, D., Budhia, R.K., Lingley-Papadopoulos, C.A., Archambault, T.: The Totem system. In: Proceedings of the 25th Annual International Symposium on Fault-Tolerant Computing, Pasadena, CA (June 1995)
59. Moser, L.E., Melliar-Smith, P.M., Narasimhan, P.: The Eternal System. In: Workshop on Dependable Distributed Object Systems, OOPSLA'97, Atlanta, Georgia (October 1997)

60. Ostrowski, K., Birman, K., Dolev, D.: Live Distributed Objects: Enabling the Active Web. IEEE Internet Computing (Nov./Dec. 2007)
61. Ostrowski, K., Birman, K., Dolev, D.: QuickSilver Scalable Multicast. In: Network Computing and Applications (NCA), Cambridge, MA (2008)
62. Ostrowski, K., Birman, K., Dolev, D., Ahnn, J.H.: Programming with live distributed objects. In: Vitek, J. (ed.) ECOOP 2008. LNCS, vol. 5142, pp. 463–489. Springer, Heidelberg (2008)
63. Randell, B., Xu, J.: The Evolution of the Recovery Block Concept. In: Lyu, M.R. (ed.) Software Fault Tolerance, pp. 1–21. John Wiley & Sons, Chichester (1995)
64. Reed, B., Junqueira, F., Konar, M.: Zookeeper: Because Building Distributed Systems is a Zoo. Submitted for publication (Oct. 2007)
65. Ricciardi, A., Birman, K.: Using Process Groups to Implement Failure Detection in Asynchronous Environments. In: PODC, pp. 341–353 (1991)
66. Schiper, A., Sandoz, A.: Uniform reliable multicast in a Virtually Synchronous Environment. In: Proc. 13th ICDCS, Pittsburgh (May 1993)
67. Schiper, A., Sandoz, A.: Primary Partition "Virtually-Synchronous Communication" Harder than Consensus. In: Tel, G., Vitányi, P.M.B. (eds.) WDAG 1994. LNCS, vol. 857, pp. 39–52. Springer, Heidelberg (1994)
68. Schneider, F.: Implementing fault-tolerant services using the state machine approach: A tutorial. ACM Computing Surveys 22(4), 299–319 (1990)
69. Schneider, F., Schlichting, R.: Fail-stop processors: An approach to designing fault-tolerant computing systems. TOCS 1(3), 222–238 (1983)
70. Skeen, D.: Nonblocking Commit Protocols. In: Proc. ACM SIGMOD, pp. 133–142 (1981)
71. Skeen, D.: Determining the Last Process to Fail. In: ACM PODS, pp. 16–24 (1983)
72. Van Renesse, R., Birman, K.: Reliable Distributed Computing with the Isis Toolkit. IEEE Computer Society Press, Los Alamitos (1994)
73. Van Renesse, R., Birman, K., Maffeis, S.: Horus: A Flexible Group Communication System. Communications of the ACM 39(4), special issue on Group Communication Systems (1996)

Chapter 7
From Viewstamped Replication to Byzantine Fault Tolerance

Barbara Liskov

Abstract The paper provides an historical perspective about two replication protocols, each of which was intended for practical deployment. The first is Viewstamped Replication, which was developed in the 1980's and allows a group of replicas to continue to provide service in spite of a certain number of crashes among them. The second is an extension of Viewstamped Replication that allows the group to survive Byzantine (arbitrary) failures. Both protocols allow users to execute general operations (thus they provide state machine replication); both were developed in the Programming Methodology group at MIT.

7.1 Introduction

This paper describes two replication algorithms. The first, Viewstamped Replication, was developed in the 1980's; it handles failures in which nodes fail by crashing. The second, PBFT (for "Practical Byzantine Fault Tolerance"), was developed in the late 1990's and handles Byzantine failures in which failed nodes can behave arbitrarily and maliciously. Both replication techniques were developed in my research group, the Programming Methodology Group at the Massachusetts Institute of Technology.

The paper has three goals:

- To describe Viewstamped Replication. The protocol is not very complex but this was not evident in the papers that described it since they presented it in the context of specific applications that used it. The goal in this paper is to strip out the extra information and focus on the basics of the protocol.
- To show how PBFT is based on Viewstamped Replication. I believe that because my group had developed Viewstamped Replication, we were in an advantageous position relative to other groups when it came to working on replication techniques that survived Byzantine failures. Furthermore, PBFT can be viewed as an extension of Viewstamped Replication; the paper shows how this works.
- To provide some historical information about what was happening when these two protocols were invented.

B. Charron-Bost, F. Pedone, and A. Schiper (Eds.): Replication, LNCS 5959, pp. 121–149, 2010.

7.2 Prehistory

I began work in distributed computing in about 1980. Prior to that time I had been working on data abstraction [21, 22] and the design of the CLU programming language [20]. In the work on CLU I decided to focus on sequential programs since there seemed to be enough other things to worry about. The work on CLU led to the invention of a number of novel programming language constructs in addition to support for data abstraction, including support for parametric polymorphism, iteration abstraction, and exception handling. However, the design of CLU ignored all issues of concurrency.

I always intended to return to consideration of concurrency when the design of CLU was complete. However, when this happened in the late 1970's, distributed computing had become a possibility. At that point the Internet existed and it was being used to send email and do file transfer. Additionally, it was hoped that the Internet could be used to run applications distributed over many machines, but there was little understanding of how that could be accomplished.

Therefore, I decided to focus on distributed computing rather than thinking just about parallel programs that ran on a single machine. I started a project to define a programming language for use in building distributed implementations. This work led to the invention of a programming language and system called Argus [17, 19].

Argus was an object-oriented language. Its programs were composed of objects called *guardians*, which provided operations called *handlers*. Each guardian ran entirely on one machine. However a computation running in one guardian could transfer control to another by making a *handler call*; these calls were one of the early examples of remote procedure calls.

Additionally, Argus ran computations as atomic transactions. A transaction started in some guardian, perhaps in response to input from a user. The execution of the transaction could include remote handler calls, and these in turn might do further remote calls. At the end, the transaction either committed, in which case all modifications at all guardians had to be installed, or it aborted, in which case all its modifications were undone. Additionally there could be many transactions running in parallel, and Argus ensured that they did not conflict. In other words it provided *serializability* for transactions.

One of our concerns in Argus was ensuring that effects of committed transactions survived even in the presence of failures. Clearly one way to achieve this is to record these effects on a stable storage medium, such as a disk, as part of committing the transactions. However, that approach only ensures that modifications will not be lost. It does not provide *availability* since there could be times when clients are unable to access the information; in fact clients could see less availability over what they could obtain by storing the information on their own machine since a failure of either the client machine or the machine that stored the information would make the information unavailable. Additionally, distributed computing provides the possibility of better availability for clients: with enough replicas we could ensure that the service would always be available with high probability.

The question then became how to achieve a correct and efficient replication protocol. This concern led to the development of Viewstamped Replication.

7.3 Viewstamped Replication

Viewstamped Replication, which I will refer to as VR from now on, was invented by Brian Oki and myself. The goal was to support a replicated service, running on a number of replicas. The service maintains a state, and makes that state accessible to a set of *client* machines.

VR was intended from the outset to satisfy two goals. The first was to provide a system where the user code running on the client machines could be unaware that it was dealing with a replicated service. As far as this code was concerned it was interacting with a service provided by a single server, albeit one that was more available than one might expect if the service ran on a single machine. Thus we required that the effect of running operations against the service be identical to what would happen if there were just one copy of the information [27, 2].

The second goal for VR was to provide *state machine replication* [13, 30]: clients could run general operations to observe and modify the service state. An alternative to state machine replication is to provide clients only the ability to read and overwrite individual words or blocks. To illustrate the difference between these two approaches, consider a banking system that provides operations to deposit and withdraw money from an account, as well as operations to observe an account balance and to transfer money from one account to another. These operations typically involve both reads and writes of the system state. State machine replication allows the banking system to be implemented directly: the replicated service provides operations to deposit, withdraw, etc. If only reads and writes are provided, the operations and the synchronization of concurrent requests must be implemented by the application code. Thus state machine replication provides more expressive power than the alternative, and simplifies what application code needs to do. The decision to support state machine replication meshed with the goal of Argus to make it easier to implement applications.

State machine replication requires that replicas start in the same initial state, and that operations be deterministic. Given these assumptions, it is easy to see that replicas will end up in the same state if they execute the same sequence of operations. The challenge for the replication protocol is to ensure that operations execute in the same order at all replicas in spite of failures.

VR was developed under the assumption that the only way nodes fail is by crashing: we assumed that a machine was either functioning correctly or it was completely stopped. We made a conscious decision to ignore Byzantine failures, in which nodes can fail arbitrarily, perhaps due to an attack by a malicious party. At the time, crashes happened fairly frequently and therefore they seemed the most important to cope with. Additionally, the crash model is simpler to handle than the Byzantine model, and we thought we had enough to deal with trying to invent a replication method for it.

VR was intended to work in an asynchronous network, like the Internet, in which the non-arrival of a message indicates nothing about the state of its sender. We assumed that messages might be lost, delivered late or out of order, and delivered more than once; however, we assumed that if sent repeatedly a message would eventually be delivered. Messages might be corrupted in transit, but we assumed we could distinguish good and bad messages, e.g., through checksums. We did not consider a malicious party that controls the network and therefore we did not think about the need to use cryptography to prevent spoofing.

Brian and I began working on replication in the fall of 1985. Brian completed his Ph.D. thesis in May 1988 [26] and a paper on our approach appeared in PODC in August 1988 [25]. These papers explained replication within the context of support for distributed transactions. In this paper I focus on just the replication protocol and ignore the details of how to run transactions. The description of VR provided here is very close to what appeared in 1988; I discuss the differences in Section 7.5.1.

A later project on the Harp file system applied VR to building a highly available file system. A paper on Harp appeared in SOSP in 1991 [18]. The Harp project extended VR to provide efficient recovery of failed replicas. It also introduced two important optimizations, to speed up the processing of read operations, and to reduce the number of replicas involved in normal case execution.

The work on VR occurred at about the same time as the work on Paxos [14, 15] and without knowledge of that work.

The papers on VR and Harp distinguished what was needed for replication from what was needed for the application (transaction processing in VR, a file system in Harp), but in each case a specific application was also described. In this paper I focus on VR as a generic replication service, independent of the application.

7.3.1 Replica Groups

VR ensures reliability and availability when no more than a *threshold* of f replicas are faulty. It does this by using replica groups of size $2f + 1$; this is the minimal number of replicas in an asynchronous network under the crash failure model. The rationale for needing this many replicas is as follows. We have to be able to carry out a request without f replicas participating, since those replicas might be crashed and unable to reply. However, it is possible that the f replicas we didn't hear from are merely slow to reply, e.g., because of congestion in the network. In this case up to f of the replicas that processed the operation might fail after doing so. Therefore we require that at least $f + 1$ replicas participate in processing the operation, since this way we can guarantee that at least one replica both processed the request and didn't fail subsequently. Thus the smallest group we can run with is of size $2f + 1$.

The membership of the replica group was fixed in VR. If a replica crashed, then when it recovered it rejoined the group and continued to carry out the replication protocol.

7.3.2 Architecture

The architecture for running VR is presented in Figure 7.1. The figure shows some client machines that are using VR, which is running on 3 replicas; thus $f = 1$ in this example. Client machines run the user code on top of the VR *proxy*. The user code communicates with VR by making operation calls to the proxy. The proxy then communicates with the replicas to cause the operation to be carried out and returns the result to the client when the operation has completed.

The replicas run code for the service that is being replicated using VR, e.g., the banking service. The replicas also run the VR code. The VR code accepts requests from client proxies, carries out the protocol, and when the request is ready to be executed, causes this to happen by making an up-call to the service code at the replica. The service code executes the call and returns the result to the VR code, which sends it in a message to the client proxy that made the request.

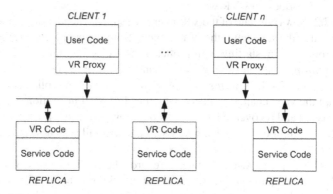

Fig. 7.1 VR Architecture; the figure shows the configuration when $f = 1$.

7.3.3 Approach

One key requirement for a replication protocol is to ensure that every operation executed by the replica group survives into the future in spite of up to f failures. The second key requirement is providing a means to handle concurrent client operations. State machine replication requires a single total ordering of client requests; the challenge is to ensure this when client requests are made concurrently.

Very early in our work on VR, we settled on an approach to replication that uses a *primary*. The primary is just one of the replicas, but it has a special responsibility: it decides on the order for client requests. This way we provide an easy solution to the ordering requirement. Additionally the primary executes the client request and returns the result to the client, but it does this only after at least $f + 1$ replicas (including itself) know about the request. Thus we ensure that no matter what happens in the future, at least one non-faulty replica knows about the request.

The downside of having a primary, however, is that it might fail, yet the protocol needs to continue. Furthermore the continuation must be a legal extension of what happened in the past: the state of the system must reflect all client operations that were previously executed, in the previously selected order.

Our solution to the problem of a faulty primary is to allow different replicas to assume this role over time. The system moves through a sequence of *views*. In each view one of the replicas is selected to be the primary. The other replicas monitor the primary, and if it appears to be faulty, they carry out a *view change* protocol to select a new primary.

Thus VR consists of three protocols, to handle processing of requests, view changes, and also node recovery. These protocols are described in the next section.

7.4 The VR Protocol

This section describes how VR works.

Figure 7.2 shows the state of the VR layer at a replica. The identity of the primary isn't recorded in the state but rather is computed from the *view-number*; the primary is chosen round-robin, starting with replica 1, as the system moves to new views. A *status* of *normal* indicates the replica is handling client requests; this case is discussed in Section 7.4.1. A *status* of *view-change* indicates a replica is engaged in carrying out the view change protocol, which is discussed in Section 7.4.2. A node that has crashed and recovered has a *status* of *recovering* while it interacts with the other replicas to find out what happened while it was failed; recovery is discussed in Section 7.4.3.

The client-side proxy also has state. It records the configuration and what it believes is the current *view-number*, which allows it to know which replica is currently the primary. In addition it records its own *client-id* and a count of the number of requests it has made. A client is allowed to have only a single outstanding request at a time. Each request is given a number by the client and later requests must have larger numbers than earlier ones. The request number is used by the replicas to avoid running requests more than once and therefore if a client crashes and recovers it must start up with a number larger than what it had before it failed; otherwise its request will be ignored. The request number is also used by the client to discard duplicate responses to its requests.

Every message sent to the client informs it of the current *view-number*; this allows the client to track the primary. Every message sent from one replica to another contains the *view-number* known to the sender. Replicas only process messages that match the *view-number* they know. If the sender has a smaller *view-number*, the receiver discards the message but sends a response containing the current *view-number*. If the sender is ahead, the replica performs a *state transfer*: it requests information it is missing from the other replicas and uses this information to bring itself up to date before processing the message.

- The *configuration*, i.e., the IP address and replica number for each of the $2f+1$ replicas. The replicas are numbered 1 to $2f+1$. Each replica also knows its own replica number.
- The current *view-number*, initially 0.
- The current *status*, either *normal*, *view-change*, or *recovering*.
- The *op-number* assigned to the most recently received request, initially 0.
- The *log*. This is an array containing *op-number* entries. The entries contain the requests that have been received so far in their assigned order.
- The *client-table*. This records for each client the number of its most recent request, plus, if the request has been executed, the result sent for that request.

Fig. 7.2 VR state at a replica.

7.4.1 Normal Operation

This section describes how VR works when the primary isn't faulty. The protocol description assumes that the *status* of each participating replica is *normal*, i.e., it is handling client requests; this assumption is critical for correctness as discussed in Section 7.4.2.

The protocol description assumes the client and all the participating replicas are in the same view; nodes handle different view numbers as described above. The description ignores a number of minor details, such as re-sending requests that haven't received responses. It assumes that each client request is a new one, and ignores suppression of duplicates. Duplicates are suppressed using the *client-table*, which allows old requests to be discarded, and the response for the most recent request to be re-sent.

The *request processing protocol* works as follows:

1. The client sends a $\langle$REQUEST *op, c, s, v*$\rangle$ message to the primary, where *op* is the operation (with its arguments) the client wants to run, *c* is the *client-id*, *s* is the number assigned to the request, and *v* is the *view-number* known to the client.
2. When the primary receives the request, it advances *op-number* and adds the request to the end of the *log*. Then it sends a $\langle$PREPARE *m, v, n*$\rangle$ message to the other replicas, where *m* is the message it received from the client, *n* is the *op-number* it assigned to the request, and *v* is the current *view-number*.
3. Non-primary replicas process PREPARE messages in order: a replica won't accept a prepare with *op-number n* until it has entries for all earlier requests in its *log*. When a non-primary replica *i* receives a PREPARE message, it waits until it has entries in its *log* for all earlier requests (doing state transfer if necessary to get the missing information). Then it adds the request to the end of its *log* and sends a $\langle$PREPAREOK *v, n, i*$\rangle$ message to the primary.
4. The primary waits for *f* PREPAREOK messages from different replicas; at this point it considers the operation to be *committed*. Then, after it has executed all earlier operations (those assigned smaller *op-numbers*), the primary executes the operation by making an up-call to the service code, and sends a $\langle$REPLY *v, s, x*$\rangle$ message to the client; here *v* is the *view-number*, *s* is the number the client provided in the request, and *x* is the result of the up-call.

5. At some point after the operation has committed, the primary informs the other replicas about the commit. This need not be done immediately. A good time to send this information is on the next PREPARE message, as piggy-backed information; only the *op-number* of the most recent committed operation needs to be sent.
6. When a non-primary replica learns of a commit, it waits until it has executed all earlier operations and until it has the request in its *log*. Then it executes the operation by performing the up-call to the service code, but does not send the reply to the client.

Figure 7.3 shows the phases of the normal processing protocol.

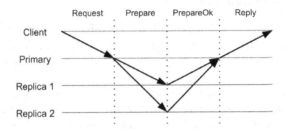

Fig. 7.3 Normal case processing in VR for a configuration with $f = 1$.

The protocol could be modified to allow non-primary replicas to process PREPARE messages out of order in Step 3. However there is no great benefit in doing things this way, and it complicates the view change protocol. Therefore VR processes PRE-PARE messages in *op-number* order.

The protocol need not involve any writing to disk. For example, replicas do not need to write the log to disk when they add the operation to the log. This point is discussed further in Section 7.4.3.

7.4.2 View Changes

View changes are used to mask failures of the primary.

Non-primary replicas monitor the primary: they expect to hear from it regularly. Normally the primary is sending PREPARE and COMMIT messages, but if it is idle (due to no requests) it sends pings. If a timeout expires without communication (and after some retries), the replicas carry out a view change to switch to a new primary. Additionally, if the client receives no reply to a request, it resends the request to all; this way it learns about the new view, and also prompts the new primary to send it the reply.

The correctness condition for view changes is that every operation that has been executed by means of the up-call to the service code at one of the replicas must survive into the new view in the order selected for it at the time it was executed. This up-call is usually done at the old primary first, and the replicas carrying out the view change may not know whether the up-call occurred. However, the up-call occurs only for committed operations. This means that the primary has received at least f PREPAREOK messages from other replicas, and this in turn implies that the operation has been recorded in the logs of at least $f + 1$ replicas (the primary and the f replicas that sent the PREPAREOK messages).

Therefore the view change protocol must obtain information from the logs of at least $f + 1$ replicas. This is sufficient to ensure that all committed operations will be known, since each must be recorded in at least one of these logs. Operations that had not committed might also survive, but this is not a problem: it is beneficial to have as many operations survive as possible.

However, it's impossible to guarantee that every client request that was preparing when the view change occurred makes it into the new view. For example, operation 25 might have been preparing when the view change happened, but none of the replicas that knew about it participated in the view change protocol and as a result the new primary knows nothing about operation 25 and might assign this number to a different operation. However if two operations are assigned the same number, how can we ensure that the right one is executed at that point in the order?

To solve this problem, we introduced the notion of a *viewstamp*. A viewstamp is a pair ⟨*view-number, op-number*⟩, with the natural order: the *view-number* is considered first, and then the *op-number* for two viewstamps with the same *view-number*. Operations are assigned viewstamps: each operation processed by the primary of view v has a viewstamp with that view number, and we associate a viewstamp with every entry in the log. VR guarantees that viewstamps are unique: different client requests are never assigned the same viewstamp. Should a replica receive information about two different operations with the same *op-number* it retains the operation with the higher viewstamp.

VR got its name from these viewstamps.

Viewstamps are used in the *view change protocol*, which works as follows. Again the presentation ignores minor details having to do with filtering of duplicate messages and with re-sending of messages that appear to have been lost.

1. A replica i that suspects the primary is faulty advances its *view-number*, sets its *status* to *view-change*, and sends a ⟨DOVIEWCHANGE v, l, k, i⟩ to the node that will be the primary of the next view (recall that the identity of the primary can be determined from the view number). Here v is its *view-number*, l is the replica's log, and k is the *op-number* of the latest committed request known to the replica.
2. When the new primary receives $f + 1$ of these messages from different replicas, including itself, it selects as the new *log* the *most recent* of those it received in these messages: this is the one whose topmost entry has the largest viewstamp. It sets the *op-number* to that of the latest entry in the new *log*, changes its *status* to *normal*, and informs the other replicas of the completion of the view change by sending a ⟨STARTVIEW v, l, k⟩ message, where l is the new log and k is the *op-number* of the latest committed request it heard about in the responses.
3. The new primary executes (in order) any committed operations that it hadn't executed previously, sends the replies to the clients, and starts accepting client requests.

4. When other replicas receive the STARTVIEW message, they replace their *log* with that in the message, set their *op-number* to that of the latest entry in the log, set their *view-number* to the view number in the message, and change their *status* to *normal*. Then they continue the protocol for all operations not yet known to be committed by sending PREPAREOK messages for these operations.

A view change may not succeed, e.g., because the new primary fails. In this case the replicas will start a further view change, with yet another primary.

To avoid storing a viewstamp in every log entry, VR maintained this information in an auxiliary *view-table*. The *view-table* contained for each view up to and including the current one the *op-number* of the latest request known in that view.

The *view-table* can be used to improve the performance of the view change protocol. The protocol described above is costly because the DOVIEWCHANGE and STARTVIEW messages contain the full log and therefore are large. The cost can be greatly reduced by sending only a suffix of the log in the messages. To send less than the full log, however, requires a way to bring a replica that has missed some earlier view changes up to date. That replica may have requests in its log that were renumbered in subsequent view changes that it didn't participate in. The *view-table* can be used to quickly determine which of its log entries need to be replaced; then it can be brought up to date by providing it with the requests it is missing.

The *view table* can also be used during state transfer to identify the information needed to bring the replica up to date.

Correctness

Safety. The correctness condition for view changes is that every committed operation survives into all subsequent views in the same position in the serial order. This condition implies that any request that had been executed retains its place in the order.

Clearly this condition holds in the first view. Assuming it holds in view v, the protocol will ensure that it also holds in the next view, v'. The reasoning is as follows:

Normal case processing ensures that any operation o that committed in view v is known to at least $f + 1$ replicas, each of which also knows all operations ordered before o, including (by assumption) all operations committed in views before v. The view change protocol starts the new view with the most recent log received from $f + 1$ replicas. Since none of these replicas accepts PREPARE messages from the old primary after sending the DOVIEWCHANGE message, the most recent log contains the latest operation committed in view v (and all earlier operations). Therefore all operations committed in views before v' are present in the log that starts view v' in their previously assigned order.

It's worth noting that it is crucial that replicas stop accepting PREPARE messages from earlier views once they start the view change protocol. Without this constraint the system could get into a state in which there are two active primaries: the old one, which hasn't failed but is merely slow or not well connected to the network, and the new one. If a replica sent a PREPAREOK message to the old primary after sending its log to the new one, the old primary might commit an operation that the new primary doesn't learn about in the DOVIEWCHANGE messages.

Liveness. The protocol executes client requests provided a group of at least $f + 1$ non-failed replicas is able to communicate. This follows because if the replicas are unable to execute the client request in the current view, they will move to a new one. Replicas monitor the primary and start a view change if the primary is unresponsive. Furthermore, once a node has advanced its *view-number* it no longer accepts messages from older views; instead it informs senders in older views about the new view. This in turn causes those replicas to advance their *view-number* and to take steps to move to that view. As a result the new primary will receive enough DOVIEWCHANGE messages to enable it to start the next view. And once this happens it will be able to carry out client requests. Additionally, clients send their requests to all replicas if they don't hear from the primary, and thus learn about new views and cause requests to be executed in a later view if necessary.

More generally liveness depends on properly setting the timeouts used to determine whether the primary is faulty so as to avoid unnecessary view changes.

7.4.3 Recovery

VR assumes a fixed group of replicas. When a replica recovers after a crash it rejoins the system, so that it can start acting as one of the group members again. A replica is considered to be failed from the moment it crashes until the moment when it is ready to rejoin the group.

If nodes record their state on disk before sending messages, a node will be able to rejoin the system immediately. The reason is that in this case a recovering node is the same as a node that has been unable to communicate for some period of time: its state is old but it hasn't forgotten anything it did before. However, running the protocol this way is unattractive since it adds a delay to normal case processing: the primary would need to write to disk before sending the PREPARE message, and the other replicas would need to write to disk before sending the PREPAREOK response.

Furthermore, it is unnecessary to do the disk write because the state is also stored at the other replicas and can be retrieved from them, using a *recovery protocol*. Retrieving state will be successful provided replicas are *failure independent*, i.e., highly unlikely to fail at the same time. If all replicas were to fail simultaneously, state will be lost if the information on disk isn't up to date; with failure independence a simultaneous failure is unlikely. Failure independence can be accomplished by placing the replicas at different geographical locations to avoid loss of availability when there is a power failure or some local problem like a fire.

VR assumed failure independence and did not require writing to disk during normal case processing. Instead it wrote to disk during the view change. This section describes a recovery protocol that assumes the disk write during a view change. A protocol that requires no disk writes even during the view change is described in Section 7.4.3.

Each replica has non-volatile state consisting of the *configuration* and the *view-number* of the latest view it knows; the rest of the state, e.g., the *log*, is volatile.

The view change protocol is modified slightly, to update the *view-number* on disk. A non-primary replica does the disk write before sending its *log* in the DoViewChange message and the primary does the disk write before sending the StartView message to the other replicas.

When a node recovers it reads the non-volatile information from disk and sets its *status* to *recovering*. It also computes a starting *view-number*: this is what it read from disk, except that if it would be the primary of this view, it advances this number by one. Then it carries out the recovery protocol.

While a replica's status is *recovering* it does not participate in either the request processing protocol or the view change protocol.

The *recovery protocol* is as follows:

1. The recovering replica, r, sends a $\langle$Recovery $v, r\rangle$ message to all other replicas, where v is its starting *view-number*.
2. A replica i replies to a Recovery message only when its status is *normal*, its *view-number* $\geq v$, and it is the primary of its view. In this case the replica sends a $\langle$RecoveryResponse $v, l, k, i\rangle$ message to the recovering replica, where v is its *view-number*, l is its *log*, and k is the latest committed request.
3. The recovering replica waits to receive a RecoveryResponse message. Then it updates its state using the information in the message. It writes the new *view-number* to disk if it is larger than what was stored on disk previously, changes its status to *normal*, and the recovery protocol is complete. The replica then sends PrepareOk messages for all uncommitted requests.

The protocol just described is expensive because *logs* are big and therefore the messages are big. A way to reduce this expense is discussed in Section 7.5.6.

Correctness

The recovery protocol is correct because it guarantees that when a recovering replica changes its status to *normal* it does so in a state at least as recent as what it knew when it failed. This condition is sufficient to ensure that any action the replica took before it fails, such as sending a DoViewChange message, will be reflected in its state.

The reason why the condition holds is because the recovering replica always starts up in a view at least as recent as the view it was in when it failed, and it gets its state from the primary of that view, which ensures it learns the latest state of the view. In more detail, there are three cases of interest:

1. If before it failed the replica had just sent a PrepareOk response to a Prepare message, when it recovers it will either hear from the primary that sent that Prepare message, or from the primary of a later view. In the former case, the *log* it receives will include the operation it sent a PrepareOk message for previously. In the latter case, the *log* will reflect a later state that takes account of its PrepareOk message if it mattered, i.e., if it led to a commit.

2. If before it failed the replica had just sent a DoVIEWCHANGE message containing its *log*, when it recovers it will either hear from the primary of that view, or from the primary of a later view. In the former case it will receive a *log* that takes account of its message if it was used by the primary; in the latter case, it will receive a *log* that reflects a later state that takes account of its message if it mattered for moving to the later view.

3. If before it failed the node had just sent a RECOVERYRESPONSE message then it was the primary when it failed and therefore when it recovers it will hear from a primary of a later view. The *log* it receives from this primary will reflect a later state that takes account of this RECOVERYRESPONSE message if it mattered for moving to the later view.

Avoiding Non-volatile Storage

It is possible to avoid any use of non-volatile storage during the protocol. This can be accomplished by adding a "pre-phase" to the view change protocol:

1. A replica *i* that notices the need for a view change advances its *view-number*, sets its status to *view-change*, and sends a ⟨STARTVIEWCHANGE *v, i*⟩ message to the other replicas, where *v* identifies the new view.

2. When replica *i* receives *f* + 1 STARTVIEWCHANGE messages from different replicas, including itself, it sends a ⟨DoVIEWCHANGE *v, l, k, i*⟩ message to the new primary.

After this point the view change protocol proceeds as described previously.

The recovery protocol also needs to be a bit different:

1. The recovering replica, *r*, sends a ⟨RECOVERY *r*⟩ message to all other replicas.

2. A replica *i* replies to a RECOVERY message only when its status is *normal*. In this case the replica sends a ⟨RECOVERYRESPONSE *v, l, k, i*⟩ message to the recovering replica, where *v* is its *view-number*. If *i* is the primary of its view, *l* is its *log*, and *k* is the latest committed request; otherwise, these values are *nil*.

3. The recovering replica waits to receive *f* + 1 RECOVERYRESPONSE messages from different replicas, including one from the primary of the latest view it learns of in these messages. Then it updates its state using the information from the primary, changes its status to *normal*, and the recovery protocol is complete. The replica then sends PREPAREOK messages for all uncommitted requests.

This protocol works (in conjunction with the revised view change protocol) because it is using the volatile state at *f* + 1 replicas as stable state. When a replica recovers it doesn't know what view it was in when it failed and therefore it can't send this information in the RECOVERY message. However, when it receives *f* + 1 responses to its RECOVERY message, it is certain to learn of a view at least as recent as the one that existed when it sent its last PREPAREOK, DoVIEWCHANGE, or RECOVERYRESPONSE message.

7.5 Discussion of VR

7.5.1 Differences from the Original

The protocol described in the previous section is close to what was described in the VR papers, but there are a few differences. In all cases, the technique described here was adopted from our later work on Byzantine fault tolerance.

First, in the original protocol only replicas that participated in the view change for a particular view were considered to be in that view. This means that view changes happened more frequently than in the protocol described in this paper. In the protocol described here, view changes happen only to mask a failed primary (or a primary that appears to be failed, but is merely slow or has trouble communicating). In the original protocol, a view change was also needed when a non-primary replica failed or became partitioned from the group, and another view change was needed when the replica recovered or the partition healed.

Second, in the original protocol the primary was chosen differently. Rather than being selected deterministically based on the *view-number*, as discussed here, it was chosen at the end of the view change to be the replica with the largest log. This allowed the old primary to continue in this role in view changes that were run for other reasons than failure of the primary.

Third, in the original protocol, replicas competed to run a view change. Several replicas might be running the protocol at once; each of them collected state information from the other replicas and since they might end up with a different initial state for the next view, there had to be a way to choose between them. The approach presented in this paper takes advantage of our way of choosing the primary (using just the *view-number*) to avoid this problem by having the primary of the next view determine the initial state of the view.

A final point is that in the original protocol, replicas exchanged "I'm alive" messages. These exchanges allowed them to notice failures of other replicas and thus do view changes; they were needed because a failure or recovery of any replica led to a view change. The protocol described here instead depends on the client sending to all replicas when it doesn't get a response.

7.5.2 Two-Phase Commit

Clearly VR was heavily influenced by the earlier work on two-phase commit [10]. Our primary is like the coordinator, and the other replicas are like the participants. Furthermore the steps of the protocol are similar to those in 2PC and even have names (prepare, commit) that come from 2PC. However, unlike in two-phase commit, there is no window of vulnerability in VR: there is never a time when a failure of the primary prevents the system from moving forward (provided there are no more than f simultaneous failures). In fact, VR can be used to replicate the coordinator of two-phase commit in order to avoid this problem.

7.5.3 Optimizations

Latency

As illustrated in Figure 7.3, the VR protocol requires four message delays to process operations. This delay can be reduced for both read operations that observe but do not modify the state and *update* operations that both observe and modify the state.

Read Operations. The paper on Harp [18] proposed a way to reduce the delay to two messages for reads. The primary immediately executed such a request by making an up-call to the service code, and sent the result to the client, without any communication with the other replicas. This communication is not needed because read operations don't modify state and therefore need not survive into the next view. This approach not only reduced the latency of reads (to the same message exchange that would be needed for a non-replicated service); it also reduced bandwidth utilization and improved throughput since PREPARE messages for read operations didn't need to be sent to the other replicas (although it isn't clear that Harp took advantage of this).

However, executing read operations this way would not be correct if it were possible that a view change had occurred that selected a new primary, yet the old one didn't know about this. Such a situation could occur, for example, if there were a network partition that isolated the old primary from the other replicas, or if the old primary were overloaded and stopped participating in the protocol for some period of time. In this case the old primary might return a result for the read operations based on old state, and this could lead to a violation of external consistency [9]. To prevent this violation, Harp used *leases*: the primary processed reads unilaterally only if it held valid leases from f other replicas, and a new view could start only when the leases at all participants in the view change protocol had expired. The Harp mechanism depended on loosely-synchronized clocks for correctness [24]. In fact it is easy to see that loosely synchronized clock rates (i.e., assuming a bound on the skew of the rates at which the clocks tick) are all that is needed.

Updates. One message delay can be removed from operations that modify the service state as follows. When a replica receives the PREPARE message, in addition to sending a PREPAREOK message to the primary it does the up-call (after it has executed all earlier requests) and sends a reply to the client. The client must wait for $f + 1$ replies; this way we are certain that the operation has committed since it is known at this many replicas.

The approach leads to a delay of 3 messages to run an update. The revised protocol requires more messages, since the non-primaries must reply to the client (as well as to the primary). However, these messages can be small: the client can identify a "preferred" replier, and only this replica needs to send the full reply; the others just send an ack.

A final point is that reduced latency for updates is possible only with some help from the service code. The problem is that the update requests are being executed speculatively, since up-calls are made before the operation commits. Therefore it's possible that a view change will make it necessary to undo the effects of that up-call on the service state.

The optimization for updates was not proposed in Harp, but instead is based on later work done on Byzantine-fault tolerance as discussed in Section 7.8.2.

Witnesses

Another innovation in Harp was a way to avoid having all replicas run the service. In Harp the group of $2f + 1$ replicas included $f + 1$ *active* replicas that stored the system state and executed operations. The other f replicas, which were referred to as *witnesses*, did not. The primary was always an active replica. The witnesses didn't need to be involved in the normal case protocol at all as long as the $f + 1$ active replicas were processing operations. Witnesses were needed for view changes, and also to fill in for active replicas when they weren't responding. However most of the time witnesses could be doing other work; only the active replicas had to be dedicated to the service.

7.5.4 Performance in the Normal Case

Avoiding disk writes during operation execution provides the opportunity for VR to outperform a non-replicated service in the case where the message delay to the replicas is less than the delay due to a disk I/O.

The Harp paper shows this effect. The paper presents results for NFS [29] running the Andrew benchmark [11] and also Nhfstone [31], for a configuration where the communication delay between the replicas was about 5 ms. In both cases Harp was able to do better than an unreplicated system. The paper reports that in addition the system saturated at a higher load than the unreplicated system did. In these experiments, the gain came from avoiding synchronous disk I/O in the foreground; these disk writes are required for update operations done at a single machine by the NFS specification.

At the time we did the work on Harp, a delay of 5 ms was possible only on a local area net. Harp ran in such a setting; Harp placed all replicas in the same data center connected by a local area network. This was not an ideal set up, because, as mentioned earlier, the replicas ought to be failure independent. The paper on Harp proposed a partial solution for the failure-independence problem, by handling power failures. Each replica had an Uninterruptible Power Supply, to allow nodes to write some information to disk in the case of a power failure. Harp pushed the log to disk on a regular basis (in the background), so that it would be able to write what remained in volatile memory to disk in the case of a power failure.

Today we need not sacrifice failure independence to outperform an unreplicated system. Instead we can place replicas in different data centers to achieve failure independence, yet still have a communication delay that is smaller than writing to disk.

7.5.5 Performance of View Changes

The Harp project also addressed the problem of efficient view changes.

The view change protocol is lightweight: there is only a single message delay from the time the replicas decide a view change is needed until the new primary has the state of the new view. After this point the primary can run the protocol for uncommitted requests and it can accept new requests. However it cannot execute these requests until it has executed all earlier ones.

Harp ensured that a new primary can start processing new requests with little delay. It accomplished this by having non-primary replicas execute operations eagerly, so that they were almost up to date when they took over as primary.

7.5.6 State Management

When a replica recovers from a crash it needs to bring itself up to date. The question is how to do this efficiently.

One way for a replica to recover its state after a crash is to start with the initial application state and re-run the log from the beginning. But clearly this is not a practical way to proceed, since the log can get very large, and recovery can take a long time, even if we eliminate read operations and updates whose modifications are no longer needed, e.g., modifications of files that were subsequently deleted.

Harp had a more efficient solution that took advantage of non-volatile state at the replica, namely the state of the service running at the replica. Given this state, it is only necessary to run the requests in the suffix of the log after the latest request executed before the replica failed. Doing things this way allowed the size of the log to be reduced, since only the suffix was needed, and greatly shortened the time needed to recover.

The solution in Harp was to retain a log suffix large enough to allow any active replica to recover. (Recall that Harp had $f + 1$ active replicas and f witnesses that did not store state nor participate in normal processing when the active replicas were not faulty.) Each active replica tracked when effects of requests made it to disk locally. As soon as the effects of a request had made it to disk at all active replicas, the request could be removed from the log. In Harp this point was reached speedily in the normal case of no failures of active replicas because even non-primary replicas executed requests eagerly, as discussed in the preceding section. Removal of log entries stalled while an active replica was out of service and therefore the log was certain to contain all requests that replica might not have processed. When an active replica recovered, it fetched the log from the other replicas, and re-ran the requests in log order.

This approach ensures that all requests needed to recover the replica state exist in the log. But it leads to the possibility that an operation might be executed both before a node fails and again as part of recovery. Note that even if a replica wrote the latest viewstamp to disk each time it executed an operation, it cannot know for sure whether the service code executed the operation before the failure. And in general we would like to avoid writing the viewstamp to disk on each operation.

Of course there is no difficulty in re-executing operations on the service state if those operations are *idempotent*. The solution in Harp was to make operations idempotent by doing extra processing. It pre-processed operations at the primary to predict their outcome, and stored this extra information along with the request in the *log*. For example, if the request created a file in a directory, Harp predicted the slot into which the file would be placed and stored the slot number in the log. Therefore, when the operation re-ran, the file would be placed in that slot, even though this is not where it would have gone based on the current state (which recorded the result of operations ordered after that one).

In the work on Byzantine-fault tolerance, we came up with a different approach that avoided the need to make operations idempotent. That approach is discussed briefly in Section 7.8.4.

7.5.7 Non-deterministic Operations

State machine replication requires that each operation be deterministic. However, applications frequently have non-deterministic operations. For example, reads and writes are non-deterministic in NFS because they require setting "time-last-read" and "time-last-modified". If this is accomplished by having each replica read its clock independently, the states at the replicas will diverge.

The paper on Harp explained how to solve the problem, using the same pre-processing approach that was used to provide idempotency. The primary preprocessed the operation to predict the outcome and sent the information to the other replicas in the PREPARE message. All replicas then used the predicted outcome when the request was executed.

7.6 Byzantine Fault Tolerance

After the end of the Harp project, we stopped working on replication protocols for a while. Then toward the end of 1997, DARPA published a Broad Area Announcement (BAA) requesting proposals on the topic of survivability, and I asked Miguel Castro, who was a student in my group at the time, to think about how we might respond.

By this time there was a realization that malicious attacks and Byzantine behavior needed to be dealt with, and this kind of issue was central to the BAA. Looking at this BAA got us interested in Byzantine-fault-tolerant replication protocols, and we began trying to invent such a protocol. This work led to PBFT, the first practical replication protocol that handles Byzantine faults.

A first paper on PBFT was published in OSDI 1999 [5]. That paper described the basic approach using public-key cryptography and it did not include the recovery mechanism. The complete protocol is described in in OSDI 2000 [6], in TOCS [7], and also in Miguel's Ph.D. thesis [4].

In this section I do not attempt to describe PBFT, which is well-covered in the literature. What I do instead is to present a simplified version of PBFT, similar to what was described in the first OSDI paper, with the goal of showing how PBFT grew out of VR. In retrospect PBFT can be seen as an extension of VR to handle the possibility of Byzantine-faulty nodes. However, it was far from straightforward to come up with the extension at the time we were doing the work.

In addition to extending VR to handle Byzantine nodes, PBFT introduced an innovation in the form of proactive recovery, and provided a number of optimizations to improve performance; a brief discussion is provided in Section 7.8.

7.6.1 Approach

Like VR, PBFT ensures reliability and availability when up to f replicas are faulty. However, it allows replicas to fail in a Byzantine manner. This means they can behave arbitrarily: in addition to not replying to requests, or to replying in obviously bad ways, they can also appear to be working correctly as far as other nodes can tell. For example, they might appear to accept modification requests, yet discard the state.

PBFT uses $3f + 1$ replicas to tolerate up to f faulty nodes; this many replicas is known to be the minimum required in an asynchronous network [3]. The system must be able to execute a request using responses from $2f + 1$ replicas. It can't require more than this many replies because the other f replicas might be faulty and not replying. However, the f replicas we do not hear from might merely be slow to reply, and therefore up to f of the replies might be from faulty nodes. These replicas might later deny processing the request, or otherwise act erroneously.

We can mask such bad behavior, however, since we have replies from at least $2f + 1$ replicas, and therefore we can be sure that at least $f + 1$ honest replicas know about the request. Since every request will execute with $2f + 1$ replicas, we can guarantee that at least one honest replica that knows of this request will also participate in the processing of the next request. Therefore we have a basis for ensuring ordered execution of requests.

Like VR, PBFT uses a primary to order client requests and to run a protocol in a way that ensures that each request that is executed will survive into the future, in spite of failures, in its assigned place in the order. However, in PBFT we have to allow for the fact that replicas might be Byzantine, which leads to differences in the PBFT protocol compared to the VR protocol.

Additionally PBFT needs to allow for an adversary that controls the network. The adversary can remove messages, cause them to be delivered late and out of order, and corrupt them; it can also create new messages and attempt to spoof the protocol. To prevent spoofing, PBFT uses cryptography; all messages are signed by the sender, and we assume that the secret key used by an honest node to sign messages is not known to the adversary. PBFT also needs to avoid replay attacks, but the needed ingredients are already present in the VR protocol, e.g., viewstamps, since VR had to handle replays, although in that case we assumed the network was not acting maliciously.

The architecture for PBFT is similar to that shown in Figure 7.1, except that now there must be $3f + 1$ replicas to survive f failures instead of $2f + 1$. Another point is that PBFT was explicitly based on this architecture: PBFT separated the protocol layer from the application layer. The code for PBFT was made available as a library that could be loaded on the clients and the replicas.

7.7 The PBFT Protocol

One way in which PBFT handles Byzantine faulty nodes is by doing each step of the protocol at at least $2f + 1$ replicas, rather than the $f + 1$ needed in VR. However this change alone is not sufficient to provide a correct protocol. The problem is that in VR some decisions are made by just one replica. For example, in normal case processing the primary tells the other replicas the viewstamp assigned to each client request. In VR the other replicas act on this information; since we assume that the primary is honest, we can rely on the viewstamp it assigns and also we can assume it reports honestly on the client request.

In PBFT, however, the primary might be lying. For example, it might assign the wrong viewstamp, one assigned in the past to a different request. Or, it might provide a bogus client operation or replay a previous request by the client. Another possibility is that it might send different PREPARE messages to the other replicas, e.g., instructing some of them to perform request $r1$ at viewstamp v and others to perform request $r2$ at the same viewstamp. Note that the interesting case here is when the primary does something that can't be recognized as bad just by looking at the message! It's much easier to handle cases where the message is not sent or is garbled.

Our solution to handling these misbehaviors of the primary was to add an extra phase to the protocol, at the beginning, prior to the prepare phase. We called this the *pre-prepare* phase. Additionally replicas check various details of what the primary is doing and refuse to process messages that are not what they should be.

The following is a description of a simplified version of the PBFT protocol. The protocol is based on the one presented in [5] and uses public-key cryptography rather than symmetric cryptography. Both clients and replicas have known public keys and use their secret keys to sign their messages; all messages are signed in this way. In the full version of PBFT, public key cryptography is avoided almost always. This improves the performance of the protocol but also complicates it, as discussed further in Section 7.8.1.

The protocol presented here requires that replicas process requests in order, similar to what was done in VR. For example, a replica won't process a PREPARE message for a particular viewstamp unless it knows about all requests that have been assigned earlier viewstamps. The unsimplified version of PBFT relaxed this constraint and allowed various protocol messages to be processed out of order.

The state of a PBFT replica is the same as was presented before, in Figure 7.2, with one important difference. In VR the log contains just the request messages sent by the client. In PBFT, each log entry also contains some of the protocol messages used to run the request assigned to that *op-number*.

The simplified *request processing protocol* works as follows. As in VR, replicas process requests only when their *status* is *normal*. Also they ignore requests from earlier views and if they learn of a later view, or if they learn they are missing entries in their log, they bring themselves up to date before processing the request.

1. The client c sends a $\langle$REQUEST $op, c, s, v\rangle_{\sigma_c}$ message to the primary, where op is the request, c is the *client-id*, s is the number the client assigned to the request, v is the *view-number* known to the client, and σ_c is the client's signature over the message.
2. If this is not a new request, or if the signature isn't valid, the request is discarded. Otherwise the primary advances *op-number* and adds the request to the end of the *log*. Then it sends a $\langle\langle$PREPREPARE $d, v, n\rangle_{\sigma_p} m\rangle$ message to the other replicas, where m is the client message, d is a digest (a cryptographic hash) of m, n is the *op-number* assigned to the request, and σ_p is the primary's signature.
3. A replica i discards PREPREPARE requests with invalid signatures, or if it had already accepted a different request at that viewstamp. If the request is valid, it waits until it has PREPREPARE entries in its *log* for all requests with earlier *op-numbers*. Then it adds the PREPREPARE message to its *log* (and updates the *client-table*) and sends a $\langle$PREPARE $d, v, n, i\rangle_{\sigma_i}$ message to all replicas, where d is the digest of the client request and σ_i is i's signature.
4. When replica i receives valid PREPARE messages for which it has the matching PREPREPARE message in its log, it adds them to the log. When it has the PREPREPARE message from the primary and $2f$ valid matching PREPARE messages, all from different non-primary replicas, including itself, for this request and all earlier ones, we say the request is *prepared at replica i*. At this point, replica i sends a $\langle$COMMIT $d, v, n, i\rangle_{\sigma_i}$ message to all other replicas.
5. When replica i receives $2f + 1$ valid COMMIT messages, all from different replicas including itself, and when additionally the request is prepared at replica i, replica i executes the request by making an up-call to the service code, but only after it has executed all earlier requests. Then it returns the result to the client.

The first thing to notice about the protocol is the extra *pre-prepare* phase. Since we can't trust the primary to tell the truth we instead use $2f + 1$ replicas; if this many replicas agree, we can rely on what they say since at least $f + 1$ of them will be honest, and at least one honest replica will know what has happened before, e.g., whether some other request has already been assigned that viewstamp.

Here we are relying on a principle at work in a Byzantine setting: *we can trust the group but not the individuals*. This principle is used in every step of the protocol; messages from a sufficient number of replicas are needed to ensure that it is correct to take that step.

Thus each replica needs to see $2f + 1$ valid matching COMMIT messages to decide that it can execute the request. Additionally the client needs to see matching reply messages. In this case, however, $f + 1$ matching responses is sufficient because at least one of them comes from an honest replica, and an honest replica won't send such a response unless the request has gone through the complete protocol.

The phases of the protocol are illustrated in Figure 7.4. It may seem that the PBFT protocol has an extra commit phase as well as the pre-prepare phase. However, the COMMIT messages in PBFT correspond to the PREPAREOK messages in VR.

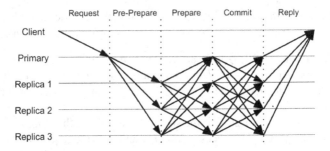

Fig. 7.4 Normal case processing in PBFT.

The protocol uses all-to-all communication for the PREPARE and COMMIT messages and therefore uses $O(n^2)$ communication. All-to-all communication wasn't needed for VR. It could be avoided in PBFT by funneling messages through the primary, but the primary would need to sends copies of the messages it received, since ultimately all replicas need to be able to see the messages of all the others. Thus if we funneled messages through the primary, its messages would be bigger (i.e., there would be no change in bandwidth utilization), and the protocol latency would increase.

7.7.1 View Changes

The main problem with view changes in a Byzantine setting is figuring out which operations must make it into the new view. We must ensure that any operations that executed at an honest replica survive into the next view in their assigned order. In PBFT, an honest replica will execute an operation only after it receives $2f + 1$ COMMIT messages. The problem now, however, is that it's possible that only one honest replica that received this many messages participates in the view change protocol, and furthermore, dishonest replicas might also participate in the view change protocol and claim that some other operation should receive that viewstamp.

For example, suppose that request $r1$ has executed at viewstamp v at some honest replica, and then a view change occurs. The view change protocol will hear from at least one honest replica that knows about $r1$. However, as many as f dishonest replicas might participate in the view change protocol and claim that some other request $r2$ has been assigned to v. In fact, if the primary is bad and assigns different requests to the same viewstamp, $2f$ replicas might claim this: the f liars and also f honest replicas that were told that $r2$ should run at viewstamp v.

Clearly we can't resolve this question by relying on a majority opinion!

The way PBFT resolves this dilemma is to rely on *certificates*. A certificate is a collection of matching valid signed messages from $2f + 1$ different replicas. A certificate represents a proof that a certain thing has happened, e.g., that a request has prepared. Since the messages are signed using public key cryptography, any replica is able to evaluate a certificate and decide for itself whether it is valid.

The certificates are composed of the messages replicas receive while running the protocol. In particular we use a *prepare certificate* consisting of a $\langle$PREPREPARE d, v, $n\rangle_{\sigma_p}$ message and $2f$ PREPARE messages, all for the same request (represented as a digest) with the same viewstamp. A replica has such a certificate for each request that has prepared at it.

The view change protocol works as follows:

1. A replica i that decides there needs to be a view change advances its viewstamp and sends a $\langle$DOVIEWCHANGE v, P, $i\rangle_{\sigma_i}$ to the new primary, where v is the new viewstamp and P is the set of prepare certificates known to i. Since i processes the protocol in request order, there will be prepare certificates for a prefix of its log entries.
2. When the new primary receives $2f + 1$ such messages from different replicas, including itself, it sets its viewstamp to the one in the messages and constructs a new log containing an entry for each prepare certificate it received. Then it sets its *status* to *normal* and sends a $\langle$STARTVIEW *mlist*, v, $O\rangle$ message to the other replicas, where *mlist* is the set of $2f + 1$ DOVIEWCHANGE messages it received, all from different replicas, and O is a set of $\langle$PREPREPARE d, v, $n\rangle_{\sigma_p}$ messages, one for each request in the log.
3. When replica i receives a valid STARTVIEW message, it processes the messages in the *mlist* and reconstructs its log. Then it sets its *status* to *normal* and re-runs the protocol for each request in O (but it only executes requests that it hasn't already executed).

Certificates are used in step 1 of this protocol, so that a replica can reliably inform the primary about the requests that have prepared at it. They are also used in step 2 of the protocol. In this case the certificate consists of the $2f + 1$ DOVIEWCHANGE messages; these allow the other replicas to construct a valid log and to check that the set O is correct. Note that all honest replicas will construct the same log given the same set of DOVIEWCHANGE messages.

It's easy to see the relationship of this protocol to the view change protocol in VR. Of course the protocol now needs to run at $2f + 1$ replicas rather than $f + 1$. Furthermore, since individual replicas aren't trusted in a Byzantine environment, replicas have to prove what they have using certificates, rather than just reporting. A final difference is that to rerun the protocol in the next view, the primary must produce the PREPREPARE messages for all the requests, since these will need to be combined with PREPARE messages to produce certificates in later views. In VR, replicas ran the protocol for preparing requests without requiring the additional PREPREPARE messages.

The protocol above handles view changes where all honest replicas notice a problem with the primary, e.g., that it hasn't sent messages for some time period. In addition, an individual replica can force a view change by proving that the primary is lying. The proof consists of contradictory messages, e.g., two PREPREPARE messages for the same viewstamp but different requests.

The protocol is robust against bad replicas trying to force a view change when one isn't needed. Each replica decides independently about whether a view change is necessary and therefore $f + 1$ honest replicas must make this decision before the view change will happen.

The protocol isn't very efficient because the DOVIEWCHANGE and STARTVIEW messages are very large. PBFT solves this problem by taking a *checkpoint* period-ically. A checkpoint summarizes a prefix of the log. Once the checkpoint has been taken, all entries in the log below that point are discarded. Only the portion of the log beyond the checkpoint need be sent in the view change messages. Checkpoints are discussed further in Section 7.8.4.

Correctness

The correctness condition we need to satisfy is that every operation executed by an honest replica makes it into the next view in the order assigned to it previously. This condition is satisfied because an operation executes at an honest replica only after the replica receives $2f + 1$ COMMIT messages for it. Here we are concerned only with what happens at correct replicas, because dishonest replicas can do anything.

If an honest replica receives this many COMMIT messages, this means that that request has prepared at at least $f + 1$ honest replicas, and each of these replicas has a prepare certificate for it and also for all earlier requests. Furthermore at least one of these $f + 1$ honest replicas will participate in the view change and report these requests with their certificates. Therefore the request will end up in the new log in the position assigned to it previously.

7.8 Discussion of PBFT

This section provides a brief discussion of some of the issues addressed by the full PBFT protocol; more information can be found in [5, 6, 7, 4].

7.8.1 Cryptography

PBFT uses symmetric cryptography most of the time. It uses public keys only to establish secret keys between pairs of replicas and also between replicas and clients.

Using symmetric cryptography represents an important optimization, since it is much more efficient than public key cryptography. However, it has a fairly substan-tial impact on the protocol because it is now more difficult for replicas to provide proofs. With public keys a certificate containing $2f + 1$ valid matching messages acts as a proof: any of the other replicas can vouch for the validity of these messages since all of them do this using the sender's public key. With symmetric cryptogra-phy this simple technique no longer works, and PBFT contains mechanisms to get around this shortcoming.

7.8.2 Optimizations

PBFT provides a number of important optimizations. Most significant are optimiza-tions that reduce the latency for request processing from 5 message delays, as shown in Figure 7.4, to 2 (for reads) and 4 (for updates), and an optimization to reduce the overhead of running the protocol by batching.

Read Operations

The simple and very robust VR technique of having the primary carry out the read doesn't work for PBFT since the primary can lie. Instead the client sends the request to all replicas, which execute the request immediately and send the reply to the client. The client waits for $2f + 1$ matching replies (actually one full reply and $2f$ digests). If it succeeds in getting this many matching replies it accepts the answer and the operation is over. Otherwise the operation must run through the primary in the normal way.

This optimization succeeds provided there is no contention (and also assuming that the replicas aren't faulty). Each replica runs the request when it arrives, which means that different replicas will run it at different spots in the serial order. However, even so they will produce the same answer provided there is no update operation that modifies the portion of the state being observed by the read and that happens at about the same time as the read.

Update Operations

Rather than waiting until they receive $2f + 1$ COMMIT messages, replicas instead execute an update operation at the time they send their COMMIT message for it (and after executing all operations before it). The client waits for $2f + 1$ matching responses (again, one full reply and $2f$ digests). This way we are sure that the operation will survive into the new view, since at least one of the replicas that sent the response is honest and will be consulted in the next view change. Waiting for only $f + 1$ replies, as is done in the base protocol, isn't sufficient since with this many replies, it is possible that only one honest replica knows of the prepare, and it might not be consulted in the next view change.

A final point is that this way of running updates is the basis for the update optimization for VR that was discussed in Section 7.5.3.

Batching

PBFT is a fairly heavyweight protocol in terms of the amount of message traffic required to run it. However, this traffic can be greatly reduced through batching. Batching simply means running the protocol for a number of requests at once.

Batching has no impact on latency when the system isn't busy: in this case the primary doesn't batch, but instead starts the protocol for each operation when its request message arrives. However, when the load goes up, the primary switches to running requests in batches. Batching thus reduces the overhead of running the protocol by amortizing the cost across all the requests in the batch, without much impact on latency, since when the system is busy the next batch fills up quickly.

7.8.3 Selecting the Primary

The idea of selecting the primary round-robin based on the current view-number comes from PBFT. PBFT requires a way of choosing the primary that cannot be affected by the adversary. In the original version of VR the same node could continue as primary as long as it participated in the view changes. In a Byzantine setting this wouldn't work because the primary might be malicious.

7.8.4 Recovery

PBFT provides a full recovery solution that supports doing disk writes in the background; it does not require disk writes during either normal case processing or view changes, and does not require making requests idempotent. The technique also provides for efficient application-level state transfer using Merkle trees [23], and a way of keeping the log small by taking checkpoints. The recovering replica uses the application-level state transfer to recover its state to the most recent checkpoint, and then runs the log from that point on to get up to date.

Checkpoints require some help from the application, both to create the checkpoint, and to revert to a checkpoint. Reverting is needed to support the update optimization. Since the update is performed speculatively before it commits, it might need to be undone in case of a view change. In PBFT, undoing is accomplished by reverting to the previous checkpoint and then running forward using the log. The application can make use of conventional copy-on-write techniques to support checkpoints.

In addition PBFT provides a *proactive* recovery mechanism, in which nodes are shut down periodically and restarted with their memory intact but with a correct copy of the code. Proactive recovery reduces the likelihood of more than f replicas being faulty simultaneously because their code has been corrupted by a malicious attack.

7.8.5 Non-determinism

VR handles the requirement for determinism by having the primary predict the outcome, as discussed in Section 7.5.7. PBFT can't use this technique since the primary might lie. Instead, PBFT relies on the group to predict the outcome: the primary runs a first phase in which it collects predictions from $2f + 1$ different replicas, including itself, and places these predictions in the PrePrepare message. Later, when the request is executed, replicas compute the outcome using a deterministic function of this information.

7.9 Conclusions

This paper has described two replication protocols. The first is Viewstamped Replication, which was a very early state machine replication protocol that handled machines that failed by crashing. The descriptions of VR that appeared in the literature describe the protocol along with an application that uses it. The presentation here strips out the application details and presents the protocol in an application-independent way; additionally, some details have been changed so that the protocol described here is close to what was described in the literature, but not identical.

VR allowed failed nodes to restart and then run a recovery protocol to recover their state. The protocol was based on the assumption that replicas were failure independent, and therefore we were able to avoid the use of non-volatile storage during normal request processing. VR did make use of a disk write as part of a view change. The paper describes a variation on the protocol that avoids the need for disk writes entirely, even during view changes.

The paper also presented a simplified version of PBFT. PBFT was the first practical replication protocol that supported state machine replication in a way that survived Byzantine failures. PBFT grew out of VR. It required the use of $3f + 1$ replicas rather than $2f + 1$. It added an extra phase to normal case processing, to prevent a malicious primary from misleading the other replicas. Also, it used the notion of certificates to ensure that all committed operations make it into the next view in spite of whatever faulty replicas might attempt to do.

Since PBFT was invented there has been quite a bit of research on related protocols. This work covers a number of topics, including: techniques for heterogeneous replication to avoid the problem of correlated failures causing many replicas to fail simultaneously [28, 32]; study of system properties when more than f replicas fail simultaneously [16]; avoiding the use of a primary, either entirely or during normal case processing [1, 8]; reducing the number of replicas that must run the application [34]; and reducing the latency of normal case processing [12, 33].

References

1. Abd-El-Malek, M., Ganger, G.R., Goodson, G.R., Reiter, M.K., Wylie, J.J.: Fault-scalable Byzantine Fault-Tolerant Services. In: SOSP 2005, Brighton, United Kingdom (Oct. 2005)
2. Bernstein, P.A., Goodman, N.: The Failure and Recovery Problem for Replicated Databases. In: Second ACM Symposium on the Principles of Distributed Computing, Aug. 1983, pp. 114–122 (1983)
3. Bracha, G., Toueg, S.: Asynchronous Consensus and Broadcast Protocols. Journal of the ACM 32(4), 824–840 (1985)
4. Castro, M.: Practical Byzantine Fault Tolerance. Technical Report MIT-LCS-TR-817, Laboratory for Computer Science, MIT, Cambridge, ph.D. thesis (Jan. 2000)
5. Castro, M., Liskov, B.: Practical Byzantine Fault Tolerance. In: Proceedings of OSDI 1999, New Orleans, LA (Feb. 1999)
6. Castro, M., Liskov, B.: Proactive Recovery in a Byzantine-Fault-Tolerant System. In: Proceedings of the Fourth Symposium on Operating Systems Design and Implementation (OSDI), San Diego, CA (Oct. 2000)
7. Castro, M., Liskov, B.: Practical Byzantine Fault Tolerance and Proactive Recovery. ACM Transactions on Computer Systems 20(4), 398–461 (2002)
8. Cowling, J., Myers, D., Liskov, B., Rodrigues, R., Shrira, L.: HQ Replication: A Hybrid Quorum Protocol for Byzantine Fault Tolerance. In: Proceedings of the Seventh Symposium on Operating Systems Design and Implementations (OSDI), Seattle, Washington (Nov. 2006)
9. Gifford, D.K.: Information Storage in a Decentralized Computer System. Technical Report CSL-81-8, Xerox Corporation, ph.D. thesis (Mar. 1983)

10. Gray, J.N.: Notes on database operating systems. In: Flynn, M.J., Jones, A.K., Opderbeck, H., Randell, B., Wiehle, H.R., Gray, J.N., Lagally, K., Popek, G.J., Saltzer, J.H. (eds.) Operating Systems. LNCS, vol. 60, pp. 393–481. Springer, Heidelberg (1978)
11. Howard, J., Kazar, M., Menees, S., Nichols, D., Satyanarayanan, M., Sidebotham, R., West, M.: Scale and Performance in a Distributed File System. ACM Transactions on Computer Systems 6(1), 51–81 (1988)
12. Kotla, R., Alvisi, L., Dahlin, M., Clement, A., Wong, E.: Zyzzyva: Speculative Byzantine Fault Tolerance. In: Proceedings of SOSP 2007, Stevenson, WA (October 2007)
13. Lamport, L.: Time, Clocks, and the Ordering of Events in a Distributed System. Comm. of the ACM 21(7), 558–565 (1978)
14. Lamport, L.: The Part-Time Parliament. Research Report 49, Digital Equipment Corporation Systems Research Center, Palo Alto, CA (Sep. 1989)
15. Lamport, L.: The Part-Time Parliament. ACM Transactions on Computer Systems 10(2) (1998)
16. Li, J., Mazieres, D.: Beyond One-third Faulty Replicas in Byzantine Fault Tolerant Systems. In: Proceedings of the 4th NSDI, Apr. 2007, USENIX, Cambridge, MA, USA (2007)
17. Liskov, B.: Distributed Programming in Argus. Comm. of the ACM 31(3), 300–312 (1988)
18. Liskov, B., Ghemawat, S., Gruber, R., Johnson, P., Shrira, L., Williams, M.: Replication in the Harp File System. In: Proceedings of the Thirteenth ACM Symposium on Operating System Principles, Pacific Grove, California, pp. 226–238 (1991)
19. Liskov, B., Scheifler, R.W.: Guardians and Actions: Linguistic Support for Robust, Distributed Programs. ACM Transactions on Programming Languages and Systems 5(3), 381–404 (1983)
20. Liskov, B., Snyder, A., Atkinson, R., Schaffert, J.C.: Abstraction Mechanisms in CLU. Comm. of the ACM 20(8), 564–576 (1977), also in Zdonik, S. and Maier, D. (eds.) Readings in Object-Oriented Database Systems
21. Liskov, B., Zilles, S.: Programming with Abstract Data Types. In: Proceedings of the ACM SIGPLAN Conference on Very High Level Languages, vol. 9, Apr. 1974, pp. 50–59. ACM Press, New York (1974)
22. Liskov, B., Zilles, S.: Specification Techniques for Data Abstractions. IEEE Transactions on Software Engineering 1(1) (1975)
23. Merkle, R.C.: A Digital Signature Based on a Conventional Encryption Function. In: Pomerance, C. (ed.) CRYPTO 1987. LNCS, vol. 293, pp. 369–378. Springer, Heidelberg (1988)
24. Mills, D.L.: Network time protocol (version 1) specification and implementation. DARPA-Internet Report RFC 1059 (Jul. 1988)
25. Oki, B., Liskov, B.: Viewstamped Replication: A New Primary Copy Method to Support Highly-Available Distributed Systems. In: Proc. of ACM Symposium on Principles of Distributed Computing, pp. 8–17 (1988)
26. Oki, B.M.: Viewstamped Replication for Highly Available Distributed Systems. Technical Report MIT-LCS-TR-423, Laboratory for Computer Science, MIT, Cambridge, MA, ph.D. thesis (May 1988)
27. Papadimitriou, C.H.: The Serializability of Concurrent Database Updates. Journal of the ACM 26(4), 631–653 (1979)
28. Rodrigues, R., Liskov, B., Castro, M.: BASE: Using Abstraction to Improve Fault Tolerance. ACM Transactions on Computer Systems 21(3) (2003)
29. Sandberg, R., et al.: Design and Implementation of the Sun Network Filesystem. In: Proceedings of the Summer 1985 USENIX Conference, Jun. 1985, pp. 119–130 (1985)
30. Schneider, F.: Implementing Fault-Tolerant Services using the State Machine Approach: a Tutorial. ACM Computing Surveys 22(4), 299–319 (1990)
31. Shein, B., et al.: NFSSTONE - A Network File Server Performance Benchmark. In: USENIX Summer '89 Conference Proceedings, pp. 269–274 (1989)
32. Vandiver, B., Liskov, B., Madden, S., Balakrishnan, H.: Tolerating Byzantine Faults in Database Systems using Commit Barrier Scheduling. In: Proceedings of SOSP 2007, Stevenson, WA (October 2007)

33. Wester, B., Cowling, J., Nightingale, E., Chen, P., Flinn, J., Liskov, B.: Tolerating Latency in Replicated State Machines through Client Speculation. In: Proceeding of the 6th NSDI, Boston, MA (April 2009)
34. Yin, J., Martin, J., Venkataramani, A., Alvisi, L., Dahlin, M.: Separating Agreement from Execution for Byzantine Fault Tolerant Services. In: Proceedings of the 19th ACM Symposium on Operating Systems Principles (Oct. 2003)

Chapter 8
Implementing Trustworthy Services Using Replicated State Machines

Fred B. Schneider and Lidong Zhou

Abstract A thread of research has emerged to investigate the interactions of replication with threshold cryptography for use in environments that satisfy weak assumptions. The result is a new paradigm known as distributed trust, and this chapter attempts to survey that landscape.

8.1 Introduction

"Divide and conquer" can be a powerful tool for disentangling complexity when designing a computing system. However, some aspects of a system design are inseparable. Treating these as though they were independent leads to one interfering with the other, and "divide and be conquered" perhaps better characterizes the consequences. For some years, we have been investigating how to construct systems that continue functioning despite component failures and despite attacks. A question we have pondered is to what extent does divide and conquer apply? Somewhat less than you might hope is, unfortunately, the answer.

One could argue that attacks can be seen as just another cause for component failure. The *Byzantine fault model* asserts that a faulty component can exhibit arbitrarily malicious (so-called "Byzantine") behavior; a system that tolerates Byzantine faults should then be able to handle anything. Moreover, because any component can be viewed abstractly in terms of its state and a set of possible next-state transitions—in short, a *state machine*—fault-tolerant services could be built by assembling enough state machine copies so that outputs from the ones exhibiting Byzantine behavior are outvoted by the correctly functioning ones. The fault-tolerance of the ensemble thus exceeds the fault-tolerance of any individual state machine, and a *distributed fault-tolerance* is the result.

A closer look at such *replicated state machines*, however, reveals problems when attacks are possible. Specific difficulties with the approach and how we can over-

B. Charron-Bost, F. Pedone, and A. Schiper (Eds.): Replication, LNCS 5959, pp. 151–167, 2010.

come these are described later in this chapter, but the overall vision remains compelling: placing more trust in an ensemble than in any of its individual components. In analogy with distributed fault-tolerance, then, we are seeking ways to implement *distributed trust*.

8.2 The State-Machine Approach

The details for using replicated state machines and implementing a Byzantine fault-tolerant service [19, 29] are well-known.

1. Start with a server, structured as a deterministic state machine, that reads and processes client submitted *requests*, which are the sole means to change the server's state or cause the server to produce an output.
2. Run replicas of that server on distinct hosts. These hosts communicate through narrow-bandwidth channels and thus form a distributed system.
3. Employ a replica-coordination protocol to ensure that all non-faulty server replicas process identical sequences of requests.

Correctly operating server replicas will produce identical outputs for each given client request. Moreover, the majority of the outputs produced for each request will come from correct replicas provided that at most t server replicas are faulty and that the service comprises at least $2t + 1$ server replicas. So, we succeed in implementing availability and integrity for a service that tolerates at most t faulty replicas by defining the service's output to be any response produced by a majority of the server replicas. Implicit in the approach are two assumptions: First, we assume that a replica-coordination protocol exists. Second, we assume *processor independence*— that the individual state-machine replicas do not influence each other if executed on separate hosts in a distributed system. That is, the probability pr_m of m replicas exhibiting Byzantine behavior is approximately $(pr_1)^m$, where pr_1 is the probability of a single replica exhibiting Byzantine behavior.

A *trustworthy* service must tolerate attacks as well as failures. Availability, integrity, and confidentiality are typically of concern. The approach outlined above is thus seriously deficient:

• Confidentiality is not just ignored, but n-fold replication actually increases the number of sites that must resist attack because they store copies of confidential information. Even services that do not operate on confidential data per se are likely to store cryptographic keys (so responses can be authenticated). Because these keys must be kept secret, support for confidentiality is needed even for implementing integrity.
• Any vulnerability in one replica is likely present in all, enabling attacks that succeed at one replica to succeed at all. The independence assumption, manifestly plausible for hardware failures and many kinds of software failures (such as Heisenbugs), is thus unlikely to be satisfied once vulnerabilities and attacks

are taken into account. So the probability that more than t servers are compromised is now approximately pr_1 rather than $(pr_1)^m$; therefore, replication does not improve the service's trustworthiness.

- Replica-coordination protocols are typically designed assuming the *synchronous* model of distributed computation. This is problematic because denial-of-service (DoS) attacks can invalidate such timing assumptions. Once an attacker has invalidated an assumption on which the system depends, correct system operation is no longer guaranteed.

Using cryptography or using algorithms for coordination can remedy a few of these deficiencies; other deficiencies drive current research. This chapter's goal is to provide a principled account of that landscape: instead of dwelling on individual features, we'll show how each contributes to implementing trustworthy services with replicated state machines. Each of the landscape's individual features is well understood in one or another research community, and some of the connections are as well, but what is involved in putting them together is not widely documented nor broadly understood. Space limitations, however, allow only a superficial survey of the related literature, so view this chapter as a starting point and consult the articles we cite (and their reference lists) for a more in-depth study. Finally, it's worth emphasizing that the replication-based approaches we discuss only address how to implement a more-trustworthy version of some service whose semantics are defined by a single state machine. We thus do not address vulnerabilities intrinsic in what that single state machine does. To solve the real trustworthiness problem requires determining that a state machine's semantics cannot be abused; unfortunately, this is still an open research problem.

8.3 Compromise and Proactive Recovery

Two general components are involved in building trustworthy services: processors and channels. Processors serve as hosts; channels enable hosts to communicate.

A *correct* component only exhibits intended behavior; a *compromised* component can exhibit other behavior. Component compromise is caused by failures or attacks. We make no assumption about the behavior of compromised components, but we do conservatively assume that a component C compromised by a successful attack is then controlled by the adversary, with secrets C stores then becoming known to the adversary.

Secrets the adversary learns by compromising one component might subsequently lead to the compromise of other components. For example, a correct channel protects the confidentiality, integrity, and authenticity of messages it carries. This channel functionality is typically implemented cryptographically, with keys stored at those hosts serving as the channel's endpoints. An attack that compromises a host thus yields secrets that then allow the adversary to compromise all channels attached to the host.

Because channel compromise is caused by host compromise, a service's trustworthiness is often specified solely in terms of which or how many host compromises it can tolerated; the possibility of channel compromise distinct from host compromise is ignored in such a specification. This simplification—also adopted in this chapter—is most defensible when the network topology provides several physically independent paths to each host, because then the channel connecting a host is unlikely to fail independent of that host.

The system builder has little control over how and when a component transitions from being correct to being compromised. A *recovery protocol* provides the means to reverse such transitions. For a faulty component, the recovery protocol might involve replacing or repairing hardware. For a component that has been attacked, the recovery protocol must

- evict the adversary, perhaps by restoring code from clean media (ideally with the recently exploited vulnerabilities patched);
- reconstitute state, perhaps from other servers; and
- replace any secret keys the adversary might have learned.

The reason that a component should execute a recovery protocol after detecting a failure or attack is obvious. Less obvious are benefits that accrue from a component executing a recovery protocol periodically, even though no compromise has been detected [15]. To wit, such *proactive recovery* defends against undetected attacks and failures by transforming a service that tolerates t compromised hosts over its lifetime into a system that tolerates up to t compromised hosts during each *window of vulnerability* delimited by successive executions of the recovery protocol. The adversary that cannot compromise $t + 1$ hosts within a window of vulnerability is foiled and forced to begin anew on a system with all defenses restored to full strength.

DoS attacks slow execution, thereby lengthening the window of vulnerability and increasing the interval available to perpetrate an attack. Whether such a lengthened window of vulnerability is significant will depend on whether the adversary can compromise more than t servers during the window. But whatever the adversary, systems with proactive recovery can, in principle, be more resilient than those without it, simply because proactive recovery (if implemented correctly) affords an opportunity for servers to recover from past compromises—including some compromises that haven't been detected.

8.4 Service Key Refresh and Scalability

With the state machine approach, a client, after making a request, awaits responses from servers. When the compromise of up to t servers must be tolerated, the same response received from fewer than t servers cannot be considered correct. But if the response is received from $t + 1$ or more servers, then that response was necessarily produced by a correct server. So sets of $t + 1$ servers together *speak for* the service, and clients require some means to identify when equivalent responses have come from $t + 1$ distinct server replicas.

One way to ascertain the origin of responses from (correct) servers is to employ digital signatures. Each server's response is digitally signed using a private key known only to that server; the receiver validates a response's origin by checking the signature using that server's public key. A server's private key thus speaks for that server. Less expensive schemes, involving message authentication codes (MAC) and shared secrets, have also been developed; such schemes contribute to the performance reported for toolkits (for example, BFT mentioned in table 2) that have recently become available to system builders.

8.4.1 Service Private Keys

The use of secrets—be it private keys or shared secret keys—for authenticating server replicas to clients impacts the scalability of a service that employs proactive recovery. This is because servers must select new secrets at the start of each window of vulnerability, and clients must then be notified of the changes. If the number of clients is large then performing the notifications will be expensive, and the resulting service ceases to be scalable.

To build a service that is scalable, we seek a scheme whereby clients don't need to be informed of periodic changes to server keys. Because sets of $t + 1$ or more servers speak for the service, a client could identify a correct response from the service if the service has a way to digitally sign responses if and only if a set of servers that speak for the service agree on that response:

TC1: Any set of $t + 1$ or more server replicas can cooperate and digitally sign a
message on behalf of the service.

TC2: No set of t or fewer server replicas can contrive to digitally sign a message
on behalf of the service.

TC1 implies that information held by $t + 1$ or more servers enables them to together construct a digital signature for a message (namely, for the service's response to a request), whereas TC2 implies that no coalition of t or fewer servers has enough information to construct such a digital signature. In effect, TC1 and TC2 characterize a new form of private key for digital signatures—a key associated with the service rather than with the individual servers. This private key speaks for the service but is never entirely materialized at individual servers comprising the service.

A private key satisfying TC1 and TC2 can be implemented using secret sharing [30, 2]. An $(n, t + 1)$ secret sharing for a secret s is a set of n random *shares* such that: s can be recovered with knowledge of $t + 1$ shares, and no information about s can be derived from t or fewer shares. Not only do protocols exist to construct $(n, t + 1)$ secret sharings but *threshold digital signature* protocols [3, 10] exist that allow construction of a digital signature for a message from $t + 1$ *partial signatures*, where each partial signature is computed using as inputs the message along with only a single share of the private key. Thus, a system can implement TC1 and TC2 using $(n, t + 1)$ secret sharing and dividing the service private key among the server replicas—one share per replica—and then having servers use threshold digital signatures to collaborate in signing responses.

If the shares are fixed then, over time, an attacker might compromise $t + 1$ servers, obtain $t + 1$ shares, and thus be able to speak for the service, generating correctly signed bogus service responses. Such an attacker is known as a *mobile adversary* [25], because it attacks and controls one server for a limited time before moving to the next. The defense against mobile adversary attacks is, as part of proactive recovery, for servers periodically to create a new and independent secret sharing for the service's private key, and then delete the old shares, replacing them with new ones. Because the new and old secret sharings are independent, the mobile adversary can't combine new shares and old shares to obtain the service's signing key. And because old shares are deleted when replaced by new shares, a mobile adversary must compromise more than t servers within a single window of vulnerability in order to succeed.

8.4.2 Proactive Secret Sharing

Protocols to create new, independent sharings of a secret are called *proactive secret sharing* protocols and have been developed for the synchronous model [15] as well as for the *asynchronous model*, which makes no assumptions about process execution speeds and message delivery delays [4, 37]. Proactive secret sharing protocols are tricky to design: First, the new sharing must be computed without ever materializing the shared secret at any server. (A server that materialized the shared secret, if compromised, could reveal the service's signing key to the adversary.) And, second, the protocol must work correctly in the presence of as many as t compromised servers, which might provide bogus shares to the protocol.

8.5 Server Key Refresh

Secure communication channels between servers are required for proactive secret sharing and for various other protocols that servers execute. Because a host stores the keys used to implement the secure channels with which it communicates, we conclude that, not withstanding the use of secret sharing and threshold cryptography for service private keys, there will be other cryptographic keys stored at servers. If these other keys can be compromised then they too must be refreshed during proactive recovery. Three classes of solutions for server key refresh have been proposed.

8.5.1 Trusted Hardware

Although not in widespread use today, special-purpose cryptographic hardware that stores keys and performs cryptographic operations encryption, decryption and digital signing) does exist. This hardware is designed so that, if correctly installed, it will not divulge keys or other secret parameters, even if the software on the attached host has been compromised. When keys stored by a server cannot be revealed, there is no reason to refresh them. So, storing server keys in this hardware eliminates the need to refresh server keys as part of proactive recovery for as long as that hardware can be trusted.

However, using special-purpose cryptographic hardware for all cryptographic operations doesn't prevent a compromised server from performing cryptographic operations for the adversary. The adversary might, for example, cause the server to generate signed or encrypted messages for later use in attacks. A defense against such attacks is to maintain an integer counter in stable memory (so that the counter's value will persist across failures and restarts) that's part of the special-purpose cryptographic hardware. This counter is incremented every time a new window of vulnerability starts, and the current counter value is included in every message that is encrypted or signed using the tamper-proof hardware. A server can now ignore any message it receives that has a counter value too low for the current window of vulnerability.

The need for special-purpose hardware would seem to limit adoption of this approach. However, recent announcements from industry groups like the Trusted Computing Group (https://www.trustedcomputinggroup.org/home) and hardware manufacturers like IBM and Intel imply that standard PC computing systems soon will support reasonable approximations to this hardware functionality, at least for threats common on the Internet today.

8.5.2 Offline Keys

In this approach to server key refresh, new keys are distributed using a separate secure communications channel that the adversary cannot compromise. This channel typically is implemented cryptographically by using secrets that are stored and used in an off-line stand-alone computer, thereby ensuring inaccessibility to a network-borne adversary. For example, an administrative public/private key pair could be associated with each server H. The administrative public key $\hat{K}_H$ is stored in ROM on all servers; the associated private key $\hat{k}_H$ is stored offline and is known only to $H's$ administrator. Each new server private key k_A for a host A would be generated offline. The corresponding public key K_A would then be distributed to all servers by including K_A in a certificate signed using the administrative private key $\hat{k}_A$ of server A.

8.5.3 Attack Awareness

Instead of relying on a full-fledged tamper-proof co-processor, a scheme suggested by Ran Canetti and Amir Herzberg[7] uses nonmodifiable storage (such as ROM) to store a special service-wide public key whose corresponding private key is shared among servers using an $(n, t + 1)$ secret sharing. To refresh its server key pair, a server H generates its new private-public key pair, signs the new public key using the old private key, and then requests that the service *endorse* the new public key. A certificate that associates the new public key with server H, signed using the special service private key, represents the endorsement.

The service private key is refreshed periodically using proactive secret sharing, thereby guaranteeing that an attacker cannot learn the service private key, provided the attacker cannot compromise more than t servers in a window of vulnerability.

Therefore, an attacker cannot fabricate a valid endorsement because servers can detect bogus certificates using the service public key stored in their ROM. A server becomes aware of an attack if it doesn't receive a valid certificate for its new public key within a reasonable amount of time or if it receives two conflicting requests that are both signed by the same server's private key during the same window of vulnerability. In either case, system administrators should implement actions in order to re-introduce the server into the system and remove the possible imposter.

8.6 Processor Independence

We approximate the processor independence assumption to the extent that a single attack or host failure cannot compromise multiple hosts. Independence is reduced, for example, when hosts

- employ common software (and thus replicas have the same vulnerabilities),
- are operated by the same organization (because a single maleficent operator could then access and compromise more than a singled host), or
- rely on a common infrastructure, such as name servers or routers used to support communications, compromising that infrastructure violates an assumption that hosts need to function.

One general way to characterize a service's trustworthiness is by describing which sets of components could together be compromised without disrupting the service's correct operation. Each vulnerability V partitions server replicas into groups, in which replicas in a given group share that vulnerability. For instance, attacks exist that compromise server replicas running Linux but not those running Windows (and vice versa), which leads to a partitioning according to the OS; the effects of a maleficent operator are likely localized to server replicas under that operator's control, which leads to a partitioning according to system operator.

Sets of a system's servers whose compromise must be tolerated for the service's correct operation of the service can be specified using an *adversary structure* [16, 22]. This is a set $\mathscr{A} = \{S_1,\ldots,S_r\}$ whose elements are sets of system servers that we assume the adversary can compromise during the same window of vulnerability. A trustworthy service is then expected to continue operating as long as the set of compromised servers is an element of $\mathscr{A}$. Thus, the adversary structure $\mathscr{A}$ for a system intended to tolerate attacks on the OS would contain sets S_i whose elements are servers all running the same OS.

When there are n server replicas and $\mathscr{A}$ contains all sets of servers of size at most t, the result is known as an (n,t) *threshold* adversary structure [30]. The basic state-machine approach described earlier involves a threshold adversary structure, as does much of the discussion throughout this chapter. Threshold adversary structures correspond to systems in which server replicas are assumed to be independent and equally vulnerable. They are, at best, approximations of reality. The price of embracing such approximations is that single events might actually compromise all of the servers in some set that isn't an element of the adversary structure—the service would then be compromised.

Protocols designed for threshold adversary structures frequently have straightforward generalizations to arbitrary adversary structures. What is less well understood is how to identify an appropriate adversary structure for a system, because doing so requires identifying all common vulnerabilities. Today's systems often employ commercial off-the-shelf (COTS) components, so access to their internal details is restricted. Yet those internal details are what is needed in identifying common vulnerabilities.

Independence by Avoiding Common Vulnerabilities

Eliminating software bugs eliminates vulnerabilities that would impinge on replica independence. Constructing bug-free software is quite difficult, however. So instead, we turn to another means of increasing replica independence: diversity. In particular, the state machine approach doesn't require that server replicas be identical in either their design or their implementation—only that different replicas produce equivalent responses for each given request. Such diversity can be obtained in three ways.

Develop Multiple Server Implementations. This, unfortunately, can be expensive. The cost of all facets of system development is multiplied, because each replica now has its own design, implementation, and testing costs. In addition, interoperation of diverse components is typically more difficult to orchestrate, not withstanding the adoption of standards. Moreover, experiments have shown that distinct development groups working from a common specification will produce software that have the same bugs [18].

Employ Pre-existing Diverse Components. Here, system developers use pre-existing diverse components that have similar functionality and then write software wrappers so that all implement the same interface and the same state-machine behavior [29, 28].

One difficulty is in procuring diverse components that do have the requisite similar functionality. Some OSs have multiple, diverse implementations (for example, BSD UNIX vs. Linux) but other OSs do not; application components used in building a service are unlikely to have multiple diverse realizations. A second difficulty arises when components don't provide access to internal non-deterministic choices they make during execution (such as creating a "handle" that will be returned to a client), which makes writing the wrapper quite difficult [28]. And, finally, there still remains a chance that the diverse components will share vulnerabilities because they are written to the same specification (exhibiting a phenomenon like that reported in John Knight and Nancy G. Leveson's work [18]) or because they are built using some of the same components or tools.

Introduce Diversity Automatically during Compilation, Loading, or in the Run-Time Environment.[12, 34] Code can typically be generated and storage allocated in several ways for a given high-level language program; making choices in producing different executables introduces diversity. Different executables for the same high-level language program are still implementations of the same algorithms, though, so executables obtained in this manner will continue to share any flaws in those algorithms.

8.7 Replica Coordination

In the state-machine approach, not only must state-machine replicas exhibit independence, but all correct replicas must reach consensus about the contents and ordering of client requests. Therefore, the replica-coordination protocol must include some sort of *consensus protocol* [26] to ensure that

- all correct state machine replicas agree on each client's request, and
- if the client sends the same request R to all replicas, then R is the consensus they reach for that request.

This specification involves both a safety property and a liveness property. The *safety property* prohibits different replicas from agreeing on different values or orderings for any given request; the *liveness property* stipulates that an agreement is always reached.

Consensus protocols exist only for systems satisfying certain assumptions [11]. In particular, deterministic consensus protocols don't exist for systems with unboundedly slow message delivery or process execution speeds—that is, systems satisfying the asynchronous model. This limitation arises because, to reach consensus in such a system, participating state-machine replicas must distinguish between those replicas that have halted (due to failures) and thus should be ignored, and those replicas that, although correct, are executing very slowly and thus cannot be ignored.

The impossibility of implementing a deterministic consensus protocol in the asynchronous model leaves three options.

Option I: Abandon Consensus

Instead of arranging that every state-machine replica receive every request, we might instead employ servers that are not as tightly coordinated. One well-known example is the use of a *quorum system* to implement a storage service from individual *storage servers*, each of which supports local read and write operations. Various robust storage systems [21, 23, 33] have been structured in this way, as have richer services such as the Cornell online certification authority (COCA; detailed in Table 1) [36], which implements operations involving both reading and writing service state.

To constitute a quorum system, servers are associated with groups (where each operation is executed on all servers in some group). Moreover, these groups are defined so that pairs of groups intersect in one or more servers—one operation's effect can thus be seen by any subsequent operation. Various quorum schemes differ in the size of the intersection of two quorums. For example, if faulty processors simply halt then as many as t faulty processors can be tolerated by having $2t + 1$ processors in each group and $t + 1$ in the intersection. If faulty processors can exhibit arbitrary behavior, then a *Byzantine quorum system* [22], involving larger groups and a larger intersection, is required.

A second example of abandoning consensus replication can be seen in the Asynchronous Proactive Secret Sharing (APSS) protocol [37]. Here, each participating server computes a new sharing of some secret; a consensus protocol would seem the obvious way for all correct servers to agree on which new sharing to adopt. But instead in APSS, each server embraces all of the new sharings; a consensus protocol for the asynchronous model is then not needed. Clients of APSS refer to individual shares by using names that tell a server which sharing is involved. So here, establishing consensus turns out to be unnecessary after the problem specification is changed slightly—APSS creates at most n new and independent sharings of a secret and is started with n sharings, rather than creating a single new sharing from a single sharing.

Certain service specifications cannot be implemented without solving a consensus problem, so abandoning consensus is not always an option. But it sometimes can be an option, albeit one that is too rarely considered.

Option II: Employ Randomization

Mike Fischer and colleagues' impossibility result [11] doesn't rule out protocols that use randomization, and practical randomized asynchronous Byzantine agreement protocols have been developed. One example is Cristian Cachin and colleagues' consensus protocol [5], which builds on some new cryptographic primitives, including a noninteractive threshold signature scheme and a threshold coin-tossing scheme; the protocol is part of the Secure Intrusion-Tolerant Replication Architecture (Sintra) toolkit [6] developed at the IBM Zurich Research Center. Sintra supports a variety of broadcast primitives needed for coordination in replicated systems.

Option III: Sacrifice Liveness (Temporarily)

A service cannot be very responsive when processes and message delivery have become glacially slow, so a consensus protocol's liveness property might temporarily be relaxed in those circumstances. After all, there are no real-time guarantees in the asynchronous model. The crux of this option, then, is to employ a consensus protocol that satisfies its safety property only while the system satisfies assumptions somewhat stronger than found in the asynchronous model but that always satisfies its safety property (so that different state-machine replicas still agree on requests they process). Leslie Lamport's Paxos protocol [20] is a well-known example of trading liveness for the weaker assumptions of the asynchronous model. Other examples include the protocol of Gregory Chockler, Dahlia Malkhi and Mike Reiter's protocol [9] and BFT [8].

8.8 Computing with Server Confidential Data

Some services involve data that must be kept confidential. Unlike secrets used in connection with cryptography (namely keys), such server data cannot be changed periodically as part of proactive recovery; values now have significance beyond just being secret and they could be part of computations that support the services' semantics.

Adversaries can gain access to information stored unencrypted on a server if that server is compromised. Thus, confidential service data must always be stored in some sort of encrypted form—either replicated or partitioned among the servers. Unfortunately, few algorithms have been found that perform interesting computations on encrypted data (although some limited search operations are now supported [31]). Even temporarily decrypting the data on a server replica or storing it on a backup in unencrypted form risks disclosing secrets to the adversary.

One promising approach is to employ *secure multi-party computations* [14]. Much is known about what can and cannot be done as a secure multiparty computation; less is known about what is practical, and the prognosis is not good for efficiently supporting arbitrary computations (beyond cryptographic operations like decryption and signing).

It's not difficult to implement a service that simply stores confidential data for subsequent retrieval by clients. An obvious scheme has the client encrypt the confidential data and forward that encrypted data to a storage service for subsequent retrieval. Only the client and other principals with knowledge of the decryption key would then be able to make sense of the data they retrieve. Note that the service here has no way to control which principals are able to access unencrypted confidential data.

In cases in which we desire the service—and not the client that initially stores the confidential data—to implement access control, then simply having a client encrypt the confidential data no longer works. The key elements of the solution to this problem have already been described, though:

- The confidential data (or a secret key to encrypt the data) is encrypted using a service public key.
- The corresponding private key is shared among replicas using an $(n, t + 1)$ secret sharing scheme and refreshed periodically using proactive secret sharing.
- A copy of the encrypted data is stored on every replica to preserve its integrity and availability in face of server compromises and failures.

Two schemes have been proposed for clients to retrieve the encrypted data.

- *Re-encryption.* A re-encryption protocol produces a ciphertext encrypted under one key from a ciphertext encrypted under another and does so without the plaintext becoming available during intermediate steps. Such protocols exist for public-key cryptosystems in which the private key is shared among a set of servers [17]. To retrieve a piece of encrypted data, the service executes a re-encryption protocol on data encrypted under the service public key; the result is data encrypted under the public key of an authorized client.

- *Blinding.* A client chooses a random blinding factor, encrypts it using the service public key, and sends that to the service. If the service deems that client authorized for access, then the service multiplies the encrypted data by this blinding factor and then employs threshold decryption to compute unencrypted but blinded data, which is sent back to the client. The client, knowing the blinding factor, can then recover the data from that blinded data.

Blinding can be considered a special case of re-encryption, because it's essentially encryption with a one-time pad (the random blinding factor). Unlike the re-encryption scheme in Markus Jakobsson's work [17], which demands no involvement of the client and produces a ciphertext for a different key in the same encryption scheme, our use of blinding requires client participation and yields a ciphertext under a different encryption scheme. So, re-encryption can be used directly for cases in which a client itself is a distributed service with a service public key, whereas the blinding-based scheme cannot be used without further modification. In fact, a re-encryption scheme based on blinding appears in other work [35]; in it, ciphertext encrypted under the service public key is transformed into ciphertext encrypted under the client public key (as with the re-encryption scheme in Jakobsson's work), thereby allowing a flexible partition of work between client and service.

Table 8.1 Systems that employ elements of distributed trust.

SYSTEM	DESCRIPTION
BFS [8]	An NFS file system implementation built using the BFT toolkit (see Table 2 for a description of the toolkit).
Cornell Online Certificate Authority (COCA) [36]	COCA is a trustworthy distributed certification authority. It avoids consensus protocols by using a Byzantine quorum system, which employs threshold cryptography to produce certificates signed by the service, using proactive recovery in conjunction with offline administrator keys for maintaining authenticated communication links. COCA assumes the asynchronous model.
Cornell Data Exchange (CODEX) [24]	CODEX is a robust and secure distribution system for confidential data. It stores private keys using secret sharing with proactive refresh, uses threshold cryptography, and employs a distributed blinding protocol to send confidential information from the service to a client or another distributed service. CODEX assumes the asynchronous model.
E-Vault[13]	A secure distributed storage system, E-Vault employs threshold cryptography to maintain private keys, uses blinding for retrieving confidential data, and implements proactive secret sharing. E-Vault assumes the synchronous system model.

8.9 Discussion

Tables 8.1 and 8.2 summarize the various systems that have been built using the elements we've just outlined. Clearly, there's much to be learned about how to engineer systems based on these elements, and only a small part of the landscape has been explored.

Table 8.2 Toolkits for implementing distributed trust.

SYSTEM	DESCRIPTION
BFT[8]	BFT is a toolkit for implementing replicated state machines in the asynchronous model. Services tolerate Byzantine failures and use a proactive recovery mechanism for periodically re-establishing secure links among replicas and restoring each replica's code and state. BFT employs consensus protocols and sacrifices liveness to circumvent the impossibility result for consensus in the asynchronous model. For proactive recovery, BFT assumes a secure cryptographic coprocessor and a watchdog timer. BFT doesn't provide support for storing confidential information or for maintaining a service private key that is required for scalability.
Intrusion Tolerance via Threshold Cryptography (ITTC)[32]	The ITTC toolkit includes a threshold RSA implementation with distributed key generation and share refreshing, which is done when instructed by an administrator. No clear system model is provided, but the protocols seem to be suitable for use in the asynchronous model.
Phalanx [23]	Phalanx is middleware for implementing scalable persistent survivable distributed object repositories. In Phalanx, a Byzantine quorum system allows Byzantine failures to be tolerated, even in the asynchronous model. Randomized protocols are used to circumvent the impossibility result for consensus in the asynchronous model. Phalanx does not provide support for storing confidential information or for maintaining confidential service keys; it also does not implement proactive recovery.
Proactive security toolkit (IBM) [1]	This is a toolkit for maintaining proactively secure communication links, private keys, and data storage in synchronous systems. The design employs the attack-awareness approach (with ROM) for refreshing the servers' public-private key pairs.
Secure INtrusion-Tolerant Replication Architecture (Sintra)[6]	Sintra is a toolkit that provides a set of group communication primitives for implementing a replicated state machine in the asynchronous model, where servers can exhibit Byzantine failures. Randomized protocols are used to circumvent the impossibility result for consensus in the asynchronous model. Sintra does not provide support for storing confidential information or for maintaining a service private key that is required for scalability, although the design of an asynchronous proactive secret sharing protocol is documented elsewhere.

A system's trustworthiness is ultimately tied to a set of assumptions about the environment in which that system must function. Systems users should prefer weaker assumptions, because then there is less risk that these assumptions will be violated by natural events or attacks. However, adopting this view, renders irrelevant much prior work in fault-tolerance and distributed algorithms.

Until recently, the synchronous model of computation has generally been assumed, but there are good reasons to investigate algorithms and system architectures for asynchronous models of computation: specifically, concern about DoS attacks and interest in distributed computations that span wide-area networks. Also, most of the prior work on replication has ignored confidentiality, yet confidentiality is not orthogonal to replication and poses a new set of challenges, so it cannot be ignored. Moreover, because confidentiality is not a property of an individual component's state or state transitions, usual approaches to specification and system refinement, which are concerned with what actions components perform, are not germane.

The system design approach outlined in this chapter has been referred to as implementing *distributed trust* [27], because it allows a higher level of trust to be placed in an ensemble than could be placed in a component. There is no magic here. Distributed trust requires that component compromise be independent. To date, only a few sources of diversity have been investigated, and only a subset of those has enjoyed practical deployment. Real diversity is messy and often brought about by random and unpredictable natural processes, in contrast to how most computations are envisaged (as a preconceived sequence of state transitions). Think about how epidemics spread (from random, hence diverse, contacts between individuals) to wipe out a population (a form of "reliable broadcast"); think about how individuality permits a species to survive or how diverse collections of species allow an ecosystem to last.

Finally, if cryptographic building blocks, like secret sharing and threshold cryptography, seem a bit arcane today, it is perhaps worth recalling that 20 years ago, research in consensus protocols was considered a niche concern that most systems builders ignored as impractical. Today, systems designers understand and regularly use such protocols to implement systems that can tolerate various kinds of failures even though hardware is more reliable than ever. The promising technologies for trustworthiness, such as secret sharing and threshold cryptography, are also seen today as a niche concern. This cannot persist for long, given our growing dependence on networked computers, which, unfortunately, makes us hostage not only to failures but also to attacks.

Acknowledgements Helpful comments on earlier drafts of this paper were provided by Martin Abadi, Úlfar Erlingsson, Andrew Myers, Mike Schroeder, Gun Sirer, and Ted Wobber. We are also very grateful to three anonymous reviewers for insightful suggestions and pointers to literature we overlooked, all of which helped us to clarify the exposition.

Discussions with Robbert van Renesse were instrumental in developing our first prototype systems that embodied these ideas; Mike Marsh worked on a second system, leading to our work on distributed blinding.

This work was supported in part by ARPA/RADC grant F30602-96-1-0317, AFOSR grant F49620-03-1-0156, Defense Advanced Research Projects Agency (DARPA) and Air Force Research Laboratory Air Force Material Command USAF under agreement number F30602-99-1-0533, National Science Foundation Grants 9703470 and 0430161, and grants from Intel Corporation and Microsoft Corporation. The views and conclusions contained herein are those of the authors and should not be interpreted as necessarily representing the official policies or endorsements, either expressed or implied, of these organizations or the U.S. Government.

References

1. Barak, B., Herzberg, A., Naor, D., Shai, E.: The proactive security toolkit and applications. In: Proceedings of the 6th ACM Conference on Computer and Communications Security (CCS'99), November 1999, pp. 18–27. ACM SIGSAC (1999)
2. Blakley, G.: Safeguarding cryptographic keys. In: Merwin, R., Zanca, J., Smith, M. (eds.) Proceedings of the 1979 National Computer Conference. AFIPS Conference Proceedings, vol. 48, pp. 313–317. AFIPS Press, New York (1979)

3. Boyd, C.: Digital multisignatures. In: Baker, H., Piper, F. (eds.) Cryptography and Coding, pp. 241–246. Clarendon Press, Oxford (1989)
4. Cachin, C., Kursawe, K., Lysyanskaya, A., Strobl, R.: Asynchronous verifiable secret sharing and proactive cryptosystems. In: Proceedings of the 9th ACM Conference on Computer and Communications Security, November 2002, pp. 88–97. ACM Press, New York (2002)
5. Cachin, C., Kursawe, K., Shoup, V.: Random oracles in Constantinople: Practical asynchronous Byzantine agreement using cryptography. In: Proceedings of the 19th ACM Symposium on Principles of Distributed Computing (PODC 2000), July 2000, pp. 123–132. ACM Press, New York (2000)
6. Cachin, C., Poritz, J.A.: Secure intrusion-tolerant replication on the Internet. In: Proceedings of the International Conference on Dependable Systems and Networks (DSN-2002), June 2002, pp. 167–176. IEEE Computer Society Press, Los Alamitos (2002)
7. Canetti, R., Herzberg, A.: Maintaining security in the presence of transient faults. In: Desmedt, Y.G. (ed.) CRYPTO 1994. LNCS, vol. 839, pp. 425–438. Springer, Heidelberg (1994)
8. Castro, M., Liskov, B.: Practical Byzantine fault tolerance and proactive recovery. ACM Transactions on Computer Systems 20(4), 398–461 (2002)
9. Chockler, G., Malkhi, D., Reiter, M.K.: Backoff protocols for distributed mutual exclusion and ordering. In: Proceedings of the International Conference on Distributed Systems, pp. 11–20. IEEE Computer Society Press, Los Alamitos (2001)
10. Desmedt, Y., Frankel, Y.: Threshold cryptosystems. In: Brassard, G. (ed.) CRYPTO 1989. LNCS, vol. 435, pp. 307–315. Springer, Heidelberg (1990)
11. Fischer, M.J., Lynch, N.A., Paterson, M.S.: Impossibility of distributed consensus with one faulty process. Journal of the ACM 32(2), 374–382 (1985)
12. Forrest, S., Somayaji, A., Ackley, D.: Building diverse computer systems. In: Proceedings of the Sixth Workshop on Hot Topics in Operating Systems, Cape Cod, MA, May 1997, pp. 67–72. IEEE Computer Society Press, Los Alamitos (1997)
13. Garay, J.A., Gennaro, R., Jutla, C., Rabin, T.: Secure distributed storage and retrieval. Theoretical Computer Science 243(1–2), 363–389 (2000)
14. Goldreich, O., Micali, S., Wigderson, A.: How to play ANY mental game. In: Proceedings of the 19th Annual Conference on Theory of Computing, STOC'87, May 25–27, 1987, pp. 218–229. ACM Press, New York (1987)
15. Herzberg, A., Jarecki, S., Krawczyk, H., Yung, M.: Proactive secret sharing or: How to cope with perpetual leakage. In: Coppersmith, D. (ed.) CRYPTO 1995. LNCS, vol. 963, pp. 339–352. Springer, Heidelberg (1995)
16. Hirt, M., Maurer, U.: Player simulation and general adversary structures in perfect multiparty computation. Journal of Cryptology 13(1), 31–60 (2000)
17. Jakobsson, M.: On quorum controlled asymmetric proxy re-encryption. In: Imai, H., Zheng, Y. (eds.) PKC 1999. LNCS, vol. 1560, pp. 112–121. Springer, Heidelberg (1999)
18. Knight, J., Leveson, N.G.: An experimental evaluation of the assumption of independence in multi-version programming. IEEE Transactions on Software Engineering 12(1), 96–109 (1986)
19. Lamport, L.: Time, clocks, and the ordering of events in a distributed system. Communications of the ACM 21(7), 558–565 (1978)
20. Lamport, L.: The part-time parliament. ACM Transactions on Computer Systems 16(2), 133–169 (1998)
21. Liskov, B., Ladin, R.: Highly available distributed services and fault-tolerant distributed garbage collection. In: Proceedings of the Fifth Annual ACM Symposium on Principles of Distributed Computing, Calgary, Alberta, Canada, August 1986, pp. 29–39. ACM Press, New York (1986)
22. Malkhi, D., Reiter, M.: Byzantine quorum system. Distributed Computing 11(4), 203–213 (1998)
23. Malkhi, D., Reiter, M.: Secure and scalable replication in Phalanx. In: Proceedings of the 17th Symposium on Reliable Distributed Systems, West Lafayette, IN, USA, October 20–22, 1998, pp. 51–58. IEEE Computer Society Press, Los Alamitos (1998)

24. Marsh, M.A., Schneider, F.B.: CODEX: A robust and secure secret distribution system. IEEE Transactions on Dependable and Secure Computing 1(1), 34–47 (2003)
25. Ostrovsky, R., Yung, M.: How to withstand mobile virus attacks. In: Proceedings of the 10th Annual Symposium on Principles of Distributed Computing (PODC'91), Montreal, Quebec, Canada, August 19–21, 1991, pp. 51–59. ACM, New York (1991)
26. Pease, M., Shostak, R., Lamport, L.: Reaching agreement in the presence of faults. Journal of the ACM 27(2), 228–234 (1980)
27. Reiter, M.K.: Distributing trust with the Rampart toolkit. Communications of the ACM 39(4), 71–74 (1996)
28. Rodrigues, R., Castro, M., Liskov, B.: BASE: using abstraction to improve fault tolerance. In: Proceedings of the 18th ACM Symposium on Operating System Principles, Banff, Canada, October 2001, pp. 15–28. ACM, New York (2001)
29. Schneider, F.B.: Implementing fault-tolerant services using the state machine approach: a tutorial. ACM Computing Surveys 22(4), 299–319 (1990)
30. Shamir, A.: How to share a secret. Communications of the ACM 22(11), 612–613 (1979)
31. Song, D., Wagner, D., Perrig, A.: Practical techniques for searches on encrypted data. In: Proceedings of the 2000 IEEE Symposium Security and Privacy, Oakland, CA USA, May 2000, pp. 44–45. IEEE Computer Society Press, Los Alamitos (2000)
32. Wu, T., Malkin, M., Boneh, D.: Building intrusion tolerant applications. In: Proceedings of the 8th USENIX Security Symposium, Washington, D.C. USA, August 22–26, 1999, pp. 79–91. USENIX Association (1999)
33. Wylie, J.J., Bigrigg, M.W., Strunk, J.D., Ganger, G.R., Kiliçҫöte, H., Khosla, P.K.: Survivable information storage systems. IEEE Computer 33(8), 61–68 (2000)
34. Xu, J., Kalbarczyk, Z., Iyer, R.K.: Transparent runtime randomization for security. Tech. Rep. UILU-ENG-03-2207 (CRHC-03-03), Center for Reliable and High-Performance Computing, University of Illinois at Urbana-Champaign, Urbana-Champaign, IL (May 2003)
35. Zhou, L., Marsh, M.A., Schneider, F.B., Redz, A.: Distributed blinding for distributed El-Gamal re-encryption. In: Proceedings of the 25th International Conference on Distributed Computing Systems, Columbus, Ohio, USA, June 2005, pp. 814–824. IEEE Computer Society, Los Alamitos (2005)
36. Zhou, L., Schneider, F.B., van Renesse, R.: COCA: A secure distributed on-line certification authority. ACM Transactions on Computer Systems 20(4), 329–368 (2002)
37. Zhou, L., Schneider, F.B., van Renesse, R.: APSS: Proactive secret sharing in asynchronous systems. ACM Trans. on Information and Sytem Security 8(3) (2005)

Chapter 9
State Machine Replication with Byzantine Faults

Christian Cachin

Abstract This chapter gives an introduction to protocols for state-machine replication in groups that are connected by asynchronous networks and whose members are subject to arbitrary or "Byzantine" faults. It explains the principles of such protocols and covers the following topics: broadcast primitives, distributed cryptosystems, randomized Byzantine consensus protocols, and atomic broadcast protocols.

9.1 Introduction

Coordinating a group of replicas to deliver a service, while some of them are actively trying to prevent the coordination effort, is a fascinating topic. It stands at the heart of Pease, Shostak, and Lamport's classic work [24] on reaching agreement in the presence of faults, which ignited an impressive flow of papers elaborating on this problem over the last 30 years.

In this chapter, we survey protocols to *replicate a state machine* in an *asynchronous network* over a group of n *parties* or *replicas*, of which up to t are subject to so-called *Byzantine* faults. No assumptions about the behavior of the faulty parties are made; they may deviate arbitrarily from the protocol, as if corrupted by a malicious adversary. The key mechanism for replicating a deterministic service among the group is a protocol for the task of *atomic broadcast* [16, 31, 32]. It guarantees that every correct party in the group receives the same sequence of requests from the clients. This approach allows to build highly resilient and intrusion-tolerant services on the Internet, as discussed in Chapter 8.

The model considered here is motivated by practice. The parties are connected pairwise by reliable authenticated channels. Protocols may use cryptographic methods, such as public-key cryptosystems and digital signatures. A trusted entity takes care of initially generating and distributing private keys, public keys, and certificates, such that every party can verify signatures by all other parties, for example. The system is asynchronous: there are no bounds on the delivery time of messages and no synchronized clocks. This is an important aspect because systems whose cor-

B. Charron-Bost, F. Pedone, and A. Schiper (Eds.): Replication, LNCS 5959, pp. 169–184, 2010.

rectness relies on timing assumptions are vulnerable to attackers that simply slow down the correct parties or delay the messages sent between them.

The chapter is organized as follows. We first introduce some building blocks for atomic broadcast; they consist of two broadcast primitives, distributed cryptosystems, and randomized Byzantine consensus protocols. Then we present the structure of some recent asynchronous atomic broadcast protocols. Finally, we illustrate some issues with service replication that arise specifically in the presence of Byzantine faults. We focus on the asynchronous model and leave out many other protocols that have been formulated for synchronous networks.

9.2 Building Blocks

9.2.1 Broadcast Primitives

We present two broadcast primitives, which are found in one way or other in all consensus and atomic broadcast protocols tolerating Byzantine faults. As such protocols usually invoke multiple instances of a broadcast primitive, every message is tagged by an identifier of the instance in practice (and where applicable, the identifier is also included in every cryptographic operation).

Every broadcast instance has a designated sender, which *broadcasts* a *request m* to the group at the start of the protocol. All parties should later *deliver m*, though termination is not guaranteed with a faulty sender. To simplify matters, we assume that the sender is a member of the group (i.e., that requests from clients to the service are relayed through one replica) and that all requests are unique.

Consistent Broadcast

Consider a group of n parties $P_1, \ldots, P_n$. In *consistent broadcast*, a designated sender P_s first executes *c-broadcast* with request m and thereby starts the protocol. All parties terminate the protocol by executing *c-deliver* with request m. Consistent broadcast ensures only that the delivered request is the same for all receivers. In particular, it does not guarantee that *every* party delivers a request with a faulty sender.

The following definition is implicit in the work of Bracha and Toueg [37, 2] but has been formulated more recently [3] to be in line with the corresponding notions for systems with crash failures [12]. Recall that it models only one instance of consistent broadcast.

Definition 9.1 (Consistent Broadcast). A protocol for consistent broadcast satisfies:

Validity: If a correct sender P_s *c-broadcasts* m, then all correct parties eventually *c-deliver m*.

Consistency: If a correct party *c-delivers m* and another correct party *c-delivers m'*, then $m = m'$.

Integrity: Every correct party *c-delivers* at most one request. Moreover, if the sender P_s is correct, then the request was previously *c-broadcast* by P_s.

The *echo broadcast* protocol below implements consistent broadcast with a *linear* number of messages and uses digital signatures. Its idea is that the sender distributes the request to all parties and expects $\lceil \frac{n+t+1}{2} \rceil$ parties to act as witnesses for the request; they attest this by signing their reply to the sender. In all *upon* clauses of the protocol description that involve receiving a message, only the first message from each party is considered.

Algorithm 9.1 Echo broadcast [29] (all parties use digital signatures).

upon *c-broadcast(m)* **do**   {*only P_s*}
   send message $(\texttt{send}, m)$ to all

upon receiving a message $(\texttt{send}, m)$ from P_s **do**
   compute signature σ on $(\texttt{echo}, s, m)$
   send message $(\texttt{echo}, m, \sigma)$ to P_s

upon receiving $\lceil \frac{n+t+1}{2} \rceil$ messages $(\texttt{echo}, m, \sigma_i)$ with valid σ_i **do**   {*only P_s*}
   let Σ be the list of all received signatures σ_i
   send message $(\texttt{final}, m, \Sigma)$ to all

upon receiving a message $(\texttt{final}, m, \Sigma)$ from P_s with $\lceil \frac{n+t+1}{2} \rceil$ valid signatures in Σ **do**
   c-deliver(m)

Theorem 9.1. *Algorithm 9.1 implements consistent broadcast for $n > 3t$.*

Proof sketch. Validity and integrity are straightforward to verify. Consistency follows from the observation that the request m in any $\texttt{final}$ message with $\lceil \frac{n+t+1}{2} \rceil$ valid signatures in Σ is unique. To see this, consider the set of parties that issued the $\lceil \frac{n+t+1}{2} \rceil$ signatures: because there are only n distinct parties, every two sets of signers overlap in at least one correct party. Such sets are also called *Byzantine quorums* [19]; quorum systems are the subject of Chapter 10.

The message complexity of echo broadcast is $O(n)$ and its communication complexity is $O(n^2(k + |m|))$, where k denotes the length of a digital signature. Using a non-interactive threshold signature scheme [34], the communication complexity can be reduced to $O(n(k + |m|))$ [3].

Reliable Broadcast

Reliable Broadcast is characterized by an *r-broadcast* event and an *r-deliver* event analogous to consistent broadcast. Reliable broadcast additionally ensures agreement on the delivery of the request in the sense that either all correct parties deliver some request or none delivers any request; this property has been called *totality* [3]. In the literature, consistency and totality are often combined into a single condition called *agreement*. This primitive is also known as the "Byzantine generals problem."

Definition 9.2 (Reliable Broadcast). A protocol for reliable broadcast is a consistent broadcast protocol that satisfies also:

Totality: If some correct party *r-delivers* a request, then all correct parties eventually *r-deliver* a request.

The classical implementation of reliable broadcast by Bracha [2] uses two rounds of message exchanges among all parties. Intuitively, it works as follows. After receiving the request from the sender, a party echoes it to all. After receiving such echos from a Byzantine quorum of parties, a party indicates to all others that it is ready to deliver the request. When a party receives a sufficient number of those indications, it delivers the request.

Algorithm 9.2 Bracha broadcast [2].

upon *r-broadcast*(m) **do**   {*only* P_s}
     send message (send, m) to all

upon receiving a message (send, m) from P_s **do**
     send message (echo, m) to all

upon receiving $\lceil \frac{n+t+1}{2} \rceil$ messages (echo, m) and not having sent a ready-message **do**
     send message (ready, m) to all

upon receiving $t + 1$ messages (ready, m) and not having sent a ready-message **do**
     send message (ready, m) to all

upon receiving $2t + 1$ messages (ready, m) **do**
     r-deliver(m)

Theorem 9.2. *Algorithm 9.2 implements reliable broadcast for $n > 3t$.*

Proof sketch. Consistency follows from the same argument as in Theorem 9.1, since the request m in any ready message of a correct party is unique. Totality is implied by the "amplification" of ready messages from $t + 1$ to $2t + 1$ with the fourth *upon* clause of the algorithm. Specifically, if a correct party has *r-delivered* m, it has received a ready message with m from $2t + 1$ distinct parties. Therefore, at least $t + 1$ correct parties have sent a ready message with m, which will be received by all correct parties and cause them to send a ready message as well. Because $n - t \geq 2t + 1$, all correct parties eventually receive enough ready messages to terminate.

The message complexity of Bracha broadcast is $O(n^2)$ and its communication complexity is $O(n^2|m|)$. Because it does not need digital signatures, which are usually computationally expensive operations, Bracha broadcast is often preferable to echo broadcast depending on the deployment conditions.

Several complex consensus and atomic broadcast protocols use either the consistent or the reliable broadcast primitive, and one can often substitute either primitive for the other one in these protocols, with appropriate modifications. Selecting one of these primitives for an implementation involves a trade-off between computation time and message complexity. It is an interesting question to determine the experimental conditions under which either primitive is more suitable; Moniz et al. [23] present some initial answers.

9.2.2 Distributed Cryptography

Distributed cryptography spreads the operation of a cryptosystem among a group of parties in a fault-tolerant way [10]; even if an adversary learns the secrets of all faulty parties, the protection of the cryptosystem must remain intact. Such schemes are also called *threshold cryptosystems*. They are based on *secret sharing* methods, and distributed implementations are typically known only for public-key cryptosystems because of their algebraic properties.

Secret Sharing

In a $(t+1)$-*out-of-n secret sharing scheme*, a secret s, element of a finite field $\mathbb{F}$ with q elements, is shared among n parties such that the cooperation of at least $t+1$ parties is needed to recover s. Any group of t or fewer parties should not get any information about s.

Algorithm 9.3 Polynomial secret sharing [33].

To *share* $s \in \mathbb{F}_q$, a *dealer* $P_d \notin \{P_1,\ldots,P_n\}$ chooses uniformly at random a polynomial $f(X) \in \mathbb{F}_q[X]$ of degree t subject to $f(0) = s$, generates *shares* $s_i = f(i)$, and sends s_i to P_i for $i = 1,\ldots,n$. To recover s among a group of $t+1$ parties with indices $\mathscr{S}$, every member of the group reveals its share and the parties together recover the secret by computing

$$ s = f(0) = \sum_{i \in \mathscr{S}} \lambda_{0,i}^{\mathscr{S}} s_i, $$

where

$$ \lambda_{0,i}^{\mathscr{S}} = \prod_{j \in \mathscr{S}, j \neq i} \frac{j}{j-i} $$

are the (easy-to-compute) Lagrange coefficients.

Theorem 9.3. *In Algorithm 9.3, every group of t or fewer parties has no information about s, i.e., their shares are statistically independent of s.*

We refer to the literature for definitions and for a proof of the theorem [36]. Secret sharing schemes do not directly give fault-tolerant replicated implementations of cryptosystems; if the secret key were reconstructed for performing a cryptographic operation, all security would be lost because the key would be exposed to the faulty parties. So-called *threshold cryptosystems* perform these operations securely; as an example, a threshold public-key cryptosystem based on the ElGamal cryptosystem is presented next (details can be found in books on modern cryptography [22, 36, 13]).

Discrete Logarithm-Based Cryptosystems

Let G be a group of prime order q such that g is a generator of G. The *discrete logarithm problem (DLP)* means, for a random $y \in G$, to compute $x \in \mathbb{Z}_q$ such that $y = g^x$. The *Diffie-Hellman problem (DHP)* is to compute $g^{x_1 x_2}$ from random $y_1 = g^{x_1}$ and $y_2 = g^{x_2}$.

It is conjectured that there exist groups in which solving the DLP and the DHP is *hard*, for instance, the multiplicative subgroup $G \subset \mathbb{Z}_p^*$ of order q, for some prime $p = mq + 1$ (recall that q is prime). This choice with $|p| = 2048$ and $|q| = 256$ is considered secure today and used widely on the Internet, for example.

A *public-key cryptosystem* consists of three algorithms, K, E, and D. The key-generation algorithm K outputs a pair of keys (pk, sk). The encryption and decryption algorithms, E and D, have the property that for all (pk, sk) generated by K and for any plaintext message m, it holds $D(sk, E(pk, m)) = m$.

A public-key cryptosystem is *semantically secure* if no efficient adversary A can distinguish the encryptions of any two messages. Semantic security provides security against so-called *passive* attacks, in which an adversary follows the protocol but tries to infer more information than it is entitled to. An adversary mounting an *active* attack may additionally fabricate ciphertext, submit it for decryption, and obtain the results.

ElGamal Cryptosystem and Threshold ElGamal

The *ElGamal cryptosystem* is based on the DHP: K selects a random secret key $x \in \mathbb{Z}_q$ and computes the public key as $y = g^x$. The encryption of $m \in \{0,1\}^k$ under public-key y is the tuple $(A, B) = (g^r, m \oplus H(y^r))$, computed using a randomly chosen $r \in \mathbb{Z}_q$ and a collision-resistant cryptographic hash function $H : G \to \{0,1\}^k$. The decryption of a ciphertext (A, B) is $\hat{m} = H(A^x) \oplus B$. One can easily verify that $\hat{m} = m$ because $A^x = g^{rx} = g^{xr} = y^r$, and therefore, the argument to H is the same in encryption and decryption. The cryptosystem is semantically secure under the assumption that the DHP is hard.

Algorithm 9.4 Threshold ElGamal Cryptosystem.

Let the secret key x be *shared* among $P_1, \ldots, P_n$ using a polynomial f of degree t over $\mathbb{Z}_q$ such that P_i holds a share $x_i = f(i)$. The public key $y = g^x$ is known to all parties. Encryption is the same as in standard ElGamal above. For decryption, a client sends a decryption request containing a ciphertext (A, B) to all parties. Upon receiving a decryption request, party P_i computes a *decryption share* $d_i = A^{x_i}$ and sends it to the client. Upon receiving decryption shares from a set of $t + 1$ parties with indices $\mathscr{S}$, the client recovers the plaintext as

$$\hat{m} = H\left(\prod_{i \in \mathscr{S}} d_i^{\lambda_{0,i}^{\mathscr{S}}}\right) \oplus B.$$

Theorem 9.4. *Algorithm 9.4 implements a $(t+1)$-out-of-n threshold cryptosystem that tolerates the passive corruption of $t < n/2$ parties.*

Proof sketch. The decryption is correct because

$$\prod_{i \in \mathscr{S}} d_i^{\lambda_{0,i}^{\mathscr{S}}} = \prod_{i \in \mathscr{S}} A^{x_i \lambda_{0,i}^{\mathscr{S}}} = A^{\sum_{i \in \mathscr{S}} x_i \lambda_{0,i}^{\mathscr{S}}} = A^x$$

from the properties of secret sharing. The system is as secure as the ElGamal cryptosystem because ciphertexts are computed in the same way. Moreover, the decryption shares ($d_i = A^{x_i}$) do not reveal any "useful information" about the shares of the secret key (x_i).

This is a *non-interactive* threshold cryptosystem, as no interaction among the parties is needed. It can also be made secure against active attacks [35]. Non-interactive threshold cryptosystems can easily be integrated in asynchronous protocols.

9.2.3 Byzantine Consensus

One step up from the broadcast primitives is a protocol to reach consensus despite Byzantine faults. It is a prerequisite for implementing atomic broadcast. All atomic broadcast protocols, at least in the model with static groups considered here, either explicitly invoke a consensus primitive or implicitly contain one.

The *Byzantine consensus* problem, also called *Byzantine agreement*[1], is characterized by two events *propose* and *decide*; every party executes *propose(v)* to start the protocol and *decide(v)* to terminate it for a value *v*. In *binary* consensus, the values are bits.

Definition 9.3 (Byzantine Consensus). A protocol for binary Byzantine consensus satisfies:

Validity: If all correct parties *propose v*, then some correct party eventually *decides v*.

Agreement: If some correct party *decides v* and another correct party *decides v'*, then $v = v'$.

Termination: Every correct party eventually *decides*.

The result of Fischer, Lynch, and Paterson [11] implies that every asynchronous protocol solving Byzantine consensus has executions that do not terminate. State machine replication in asynchronous networks is also subject to this limitation. Roughly at the same time, however, randomized protocols to circumvent this impossibility were developed [26, 1, 37]. They make the probability of non-terminating executions arbitrarily small. More precisely, given a logical time measure T, such as the number of steps performed by all correct parties, define *termination with probability 1* as

$$\lim_{T \to \infty} \Pr[\text{some correct party has not } decided \text{ after time } T] = 0.$$

---

[1] We prefer the name *Byzantine consensus* because *Byzantine agreement* is overloaded and has been used for technically different problems.

Algorithm 9.5 Binary randomized Byzantine consensus [37].

Suppose a trusted dealer has *shared* a sequence $s_0, s_1, \ldots$ of random bits, called *coins*, among the parties, using $(t+1)$-out-of-n secret sharing. A party can access the coin s_r using a *recover*(r) operation, which involves a protocol that exchanges some messages to reveal the shares to all parties, and gives the same coin value to every party.

The two *upon* clauses in the pseudo-code below are executed concurrently.

upon *propose*(v) **do**
    $r \leftarrow 0$
    decided $\leftarrow$ false
    loop
        send the signed message $(\texttt{1-vote}, r, v)$ to all
        wait for receiving properly signed $(\texttt{1-vote}, r, v')$ messages
            from $n - t$ distinct parties
        $\Pi \leftarrow$ set of received $\texttt{1-vote}$ messages including the signatures
        $v \leftarrow$ value v' that is contained most often in Π
        r-broadcast the message $(\texttt{2-vote}, r, v, \Pi)$
        wait for *r-delivery* of $(\texttt{2-vote}, r, v', \Pi)$ messages from $n - t$ distinct
            senders with valid signatures in Π and correctly computed v'
        $b \leftarrow$ value v' contained most often among the r-delivered $\texttt{2-vote}$ msgs.
        $c \leftarrow$ number of r-delivered $\texttt{2-vote}$ messages with $v' = b$
        $s_r \leftarrow recover(r)$
        if $c = n - t$ **then**
            $v \leftarrow b$
        else
            $v \leftarrow s_r$
        if $b = s_r$ **then**
            send the message $(\texttt{decide}, v)$ to all   {note that $v = s_r = b$}
        $r \leftarrow r + 1$

upon receiving $t + 1$ messages $(\texttt{decide}, b)$ **do**
    if *decided* $=$ false **then**
        send the message $(\texttt{decide}, b)$ to all
        decided $\leftarrow$ true
        decide(b)

A consensus protocol that terminates with probability 1 is Algorithm 9.5. It works as follows. Every party maintains a value v, called its *vote*, and the protocol proceeds in global asynchronous rounds. Every round consists of two voting steps among the parties with all-to-all communication. In the first voting step, the parties simply exchange their votes, and every party determines the majority of the received votes. In the second voting step, every party relays the majority vote to all others, this time using reliable broadcast and accompanied by a set Π that serves as a *proof* for justifying the choice of the majority. The set Π contains messages and signatures from the first voting step. After receiving reliable broadcasts from $n - t$ parties, every party determines the majority of this second vote and adopts its outcome as its vote v if the tally is unanimous; otherwise, a party sets v to the shared coin for the round. If the coin equals the outcome of the second vote, then the party decides.

Lemma 9.1. *If all correct parties start some round r with vote v_0, then all correct parties terminate round r with vote v_0.*

Proof. It is impossible to create a valid Π for a 2-vote message with a vote $v \neq v_0$ because v must be set to the majority value in $n - t$ received 1-vote messages and $n - t > 2t$.

Lemma 9.2. *In round $r \geq 0$, the following holds:*

1. *If a correct party sends a* decide *message for v_0 at the end of round r, then all correct parties terminate round r with vote v_0.*
2. *With probability at least $\frac{1}{2}$, all correct parties terminate round r with the same vote.*

Proof. Consider the assignment of b and c in round r. If some correct party obtains $c = n - t$ and $b = v_0$, then no correct party can obtain a majority of 2-vote messages for a value different from v_0 (there are only n 2-vote messages and they satisfy the consistency of reliable broadcast). Those correct parties with $c = n - t$ set their vote v to v_0; every other correct party sets v to s_r. Hence, if $s_r = v_0$, all correct parties terminate round r with vote v_0.

Claim *a)* now follows upon noticing that a correct party only sends a decide message for v_0 when $v_0 = b = s_r$.

Claim *b)* follows because the first correct party to assign b and c does so *before* any information about s_r is known (to the adversary). To see this note that at least $t + 1$ shares are needed for recovering s_r, but a correct party only reveals its share *after* assigning b and c. Thus, s_r and v_0 are statistically independent and $s_r = v_0$ holds with probability $\frac{1}{2}$.

Theorem 9.5. *Algorithm 9.5 implements binary Byzantine consensus for $n > 3t$, where termination holds with probability 1.*

The theorem follows easily from the two lemmas. The protocol achieves optimal resilience because reaching agreement in asynchronous networks with $t \geq n/3$ Byzantine faults is impossible, despite the use of digital signatures [37]. Since Algorithm 9.5 terminates with probability at least $\frac{1}{2}$ in every round, the expected number of rounds is two, and the expected number of messages is $O(n^3)$.

Using Cryptographic Randomness

The problem with Algorithm 9.5 is that every round in the execution uses up one shared coin in the sequence $s_0, s_1, \ldots$. As coins cannot be reused, this is a problem in practice. A solution for this is to obtain the shared coins from a threshold-cryptographic function. Malkhi and Reiter [20] observe that a non-interactive and deterministic threshold signature scheme yields unpredictable bits, which is sufficient.

More generally, one may obtain the coin value s_r from the output of a distributed *pseudorandom function (PRF)* [13] evaluated on the round number r and the protocol instance identifier. A PRF is parameterized by a secret key and maps every input string to an output string that looks random to anyone who does not have the secret key. A practical PRF construction is a block cipher with a secret key; distributed implementations, however, are only known for functions based on public-key cryptosystems. Cachin et al. [4] describe a suitable distributed PRF based on the Diffie-Hellman problem. With their implementation of the shared coin, Algorithm 9.5 is quite practical and has expected message complexity $O(n^3)$. It can further be improved to a randomized asynchronous Byzantine consensus protocol with $O(n^2)$ expected messages [4].

9.3 Atomic Broadcast Protocols

Atomic broadcast delivers multiple requests in the same order to all parties. Whereas instances of reliable broadcast may be independent of each other, the total order of atomic broadcast links these together and requires more complex implementations. The details of the protocols in this section are therefore omitted.

Analogously to reliable broadcast, atomic broadcast is characterized by an *a-broadcast* event, executed by the sender of a request, and an *a-deliver* event. Every party may a-broadcast multiple requests; also a-deliver generally occurs multiple times. The following definition [3] is adapted from the corresponding one in the crash-failure model [12].

Definition 9.4 (Atomic Broadcast). A protocol for atomic broadcast consists of a set of protocol instances for reliable broadcast that satisfy also:

Total order: If two correct parties P_i and P_j both *a-deliver* two requests m and m', then P_i *a-delivers* m before m' if and only if P_j *a-delivers* m before m'.

Since we are not explicit about instances of reliable broadcast in this definition, we must change the *integrity* property in Definition 9.2 (originating in Definition 9.1) appropriately: We require instead that every possible request m is a-delivered at most once, and that if all parties are correct, then m was previously a-broadcast by some party.

Some early atomic broadcast protocols [29, 25] used dynamic groups with a membership service that might evict faulty parties from the group, even if they only appear to be slow. When an attacker manages to exploit network delays accordingly, this may lead to the problematic situation where the correct parties are in a minority, and the protocol violates safety.

The more recent protocols, on which we focus here, never violate safety because of network instability. We distinguish between two kinds of atomic broadcast protocols, which we call *consensus-based* and *sequencer-based* according to the survey of atomic broadcast protocols of Défago et al. [9]. We next review the principles of these protocols, starting with the historically older protocols based on consensus. A third option, considered afterwards, is to combine leader- and consensus-based protocols into *hybrid* atomic broadcast protocols.

9.3.1 Consensus-Based Atomic Broadcast

The canonical implementation of atomic broadcast uses a consensus primitive to determine the next request that should be a-delivered. Such a protocol proceeds in asynchronous rounds and uses one instance of (multi-valued) Byzantine consensus in every round to agree on a set of requests, which are then a-delivered in a fixed order at the end of the round. The same approach has been applied in the crash-failure model by algorithms using the mechanism of *message ordering by agreement on a message set* [9] (see also Chapter 3 and [12]).

Incoming requests are buffered and proposed for delivery in the next available round. The validity notion of Byzantine consensus, however, must be amended for this to work: the standard validity condition only guarantees that a particular decision is reached when all parties make the same proposal. This will rarely be the case in practice, where every party receives different requests to a-broadcast.

A suitable notion of validity for *multi-valued Byzantine consensus* has been introduced by Cachin et al. [3]; it defines a test for determining if a proposed value is acceptable and externalizes it. Moreover, to agree on a value from a domain of arbitrary size, Algorithm 9.5 must be extended in non-trivial ways. Note that it would be infeasible in practice to agree bit-by-bit on values from large domains such as the set of all requests. A suitable protocol for multi-valued Byzantine consensus has been formulated [3], and it uses a binary Byzantine consensus protocol as a subroutine. This protocol incurs a communication overhead of $O(n^2)$ messages over the primitive for binary consensus.

With multi-valued (randomized) Byzantine consensus, a protocol for asynchronous atomic broadcast can be implemented easily as sketched before. In every round of consensus, the validity test ensures that a batch of requests is only acceptable when it has been assembled from the request buffers of at least $t + 1$ parties. This implies that the requests from the buffer of at least one correct party are delivered in that round. The resulting atomic broadcast protocol satisfies the relaxation of Definition 9.4 to termination with probability 1 in the validity condition. Several protocols of this kind have been prototyped in practical systems [5, 23, 28].

Note that the randomized nature of these atomic broadcast protocols does not hurt in practice: they never violate safety (unless a cryptographic mechanism is broken) and the worst-case probability that they take a large number of rounds to terminate is, in fact, exponentially small and comparable to the probability that the adversary guesses a cryptographic key.

9.3.2 Sequencer-Based Atomic Broadcast

Consensus-based protocols send all requests through a Byzantine consensus subroutine to determine their order; but consensus is a rather expensive protocol. A more efficient approach is taken by the *PBFT protocol* of Castro and Liskov [7], which relies on a single party, called the *sequencer*, to determine the request order. Because the sequencer may be faulty, its actions must be checked by the other parties in a distributed protocol. PBFT can actually a be viewed as a Byzantine-fault-tolerant version of the Paxos protocol [17, 18] or of viewstamped replication (see Chapter 7).

Since it does not use randomization, it may not terminate in asynchronous networks due to the FLP impossibility result [11]; therefore it uses a partially synchronous model.

The PBFT protocol proceeds in *epochs* (also called *views*, where an epoch consists of a *normal-operation phase* and a *recovery phase*. During every epoch, a designated party acts as the sequencer for the normal-operation phase, determines the delivery order of requests, and commits every request through reliable broadcast with Bracha's protocol (Algorithm 9.2). Because the sequencer runs the reliable broadcasts in a sequence, this guarantees that all correct parties receive and a-deliver the requests in the same order. This approach ensures safety even when the sequencer is faulty, but may violate liveness when the sequencer stops r-broadcasting requests.

When the sequencer appears faulty in the eyes of enough other parties, the protocol switches to the recovery phase. This step is based on timeouts that must occur on at least $t+1$ parties. Once sufficiently many parties have switched to the recovery phase, the protocol aborts the still ongoing reliable broadcasts, and the recovery phase eventually starts at all correct parties. The goal of the recovery phase is to agree on a new sequencer for the next epoch and on the a-delivery of the requests that the previous sequencer may have left in an inconclusive state.

Progress during the recovery phase and in the subsequent epoch requires the timely cooperation of the new sequencer. In asynchronous networks, it is possible that no requests are delivered before the epoch ends again, and the protocol loses liveness. However, it is assumed that this occurs rarely in practice. This protocol uses the *fixed-sequencer mechanism* for message ordering within every epoch [9] and rotates the sequencer for every new epoch.

Despite its inherent complexity, the recovery phase of PBFT is still more efficient than one round in the consensus-based atomic broadcast protocols. The PBFT protocol has message complexity $O(n^2)$, ensures safety always and liveness only during periods where the network is stable enough; it is considered practical by many system implementors. Several atomic broadcast protocols inspired by PBFT have appeared recently [21, 8, 14], which are even more efficient than PBFT under certain conditions. Chapter 10 explores the use of Byzantine quorum systems in PBFT and related protocols.

9.3.3 Hybrid Atomic Broadcast

Combining the efficiency of the sequencer-based approach during normal operation with the strong guarantees of the (randomized) consensus-based approach for recovery, protocols have been proposed that take the best features from both approaches.

The protocol of Kursawe and Shoup [15] is divided into epochs and uses reliable broadcast during the normal-operation phase, like the PBFT protocol. For recovery, however, it employs randomized Byzantine consensus and ensures that some requests are a-delivered in any case. It therefore guarantees safety *and* liveness and has the same efficiency as PBFT during stable periods.

Ramasamy and Cachin [27] replace the reliable broadcast primitive in the Kursa-we-Shoup protocol by consistent broadcast. The resulting protocol is attractive for its low message complexity, only $O(n)$ expected messages per request, amortized over protocol executions with long periods of stability, compared to $O(n^2)$ for all other atomic broadcast protocols in the Byzantine fault model. The improvement comes at the cost of adding complexity to the recovery phase and, more importantly, by using a digital signature scheme with public-key operations during the normal-operation phase.

9.4 Service Replication

A fault-tolerant service implemented using replication should present the same interface to its clients as when implemented using a single server. Sending requests to the replicated deterministic service via atomic broadcast enables the replicas to process the same sequence of requests and to maintain the same state [32]. If failures are limited to benign crashes, the client may obtain the correct service response from any replica.

When the replicas are subject to Byzantine faults, additional concerns arise: First, services involving cryptographic operations and secret keys must remain secure despite the leakage of keys from corrupted replicas; second, clients must not rely on the response message from any single replica because the replica may be faulty and give a wrong answer; and third, faulty replicas may violate the causality between requests sent to the replicated service. We review methods to address each of these concerns next.

9.4.1 Replicating Cryptographic Services

The service may involve cryptographic operations with keys that should be protected, for example, when the service receives requests that are encrypted with a service-specific key, or when it signs responses using digital signatures. In this case, a break-in to single replica will leak all secrets to the adversary. To defend against this attack, the cryptographic operations of the service should be implemented using threshold cryptography. This leaves the service interface for clients unchanged and hides the distributed implementation of the service, because they need to know only one public key for the service, instead of n public keys for the group of replicas [30].

An important example of such a service is a certification authority (CA), which binds public keys to names and asserts this with its digital signature. Since CAs often serve as the root of trust for large systems, implementing them in an intrusion-tolerant way is a good method to protect them. This principle has been demonstrated in prototype systems [30, 39, 6].

9.4.2 Handling Responses Securely

As the response from any single replica may be forged, clients must generally receive at least $t+1$ responses and infer the service response from them. If all $t+1$

responses are equal, then at least one of them was sent by a correct party, which ensures that the response is correct. Collecting responses and deciding for a correct one involves a modification of the client-side service interface. Usually this modification is simple and can be hidden in a library. But if no such modification is possible, there is an alternative for services that rely on cryptographically protected responses: use threshold cryptography to authenticate the response, for example, with a digital signature. Then it is sufficient that the client verifies the authenticity of the response once because it carries the approval of at least $t + 1$ parties that executed the request [30]. In this context, Yin et al. [38] observed that only $2t + 1$ parties need to execute requests and maintain the state of the service, instead of all n parties.

9.4.3 Preserving Causality of Requests

When a client atomically broadcasts a request to the replicated service, the faulty replicas may be able to create a derived request that is a-delivered and executed *before* the client's request. This violates the safety of the service, more precisely, the causal order among requests. For example, consider a service that registers names in a directory on a first-come, first-served basis. When a faulty party peeks inside the atomic broadcast protocol and observes that an interesting name is being registered, it may try to quickly register the name for one of its conspirators.

One can ensure a causal order among the requests to the service with the following protocol [30], which combines a threshold cryptosystem (Section 9.2.2) with an atomic broadcast protocol (Section 9.3). To a-broadcast a request, the client first encrypts it with a $(t + 1)$-out-of-n threshold public-key cryptosystem under the public key of the service. Then, it a-broadcasts the resulting ciphertext. Upon a-delivery of a ciphertext, a replica first computes a decryption share for the ciphertext, using its share of the corresponding decryption key, and sends the decryption share to all replicas. Then it waits for $t + 1$ decryption shares to arrive, recovers the original request, and a-delivers it.

This protocol can be seen as an atomic broadcast protocol that respects causal order in the Byzantine-fault model [3].

9.5 Conclusion

In the recent years, we have seen a revival of the research on protocols for Byzantine consensus and atomic broadcast subject to Byzantine faults. This is because such protocols appear to be much more practical nowadays and because there is demand for realizing intrusion-tolerant services on the Internet. This chapter has presented the building blocks for such protocols, some 25 years old, and some very recent, and shown how they fit together for securing distributed on-line services.

References

1. Ben-Or, M.: Another advantage of free choice: Completely asynchronous agreement protocols. In: Proc. 2nd ACM Symposium on Principles of Distributed Computing (PODC), pp. 27–30 (1983)
2. Bracha, G.: Asynchronous Byzantine agreement protocols. Information and Computation 75, 130–143 (1987)
3. Cachin, C., Kursawe, K., Petzold, F., Shoup, V.: Secure and efficient asynchronous broadcast protocols. In: Kilian, J. (ed.) CRYPTO 2001. LNCS, vol. 2139, pp. 524–541. Springer, Heidelberg (2001)
4. Cachin, C., Kursawe, K., Shoup, V.: Random oracles in Constantinople: Practical asynchronous Byzantine agreement using cryptography. Journal of Cryptology 18(3), 219–246 (2005)
5. Cachin, C., Poritz, J.A.: Secure intrusion-tolerant replication on the Internet. In: Proc. International Conference on Dependable Systems and Networks (DSN-DCCS), Jun. 2002, pp. 167–176 (2002)
6. Cachin, C., Samar, A.: Secure distributed DNS. In: Proc. International Conference on Dependable Systems and Networks (DSN-DCCS), Jun. 2004, pp. 423–432 (2004)
7. Castro, M., Liskov, B.: Practical Byzantine fault tolerance and proactive recovery. ACM Transactions on Computer Systems 20(4), 398–461 (2002)
8. Cowling, J., Myers, D., Liskov, B., Rodrigues, R., Shrira, L.: HQ replication: A hybrid quorum protocol for Byzantine fault tolerance. In: Proc. 8th Symp. Operating Systems Design and Implementation (OSDI) (2006)
9. Défago, X., Schiper, A., Urbán, P.: Total order broadcast and multicast algorithms: Taxonomy and survey. ACM Computing Surveys 36(4), 372–421 (2004)
10. Desmedt, Y.: Threshold cryptography. European Transactions on Telecommunications 5(4), 449–457 (1994)
11. Fischer, M.J., Lynch, N.A., Paterson, M.S.: Impossibility of distributed consensus with one faulty process. Journal of the ACM 32(2), 374–382 (1985)
12. Hadzilacos, V., Toueg, S.: Fault-tolerant broadcasts and related problems. In: Mullender, S.J. (ed.) Distributed Systems, Addison-Wesley, Reading (1993)
13. Katz, J., Lindell, Y.: Introduction to Modern Cryptography: Principles and Protocols. Chapman and Hall, Boca Raton (2007)
14. Kotla, R., Alvisi, L., Dahlin, M., Clement, A., Wong, E.: Zyzzyva: Speculative Byzantine fault tolerance. In: Proc. 21st ACM Symposium on Operating System Principles (SOSP) (2007)
15. Kursawe, K., Shoup, V.: Optimistic asynchronous atomic broadcast. In: Caires, L., Italiano, G.F., Monteiro, L., Palamidessi, C., Yung, M. (eds.) ICALP 2005. LNCS, vol. 3580, pp. 204–215. Springer, Heidelberg (2005)
16. Lamport, L.: Time, clocks, and the ordering of events in a distributed system. Communications of the ACM 21(7), 558–565 (1978)
17. Lamport, L.: The part-time parliament. ACM Transactions on Computer Systems 16(2), 133–169 (1998)
18. Lamport, L.: Paxos made simple. SIGACT News 32(4), 51–58 (2001)
19. Malkhi, D., Reiter, M.K.: Byzantine quorum systems. Distributed Computing 11(4), 203–213 (1998)
20. Malkhi, D., Reiter, M.K.: An architecture for survivable coordination in large distributed systems. IEEE Transactions on Knowledge and Data Engineering 12(2), 187–202 (2000)
21. Martin, J.P., Alvisi, L.: Fast Byzantine consensus. IEEE Transactions on Dependable and Secure Computing 3(3), 202–215 (2006)
22. Menezes, A.J., van Oorschot, P.C., Vanstone, S.A.: Handbook of Applied Cryptography. CRC Press, Boca Raton (1997)
23. Moniz, H., Neves, N.F., Correia, M., Veríssimo, P.: Randomized intrusion-tolerant asynchronous services. In: Proc. International Conference on Dependable Systems and Networks (DSN-DCCS), pp. 568–577 (2006)

24. Pease, M., Shostak, R., Lamport, L.: Reaching agreement in the presence of faults. Journal of the ACM 27(2), 228–234 (1980)
25. Potter Kihlstrom, K., Moser, L.E., Melliar-Smith, P.M.: The SecureRing group communication system. ACM Transactions on Information and System Security 4(4), 371–406 (2001)
26. Rabin, M.O.: Randomized Byzantine generals. In: Proc. 24th IEEE Symposium on Foundations of Computer Science (FOCS), pp. 403–409 (1983)
27. Ramasamy, H.V., Cachin, C.: Parsimonious asynchronous byzantine-fault-tolerant atomic broadcast. In: Anderson, J.H., Prencipe, G., Wattenhofer, R. (eds.) OPODIS 2005. LNCS, vol. 3974, pp. 88–102. Springer, Heidelberg (2006)
28. Ramasamy, H.V., Seri, M., Sanders, W.H.: Brief announcement: The CoBFIT toolkit. In: Proc. 26th ACM Symposium on Principles of Distributed Computing (PODC), pp. 350–351 (2007)
29. Reiter, M.K.: Secure agreement protocols: Reliable and atomic group multicast in Rampart. In: Proc. 2nd ACM Conference on Computer and Communications Security, pp. 68–80 (1994)
30. Reiter, M.K., Birman, K.P.: How to securely replicate services. ACM Transactions on Programming Languages and Systems 16(3), 986–1009 (1994)
31. Schneider, F.B.: Byzantine generals in action: Implementing fail-stop processors. ACM Transactions on Computer Systems 2(2), 145–154 (1984)
32. Schneider, F.B.: Implementing fault-tolerant services using the state machine approach: A tutorial. ACM Computing Surveys 22(4), 299–319 (1990)
33. Shamir, A.: How to share a secret. Communications of the ACM 22(11), 612–613 (1979)
34. Shoup, V.: Practical threshold signatures. In: Preneel, B. (ed.) EUROCRYPT 2000. LNCS, vol. 1807, pp. 207–220. Springer, Heidelberg (2000)
35. Shoup, V., Gennaro, R.: Securing threshold cryptosystems against chosen ciphertext attack. Journal of Cryptology 15(2), 75–96 (2002)
36. Smart, N.: Cryptography — An Introduction. McGraw-Hill, London (2003)
37. Toueg, S.: Randomized Byzantine agreements. In: Proc. 3rd ACM Symposium on Principles of Distributed Computing (PODC), pp. 163–178 (1984)
38. Yin, J., Martin, J.P., Alvisi, A.V.L., Dahlin, M.: Separating agreement from execution in Byzantine fault-tolerant services. In: Proc. 19th ACM Symposium on Operating System Principles (SOSP), pp. 253–268 (2003)
39. Zhou, L., Schneider, F.B., van Renesse, R.: COCA: A secure distributed online certification authority. ACM Transactions on Computer Systems 20(4), 329–368 (2002)

Chapter 10
Selected Results from the Latest Decade of Quorum Systems Research

Michael G. Merideth and Michael K. Reiter

Abstract Over the past decade, work on quorum systems in non-traditional scenarios has facilitated a number of advances in the field of distributed systems. This chapter surveys a selection of these results including: Byzantine quorum systems that are suitable for use when parts of the system cannot be trusted; algorithms for the deployment of quorum systems on wide area networks so as to allow for efficient access and to retain load dispersion properties; and probabilistic quorum systems that yield benefits for protocols and applications that can tolerate a small possibility of inconsistency. We also present a framework grounded in Byzantine quorum systems that can be used to explain, compare, and contrast several recent Byzantine fault-tolerant state-machine and storage protocols. The framework provides a path to understanding the number of servers required, the number of faults that can be tolerated, and the number of rounds of communication employed by each protocol.

10.1 Introduction

Given a universe U of servers, a *quorum system* over U is a collection $\mathcal{Q} = \{Q_1, \ldots, Q_m\}$ such that each $Q_i \subseteq U$ and

$$|Q \cap Q'| > 0 \tag{10.1}$$

for all $Q, Q' \in \mathcal{Q}$. Each Q_i is called a *quorum*. The intersection property (10.1) makes quorum systems a useful primitive for coordinating actions in a distributed system. For example, if each write is performed at a quorum of servers, then a client who reads from a quorum will observe the last written value. Because of their utility in such applications, quorum systems have a long history in distributed computing.

In this paper, we survey a number of advances that have occurred in using quorum systems to implement distributed services in the last ten years or so. These recent advances derive primarily from the use of quorum systems in non-traditional scenarios. We begin by focusing on their use in systems that suffer Byzantine faults [15], which introduce the possibility of not being able to trust all servers in the intersec-

B. Charron-Bost, F. Pedone, and A. Schiper (Eds.): Replication, LNCS 5959, pp. 185–206, 2010.
© Springer-Verlag Berlin Heidelberg 2010

tion of two different quorums. In Section 10.2, we summarize the basic properties of Byzantine quorum systems, including the minimum universe sizes they require and their best-case load-dispersing properties. We also summarize weaker, probabilistic variants of Byzantine quorum systems that can offset these costs in some cases.

The use of distributed protocols in wide-area networks (e.g., in support of edge computing or content distribution) motivates another set of results that we summarize in Section 10.3. Namely, these results focus on how to position servers and quorums in networks so as to minimize the delays that clients suffer by accessing them. Interestingly, there can be a tension between achieving good load dispersion and having low delay for accessing quorums because, when seeking to balance the load, a client might be required to bypass a nearby but heavily loaded server for another that is further away but more lightly loaded. We briefly summarize some results that have been developed to balance this trade-off.

We then return to Byzantine quorums in Section 10.4, but with an eye toward their use in Byzantine-fault-tolerant state-machine-replication protocols. We present a framework grounded in Byzantine quorum systems that can be used to explain, compare, and contrast several recent such protocols. The Byzantine quorum systems framework particularly helps to elucidate the commonalities among these protocols, and we further believe that this framework should be useful in explaining future such protocols.

10.2 Quorum Systems for Byzantine Faults

In systems that may suffer Byzantine faults, the intersection property (10.1) is typically not adequate as a mechanism to enable consistent data access. Because (10.1) requires only that the intersection of quorums be non-empty, it could be that two quorums intersect in only a single server, for example. In a system in which up to $b > 0$ servers might suffer Byzantine faults, this single server might be faulty and, consequently, could fail to convey the last written value to a reader, for example.

For this reason, Malkhi and Reiter [18] proposed various ways of strengthening the intersection property (10.1) so as to enable quorum systems to be used in Byzantine environments. Our presentation here assumes that there is an (unknown) set B of up to b servers that are faulty. Malkhi and Reiter considered three stronger properties as alternatives. All of these alternatives require that for some $Q \in \mathcal{Q}$,

$$|B \cap Q| = 0. \tag{10.2}$$

In words, for any set of server faults B, there is a quorum Q that does not intersect B. Without this constraint, the faulty servers could prevent progress in the system by simply not responding, since a client typically requires a response from a full quorum of servers to make progress.

The first and simplest alternative to (10.1) is

$$|Q \cap Q' \setminus B| > 0 \tag{10.3}$$

for all $Q, Q' \in \mathcal{Q}$. That is, the intersection of any two quorums contains at least one non-faulty server. For example, if a non-faulty client acquires a lock by accessing Q, then any subsequent client that attempts to acquire this lock at another quorum Q' will notice that some other client already requested the lock, regardless of the behavior of the faulty servers. Quorum systems satisfying (10.3) are called *dissemination* quorum systems.

The second alternative to (10.1) is

$$|Q \cap Q' \setminus B| > |Q' \cap B| \tag{10.4}$$

for all $Q, Q' \in \mathcal{Q}$. In words, the intersection of any two quorums contains more non-faulty servers than the faulty ones in either quorum. As such, the responses from these non-faulty servers will outnumber those from faulty ones. These quorum systems are called *masking* quorum systems.

Finally, the third alternative to (10.1) is

$$|Q \cap Q' \setminus B| > |(Q' \cap B) \cup (Q' \setminus Q)| \tag{10.5}$$

for all $Q, Q' \in \mathcal{Q}$. In words, the number of non-faulty servers in the intersection of Q and Q' (i.e., $|Q \cap Q' \setminus B|$) exceeds the number of faulty servers in Q' (i.e., $|Q' \cap B|$) together with the number of servers in Q' but not Q. The rationale for this property can be seen by considering the servers in Q' but not Q as "outdated", in the sense that if Q was used to perform a write to the system, then those servers in $Q' \setminus Q$ are unaware of the write. As such, if the faulty servers in Q' behave as the outdated ones do, their behavior (i.e., their responses) will dominate that from the non-faulty servers in the intersection ($Q \cap Q' \setminus B$) unless (10.5) holds. Quorum systems satisfying (10.5) are called *opaque* quorum systems.

The increasingly stringent properties (10.3) – (10.5) come with costs in terms of the smallest system sizes that can be supported while tolerating a number b of faults, as shown in the following theorem.

Theorem 10.1 ([18]). *Let $n = |U|$, and let $\mathcal{Q}$ be a quorum system over U.*

- *If $\mathcal{Q}$ is a dissemination quorum system (10.3), then $b < n/3$.*
- *If $\mathcal{Q}$ is a masking quorum system (10.4), then $b < n/4$.*
- *If $\mathcal{Q}$ is an opaque quorum system (10.5), then $b < n/5$.*

10.2.1 Access Strategies and Load

Naor and Wool [24] introduced the notion of an *access strategy* by which clients select quorums to access. An access strategy $p : \mathcal{Q} \to [0, 1]$ is simply a probability distribution on quorums, i.e., $\sum_{Q \in \mathcal{Q}} p(Q) = 1$. Intuitively, when a client accesses the system, it does so at a quorum selected randomly according to the distribution p.

The formalization of an access strategy is useful as a tool for discussing the load dispersing properties of quorum systems. Specifically, it permits us to talk about the probability with which a server is accessed in any given quorum access, i.e.,

$$\ell_p(u) = \sum_{Q \ni u} p(Q), \tag{10.6}$$

and then the maximally loaded server under a given access strategy p, i.e.,

$$\mathscr{L}_p(\mathscr{Q}) = \max_{u \in U} \ell_p(u). \tag{10.7}$$

Finally, this enables us to define the *load* [24] of a quorum system as

$$\mathscr{L}(\mathscr{Q}) = \min_p \mathscr{L}_p(\mathscr{Q}). \tag{10.8}$$

In words, $\mathscr{L}(\mathscr{Q})$ is the probability with which the busiest server is accessed in a client access, under the best possible access strategy p.

Theorem 10.2 ([24, 19]). *Let $\mathscr{Q}$ be a quorum system of U, $n = |U|$.*

- *If $\mathscr{Q}$ is a regular quorum system (10.1), then $\mathscr{L}(\mathscr{Q}) \geq \sqrt{\frac{1}{n}}$.*
- *If $\mathscr{Q}$ is a dissemination quorum system (10.3), then $\mathscr{L}(\mathscr{Q}) \geq \sqrt{\frac{b}{n}}$.*
- *If $\mathscr{Q}$ is a masking quorum system (10.4), then $\mathscr{L}(\mathscr{Q}) \geq \sqrt{\frac{2b}{n}}$.*
- *If $\mathscr{Q}$ is an opaque quorum system (10.5), then $\mathscr{L}(\mathscr{Q}) \geq \frac{1}{2}$.*

All of these lower bounds are tight, in the sense that there are known quorum systems $\mathscr{Q}$ (of the respective types) and access strategies p that meet these lower bounds asymptotically [24, 18, 19]. The last of the results listed in Theorem 10.2 is particularly unfortunate, since it shows that systems that utilize opaque quorum systems cannot effectively disperse processing load across more servers (i.e., by increasing n). We see one way to address this in Section 10.2.2.

10.2.2 Probabilistic Quorum Systems

The lower bounds on universe size presented in Theorem 10.1 present an obstacle to the use of quorum systems in practice. Moreover, the constant lower bound on the load of opaque quorum systems imposes a theoretical limit on the scalability of systems that use them.

One way to circumvent these lower bounds is to relax the quorum intersection properties themselves, and one such way is to ask them to hold only with high probability. More specifically, we can relax any of (10.3), (10.4) and (10.5) to hold only with probability $1 - \varepsilon$, where probabilities are taken with respect to the selection of quorums according to an access strategy p [20, 22]. This technique yields masking quorum system constructions tolerating $b < 2.62/n$ and opaque quorum system constructions tolerating $b < 3.15/n$. These bounds hold in the sense that for any $\varepsilon > 0$ there is an n_0 such that for all $n > n_0$, the required intersection property ((10.4) or (10.5) for masking and opaque quorum systems, respectively) holds with probability at least $1 - \varepsilon$. Unfortunately, this technique alone does not materially improve the load of these systems [20].

An additional modification, however, can improve this situation even further. Merideth and Reiter [23] propose the use of *write markers* for further improving the resilience and load of these systems. Intuitively, in each write access to a quorum of servers, a write marker is placed at the accessed servers in order to evidence the quorum used in that access. This write marker identifies the quorum used; as such, faulty servers not in this quorum cannot respond to subsequent quorum accesses as though they were. By using this method to constrain how faulty servers can collaborate, the resilience of probabilistic masking quorum systems can be improved to $b < n/2$, and the resilience of probabilistic opaque quorum systems can be improved to $b < n/2.62$. In addition, probabilistic opaque quorum systems with load $O(b/n)$ can also be achieved via this technique, breaking the constant lower bound on load for opaque systems.

In addition to introducing a probability ε of error, probabilistic quorum systems require mechanisms to ensure that accesses are performed according to the required access strategy p, if the clients cannot be trusted to do so (e.g., see [22, 23] for such mechanisms). Moreover, the communication network must be assumed not to bias different clients' accesses toward different (and not adequately intersecting) quorums, and so these approaches require a stronger system model than do strict quorum systems.

10.3 Minimizing Delays of Quorum Accesses

Before explaining the use of quorum systems in protocols in Section 10.4, we first consider the performance impacts of quorums generically. The performance implications for a protocol utilizing quorums primarily lie in the costs of accessing a full quorum, in addition to the processing delays incurred at the servers in the accessed quorum. Most early research in quorum systems assumed an abstract setting that does not ascribe any costs or delays to quorum accesses or heterogeneous limits on the processing capabilities of different servers. Recent research, however, has made strides in taking these into account.

To frame this progress, suppose that the communication network can be represented by an undirected graph $G = (V, E)$, where each edge $e \in E$ has a positive "length" $l(e)$. This induces a distance function $d : V \times V \rightarrow \mathbb{R}^+$ obtained by setting $d(v, v')$ to be the sum of lengths of the edges comprising the path from v to v' that minimizes this sum (i.e., the shortest path). This can naturally be extended to a distance $\delta : V \times 2^V \rightarrow \mathbb{R}^+$ defined as $\delta(v, Q) = \max_{v' \in Q} d(v, v')$.

In this context, several authors have made progress on placing servers U at graph nodes V and defining a quorum system $\mathcal{Q}$ over them so as to optimize the costs of clients (typically the elements of V) accessing quorums.

- Fu [5] introduced the following problem: Find a quorum system $\mathcal{Q}$ over universe V to minimize $\text{avg}_{v \in V} \min_{Q \in \mathcal{Q}} \delta(v, Q)$, i.e., the average cost for each client to reach its *closest* quorum. That work presented optimal algorithms when G has certain characteristics, e.g., G is a tree, cycle or cluster network.

- For general networks, Tsuchiya et al. [30] gave an efficient algorithm to find $\mathcal{Q}$ so as to minimize $\max_{v \in V} \min_{Q \in \mathcal{Q}} \delta(v, Q)$, i.e., the maximum cost any client pays to reach its closest quorum.
- Kobayashi et al. [12] presented a branch-and-bound algorithm to produce a quorum system $\mathcal{Q}$ to minimize $\mathrm{avg}_{v \in V} \min_{Q \in \mathcal{Q}} \delta(v, Q)$. Their algorithm could be evaluated only on topologies with up to 20 nodes due to its exponential running time, and they conjectured that the problem of finding a quorum system to minimize $\mathrm{avg}_{v \in V} \min_{Q \in \mathcal{Q}} \delta(v, Q)$ is NP-hard.
- Lin [16] showed that designing a quorum system $\mathcal{Q}$ to minimize $\mathrm{avg}_{v \in V} \min_{Q \in \mathcal{Q}} \delta(v, Q)$ is indeed NP-hard, and gave a 2-approximation for the problem.

None of these works consider the load of the quorum system; indeed, Lin's 2-approximation [16] yields a quorum system with very high load: the output consists of only a single quorum containing a single node v minimizing $\sum_{v' \in V} d(v, v')$. Such a solution is not very desirable, since it eliminates the advantages (such as load dispersion and fault tolerance) of any distributed quorum-based algorithm. More generally, there is a tension between achieving low load and low quorum access delay, in that in order to reduce the load on a nearby server, it might be necessary for a client to access quorums that incur greater network latency but that have less heavily loaded servers.

Methods to balance this tension have been recently studied under the rubrics of "quorum placement" [10, 7] and "quorum deployment" [6]. In these frameworks, a quorum system $\mathcal{Q}$ over a universe of "logical" servers U is provided as an input to the problem, along with the graph $G = (V, E)$ that represents the network. The goal in these problems is to find a placement $f : U \rightarrow V$ that minimizes some notion of access delay. Gilbert and Malewicz [6] consider a variation of the problem in which $|\mathcal{Q}| = |V| = |U|$ and each client accesses only a single, distinct quorum. In this setting, they show

Theorem 10.3 ([6]). *There is a polynomial-time algorithm to compute bijections* $f :$ $U \rightarrow V$ *and* $q : V \rightarrow \mathcal{Q}$ *that minimize* $\mathrm{avg}_{v \in V} \gamma(v, f(q(v)))$, *where* $f(Q) = \{f(u)\}_{u \in Q}$ *and* $\gamma(v, Q) = \sum_{u \in Q} d(v, u)$.

Gupta et al. [10] consider a version of the problem in which a capacity $\mathrm{cap}(v)$ for each $v \in V$ and an access strategy p are provided as inputs. They extend the problem formulation to incorporate a placement f into the notions of load and access delay, i.e.,

$$\ell_f(v) = \sum_{u : f(u) = v} \ell_p(u),$$
$$\delta_f(v, Q) = \max_{u \in Q} d(v, f(u)).$$

They seek a placement f so that $\ell_f(v) \leq \mathrm{cap}(v)$ for all $v \in V$, and that minimizes the *expected* quorum access delay

$$\Delta_f(v) = \sum_{Q \in \mathcal{Q}} p(Q)\delta_f(v, Q),$$

averaged over all $v \in V$, i.e., that minimizes

$$\text{avg}_{v \in V} \Delta_f(v).$$

Specifically, Gupta et al. show

Theorem 10.4 ([10]). *There is a polynomial-time algorithm to compute, for any* $\alpha > 1$, *a placement* f *with* $\ell_f(v) \leq (\alpha + 1)\text{cap}(v)$ *for all* $v \in V$ *and for which*

$$\text{avg}_{v \in V} \Delta_f(v) \leq \frac{5\alpha}{\alpha - 1} \text{avg}_{v \in V} \Delta_{f^*}(v)$$

for any capacity-respecting solution f^* *(i.e., any* f^* *satisfying* $\ell_{f^*}(v) \leq \text{cap}(v)$ *for all* $v \in V$ *).*

They also provide exact polynomial-time solutions for quorum systems $\mathcal{Q}$ of certain types when the access strategy p is load-optimal for those systems, but show that solving the problem for general quorum systems and access strategies is NP-hard. Oprea and Reiter [26, 25] experiment with the algorithm specified in Theorem 10.4 in wide-area topologies, including exploring variations in which different clients can employ different access strategies. Golovin et al. [7] extend the quorum placement framework to minimize network congestion arising from quorum accesses, again while respecting capacity constraints on the processing capabilities of nodes.

10.4 Uses of Byzantine Quorums in Protocols

Byzantine variations on quorum systems have provided a basis for explaining existing agreement protocols (e.g., [29, 9]) and have contributed to the design of new ones. In this section, we present a framework by which such protocols, and specifically their use of different types of Byzantine quorum systems, can be compared.

More specifically, we consider two types of protocols in this section. The first are protocols for implementing a service offering *read* and *overwrite* operations on objects, where an overwrite operation overwrites the previous value of the object with a new value; we refer to these protocols as simple *read-overwrite* protocols.[1] The second type of protocol we consider enables the implementation of arbitrary types of operations on objects, provided that those operations are deterministic. These protocols are typically called state-machine-replication protocols, since the operations provided by the service are mapped to the state transitions of a deterministic state machine, and each service replica runs a copy of the state machine, conceptually.

Both types of protocols coordinate the treatment of client requests across multiple servers while guaranteeing *consistency*—the illusion of a single centralized service.

---

[1] In other contexts, such protocols are often called read-write protocols. Here, we use the term *overwrite* to distinguish from writes that occur in quorum systems.

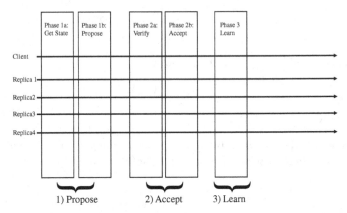

Fig. 10.1 The phases for an overwrite in a read-overwrite protocol.

To do so, these protocols order requests so that non-faulty clients perceive them to be executed in the same order. These protocols are powerful because of their ability to work even if up to b of the n total replicas and any number of the clients are faulty such that they behave arbitrarily or maliciously (i.e., Byzantine faults).

These protocols maintain consistency by using Byzantine quorum systems (see Section 10.1), which require only any quorum (subset) of the replicas to be involved in any operation. Inherently, the use of Byzantine quorum systems allows the protocols to maintain consistency while making progress even if some replicas never receive or process requests. As we show in the rest of this section, the common use of Byzantine quorum systems in these protocols also provides a basis for their comparison. We present frameworks for both read-overwrite and state-machine-replication protocols in which we identify the roles that Byzantine quorum systems play in the protocols, and the implications that result.

10.4.1 Read-Overwrite Protocols

Figure 10.1 shows the phases for an overwrite operation in a typical read-overwrite protocol. The first phase, which we call *propose*, is where the client submits the operation. In some protocols, such as the PASIS-RW protocol [8] described below, the client must first determine the current state of the system, e.g., in order to determine what the next sequence number should be. If necessary, this is done in phase 1a. In phase 1b, the client sends the operation to at least a quorum of servers. In phase 2, servers perform any necessary verification, and accept the operation. In phase 3, the client knows that the operation is complete once it has been accepted by a quorum of servers.

Figure 10.2 shows the phases for a read operation in a typical read-overwrite protocol. To perform an operation, a client contacts at least a quorum of servers in phase 1. For the service to provide linearizable semantics [11], the client must be certain that the value it reads is the result of a complete overwrite. If not, then

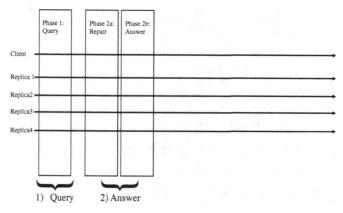

Fig. 10.2 The phases for a read in a read-overwrite protocol.

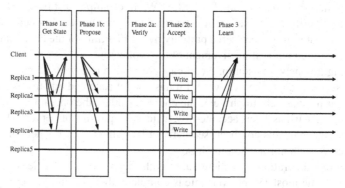

Fig. 10.3 The phases for an overwrite in the PASIS-RW protocol.

another client performing a later read might read an earlier or different value. Therefore, if the client is uncertain whether the overwrite is complete, the client repairs
it, e.g., by completing it at a quorum of servers in phase 2a. Finally, if the client
receives the same value from at least a quorum of servers in phase 2b, then it knows
the overwrite is complete. Therefore, the client uses this value as the result of the
read operation.

Use of Masking Quorum Systems

To make this more concrete, consider the PASIS-RW protocol [8]. Figures 10.3
and 10.4 show a simplified view of the protocol that omits details such as erasure
coding that are discussed in [8].

The PASIS-RW protocol uses a masking quorum system that satisfies (10.4).
In an overwrite operation, the client first determines the most recent timestamp by
querying at least a quorum in phase 1a. Let us assume that the system does not need
repair. Then, based on the retrieved state and details such as the client identifier and
the request description, the client generates a unique timestamp that is greater than

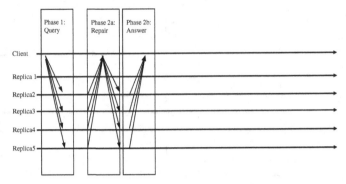

Fig. 10.4 The phases for a read in the PASIS-RW protocol.

those returned by the quorum. In PASIS-RW, timestamps must be strictly increasing so as to identify the most recent overwrite, but need not be consecutive. This fact allows timestamps to be ordered partially by the identifier of the client, and therefore to be generated without involvement of the replicas.

Using this new timestamp, the client submits the overwrite in phase 1b. A non-faulty server accepts the overwrite if it has not yet accepted one that is more recent, storing it in phase 2b. In phase 3, the client considers the operation complete upon learning that it has been accepted by at least a quorum of servers. The protocol includes mechanisms not discussed here for handling the case where the client does not receive such notification in phase 3.

In a read operation, the client submits the read request to at least a quorum of servers. If the most recent overwrite is complete, then, barring a more recent overwrite, the reading client will observe it from more than b servers. Consider the example in the figures, and assume that replica number 4 is faulty. The first client used the quorum containing replicas numbered 1 through 4 for the overwrite. The reading client queries replicas 2 through 5. Replica 5 returns a previous value, and replica 4 might forge a newer value in an attempt to hide the overwrite. However, replicas 2 and 3 each return the correct value. Since the value is returned by two replicas, which is more than b but fewer than a quorum, the client repairs the overwrite using a quorum in phase 2a. Upon learning that the value has been accepted by a quorum, the client uses the value as the result of the read in phase 2b.

Creating Self-Verifying Data

The PASIS-RW protocol just discussed uses a masking quorum system to ensure that any values generated by faulty replicas are not observed in other quorums. If the data were self-verifying, a dissemination quorum system could be used instead because replicas would be unable to generate verifiable values at all. One way to make data self-verifying is to have each client use a digital signature scheme to sign each overwrite. Unfortunately, clients may suffer Byzantine faults in our fault model, and therefore they cannot be trusted.

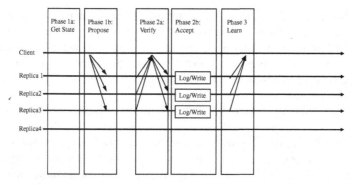

Fig. 10.5 Making data self-verifying.

One way to make an operation self-verifying without trusting clients involves using signatures from a quorum of replicas. Liskov and Rodrigues [17] show how to make operations self-verifying in a read-overwrite protocol with Byzantine clients. There are two steps: an echo protocol like that of Rampart [27] so that non-faulty servers know that other non-faulty servers are not accepting conflicting operations; and a way for clients to verify this as well during reads. For the echo protocol, the first step is to have a quorum of servers provide their signatures stating that they have *tentatively* accepted the operation. If a replica is willing to accept the operation upon the condition that other non-faulty replicas accept no conflicting operation, the replica sends a tentative accept (echo) response. Non-faulty servers only accept operations that have been tentatively accepted by a quorum of servers. Therefore, clients must send a quorum of signed echos in a second phase; in Figure 10.5, this occurs in phase 2a. Servers log the quorum of signatures along with the operation in phase 2b.

The second part of making the operation self-verifying is that the servers return the quorum of signatures to the clients during read operations. A quorum of echo responses proves that no quorum will accept a conflicting operation. This is because every two quorums overlap in some positive number of non-faulty replicas, and no non-faulty replica sends echo messages for conflicting operations. By themselves, faulty servers are too few to generate a quorum of signatures that can be verified. During a read, a client verifies the signatures before using the value, and therefore, each overwrite is self-verifying.

10.4.2 State-Machine-Replication Protocols

State-machine-replication protocols must assign a total order to requests. To minimize the amount of communication between servers, protocols like Q/U [1] and FaB Paxos [21] use opaque quorum systems [18] to order requests *optimistically*. That is, servers independently choose an ordering, without steps that would be required to reach agreement with other servers; the steps are performed only if servers choose different orderings. Under the assumption that servers independently typically choose the same ordering, the optimistic approach can provide lower overhead in the common case than protocols like BFT [4], which require that servers perform steps to agree upon an ordering *before* choosing it [1]. However, optimistic protocols have the disadvantage of requiring at least $5b + 1$ servers to tolerate b server faults, instead of as few as $3b + 1$ servers, and so they cannot tolerate as many faults for a given number of servers.

State-machine-replication protocols assign a total order to requests as follows. Each request is assigned a *permanent sequence number* that exists from the time of assignment through the life of the system and is never changed.[2] We use the term *sequence number* to indicate that there is a totally-ordered chain of requests; however, the sequence number might be implemented as a logical timestamp [1] or other suitable device. Each permanent sequence number is assigned to a *single* request. Therefore, due to the Byzantine fault model, permanent sequence numbers cannot be assigned by a single replica or client, which might assign the same permanent sequence number to multiple requests.

In order to get a permanent sequence number, a request is first assigned a *proposed sequence number*. Unlike permanent sequence numbers, the same proposed sequence number may be assigned to multiple requests. Therefore, a proposed sequence number can be selected by a single client or replica in isolation.

A quorum system is used for the assignment of permanent sequence numbers. A proposed sequence number for the request is written to the quorum system made up of the replicas. Each non-faulty replica accepts the proposed sequence number only if it has not already assigned the sequence number to a different request. A sequence number is permanent if and only if it has been accepted by a quorum of replicas. This ensures that each permanent sequence number is assigned only to a single request.

The type of quorum system used for accepting proposed sequence numbers to make them permanent implies a lower bound on n in terms of b as discussed earlier. For example, an opaque quorum system requires at least $5b + 1$ replicas, but can accept a proposed sequence number in a single round of communication. On the other hand, dissemination and masking quorum systems need only $3b + 1$ and $4b + 1$ replicas but require more rounds.

A non-faulty replica executes a request only after all lower sequence numbers are assigned permanently and it has executed their corresponding requests. Individual replicas send responses to the client upon executing the request. If a non-faulty replica is waiting to execute a request because it is unaware of the assignment of an earlier sequence number, action is taken so that the replica obtains the missing assignment.

The client determines the correct result from the set of responses it receives by determining that the result is due to a permanent sequence number assignment and from at least one non-faulty replica. This works because each non-faulty replica that executes a request with a permanent sequence number returns the same, correct result to the client because the service is deterministic. However, faulty replicas, as

---

[2] We choose the passive voice in this description because details such as which clients/replicas are involved in assigning the sequence number are protocol-specific.

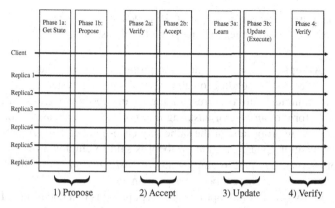

Fig. 10.6 The stages of Byzantine-quorum state-machine-replication protocols.

well as non-faulty replicas that execute requests without permanent sequence numbers (an optimization employed by some protocols), may return incorrect results.

Because of the use of the quorum system for sequence number assignments, none of the protocols surveyed become inconsistent in the face of a Byzantine-faulty proposer. However, the protocols each require a *repair* phase in order to continue to be able to make progress. The processes performing repair read from the quorum system to ensure that no permanent sequence number assignments are lost or changed. Repair is discussed further in Section 10.4.2.

The Framework

The framework depicted in Figure 10.6 is an extension of that in Figure 10.1. It consists of four high-level phases totaling seven sub-phases. In phase 1, a proposed sequence number is chosen for the client's request and sent to (at least) a quorum of replicas. In phase 2, a quorum of replicas accepts the proposed sequence number. If no quorum accepts the proposed sequence number assignment, a new proposal must be tried and the system may require repair (see Section 10.4.2). In phase 3, the request is executed according to the sequence number, and in phase 4 the client chooses the correct result. Phases 1a, 2a and 3a can be viewed as optional, as they are omitted by some protocols; however, omitting them has implications as discussed below. The remainder of this section explores each of the phases of the framework in greater detail.

Phase 1: Propose.   Phase 1 is where a proposed sequence number is selected for a client request; this is done by a *proposer*, which, dependent on the protocol, is either a replica or a client. In some protocols, it is possible that the state of the system has been updated without the knowledge of the proposer (for example due to contention by multiple proposers). In this case the proposer may first need to retrieve the up-to-date state of the system, including earlier permanent sequence number assignments.

This is the purpose of phase 1a. Phase 1b is where the proposed sequence number and request are sent to (at least) a quorum of replicas.

Phase 2: Accept. Phase 2 is where the proposed sequence number is either accepted or rejected. Depending on the type of quorum system, this may require a round of communication (corresponding to an echo phase as discussed in Section 10.4.1) for the purpose of ensuring that non-faulty replicas do not accept different conflicting proposals for the same sequence-number. If it requires this round of communication (phase 2a), the protocol is said to employ a *pessimistic accept* phase, otherwise, it is said to employ an *optimistic accept* phase. In phase 2b, the sequence number assignment becomes permanent.

The primary benefit of an optimistic accept phase is that one round of communication (phase 2a) involving at least a quorum of replicas is avoided. The disadvantage is the need for an opaque quorum system, which requires $n > 5b$. The Zyzzyva protocol [13] discussed below avoids phase 2a in some executions (e.g., when the servers are all non-faulty and messages are delivered in a timely fashion), a case referred to as *speculative accept*, without requiring an opaque quorum system.

Phase 3: Update. Phase 3 is where the update is applied, typically resulting in the execution of the requested operation. Like phase 2, this phase can be either *pessimistic* (requiring phase 3a), or *optimistic* (omitting phase 3a). Comparing phase 3a to the third phase of an overwrite operation in a read-overwrite protocol described in Section 10.4.1, we see that phase 3a allows the execution replicas to learn that the sequence number assignment has become permanent before performing the update. If phase 3a is omitted, the sequence number assignment may change and the request may need to be executed again with the permanent sequence number.

Since an optimistic update phase requires no additional round of communication before execution, it can lead to better performance. The disadvantages are that, as described below, clients must wait for a quorum of responses instead of just $b + 1$ to ensure that the sequence number assignment is permanent, and that computation may be wasted in the case that the proposed sequence number does not become permanent.

Phase 4: Verify. Phase 4 is where the client receives a set of responses. The client must verify that the update was based on a permanent sequence number assignment and performed by at least one non-faulty replica (in order to ensure that the result is correct). In general, this requires waiting for a quorum of identical responses indicating the sequence number, where the size of the quorum is dependent on the quorum system construction. However, if phase 3 is pessimistic, then no non-faulty replica will execute an operation unless the assignment is permanent. In this case, the client can rely on non-faulty replicas to verify that the sequence number is permanent, and so clients need wait for only $b + 1$ identical responses.

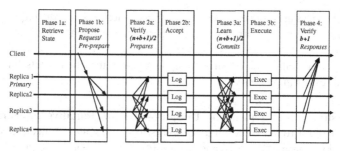

Fig. 10.7 BFT.

Use of Dissemination Quorum Systems

Pessimistic Accept and Update—BFT (without Optimizations). BFT [4] is an example of a Byzantine-fault-tolerant state-machine-replication protocol that employs a pessimistic accept phase (with a dissemination quorum system) and a pessimistic update phase. As such, it involves communication in all four phases of our framework. Figure 10.7 shows the phases of an update request of the BFT protocol in the fault-free case. The operation is very similar to a protocol presented by Bracha and Toueg [2] also used by other protocols, e.g., [28, 3, 31, 14].

In the common case, there is a single proposer (called the *primary*) that itself is a replica; therefore, phase 1a is unnecessary—the proposer already knows the next unused sequence number. In phase 1b, the proposer unilaterally chooses a proposed sequence number for the request (a non-faulty proposer should choose the next unassigned sequence number) and writes (in the sense of a quorum system write, not an overwrite) the request along with the proposal to the other replicas in a message called PRE-PREPARE.

The verification done in phase 2a is equivalent to an echo protocol (though the responses are sent directly to all other replicas instead of through the proposer). This guarantees that non-faulty replicas do not accept different updates with the same proposed sequence numbers. Each replica other than the proposer sends a PRE-PARE (i.e., echo) message including the proposal to all other replicas. If a replica obtains a quorum of matching PREPARE and PRE-PREPARE messages (including its own), it is guaranteed that no non-faulty replica will accept a proposal for the same sequence number but with a different request. Such a replica is called *prepared*. A prepared replica accepts the request in phase 2b, and logs the quorum of PREPARE and PRE-PREPARE messages as a form of proof. The sequence number assignment is permanent if and only if a quorum of replicas accepts the proposed sequence number in phase 2b.

In phase 3a, prepared replicas send COMMIT messages to all other replicas. A COMMIT message includes the quorum of PREPARE and PRE-PREPARE messages (i.e., echos) so that the sequence number assignment is self-verifying as discussed in Section 10.4.1. Because the update phase is pessimistic, in phase 3a, replicas wait to receive a quorum of COMMIT messages to make certain that the sequence number assignment is permanent. Having received a quorum of matching

COMMIT messages for sequence number i, a replica executes the request only after executing all requests corresponding to permanent sequence number assignments $1 .. i - 1$.

Since BFT employs a pessimistic update phase, the client waits for only $b + 1$ identical results in phase 4.

Pessimistic Accept, Optimistic Update—BFT w/ Tentative Execution. One way to avoid a round of communication is to employ an optimistic update phase (i.e., to skip phase 3a). Castro and Liskov [4] detail an optimistic update optimization for BFT called tentative execution (TE). In tentative execution, phase 3a is omitted; however, the dissemination quorum system used to accept sequence numbers in phase 2 remains the same. Compared with unoptimized BFT, tentative execution saves a round of communication. However, since a response from a non-faulty replica no longer necessarily corresponds to a permanent sequence number assignment, the client must wait for a quorum of identical responses in phase 4 in order to ensure that the sequence number assignment is indeed permanent. In addition, replicas that execute a request corresponding to a non-permanent sequence number assignment that later changes (e.g., due to repair) may need to re-execute the request later.

Figure 10.8 shows the stages of the BFT protocol with the tentative-execution optimization, compared with the FaB Paxos protocol [21] that is discussed below. Note the smaller quorum size of BFT due to the use of a dissemination quorum system rather than the opaque quorum system required by FaB Paxos.

Speculative Accept, Optimistic Update—Zyzzyva. Zyzzyva [13], shown in Figure 10.9, also uses tentative execution but can save an additional round of communication in "gracious" executions by additionally omitting phase 2a in such executions. Instead of waiting for a quorum of identical responses in phase 4, the client attempts to retrieve identical responses from *all* replicas. If successful, the client knows that, in any quorum, all of the non-faulty replicas in that quorum (i.e., at least $b + 1$ non-faulty replicas) will vouch for the sequence number assignment. Since these replicas are guaranteed to outnumber the faulty replicas, the sequence number assignment does not need to be self-verifying.

If the client does not receive identical responses from all servers, the execution is not gracious. In this case, phase 2a is necessary for the reasons described previously. If the client has received identical responses from at least a quorum of servers, the client executes phase 2a by sending the quorum of identical responses to the servers that each log this quorum of responses. If the client receives confirmation that at least a quorum of servers has logged this proof, then it knows that the sequence number assignment is self-verifying. Given this knowledge, the client accepts the result in phase 4.

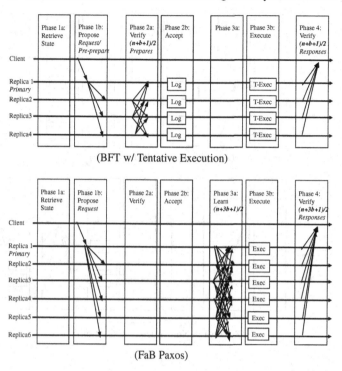

(BFT w/ Tentative Execution)

(FaB Paxos)

Fig. 10.8 Optimistic update (BFT w/ tentative-execution optimization), compared to optimistic accept (FaB Paxos).

Use of Opaque Quorum Systems

Another way to avoid a round of communication is to employ an optimistic accept phase (i.e., to skip phase 2a). Two of the protocols that we survey use both optimistic accept and optimistic update phases. Q/U [1] is a Byzantine-fault-tolerant state-machine-replication protocol based on opaque quorum systems. FaB Paxos, which normally employs only an optimistic accept phase, can, like the BFT variant described above, also employ an optimistic update optimization known as tentative execution. Since both Q/U and FaB Paxos with tentative execution always skip phase 2a (i.e., regardless of whether the execution is gracious), neither protocol can use fewer than $5b + 1$ replicas. In addition, since they also skip phase 3a, both protocols require the client to wait for a quorum of identical responses in phase 4 to make certain that the result is based on a permanent sequence number assignment; this quorum is larger than quorums in systems that employ dissemination or masking quorum systems.

Optimistic Accept, Pessimistic Update—FaB Paxos.   In relation to our framework, FaB Paxos [21], can be viewed as BFT with an optimistic accept phase (pro-

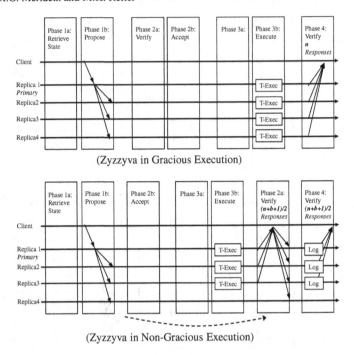

Fig. 10.9 Zyzzyva.

vided by the use of an opaque quorum system). It is seen in the lower half of Figure 10.8. Compared with BFT, FaB Paxos must use larger quorums, and therefore requires more replicas, in order to save this round of communication. While BFT with tentative execution and FaB Paxos (without tentative execution) require the same number of message delays, they have different properties. In BFT, the execution may need to be rolled back and redone if a different sequence number assignment becomes permanent. In FaB Paxos, the execution is not tentative. However, because accept is optimistic, individual servers have no proof that the sequence number assignment is permanent, and so an opaque quorum system is necessary to ensure that permanent sequence numbers are observed later, e.g., in repair.

Optimistic Accept, Optimistic Update—Q/U Protocol. Figures 10.10 and 10.11 show the Q/U protocol. In phase 1, clients act as proposers and directly issue requests to the replicas. Since there are multiple proposers, a proposer may not know the next sequence number (implemented as a logical timestamp). Therefore, the client first retrieves the update history (called a replica history set) from a quorum of replicas (phase 1a). A quorum of replica history sets is called an object history set. It identifies the latest completed update, and, therefore, the sequence number at which the next update should be applied. The client sends the object history set along with the request to a quorum of replicas (phase 1b). In phase 2b, each replica

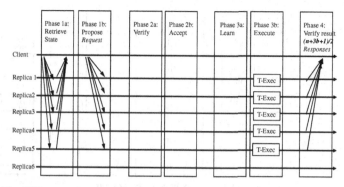

Fig. 10.10 The Q/U protocol (optimistic accept and update).

verifies that it has not executed any operation more recent than that which is reflected in the object history set, and then accepts the update. Having accepted the update, the acceptor executes the request (phase 3b). Because Q/U is an optimistic execution protocol (it skips phase 3a), the client must wait for a quorum of responses in phase 4.

In a pipelined optimization of Q/U (shown in Figure 10.11), clients cache object history sets after each operation. As such, clients can avoid phase 1a if no other clients have since updated the object.

FaB Paxos w/ Tentative Execution. The tentative-execution optimization for FaB Paxos works as it does in BFT—a replica executes the request upon accepting the sequence number assignment for it in phase 2b (assuming it has also executed the requests corresponding to all earlier permanent sequence numbers). Because this sequence number assignment may never become permanent, it may need to be rolled back. Therefore, clients must wait for a quorum of identical responses in phase 4. Figure 10.11 highlights the similarities between Q/U with the pipelined optimization described above and FaB Paxos with the tentative-execution optimization.

Other Trade-offs

BFT, Zyzzyva, and FaB Paxos use a single proposer (the primary), and so can omit phase 1a. On the other hand, Q/U allows clients to act as proposers, and therefore requires phase 1a (though it can be avoided in some cases with the pipelined optimization). The use of a single proposer has potential advantages. First, a client sends only a single request to the system (in the common case) as opposed to sending the request to an entire quorum. Therefore, if the single proposer is physically closer than the clients to the replicas, then the use of a primary might be more efficient, e.g., on a WAN with relatively large message delays. Another advantage is that request-batching optimizations can be employed because the primary is aware of requests from multiple clients. Furthermore, use of a primary can mitigate the impact of client contention. However, the use of a primary: (i) involves an extra

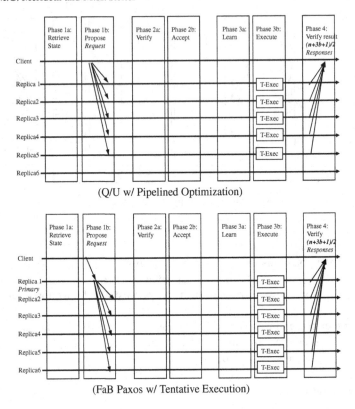

Fig. 10.11 Optimistic accept and update in Q/U and FaB Paxos (both optimized).

message delay (for the request to be forwarded from the client to the primary); and (ii) may allow a faulty primary to slow progress without being detected.

Because a proposer may be Byzantine-faulty, a repair phase may be necessary in order for the service to make progress in the presence of faults.[3] In systems such as BFT and FaB Paxos that use a dedicated proposer, the repair phase is used in part to choose a new proposer. In Q/U, this phase may also result from concurrent client updates, and is used to make sure that non-faulty replicas no longer have conflicting sequence number assignments. In BFT and FaB Paxos, repair is initiated by non-faulty replicas that have learned of some request but not have executed it after a specified length of time (*proactive repair*). In Q/U, repair is initiated by a client that has learned that the system is in a state from which no update can be completed due to conflicting proposed sequence number assignments (*need-based repair*). Because it is based on timeouts, proactive repair might sometimes be executed when it is not actually of help, e.g., when the network is being slow but the primary is not faulty.

---

[3] We do not classify protocols based on their repair phases. Therefore, we do not distinguish between BFT and SINTRA [3], for example.

10.5 Conclusion

In this paper we have highlighted a number of advances in both the theory and practice of distributed systems that were facilitated by, or an outgrowth of, work on quorum systems, particularly of a Byzantine-fault-tolerant variety. We have provided a summary of Byzantine quorum systems and several results about the universe sizes they require and their load-dispersing capabilities. We have also discussed probabilistic variations of them. We have presented techniques that have been recently developed to place quorums in networks for efficient access, in some cases while attempting to retain their load-dispersing properties.

We have also presented a framework consisting of logical phases for the comparison of Byzantine-fault-tolerant read-overwrite and state-machine-replication protocols. Our framework centers on the use of Byzantine quorum systems in each protocol, highlighting trade-offs made by the protocols in terms of the number of replicas required, the number of faults that can be tolerated, and the number of rounds of communication required.

References

1. Abd-El-Malek, M., Ganger, G.R., Goodson, G.R., Reiter, M.K., Wylie, J.J.: Fault-scalable byzantine fault-tolerant services. In: Proceedings of the 20th ACM Symposium on Operating Systems Principles, pp. 59–74 (2005)
2. Bracha, G., Toueg, S.: Asynchronous consensus and broadcast protocols. Journal of the ACM 32(4), 824–840 (1985)
3. Cachin, C., Poritz, J.A.: Secure intrusion-tolerant replication on the Internet. In: International Conference on Dependable Systems and Networks, pp. 167–176 (2002)
4. Castro, M., Liskov, B.: Practical Byzantine fault tolerance and proactive recovery. ACM Transactions on Computer Systems 20(4), 398–461 (2002)
5. Fu, A.W.: Delay-optimal quorum consensus for distributed systems. IEEE Transactions on Parallel and Distributed Systems 8(1), 59–69 (1997)
6. Gilbert, S., Malewicz, G.: The quorum deployment problem. In: Proceedings of the 8th International Conference on Principles of Distributed Systems (2004)
7. Golovin, D., Gupta, A., Maggs, B.M., Oprea, F., Reiter, M.K.: Quorum placement in networks: Minimizing network congestion. In: Proceedings of the 25th ACM Symposium on Principles of Distributed Computing, pp. 16–25 (2006)
8. Goodson, G.R., Wylie, J.J., Ganger, G.R., Reiter, M.K.: Efficient Byzantine-tolerant erasure-coded storage. In: International Conference on Dependable Systems and Networks (2004)
9. Guerraoui, R., Vukolic, M.: Refined quorum systems. In: Symposium on Principles of Distributed Computing, pp. 119–128 (2007)
10. Gupta, A., Maggs, B.M., Oprea, F., Reiter, M.K.: Quorum placement in networks to minimize access delays. In: Proceedings of the 24th ACM Symposium on Principles of Distributed Computing, pp. 87–96 (2005)
11. Herlihy, M., Wing, J.: Linearizability: A correctness condition for concurrent objects. ACM Transactions on Programming Languages and Systems 12(3), 463–492 (1990)
12. Kobayashi, N., Tsuchiya, T., Kikuno, T.: Minimizing the mean delay of quorum-based mutual exclusion schemes. Journal of Systems and Software 58(1), 1–9 (2001)
13. Kotla, R., Alvisi, L., Dahlin, M., Clement, A., Wong, E.: Zyzzyva: Speculative Byzantine fault tolerance. In: Symposium on Operating Systems Principles, pp. 45–58. ACM Press, New York (2007), http://doi.acm.org/10.1145/1294261.1294267
14. Kotla, R., Dahlin, M.: High throughput Byzantine fault tolerance. In: International Conference on Dependable Systems and Networks, p. 575 (2004)

15. Lamport, L., Shostak, R., Pease, M.: The Byzantine generals problem. ACM Transactions on Programming Languages and Systems 4(3), 382–401 (1982)
16. Lin, X.: Delay optimizations in quorum consensus. In: Eades, P., Takaoka, T. (eds.) ISAAC 2001. LNCS, vol. 2223, pp. 575–586. Springer, Heidelberg (2001)
17. Liskov, B., Rodrigues, R.: Tolerating Byzantine faulty clients in a quorum system. In: International Conference on Distributed Computing Systems (2006)
18. Malkhi, D., Reiter, M.: Byzantine quorum systems. Distributed Computing 11(4), 203–213 (1998)
19. Malkhi, D., Reiter, M.K., Wool, A.: The load and availability of Byzantine quorum systems. SIAM Journal of Computing 29(6), 1889–1906 (2000)
20. Malkhi, D., Reiter, M.K., Wool, A., Wright, R.N.: Probabilistic quorum systems. Information and Computation 170(2), 184–206 (2001)
21. Martin, J.P., Alvisi, L.: Fast Byzantine consensus. IEEE Transactions on Dependable and Secure Computing 3(3), 202–215 (2006)
22. Merideth, M.G., Reiter, M.K.: Probabilistic opaque quorum systems. In: Pelc, A. (ed.) DISC 2007. LNCS, vol. 4731, pp. 403–419. Springer, Heidelberg (2007)
23. Merideth, M.G., Reiter, M.K.: Write markers for probabilistic quorum systems. In: Baker, T.P., Bui, A., Tixeuil, S. (eds.) OPODIS 2008. LNCS, vol. 5401, pp. 5–21. Springer, Heidelberg (2008)
24. Naor, M., Wool, A.: The load, capacity and availability of quorum systems. SIAM Journal of Computing 27(2), 423–447 (1998)
25. Oprea, F.: Quorum placement on wide-area networks. Ph.D. thesis, Electrical & Computer Engineering Department, Carnegie Mellon University (2008)
26. Oprea, F., Reiter, M.K.: Minimizing response time for quorum-system protocols over wide-area networks. In: Proceedings of the 37th International Conference on Dependable Systems and Networks, pp. 409–418 (2007)
27. Reiter, M.K.: Secure agreement protocols: Reliable and atomic group multicast in Rampart. In: Conference on Computer and Communication Security, pp. 68–80 (1994)
28. Rodrigues, R., Castro, M., Liskov, B.: BASE: Using abstraction to improve fault tolerance. In: Symposium on Operating Systems Principles (2001)
29. Song, Y.J., van Renesse, R., Schneider, F.B., Dolev, D.: The building blocks of consensus. In: Proceedings of the 9th International Conference on Distributed Computing and Networking (2008)
30. Tsuchiya, M., Yamaguchi, M., Kikuno, T.: Minimizing the maximum delay for reaching consensus in quorum-based mutual exclusion schemes. IEEE Transactions on Parallel and Distributed Systems 10(4), 337–345 (1999)
31. Yin, J., Martin, J.P., Venkataramani, A., Alvisi, L., Dahlin, M.: Separating agreement from execution for Byzantine fault tolerant services. In: Symposium on Operating Systems Principles, pp. 253–267 (2003)

Chapter 11
From Object Replication to Database Replication

Fernando Pedone and André Schiper

Abstract This chapter reviews past research on database replication based on group communication. It initially recalls consistency criteria for object replication, compares them to serializability, a typical consistency criterion for databases, and presents a functional model to reason about replication protocols in general. Within this framework, deferred update replication is explained. We consider two instances of deferred update replication, one relying on atomic commit and the other relying on atomic broadcast. In this context, we show how group communication can simplify the design of database replication protocols and improve their availability and performance by reducing the abort rate.

11.1 Introduction

Database replication has been extensively studied in the past years. Early work in the database community dates back to the late 1970s and early 1980s, addressing both theoretical and practical concerns (e.g., one-copy serializability [2], primary copy replication [12]). Although database replication was much later considered in the distributed systems community at large, foundational work on object replication (i.e., non-transactional behavior) dates back to the late 1970s (e.g., state machine replication [6]).

In the context of distributed systems, replication has been mostly related to group communication. To understand how group communication came into play in database replication, we should recall two observations made in the mid-1990s.

First, Gray et al. showed in a seminal paper [4] that mechanisms typically used to provide strong consistency (i.e., serializability) in distributed databases were inappropriate for replication. Distributed two-phase locking, for example, has an expected deadlock rate that grows with the third power of the number of replicas. The underlying argument for this result comes from the fact that unordered lock requests may get entangled, increasing the chances of distributed deadlocks. Replication increases the number of requests, and therefore the probability of deadlocks.

B. Charron-Bost, F. Pedone, and A. Schiper (Eds.): Replication, LNCS 5959, pp. 207–218, 2010.

Second, Schiper and Raynal pointed out that transactions in replicated databases share common properties with group communication primitives [10]. For example, ordering requirements are present both in transactional systems (e.g., in relation to the isolation property) and in group communication primitives (e.g., total order delivery). Likewise, transaction atomicity or the "all-or-nothing" property is related to agreement in group communication systems.

Consequently, not only group communication and database replication were shown to have intersecting requirements, but some of the shortcomings of the mechanisms traditionally used to implement database replication could be addressed by group communication. Therefore, it is not surprising that researchers in the two communities — databases and distributed systems — set up to further investigate the pros and cons of group communication-based database replication.

In the following, we review some of the work done in the distributed systems community on database replication, focusing on group communication-based protocols. To place database and object replication protocols into perspective, we start by discussing the relationship between some of their most accepted consistency models. Different consistency models require different algorithms for database replication and object replication. It turns out, however, that despite their differences, most protocols fit a common functional model [13], which allows them to be understood and compared.

After presenting the generic functional model and recalling consistency criteria for replication (Section 11.2), we discuss how existing object replication protocols fit the model and introduce a novel object replication protocol (Section 11.3). This replication protocol naturally evolves into the deferred update technique, one of the most promising replication techniques capable to provide strong consistency.

Designing database replication systems and algorithms based on group communication leads to modular approaches, in which synchronization among servers, for example, is encapsulated in the group communication primitives. As a result, group communication (or more specifically atomic broadcast) can simplify the design of database replication protocols and improve their availability and performance by reducing the abort rate (Section 11.4).

We conclude with a discussion of why we believe both the database community and the distributed systems community have gained from this joint approach to group communication-based database replication (Section 11.5).

11.2 Replication Model and Consistency

In this section, we present a generic functional model that can be used as a common framework to reason about replication protocols for objects and databases, and briefly review linearizability and sequential consistency, two correctness criteria for object replication explained in Chapter 1.

11.2.1 Generic Functional Model

The generic functional model (see Figure 11.1) has five phases, although some replication techniques may omit some phases or iterate over the phases:

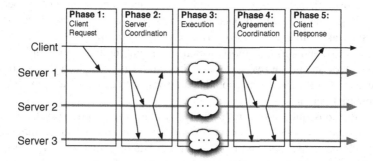

Fig. 11.1 Functional model [13] (messages are illustrative, actual message patterns depend on the particular protocol).

- *Client Request Phase.* During this phase the client submits an operation to one or more servers. If the protocol requires several servers to be contacted, the client can address them all directly or contact a single server, which will relay the request to the others in Phase 2.
- *Server Coordination Phase.* Before executing the operation submitted by the client, servers may have to synchronize to ensure that operations are performed in the right way. For example, some protocols may require a broadcast primitive with total order delivery to synchronize operations. Moreover, as just mentioned, some protocols use this phase to propagate the operations to the other servers.
- *Execution Phase.* The actual processing of the operation takes place in this phase. Although this phase does not introduce many differences among protocols, one aspect in which some protocols diverge is whether operations should be executed deterministically or not. Typically, if there is no further interaction among servers (i.e., no Phase 4), then the execution should be deterministic.
- *Agreement Coordination Phase.* In some replication techniques, servers need to undergo a coordination phase to ensure that each executed operation takes effect in the same manner at all servers. In the context of databases, agreement coordination is known as atomic commitment, during which all servers decide to either commit a transaction or abort it. Some database replication protocols use this phase to propagate update requests to the other servers.
- *Client Response Phase.* After the operation has been executed and the states of the servers are guaranteed to converge, reflecting the effects of the executed operation, the client is notified.

11.2.2 Object and Database Consistency

Linearizability and sequential consistency refer to *processes* and *single operations*. In the context of databases, correctness refers neither to processes nor to single operations: correctness refers to *transactions*. A transaction is a sequence of read and write operations followed by a commit or an abort operation. These operations should satisfy the following properties: (i) *atomicity*, either all the operations of a transaction take effect or none do; (ii) *isolation*, also known as serializability, and described next; and (iii) *durability*, which states that the transaction modifications to the database should survive system crashes. Serializability states that the (concurrent) execution of transactions should be equivalent to a serial execution involving the same transactions.

Note the consequence of serializability not referring to processes. Consider the following two cases with two clients c_1 and c_2: (i) c_1 submits some transaction t_1 and c_2 submits some transaction t_2; (ii) c_1 submits first transaction t_1 and then t_2. These two cases are indistinguishable from the point of view of serializability. The situation is different with linearizability/sequential consistency, where the following two cases are distinct: (i) client c_1 submits operation op_1 and c_2 submits operation op_2, (ii) client c_1 submits first operation op_1 and then op_2. Indeed, in case (ii) op_1 must take place before op_2, while in case (i) op_1 can take place before or after op_2.

In replicated settings, the typical isolation property is *one-copy serializability (1SR)*: the (concurrent) execution of transactions in a replicated database should be equivalent to a serial execution of the same transactions in a single replica. 1SR allows read operations to see arbitrarily old versions of the database (e.g., read-only transactions could use the initial state of the database). Although more strict definitions exist (e.g., external consistency, defined in Chapter 1, and strong serializability [3], which forces reads to see up-to-date values), most database replication protocols guaranteeing strong consistency have considered either plain one-copy serializability, as we do in the rest of this chapter, or snapshot isolation (see Chapter 12).

11.3 From Object Replication to Database Replication: Multi-primary Passive Replication

The two prominent object replication techniques are active replication and passive replication (see Chapter 2). In the context of our framework, active replication does not have Phase 4 and every server replies to the client in Phase 5; the client considers the first reply and discards the others. With passive replication, there is no Phase 2: clients submit their requests to the primary server, which executes the requests and sends the state changes to the other servers in Phase 4.

While one could implement database replication using active and passive replication, it turns out that neither is appropriate. The main reason is that database replication is not only for high availability, but also for high performance. Neither active replication nor passive replication allow us to achieve the latter. Moreover, active replication requires the execution to be deterministic, which is difficult to achieve in multi-threaded database systems.

One interesting alternative is multi-primary passive replication. Multi-primary passive replication is similar to passive replication in the sense that each operation is executed by only one replica (i.e., no Phase 2 in our functional model), which then sends a message with the resulting state updates to the other replicas (in Phase 4). Upon receiving such a message, each replica unilaterally and deterministically checks whether the update can be accepted, and if so, it updates its local state. The check is needed to account for the concurrency among multi-primaries, which may lead to mutually inconsistent updates. If the update is not accepted, its corresponding operation should be re-executed.

Multi-primary replication differs from passive replication in the sense that multiple processes act as primary, which allows increased transaction throughput. It differs from active replication in that only one replica executes the operations. In the context of databases, this technique has been called "deferred update"; in the classification of [4] (see Chapter 12), it is an eager, update everywhere approach. With the deferred update technique, a client initially chooses one database server and submits its transaction operations to this server, which will be the primary for the transaction. The technique distinguishes two parts in the lifetime of a transaction: *transaction processing*, from the beginning of the execution until before the client requests the transaction commit, and *transaction termination*, from the commit request until the transaction is completed (i.e., committed or aborted). During transaction processing, the protocol iterates through Phases 1, 3 and 5: The client submits each operation to the transaction primary (Phase 1), which computes the result (Phase 3) and sends it back to the client (Phase 5). There are no Phases 2 and 4 during transaction processing.

Upon transaction termination, there are two cases to consider: read-only transactions (also called queries) and update transactions. Read-only transactions terminate without any interaction among replicas: they are simply committed by the transaction's primary. This is not the case of update transactions. When a client requests the commit of an update transaction t (Phase 1), t must be certified. As part of the certification process, t's readset, writeset and actual updates are propagated to all replicas (Phase 2): t's readset and writeset identify the data items read and written by t, while the updates are the actual values written during t's execution. Servers must then agree whether t is one-copy serializable and commit t if so. The certification test can be executed by each server independently, thanks to a deterministic procedure, or by means of an atomic commit protocol, as explained in the next section. If the transaction passes the certification test, each server locally commits it (Phase 4); whatever the result of the certification test, the transaction outcome is then sent to the client (Phase 5).

11.4 Deferred Update Database Replication

In the following we introduce some additional definitions and present four mechanisms for terminating transactions in the deferred update approach (or multi-primary). Termination guarantees both transaction atomicity, in the sense that either all servers commit the transactions or none do it, and isolation (here one-copy serializability).

11.4.1 Additional Definitions

As described in the previous section, a transaction must be certified. The transaction is only committed if it passes certification. This suggests that transactions pass through well-defined states in the system. A transaction starts in the *executing* state, when its read and write operations are locally executed by its primary server. When the transaction requests the commit, it is propagated to all servers for certification. Upon reception at a server, the transaction enters the *committing* state and should be certified. As a result of certification, the transaction can be *committed* or *aborted*.

Given a transaction t, its various states at server s are expressed by the following mutually exclusive predicates: $Executing(t,s)$, $Committing(t,s)$, $Committed(t,s)$, and $Aborted(t,s)$. States *executing* and *committing* are transitory; states *committed* and *aborted* are final, that is, if either one of them holds at a time, then it holds at all later times.

In order for a server to certify transaction t, it must know which transactions *precede* t and which transactions have *conflicting* operations with t:

- Let s be a server that executes transaction t. A transaction t' *precedes* a transaction t, denoted $t' \rightarrow t$, if t' committed at server s before t started executing at s. If neither $t \rightarrow t'$ nor $t' \rightarrow t$ then t and t' are concurrent.
- A transaction t' has *conflicting* operations with t (or t' conflicts with t) if t' and t access the same data item, and at least one of them modifies the data item.

11.4.2 Atomic Commit-Based Termination

To better place into perspective the advantages of implementing deferred update with group communication, we show in this section how it can be implemented using atomic commit. Atomic commit guarantees that all transaction participants vote and agree on committing or aborting the transactions. If a participant votes to commit the transaction, it locally precommits it. The transaction is committed iff *all* participants precommit it. As we show in the next paragraph, atomic commit-based termination may abort transactions unnecessarily. This happens because (a) all the transaction participants should vote to precommit the transaction in order for it to be committed and (b) atomic commit does not impose an order on the certification of transactions. This drawback is addressed by an atomic broadcast-based termination, discussed in Section 11.4.3.

With atomic commit-based termination, transactions (i.e., their readsets, writesets, and updates) are propagated to all servers as part of Phase 4 (e.g., [5]). When a server s receives a transaction t, $Committing(t,s)$ holds. Server s votes either to commit t, referred to as t's precommit, or to abort t. Transaction t is committed if all servers precommit t. The precommit introduces a further transitory state in the transaction's lifetime, $PreCommit(t,s)$. Server s votes for transactions t and t' in the order it receives them, that is, if t is received by s before t', then s votes for t before it votes for t'.

A server precommits t if each transaction it knows about in the committed or precommitted states either precedes t or does not conflict with t. Let $RS(t)$ and $WS(t)$ stand for the readset and writeset of t, and let $A \rightsquigarrow B$ denote the enabling condition of the transition from state A to state B. We define the conditions for the transitions from the committing state to the precommit state, and from the precommit state to the committed state more formally as follows[1]:

$$\forall t\, \forall s : Committing(t,s) \rightsquigarrow PreCommit(t,s) \equiv$$
$$\begin{bmatrix} \forall t' \text{ s.t. } Committed(t',s) \vee PreCommit(t',s) : \\ t' \rightarrow t \vee \begin{pmatrix} WS(t') \cap RS(t) = \emptyset \\ \wedge \\ RS(t') \cap WS(t) = \emptyset \\ \wedge \\ WS(t') \cap WS(t) = \emptyset \end{pmatrix} \end{bmatrix} \quad (11.1)$$

$$\forall t\, \forall s : PreCommit(t,s) \rightsquigarrow Committed(t,s) \equiv$$
$$\forall s' : PreCommit(t,s') \vee Committed(t,s') \quad (11.2)$$

Conditions 11.1 and 11.2 guarantee that the execution is serializable. To see why, let t and t' be two transactions with conflicting operations. If by the time t starts its execution at some server s, s has already committed t' (i.e., $t' \rightarrow t$), then any modifications made by t' will be seen by t, and t is obviously serialized after t'. Thus, assume that neither $t' \rightarrow t$ nor $t \rightarrow t'$ hold. We show next that in such a case, conditions 11.1 and 11.2 allow at most one transaction to commit. The argument is by contradiction: Assume that both t and t' commit. Therefore, from condition 11.2 transactions t and t' have been precommitted by all servers. Without loss of generality, let t' enter the committing state at s before t. When s received t, transaction t' could be in the *committed* state or in the *precommit* state. In either case, by 11.1, server s will consider t' in t's certification. Since t' does not precede t, the only way for s to precommit t is if t and t' do not have intersecting readsets and writesets, a contradiction since t and t' have conflicting operations.

Although conditions 11.1 and 11.2 produce serializable executions, they may lead to unnecessary aborts. For example, consider a scenario where server s (resp. s') receives t (resp. t') for certification after it has precommitted t' (resp. t), but before committing it. Thus, t will not satisfy the precommit condition at s and t' will not satisfy the precommit condition at s', leading both transactions to abort (i.e., they both do not satisfy condition 11.2). This example shows that the outcome of certification using atomic commit depends on the interleaving of the messages

---

[1] Notice that the transition from the precommit state to the abort state is given by the complement (i.e., negation) of the transition from the precommit state to the commit state.

exchanged between servers during termination. If the interleaving is not favorable, then unnecessary aborts may happen.

Also notice that condition 11.2 quantifies over all servers. Therefore, if one server is down, certification will only be completed after the server recovers. In the next section we revisit transaction termination using an atomic broadcast primitive, a technique that avoids unnecessary aborts and does not require all servers to be up to commit transactions.

11.4.3 Atomic Broadcast-Based Termination

When transaction termination is based on the atomic broadcast primitive (see Chapter 3), transactions (or more precisely, their readsets, writesets, and updates) are atomically broadcast to all servers during Phase 4. Atomic broadcast guarantees that (a) if a server delivers a transaction, all other servers will also deliver it (*agreement property*) and (b) any two servers deliver transactions in the same order (*total order property*). Since all transactions are delivered by all replicas in the same order, the certification test can be deterministic, and therefore, all servers reach the same outcome, *committed* or *aborted*, without further communication [1, 8].

When a server s delivers t, Committing(t,s) holds. Server s certifies transactions in the order they are delivered. To certify t, server s checks whether each transaction it knows about in the committed state either precedes t or does not have a writeset that intersects t's readset. If one of these conditions holds, s locally commits t. We define the condition for the transition from the committing state to the committed state more formally as follows:

$$\forall t \, \forall s : Committing(t,s) \rightsquigarrow Committed(t,s) \equiv \left[\begin{array}{l} \forall t' \text{ s.t. } Committed(t',s): \\ t' \rightarrow t \vee WS(t') \cap RS(t) = \emptyset \end{array} \right] \quad (11.3)$$

If transaction t passes to the *committed* state at s, its updates should be applied to the database following the order imposed by the atomic broadcast primitive, that is, if t is delivered before t' and both pass the certification test, then t's updates should be applied to the database before those of t'.

Intuitively, condition 11.3 checks whether transactions can be serialized following their delivery order. Let t and t' be two transactions such that t' is delivered and committed before t. There are two cases in which t will pass certification: (i) t' committed before t started its execution, in which case any modifications made by t' would be seen by t during its execution, or (ii) t' does not update any data item read by t, in which case it does not matter if t' committed before t started.

Differently from condition 11.1 (see Section 11.4.2), condition 11.3 does not require checking write-write conflicts. Termination based on an atomic broadcast primitive requires the writes of transactions that passed certification to be processed by all replicas according to the delivery order. Therefore, all servers will process the writes of successfully certified transactions in the same order and end up in the same state after committing each transaction, even though two or more committing transactions update the same data item.

Notice that many other database replication protocols based on atomic broadcast have been proposed. The reader is referred to Chapters 12 and 13 for a detailed description of some of these protocols.

11.4.4 Reordering-Based Termination

Reordering-based termination is an extension of atomic broadcast-based termination. The idea is to dynamically build a serial order of transactions that does not necessarily follow the order in which these transactions are delivered and, in doing so, reduce the number of transactions that fail certification [8]. We illustrate the idea with an example. Assume two concurrent transactions, t and t' such that t reads data item x and updates y, and t' reads y and updates z. There are two cases to consider: (a) If t is delivered before t', then t will pass certification but t' will fail since $WS(t) \cap RS(t') = \{y\}$; (b) If t' is delivered before t, then both transactions will pass the certification test. The reordering technique reconsiders the order in which transactions are certified to avoid aborts. In the example, even if t delivered before t', the certification process will reverse their order so that both can commit.

In order to implement the reordering technique, certification must distinguish between committed transactions already applied to the database and committed transactions in the *Reorder List*. The Reorder List contains committed transactions that have not been seen by transactions in execution since their relative order may change. The number of transactions in the Reorder List is limited by a predetermined threshold, the *Reorder Factor*. Whenever the Reorder Factor is reached, one transaction in the Reorder List is removed and its updates are applied to the database.

Let $RL_s = t_0; t_1; \ldots; t_{count-1}$ be the Reorder List at server s containing *count* transactions and $pos(x)$ be a function that returns the position of transaction x in RL_s. We represent the condition for the state transition of transaction t from the committing state to the committed state more formally as follows:

$$\forall t \forall s : Committing(t,s) \rightsquigarrow Committed(t,s) \equiv$$
$$\left[\begin{array}{l} \exists i,\ 0 \leq i < count,\ \text{s.t.}\ \forall t' \in RL_s : \\[4pt] pos(t') < i \Rightarrow t' \rightarrow t \vee WS(t') \cap RS(t) = \emptyset\ \wedge \\ \qquad\qquad\qquad \wedge \\ pos(t') \geq i \Rightarrow \left(\begin{array}{c} (t' \nrightarrow t \vee WS(t') \cap RS(t) = \emptyset) \\ \wedge \\ WS(t) \cap RS(t') = \emptyset \end{array} \right) \end{array} \right] \quad (11.4)$$

If t passes the certification test, it is included in RL_s at position i, which means that transactions in positions in $[i..count-1]$ are rightshifted. If more than one position satisfies the condition in equation 11.4, then to ensure that all servers apply transactions to the database in the same order, a deterministic procedure has to be used to choose the insertion position (e.g., the rightmost position in RL_s). If after including

t in RL_s the list overflows, the leftmost transaction in the list, t_0, is applied to the database and the remaining transactions are leftshifted.

11.4.5 Generic Broadcast-Based Termination

We show now that the ordering imposed by atomic broadcast is not always needed. Consider the termination of two transactions t and t' with non-intersecting readsets and writesets. In such a case, both t and t' will pass the certification test and be committed, regardless of the order in which they are delivered. This shows that atomic broadcast is sometimes too strong, and can be favorably replaced by *generic broadcast* (see Chapter 3). Generic broadcast is similar to atomic broadcast, with the exception that applications can define order constraints on the delivery of messages: two messages are ordered only if they *conflict*, where the conflict relation is defined by the application semantics.

Based on the example above, one could define the following conflict relation $\sim$ among messages, where $m : t$ means that message m relays transaction t:

$$ m{:}t \sim m'{:}t' \equiv \begin{bmatrix} RS(t) \cap WS(t') \neq \emptyset \\ \vee \\ WS(t) \cap RS(t') \neq \emptyset \\ \vee \\ WS(t) \cap WS(t') \neq \emptyset \end{bmatrix} \tag{11.5} $$

Notice that the conflict relation $\sim$ should account for write-write conflicts to make sure that transactions that update common data items are ordered, preventing the case in which two servers end up in different states after applying such transactions in different orders.

Surprisingly, although $\sim$ provides an adequate ordering for the termination of update transactions in the deferred update technique, read-only transactions may violate serializability, due to the fact that their execution is local to a server. We illustrate the problem with an execution with two update transactions, t_x and t_y, and two read-only transactions, q_i and q_j. Transaction t_x modifies data item x and t_y modifies data item y; transactions q_i and q_j both read x and y. Since t_x and t_y do not execute conflicting operations, assume they are delivered in different orders by different servers, as follows:

- Server s_i delivers and commits t_x, then executes q_i, and finally delivers and commits t_y;
- Server s_j delivers and commits t_y, then executes q_j, and finally delivers and commits t_x.

The execution is non-serializable since for q_i, t_x precedes t_y, and for q_j, t_y precedes t_x. Therefore, termination based on generic broadcast with conflict relation $\sim$ prevents local execution of read-only transactions. We briefly describe two solutions, one optimistic and one pessimistic, to allow partial order delivery of transactions using the conflict relation $\sim$ together with the execution of read-only transactions.

The optimistic solution consists in treating read-only transactions like update transactions, that is, after the execution the transaction is broadcast (using generic broadcast) and certified. As a result, a read-only transaction may be aborted if it does not pass certification.

The pessimistic solution requires read-only transactions to pre-declare their read-sets before executing. Before reading the first data item, a read-only transaction is broadcast to all servers. Upon delivery, one server executes the transaction. In this case, no certification is needed since the generic broadcast primitive guarantees that the read-only transaction is properly ordered with respect to conflicting update transactions.

11.5 Final Remarks

Group communication-based database replication is at the intersection between database replication and distributed systems. In addition to the results accomplished combining the two areas, some of which are reviewed in this chapter, one can also point out that this research effort had a positive effect on each area alone as well.

On the one hand, group communication solved some of the problems identified by the database community in the context of replication (see discussion in Section 11.1). On the other hand, taking application semantics into account when agreeing on a sequence of messages (e.g., as implemented by Generic Broadcast [9] and Generalized Paxos [7]) was originally inspired by the semantics of transactions and the minimum guarantees needed to ensure database isolation. Since transactions have a well-defined semantics, characterizing this ordering is a relatively straightforward task for replicated databases. Defining the problem in a concrete setting was one important step toward group communication protocols that account for message semantics.

Despite the large amount of work done in database replication based on group communication, some problems are still open. One example is partial replication. Protocols for fully replicated databases have limited scalability under update-intensive workloads. The reasons for the limitations are intrinsic to the full replication approach: Each new server added to a fully replicated system allows more clients to connect and submit transactions. If most clients submit update transactions, they will add load to every individual server. Partial replication does not suffer from the same problem since the degree of replication of each data item can be controlled. Defining and efficiently implementing group communication primitives for partial replication is a new challenge for distributed system researchers [11].

Acknowledgements We would like to thank Leslie Lamport for his useful comments and suggestions.

References

1. Agrawal, D., Alonso, G., Abbadi, A.E., Stanoi, I.: Exploiting atomic broadcast in replicated databases. In: Proceedings of EuroPar (EuroPar'97) (Sep. 1997)
2. Bernstein, P., Hadzilacos, V., Goodman, N.: Concurrency Control and Recovery in Database Systems. Addison-Wesley, Reading (1987)
3. Breitbart, Y., Garcia-Molina, H., Silberschatz, A.: Overview of multidatabase transaction management. The VLDB Journal 1(2), 181–239 (1992)
4. Gray, J.N., Helland, P., O'Neil, P., Shasha, D.: The dangers of replication and a solution. In: Proc. of the 1996 ACM SIGMOD Int. Conf. on Management of Data (Jun. 1996)
5. Holliday, J., Steinke, R., Agrawal, D., El Abbadi, A.: Epidemic algorithms for replicated databases. IEEE Trans. on Knowl. and Data Eng. 15(5), 1218–1238 (2003)
6. Lamport, L.: Time, clocks, and the ordering of events in a distributed system. Comm. of the ACM 21(7), 558–565 (1978)
7. Lamport, L.: Generalized consensus and Paxos. Tech. Rep. MSR-TR-2005-33, Microsoft Research (MSR) (Mar. 2005)
8. Pedone, F., Guerraoui, R., Schiper, A.: The database state machine approach. Distributed and Parallel Databases 14(1), 71–98 (2003)
9. Pedone, F., Schiper, A.: Generic broadcast. In: Jayanti, P. (ed.) DISC 1999. LNCS, vol. 1693, pp. 94–106. Springer, Heidelberg (1999)
10. Schiper, A., Raynal, M.: From group communication to transaction in distributed systems. Comm. of the ACM 39(4), 84–87 (1996)
11. Schiper, N., Sutra, P., Pedone, F.: Genuine versus non-genuine atomic multicast protocols for wide area networks: An empirical study. In: Proc. of the 28th IEEE Symp. on Reliable Distributed Systems, SRDS (2009)
12. Stonebraker, M.: Concurrency control and consistency of multiple copies of data in distributed Ingres. IEEE Transactions on Software Engineering 5, 188–194 (1979)
13. Wiesmann, M., Pedone, F., Schiper, A., Kemme, B., Alonso, G.: Understanding replication in databases and distributed systems. In: Proc. of 20th IEEE Int. Conf. on Distributed Computing Systems (ICDCS) (April 2000)

Chapter 12
Database Replication: A Tutorial

Bettina Kemme, Ricardo Jiménez-Peris, Marta Patiño-Martínez, and
Gustavo Alonso

Abstract This chapter provides an in-depth introduction to database replication, in
particular how transactions are executed in a replicated environment. We describe
a suite of replication protocols and illustrate the design alternatives using a two-
step approach. We first categorize replication protocols by only two parameters and
present a simple example protocol for each of the resulting categories. Further parameters are then introduced, and we illustrate them by the given replication protocols and some variants.

12.1 Introduction

12.1.1 Why Replication

Database replication has been studied for more than three decades. It is concerned
with the management of data copies residing on different nodes and with each copy
controlled by an independent database engine. A main challenge of database replication is *replica control*: when data can be updated, replica control is in charge
of keeping the copies consistent and providing a globally correct execution. Consistency needs to be enforced through some protocol running across the different nodes
so that the independent database engines can make local decisions that still provide
some form of global consistency when the system is considered as a whole.

Some particular characteristics differentiate database replication from replication
approaches in other domains of distributed computing. While database replication
can be used for fault-tolerance and high-availability in a similar spirit as replication
is used in distributed computing in general, there are many other purposes of replication. Foremost, often the primary purpose of database replication is to increase the
performance and improve the scalability of database engines. Having more database
replicas distributed across geographic regions provides fast access to local copies,
having a cluster of database replicas provides high throughput. Finally, for some
applications replication is a natural choice, e.g., in the context of mobile users that
are frequently disconnected from the corporate data server, or for data warehouses,

B. Charron-Bost, F. Pedone, and A. Schiper (Eds.): Replication, LNCS 5959, pp. 219–252, 2010.
© Springer-Verlag Berlin Heidelberg 2010

which have to reformat data in order to speed up query processing. These various use cases bring to the fore a tradeoff between consistency and performance, which attracts less attention when replication is targeted at high availability, as studied in previous chapters of this book.

A further difference is that databases, by their name, are *data centric*, usually consisting of a large set of individual data items, and access to this data is enclosed in *transactions*. This means that the database supports operations which are grouped together in transactions, rather than being processed independently of one another. A transaction reflects a logical unit of execution and is defined as a sequence of read and write operations. Transactions come with a set of properties. *Atomicity* requires a transaction to either execute entirely and commit, or abort and not leave any changes in the database. *Isolation* provides a transaction with the impression that no other transaction is currently executing in the system. *Durability* guarantees that once the initiator of the transaction has received the confirmation of commit, the changes of the transaction are, indeed, reflected in the database (they can, of course, later be overwritten by other transactions). Transactions are a particularity of database systems and provide additional challenges compared to object or process replication, as the latter usually only consider individual read and write operations.

12.1.2 Organization of the Chapter

In this chapter we provide a systematic introduction to the principles of replica control algorithms. In the following, the term *replica* mostly refers to a site running the database system software and storing a copy of the entire database. But depending on the context, a replica can also refer to the physical copy of an individual data item. Replica control has to translate the operations that transactions submit on logical data items into operations on the physical data copies. Most algorithms are based on a specific form of *read-one-write-all-(available)* (ROWAA) approach where a transaction is assigned to one site (replica), where it is *local*, and all its read and write operations are executed at this local site. The write operations are also executed at all other replicas in the form of a *remote* transaction. This chapter only considers ROWAA protocols. We refer readers interested in quorum systems for database replication to [24]. Replica control also has to make sure that the copies are consistent. Ideally, all copies of a data item have the same value at all times. In reality, many different levels of consistency exist.

We first introduce two main parameters that were presented by Gray et al. [20] to provide a coarse categorization of replication algorithms. The *transaction location* determines where update transactions are executed, namely either at a *primary replica* or at *any replica*. The *synchronization strategy* determines when update propagation takes place, either before or after commit of a transaction. We use these parameters as a basis to develop a suite of replication algorithms that serve as examples and illustrate the principles behind the tasks of replica control. We keep the description at an abstract level and provide very simple algorithms in order to better illustrate the principles. Many issues are only discussed informally.

As a second step, we discuss a wide range of other parameters. In particular, we have a closer look at the level of correctness provided by different replica control solutions in regard to atomicity, isolation and durability. We also have a closer look at the choice of concurrency control mechanism (e.g., optimistic vs. pessimistic), the degree of replication (full vs. partial replication), and other design choices that can have a significant influence on the performance and practicality of the replication solution.

At the end of this chapter we present some of the research and commercial replication solutions, and how they fit into our categorization. We also discuss the relationship between replication and related areas of data management, such as materialized views, caching, and parallel database systems. They all maintain data copies, and data maintenance can, to some degree, be categorized with the parameters presented in this chapter. However, they have some fundamental differences that we would like to point out.

In a replicated database, the replica control needs to interact closely with the general transaction management. Transaction management includes concurrency control (which delivers isolation) and logging to allow an aborting transaction to roll back any changes previously made (this is part of ensuring atomicity). In most of this chapter, we assume that each site uses strict two-phase locking (2PL) for concurrency control; that is, an exclusive lock is acquired on an item before that item is written, a shared lock is acquired before reading the item, and each lock is held until the commit or abort of the transaction holding the lock. Other concurrency control techniques are possible, as we discuss briefly in Section 12.4.3. More details can be found in [7].

Another essential feature of all replica control protocols is the inter-site communication. Since we discuss ROWAA approaches, write operations must be sent to all available sites. We assume that a primitive, called multicast, is used to propagate information to all replicas. In most of the chapter, we require FIFO multicast, which means that all recipients get the messages from the same sender in the order they were sent. We will introduce more powerful multicast primitives later in the chapter when we discuss protocols that take advantage of them.

12.2 Basic Taxonomy for Replica Control Approaches

Gray et. al [20] categorize replica control solutions by only two parameters. The parameter *transaction location* indicates *where* transactions can be executed. In general, a transaction containing only read operations can be executed at any replica. Such a read-only transaction is then called a local transaction at this replica. For update transactions, i.e., transactions that have at least one write operation, there exist two possibilities. In a *primary copy* approach, all update transactions are executed at a given replica (the primary). The primary propagates the write operations these transactions perform to the other replicas (secondaries) (see Chapter 2 for primary-backup object replication). This model is also called passive replication (as in Chapters 11 and 13). In contrast, in an *update anywhere* approach, update transactions can be executed at any site, just as the read-only transactions which then transaction location: WHERE?

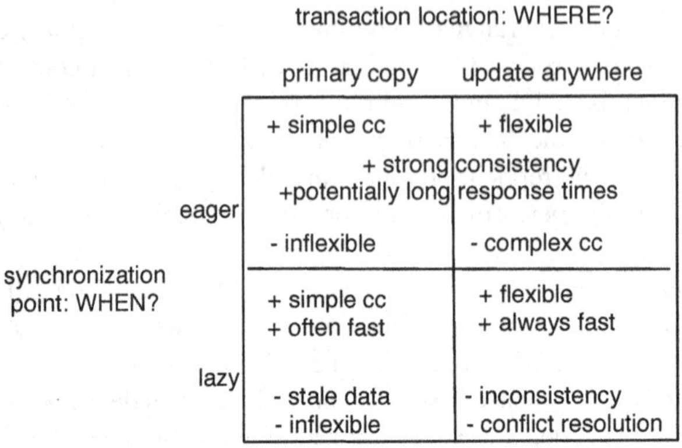

	primary copy	update anywhere
eager	+ simple cc + strong consistency + potentially long response times - inflexible	+ flexible - complex cc
lazy	+ simple cc + often fast - stale data - inflexible	+ flexible + always fast - inconsistency - conflict resolution

synchronization point: WHEN?

Fig. 12.1 Categories.

takes care of update propagation. This model is also called multi-primary (as in Chapter 11). Using a primary copy approach, conflicts between concurrent update transactions can all be detected at the primary while an update anywhere approach requires a more complex distributed concurrency control mechanism. However, a primary copy approach is less flexible as all update transactions have to be executed at a specific replica.

The *synchronization strategy* determines when replicas coordinate in order to achieve consistency. In *eager* replication, coordination for the updates of a transaction takes place before the transaction commits. With *lazy* replication, updates are asynchronously propagated after the transaction commits. Eager replication often results in longer client response times since communication takes place before a commit confirmation can be returned, but it can provide strong consistency more easily than lazy replication (see Chapter 1 for a definition of strong consistency).

Using these two parameters, there are four categories as shown in Figure 12.1, and each replica control algorithm belongs to one of these categories. The definitions so far contain some ambiguity and we will refine them later. Each category has its own implications in regard to performance, flexibility and the degree of consistency that can be achieved. We illustrate these differences by providing an example algorithm for each of the categories. At the same time, these algorithms provide an intuition for the main building blocks needed for replica control, and also reflect some other design choices that we will discuss in detail later.

In the following algorithms, a transaction T_i submits a sequence of read and write operations. A read operation $r_i(x)$ accesses data item x, a write operation $w_i(x, v_i)$ sets data item x to value v_i. At the end of execution, a transaction either submits a commit request to successfully terminate a transaction or an abort request to undo all the updates it has performed so far. We ignore the possibility that operations might fail due to application semantics (e.g., updating a non-existing record). The algorithms, as we describe them, do not consider failures, e.g., failure of replicas or the network. Our discussions, however, mention, how the protocols could be extended in this respect.

12.2.1 Eager Primary Copy

Eager primary copy protocols are probably the simplest protocol type to understand. We present a protocol that is a straightforward extension of non-replicated transaction execution.

Example Protocol

Figure 12.2 shows an example protocol using strict 2-phase-locking (2PL) for concurrency control at each replica. When a client submits a transaction T_i it sends all the operations of this transaction to one replica R. T_i is then a local transaction at R and R is responsible for returning the corresponding responses for the requests associated with T_i. Update transactions may only be submitted to the primary. Read operations are executed completely locally (lines 1-5). They acquire a shared lock before accessing the local copy of the data item. For a write operation (lines 6-12), the primary replica first acquires an exclusive lock locally and performs the update. Then it multicasts the request to the other replicas in FIFO order. Aborts can occur due to deadlock (lines 13-16). If an update transaction aborts the primary informs the secondary replicas if they had already received some write requests for this transaction. Similar actions are needed if the client decides to abort the transaction (line 17). When the client submits the commit request after completion of the transaction (lines 18-24), an update transaction needs to run a 2-phase-commit protocol (2PC) to guarantee the atomicity of the transaction (we discuss this later in detail). The primary becomes the coordinator of the 2PC. The 2PC guarantees that all decide on the same commit/abort outcome of the transaction and that all secondaries have successfully executed the transaction before it commits at the primary. Read-only transactions can simply be committed locally. After successful commit (lines 22-24), the transaction releases its lock and the local replica returns the confirmation to the client. When a secondary replica receives a write request for a transaction from the primary (lines 25-26), it acquires an exclusive lock (in the order in which messages are received), and executes the operation. Although an update transaction might be involved in a deadlock at the secondary, it is not aborted at the secondary. If it is a deadlock among update transactions only, the primary will detect such a deadlock and act appropriately. If the deadlock involves local read-only transactions, those read-only transactions need to be aborted. When a secondary receives an abort request for an update transaction it has to abort it locally.

Example Execution

Figure 12.3 shows a simple example execution under this protocol. In this and all following examples, time passes from top to bottom. Furthermore, T_1 acquiring a shared lock on data item x is denoted as $S_1(x)$, and T_1 acquiring an exclusive lock on x is denoted as $X_1(x)$. $T_1 = r_1(x), w_1(x, v_1)$ is an update transaction local at primary $R1$. $T_2 = r_2(y), r_2(x)$ is a read-only transaction local at secondary $R2$. Read operations are executed locally. The write operation of T_1 is multicast to all replicas and executed everywhere. When T_1 wants to commit it requires a 2-phase-commit

224   B. Kemme et al.

Upon: $r_i(x)$ for local transaction T_i
1: acquire shared lock on x
2: **if** deadlock **then**
3:     call *abortHandling*(T_i)
4: **else**
5:     **return** x

Upon: $w_i(x, v_i)$ for local transaction T_i {*only at primary replica*}
6: acquire exclusive lock on x
7: **if** deadlock **then**
8:     call *abortHandling*(T_i)
9: **else**
10:     $x := v_i$
11:     multicast $w_i(x, v_i)$ to secondaries in FIFO order
12:     **return** ok

Upon: *abortHandling*(T_i)
13: **if** T_i update transaction and at least one $w_i(x, v_i)$ was multicast **then**
14:     multicast *abort*(T_i) to all replicas
15: abort T_i, release locks of T_i
16: **return** aborted

Upon: abort request for local transaction T_i
17: call *abortHandling*(T_i)

Upon: commit request for local transaction T_i
18: **if** T_i update transaction **then**
19:     run 2PC among all replicas to commit T_i
20: **else**
21:     commit T_i

Upon: successful commit of transaction T_i
22: release locks of T_i
23: **if** T_i local transaction **then**
24:     **return** committed

Upon: receiving $w_j(x, v_j)$ of remote transaction T_j from primary replica
25: acquire exclusive lock on x
26: $x := v_j$

Upon: receiving *abort*(T_j) for remote transaction T_j from primary replica
27: abort T_j, release locks of T_j

Fig. 12.2 Eager Primary Copy Algorithm.

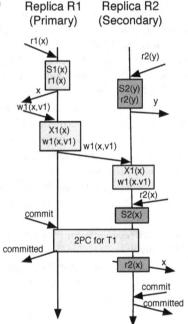

Fig. 12.3 Eager Primary Copy Example.

protocol. When T_2 requests the shared lock on x it has to wait because T_1 holds the lock. Only after T_1 commits can T_2 get the lock and complete. If there were a deadlock between T_1 and T_2, the secondary would abort read-only transaction T_2.

Discussion

Advantages   In most primary copy approaches concurrency control is nearly the same as in a non-replicated system. For our protocol, the only difference is that secondaries have request locks for update operations in the order they receive them from the primary. And in case of deadlock they have to abort local read-only trans-actions. Since secondaries execute conflicting updates in the same order as they are executed at the primary and strict 2PL is used, execution is globally serializable. This means that the concurrent execution of transactions over the physical copies is equivalent to a serial execution of the transactions over a single logical copy of the database.

As execution is eager and a 2PC is run, all copies are virtually consistent (have the same value at commit time of transactions). This means that read operations at the secondaries never read stale data. This also provides strong guarantees in case of failures. If the primary fails, active transactions are aborted. For all committed transactions it is guaranteed that the secondaries have the updates. Therefore, if one of the secondaries takes over and becomes the new primary, no updates are lost. However, if the primary has failed during a 2PC some transactions might be blocked. This could be resolved by the system administrator. Clients connected to the primary can reconnect to the new primary. Some systems provide automatic reconnection.

Disadvantages   Requiring all update transactions to execute at the primary leads to a loss of replication transparency and flexibility. Clients need to know that only the primary replica can execute update transactions. Some primary copy systems automatically redirect update transactions to the primary. However, in this case, the system needs to know at the start of a transaction whether it is an update transaction or not even if the first operation submitted is a read operation, as is the case in the example of Figure 12.3.

The price to pay for an eager protocol that uses 2PC are long execution times for update transactions as they only commit at the primary once they have completely executed at all secondaries. We discuss in Section 12.2.5 some eager protocols that do not have this behavior.

12.2.2 Eager Update Anywhere

Eager update anywhere replica control algorithms were the first replica control al-gorithms to be proposed in the literature. The early algorithms extended traditional concurrency control mechanisms to provide globally serializable execution with a large emphasis on correctly handling failures and recoveries.

Example Protocol

Figure 12.4 shows the changes to the eager primary copy algorithm of Figure 12.2 to allow for update anywhere. Both read-only and update transactions can now be local at any replica which coordinates their execution. Read operations are executed as before at the local replica. A write operation has to execute at all replicas (lines 1-11). The local replica multicasts the request to the other replicas and then acquires an exclusive lock locally and performs the update. Then, it waits for acknowledgements from all other replicas before returning the ok to the client. The acknowledgements are needed as conflicting requests might now occur in different order at the different replicas and it is not guaranteed that the remote replicas can execute the request in the same order. In fact, distributed deadlocks can occur, as we discuss below. Aborts for local transactions are handled as in the primary copy protocol. Commits are handled as before with the only difference that the 2PC can now be initiated by any replica that wants to commit a local update transaction. When a replica receives a write request from a transaction that is local at another replica (lines 12-17), it acquires an exclusive lock, executes the operations and sends an acknowledgement back to the local replica. When a deadlock is detected, it might involve remote transactions. The system can choose to abort a remote transaction; if that is the case, the replica where the transaction is local is informed accordingly. Similarly, any replica has to abort a remote transaction when it is informed by the transaction's local replica (line 18).

Example Execution

Figure 12.5 shows an example execution under this protocol indicating the special case of a distributed deadlock. This time, $T_1 = r_1(x), w_1(x, v1)$ is local at $R1$. $T_2 = r_2(y), w_2(x, v2)$ also updates x and is local at $R2$. As the lock requests in this execution were processed in different orders at the two replicas, there is a deadlock. This cannot be detected with information from a single site, but the system must have a distributed deadlock mechanism or timeout. In this execution, T_2 is chosen to abort.

Discussion

Advantages Being an update anywhere approach it is more flexible than the primary copy approach and provides transparency as it allows update transactions to be submitted to any replica. As it is again eager, using a 2PC, all data copies are virtually consistent. Failures are tolerated without loss of correctness. Given that the protocol extends strict 2PL, it provides global serializability.

Disadvantages Although the concurrency control mechanism appears very similar to the one of the eager primary copy approach, the complexity is higher as distributed deadlocks may occur. As distributed algorithms to detect distributed deadlocks are expensive, many systems use timeouts, but these are hard to set sensibly. If

Upon: $w_i(x, v_i)$ for local transaction T_i
1: multicast $w_i(x, v_i)$ to all other replicas
2: acquire exclusive lock on x
3: **if** deadlock **then**
4:    call *abortHandling(T_i)*
5: **else**
6:    $x = v_i$
7:    wait for all to return answer
8:    **if** all return ok **then**
9:       **return** ok
10:   **else**
11:      **call** *abortHandling(T_i)*

Upon: receiving $w_j(x, v_j)$ of
    remote transaction T_j from replica R'
12: acquire exclusive lock on x
13: **if** deadlock **then**
14:    send abort(T_j) to R'
15: **else**
16:    $x := v_j$
17:    send ok back to R'

Upon: commit request for local transaction T_i
18: **if** T_i update transaction **then**
19:    run 2PC among all replicas to commit T_i
20: **else**
21:    commit T_i

Upon: successful commit of transaction T_i
22: release locks of T_i
23: **if** T_i local transaction **then**
24:    **return** committed

Upon: receiving *abort(T_j)* for
    remote transaction T_j from replica R'
25: abort T_j, release locks of T_j

Fig. 12.4 Eager Update Anywhere Algorithm.

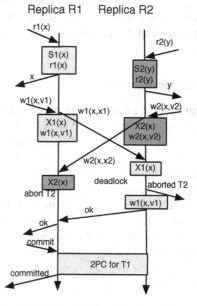

Fig. 12.5 Eager Update Anywhere Example.

too short, many transactions are aborted unnecessarily. If set too long, a few deadlocks can block large parts of the database leading quickly to deterioration. This was one of the reasons, why Gray et. al [20] indicated that traditional replication solutions do not scale.

Comparing the two protocols presented so far, the update anywhere protocol is likely to have longer response times than the primary copy protocol as each write operation has to be executed at all replicas before the next operation can start. However, this is a consequence of the protocol detail, rather than being intrinsic to the update anywhere and primary copy styles. The primary copy protocol could also wait for each write to be executed at the secondaries before proceeding, or the update anywhere protocol could simply multicast the writes as the primary copy protocol without waiting. Conflicts would then be resolved at commit time. One could even change the protocols and send all changes in a single message only at the end of transaction. We will discuss the issue of message overhead and number of messages per transaction in Section 12.4.1. At this point, we only want to point out that we have consciously chosen to present different flavors of protocols to already give an indication that there are many design alternatives.

12.2.3 Lazy Primary Copy

Compared to eager approaches, lazy approaches do not have any communication among replicas during transaction execution. A transaction can completely execute and commit at one replica and updates are only propagated to the other replicas after commit. Combining lazy with primary copy leads to a quite simple replication approach.

Example Protocol

Figure 12.6 presents a simple lock-based lazy primary copy protocol. Read-only transactions are executed as in the eager approach (lines 1-5). Update transactions may only be submitted to the primary which executes both read and write operations locally (lines 1-5 and 6-11). Therefore, when the transaction aborts during execution or when the client requests it (line 14), the abort remains local (lines 12-13). When the client submits a commit (lines 15-18), the transaction commits first locally and only after commit are all write operations multicast within a single message, often referred to as write set. These writesets are multicast in FIFO order. The multicast can be directly after the commit or some time after, e.g., in certain time-intervals. The secondaries, upon receiving such a writeset (lines 19-23) acquire locks in receiving order to make sure that they serialize conflicting transactions in the same way as the primary.

Example Execution

Figure 12.7 shows an example where $T_1 = r_1(x), w_1(x, v1), w_1(y, w1)$ executes at the primary updating x and y. Only after commit the updates are sent to the secondary. At the secondary, the locks for the updates are requested. As there is a deadlock with a local transaction $T_2 = r_2(y), r_2(x)$, the local transaction has to abort in order to apply the updates of T_1.

Discussion

Advantages   Being a primary copy approach, concurrency control remains simple while serializability is provided. It is similar to the eager primary copy approach as secondaries apply updates in receiving order. In contrast to eager approaches the response times of update transactions are not delayed by communication and coordination overhead among the replicas which can potentially lead to shorter response times.

Upon: $r_i(x)$ for local transaction T_i
1: acquire read lock on x
2: **if** deadlock **then**
3:    call $abortHandling(T_i)$
4: **else**
5:    **return** x

Upon: $w_i(x, v_i)$ for local transaction T_i {*only at primary replica*}
6: acquire exclusive lock on x
7: **if** deadlock **then**
8:    call $abortHandling(T_i)$
9: **else**
10:    $x := v_i$
11:    **return** ok

Upon: $abortHandling(T_i)$
12: abort T_i, release locks of T_i
13: **return** aborted

Upon: abort request for local transaction T_i
14: call $abortHandling(T_i)$

Upon: commit request for local transaction T_i
15: commit T_i, release locks
16: **return** committed
17: **if** T_i update transaction **then**
18:    send all w_i of T_i in single write set
       sometime after commit
       in FIFO order

Upon: receiving write set message of
   remote transaction T_j from primary replica
   in FIFO order
19: **for all** $w_j(x, v_j)$ in write set **do**
20:    acquire exclusive lock on x
21: **for all** $w_j(x, v_j)$ in write set **do**
22:    $x := v_j$
23: commit T_j, release locks

Fig. 12.6 Lazy Primary Copy Algorithm.

Fig. 12.7 Lazy Primary Copy Example.

Disadvantages While a lazy primary copy approach easily provides serializability or other strong isolation levels, lazy replication provides an inherent weaker consistency than eager replication. Lazy replication does not provide the virtual consistency shown in eager approaches. At the time a transaction commits at the primary, the data at the secondary becomes stale. Thus, read operations that access the secondaries before the writeset is processed read outdated data. Note that serializability is still provided, with read-only transactions that read stale data being serialized before the update transactions although those happened earlier in time.

More severe, if the site executing and committing an update transaction fails before propagating the writeset, the other replicas are not aware of the transaction. If another site takes over as primary, this transaction is lost. When the failed replica recovers it might try to reintegrate the changes into the existing system, but the database might have changed considerably since then. We can consider this a loss of the durability guarantee. We will discuss this later in more detail.

Although there is no communication among replicas during transaction execution, transactions are not necessarily faster than in an eager approach. If the clients and replicas are geographically distributed in a WAN, then clients that are not close to the primary copy experience long response times as they have to interact with a remote primary copy. That is, there can still be considerable communication delay between client and primary copy. To address this issue, many commercial systems partition the database, with each partition having the primary copy on a different replica. In geographically distributed applications, a database can often be partitioned by regions. Clients that are local to one region typically access mostly the partition of the database that is relevant for this region. Thus, the replica of a region becomes the primary for the corresponding partition. Therefore, for most clients the primary of the data they access will be close and client/replica interaction will be fast. A challenge with this approach is to find appropriate partitions. Also, the programmer has to be aware to write code so that each transaction only accesses data for a single partition.

12.2.4 Lazy Update Anywhere

Allowing update transactions to execute at any replica and at the same time propagate changes only after commit combines flexibility with fast execution. No remote communication, neither between replicas nor between client and replica, is necessary.

Example Protocol

Figure 12.8 shows the differences to the lazy primary copy approach. Write operations can now be processed at all replicas and each replica is responsible to multicast the writesets of its local transactions to the other replicas (lines 1-6). When a replica receives such a remote writeset, it applies the changes (lines 7-14). However, as lazy update anywhere allows conflicting transactions to execute and commit concurrently at different replica without detecting conflicts during the life-time of transactions, conflict resolution might be needed. The system has to detect for a write operation on a data item x whether there was a concurrent conflicting operation on the same data item. If such a conflict is detected, conflict resolution has to ensure that the different replicas agree on the same final value for their data copies of x. There are many ways to resolve the conflict; a common choice is the Thomas Write Rule, which discards any update with earlier timestamp than a previously applied update.

Example Execution

Figure 12.9 shows an example execution under this protocol indicating the special case of a conflict. Both $T_1 = r_1(x), w_1(x, v1)$, local at $R1$ and $T_2 = r_2(y), w_2(x, v2)$,

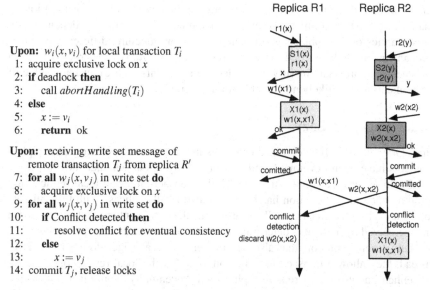

Upon: $w_i(x, v_i)$ for local transaction T_i
1: acquire exclusive lock on x
2: if deadlock then
3:      call *abortHandling*(T_i)
4: else
5:      $x := v_i$
6:      return ok

Upon: receiving write set message of
    remote transaction T_j from replica R'
7: for all $w_j(x, v_j)$ in write set do
8:      acquire exclusive lock on x
9: for all $w_j(x, v_j)$ in write set do
10:     if Conflict detected then
11:         resolve conflict for eventual consistency
12:     else
13:         $x := v_j$
14: commit T_j, release locks

Fig. 12.8 Lazy Update Anywhere Algorithm.   **Fig. 12.9** Lazy Update Anywhere Example.

local at $R2$ update x and commit. After commit, the writesets are propagated. If both $R1$ and $R2$ simply applied the update they receive from the other replica, $R1$ would eventually have the value written by T_2, and $R2$ would have the value written by T_1. Upon receiving the writeset of T_2, $R1$ has to detect that T_1 was concurrent to T_2, conflicts with T_2, and already committed. $R2$ has to detect this conflict when receiving the writeset of T_1. A resolution mechanism, e.g., via timestamps, has led both replicas to decide that T_1's update wins out, and so $R1$ discards the write of x from T_2, while $R2$ overwrites x using T_1's update. In this way, it is guaranteed that the data copies converge towards a common value.

Discussion

Advantages Lazy update anywhere provides flexibility and fast execution for all transactions. These are two very strong properties. In some situations the approach is possible and necessary, e.g., if WANs have frequent connection loss, forbidding updates would lead to large revenue loss, and either conflicts are rare or easy to resolve.

Disadvantages One has to be aware that the fundamental properties of transactions are violated. Durability is not guaranteed as a transaction might commit from the user perspective but the updates are finally lost during conflict resolution. Atomicity might be lost, if conflict resolution is done on an per-object basis. If a transaction T_i updates data items x and y, and a conflict with T_j exists only on x, then it could be possible that T_i's update on x is not considered while its update on y succeeds.

The traditional concept of serializability or other isolation levels is also not longer guaranteed. Finally, conflict resolution is potentially very complex; depending on the semantics of data objects and the application architecture, different resolution mechanisms might be needed for different parts of the database. Therefore, such an approach is appropriate in very controlled environments with exact knowledge of the application. It is likely not suitable for a general replication solution.

12.2.5 Eager vs. Lazy

Since Gray et. al. [20] categorized protocols into eager and lazy many new replica protocols have been developed, and it is not always clear whether they are eager or lazy. In eager algorithms using a 2PC, the transaction at the local replica only commits once the transaction has been executed at all replicas. With this, all data copies are virtually consistent. This results in the disadvantage that the response time perceived by a client is determined by the slowest machine in the system.

Many recent protocols that also define themselves as eager do not run a 2PC. Instead, they allow a transaction to be committed at the local replica once the local replica knows that all remote replicas will "eventually" commit it (unless the remote replica fails). This typically requires that all replicas have received the write operations or the writeset, and that it is guaranteed that each replica will decide on the same global serialization order. It is not necessary that remote replicas have actually already executed the write operations at the time the local replica commits. This means, some "agreement" protocol is executed among the replicas but it does not necessarily include processing the transaction or writing logs to disk. We use this weaker form of "eagerness" in order to accommodate many of the more recent replication solutions.

Many of these approaches use the delivery guarantees of group communication systems [13] to simplify the agreement protocol. Group communication systems provide multicast primitives with ordering guarantees (e.g., FIFO order or total order of all messages) and delivery guarantees (see Chapter 3). In particular, a multicast with uniform reliable delivery guarantees that whenever a message is delivered to any replica, it is guaranteed that it will be delivered to all replicas that are available. Now assume that transactions multicast their writesets using uniform reliable delivery. In case a replica receives a writeset of a local transaction and commits the transaction, uniform reliable delivery guarantees the writeset will be received by all other replicas, even if the local replica crashes immediately after the commit. Therefore, assuming an appropriate concurrency control method, the transaction will also commit at all other replicas. This provides the "eager" character of these protocols offering atomicity and durability without the need of a 2PC. Uniform reliable delivery itself performs some coordination among the group members before delivering a message to guarantee atomicity in the message delivery, though this is not visible to the replication algorithm. There are some subtle differences in the properties provided by uniform reliable delivery multicast compared to 2PC as the first assumes a crash-stop failure model where nodes never recover, while 2PC has a crash-recovery model that assumes sites to rejoin.

In contrast, we use the term lazy for protocols where write operations are not sent at all before commit time, or where the sending multicast occurs earlier but is not reliable. Thus, if a local replica fails after committing a transaction but before propagating its write operations successfully, then the remote replicas have no means to commit the transaction. If the others don't want to block until the local replica has recovered and sent the write operations, the transaction can be considered lost.

12.3 Correctness Criteria

So far, we have only informally reasoned about the differences in correctness that the protocols provide. In fact, the research literature does not have a single, generally agreed on understanding of what "correctness" and data consistency mean. Terms such as strong consistency, weak consistency, 1-copy-equivalence, serializability, and snapshot isolation are used but definitions vary and it is not always clear which failure assumptions are needed for a protocol to provide its properties (see Chapter 1 for consistency models for replicated data). In this section, we discuss different aspects of correctness, and how they relate to one another.

In our discussion above, the eager protocols provided a stronger level of consistency than the lazy ones. This is, however, only true in regard to atomicity. But there does not simply exist a stack of consistency levels, from a very low level to a very high level. Instead, correctness is composed of different orthogonal issues, and a replica control protocol might provide a high level of consistency in one dimension and a low level for another dimension. In regard to lazy vs. eager, all lazy protocols are weaker than eager protocols in regard to atomicity. But given two particular protocols, one lazy and one eager, the lazy protocol could provide stronger consistency than the eager protocol in regard to a different correctness dimension.

In the following, we look at several correctness dimensions individually, extract what are the possible levels of consistency for this dimension and discuss to what degree replication protocols can fulfill the criteria depending on their category.

12.3.1 Atomicity and Consistency

Atomicity in a replicated environment means that if an update transaction commits at one replica it has to commit at all other replicas and its updates are executed at all replicas. If a transaction aborts, none of the replicas may have the updates reflected in its database copy. Considering a failure-free environment only, this means that the replica and concurrency control system has to ensure that each replica takes the same decision on commit/abort for each transaction. For instance, in the primary copy protocols described in the previous section, this was achieved via a FIFO multicast of write operations or writesets and strict 2PL.

Considering a system that is able to tolerate failures, atomicity means that if a transaction commits at a replica that fails after the commit, the remaining available replicas also need to commit the transaction in order for the transaction to not be "lost". Note that available replicas can continue committing transactions while some replicas are down and thus, don't commit these transactions. Recovery has to ensure that a restarted replica receives the missing updates. In summary, available replicas commit the same set of transactions and failed replicas have committed a subset of these transactions.

Atomicity in the presence of failures can only be achieved by eager protocols as all replicas are guaranteed to receive the writeset information and all other information needed to decide on the fate of a transaction before the local replica commits the transaction. Thus, the available replicas will eventually commit the transaction. In a lazy protocol, available replicas might not know about the existence of a transaction that executed at a replica that fails shortly afterwards. In a lazy primary copy protocol, atomicity can be guaranteed if no new primary is chosen when the current primary fails. Then, upon recovery of the primary, the missing writesets can eventually be propagated. However, this would severely reduce the availability of the system. If a failover takes place to a new primary, or in a lazy update anywhere approach, one can still attempt to send the writesets after recovery. However, the transaction might conflict with other transactions that committed in the meantime, and therefore, no smooth integration of the "lost" transaction into the transaction history is possible.

In summary, while eager protocols can provide atomicity, lazy approaches can be considered non-atomic.

In the research literature, one often finds the term *strong consistency* associated with eager protocols and *weak consistency* associated with lazy protocols. The use of these terms usually remains vague. One way to define strong consistency is by what we have called virtual consistency, requiring all data copies to have the same value at transaction commit time. Only eager protocols with a 2PC or similar agreement provide virtual consistency; the weaker forms of eagerness described in Section 12.2.5 allow a transaction to commit before all replicas have executed the write operations. Nevertheless, protocols based on this weaker eager definition are usually also associated with providing strong consistency. Strong consistency is different than atomicity as it refers to the values of data items and not the outcome of transactions. It typically implies that all replicas apply conflicting updates in the same order. In theory, one might have a replica control protocol that provides atomicity (guaranteeing that all replicas commit the same set of transactions) but the execution order of conflicting transactions is different at the different replicas. However, we are not aware of such a protocol.

Weak consistency generally means that data copies can be stale or even temporarily inconsistent. Staleness arises in lazy primary copy approaches. As long as the primary has not propagated the writeset to the secondaries, the data copies at the secondaries are outdated. If the secondaries apply updates in the same serialization order as they primary, the data copies at secondaries do not contain any incorrect data but simply data from the past. A system can be designed to limit the staleness experienced by a read operation on a secondary site. For instance, for numeric values the difference between the value read and the value at the primary might be kept below a threshold like 100. Other systems use different forms of limiting the divergence, for example, the secondary copy might be required to have missed no more than a fixed number of writes which were already applied at the primary, or the limit might be on the time between when a write is done at the primary and when it gets to the secondary. These staleness levels, also referred to as freshness levels allow one to bound the discrepancy between replicas visible to the outside world. These intermediate consistency levels can be achieved by refreshing secondary copies at appropriate time points.

Lazy update anywhere protocols allow the copies to be inconsistent. As our example in Figure 12.9 has shown, each replica might have changes of a local committed transaction while missing conflicting changes from a concurrent transaction committed at a different replica. In such a scenario, the most important property to provide is *eventual consistency* [42]. It indicates that, assuming the system reaches a quiescent state without any further write operations, all copies of a data item eventually converge to the same value. Note that eventual consistency is normally defined outside the scope of transactions. As such, it is possible that if two conflicting transactions T_i and T_j update both x and y, all copies of x will eventually contain T_i's update while all copies of y will have T_j's update. One way to define eventual consistency in the context of transactions is as follows: there must exist a subset of the committed transactions and an order on this subset, such that data copies converge to the same values as if the write operations of these transactions had been executed in the given serial order.

12.3.2 Isolation

Isolation in a Non-replicated System

In non-replicated database systems, the level of isolation indicates the degree to which concurrently executing transactions are allowed to be seen by another one. The most well-known correctness criteria is *serializability*: the interleaved execution of transactions is equivalent to a serial execution of these transactions. Typically, two executions are considered equivalent if the order of any two conflicting operations is the same in both executions. Two operations conflict if they access the same data item and at least one is an update operation. The most well-known concurrency control mechanisms providing serializability are strict 2-phase-locking and optimistic concurrency control. Weaker levels of isolation are often defined by specifying a set of anomalies that are allowed to occur during the execution. For instance, *snapshot isolation* allows an anomaly that may not occur in a serializable execution[1]. Snapshot isolation can be implemented very efficiently and provides much better concurrency in applications with a large read proportion. Transactions read from a snapshot of the database that represents the committed version of the database as of start of transaction. Conflicts only exist between write operations. If two concurrent transactions want to update the same data item only one of them may

---

[1] Note that strictly speaking snapshot isolation and serializability are incomparable since snapshot isolation disallows some executions allowed by serializability (concurrent blind writes, e.g. consider two transactions, $r_1(x); r_2(y); w_1(y); w_2(x); c_1; c_2$, being the subscripts the transaction identifier) and vice versa (write skew: $r_1(x); r_2(x); w_1(y); w_2(y); c_1; c_2$).

succeed, the other has to abort. Snapshot isolation typically uses multiple versions to provide snapshots.

Global Isolation Levels

Ideally, a replicated system should provide exactly the same level of isolation as a non-replicated system. For that, definitions for isolation in a replicated system have to reduce the execution over data copies onto an execution over a single logical copy. For instance, serializability in a replicated system is provided if the execution is equivalent to a serial execution over a single logical copy of the database.

Apart from serializability, snapshot isolation has also been well studied in replicated systems. All transactions must read from snapshots that can also exist in a non-replicated system and writes by concurrent committed transactions must not conflict, even if they are executed at different replicas. In a replicated environment, snapshot isolation is very attractive due to its handling of read operations.

Atomicity vs. Isolation

In principle, isolation is orthogonal to atomicity. Both eager and lazy protocols can provide serializability or snapshot isolation across the entire system. However, this only holds if there are no failures. If there are failures, then the problem of lost transactions occurs in lazy protocols, as we have discussed before. It is not clear how these lost transactions and transactions that have read values written by these lost transactions, can be placed in the execution history to show that it is equivalent to a serial history or fulfills the snapshot isolation properties.

1-Copy-Equivalence

1-copy-equivalence requires the many physical copies to appear as one logical copy. It was introduced with failures in mind, that is, the equivalence must exist even when copies are temporarily not available; in this view, lazy protocols do not provide 1-copy-equivalence. 1-copy-equivalence can then be combined with an isolation level to consider isolation in a failure-prone environment. For example, 1-copy-serializability requires the execution over a set of physical copies, some of them possibly unavailable, to be equivalent to a serial execution over a single logical copy.

Linearizability and Sequential Consistency

Linearizability and sequential consistency are two correctness criteria defined for the concurrent execution on replicated objects. They include the notion of the execution over the replicated data to be equivalent to an execution on a single image of the object. However, none of the two has the concept of transactions which requires to take operations on different objects into account (although sequential consistency takes the order within a client program into account). Different to serializability and snapshot isolation, linearizability requires an order that is consistent with real time.

12.3.3 Session Consistency

Session consistency is yet another dimension of correctness that is orthogonal to atomicity, data consistency or isolation. It defines correctness from the perspective of a user. Users typically interact with the system in form of sessions. For instance, a database application opens a connection to the database and then submits a sequence of transactions. These transactions build a logical order from the user's perspective. Therefore, if a client first submits transaction T_i and then T_j, and T_i has written some data item x that T_j reads, then T_j should observe T_i's write (unless another transaction has overwritten x since T_i's commit). This means, informally, session consistency guarantees that a client observes its own writes.

Definitions like serializability and 1-copy-serializability do not include session consistency, since they require the execution to be equivalent to a serial order, but that may not match the order of submission within a session. In the usual non-replicated platforms, built with locking or SI, session consistency is observed. Thus a truly transparent replicated system should provide session consistency, too.

In a replicated system, without special mechanisms, replica control may not ensure session consistency For instance, in a lazy primary copy approach, the client could submit an update transaction to the primary, and then submit a read-only transaction to a secondary before the writeset of its update transaction has been propagated to the secondary. In this case, it does not observe its own writes. In order to provide session consistency, such a protocol needs to be extended. For instance, transactions can receive global transaction identifiers which are monotonically increasing within a session. The driver software at the client then keeps track of the transaction identifiers. Whenever it submits a new transaction to a replica it piggybacks the identifier of the last transaction that was committed on behalf of this client. Then, the replica to which the new transaction was submitted will make sure that the new transaction will see any state changed performed by this last or older transactions.

Other protocols provide session consistency automatically, e.g., an eager protocol with 2PL and 2PC. Assume again a primary copy approach and a client submits first update transaction T_i to the primary and then read-only transaction T_j to a secondary. Although T_i might not yet be committed at the secondary when the first operation of T_j is submitted, T_i is guaranteed to be in the prepared state or a later state holding all necessary locks. Thus, T_j will be blocked until T_i commits and will see its writes. Eager protocols that only guarantee "eventual commit" typically need a special extension, e.g., a special driver as described above, to provide session consistency.

12.4 Other Parameters

We have already seen that eager protocols do not necessarily always provide higher guarantees than lazy protocols. In the same way, lazy protocols do not always perform better than eager protocols. In fact, performance depends on many issues. Some fundamental techniques can be applied to most replica control algorithms to speed-up processing. In this section, we discuss some of them. We also discuss some other fundamental design choices for a replicated database architecture that have a great influence on the performance, feasibility, and flexibility of the replication solution.

12.4.1 Message Management

The number of message rounds within a transaction are an important parameter for a replica control protocol. Looking at our examples of Section 12.2, the eager update anywhere protocol has a message round per write operation of a transaction (writeset and acknowledgement) plus the 2PC. With this, the number of messages within a transaction is linear with the number of write operations of the transaction. In contrast, the presented lazy protocols send one message per transaction, independently of the number of operations.

The number of messages per transaction depends on protocol details rather than simply on the category. For example, eager protocols can have a constant number of messages and lazy protocols can send a message per write operation. As an example, let's have a look at two further eager update anywhere protocols. The first alternative (*Alternative 1*) to the protocol presented in Figure 12.4 (*Original protocol*) executes first all operations only on the local database copy. Only when the client submits the commit request, the local replica sends the writeset with all write operations to all other replicas. The other replicas acquire the locks, execute the operations and return when they have completed. Finally the 2PC is performed. This model has one message round for the writeset and acknowledgements plus the overhead for the 2PC. The second alternative (*Alternative 2*) also executes the transaction first locally and sends the writeset at commit time. The remote replicas acquire the locks and send the acknowledgement once they have all locks. The local replica commits the transaction once it has received all acknowledgements. No 2PC takes place. The remote replicas execute the write operations in the writeset and commit the transaction in the meantime. That is, transaction execution contains only a single message round.

It is often assumed that transaction response time increases with the number of message rounds which occur during the transaction. In WANs, where messages take a long time, this means it is usually unacceptable to include more than one message round. In LANs, however, message latency might not play such a big role, and message throughput is often high. In such an environment, response time may be influenced more by other aspects rather than rounds of message exchange.

We illustrate this along the eager update anywhere protocol of Figure 12.4 and the two alternatives presented above. Figure 12.10 shows an example execution of a transaction $T_1 = w_1(x, v1), w_1(y, w1)$ updating x and y under these three variant protocols. In this diagram, we show time by the vertical distance, and we pay special attention to the possible concurrency between activities. The original protocol of Figure 12.4 multicasts each write operation and then executes it locally. That is, in the ideal case, the write operations on the different physical copies occur concurrently, and the local replica receives all acknowledgements shortly after it has

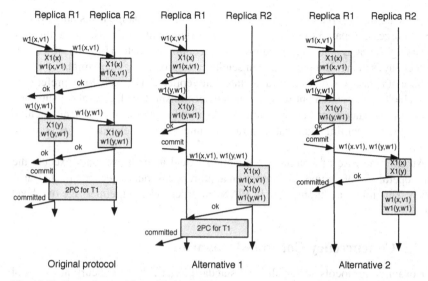

Fig. 12.10 Example execution with three different eager update anywhere protocols.

completed the operation itself. As such, execution is concurrent (this execution is also called conservative in Chapter 13). What is added is the latency of n messages rounds if there are n write operations and the latency of the 2PC. In the first alternative described above, the local replica first executes locally, then sends one message, then the remote replicas execute the write operations and then the 2PC occurs. Thus, while the number of message rounds is lower, the pure execution time is actually longer than in the original protocol as execution at the local replica and remote replicas is not performed in parallel. Finally, the last algorithm has the local execution, then one writeset message, then the time to acquire the locks successfully and finally the acknowledgement phase within the response time of the transaction. This approach has the lowest number of messages rounds and the actual execution time at the remote replicas is not included in the response time. These two alternatives are executed optimistically at the local replica (called optimistic execution in Chapter 13).

12.4.2 Executing Writes

Write operations have to be executed at all replicas. This can be done in two ways. In *statement* replication, also called *symmetric* replication, each replica executes the complete write operation, e.g., the SQL statement (update, delete, insert). In contrast, in *object* replication, also called *asymmetric* replication, only the local replica executes the operation and keeps track of the tuples changed by the operation. Then, the changed tuples are sent to the remote replicas which only apply the changes.

Applying the changes has usually much less overhead than executing the statement itself. For instance, experiments with PostgreSQL have shown that even for simple statements (update on primary key), applying the change takes only 30% of the resources compared to executing the entire statement. The reasons are the cost in parsing the SQL statement, building the execution tree, etc. However, if a statement changes many data records, then sending and processing them might be costly because of message size. In this case, statement replication is likely to be preferable.

A challenge of statement replication is determinism. One has to make sure that executing the statement has the same results at all replicas. If statements include setting the current time, generating a random number, etc. determinism is no more given.

An extreme case of statement replication would actually not only execute the write operations of an update transaction at all replicas, but the entire update transaction. This might be appropriate in WANs in order to keep the message overhead low.

12.4.3 Concurrency Control Mechanisms

Our example protocols so far all used standard strict 2PL as concurrency control mechanism. Clearly, replica control can be combined with various concurrency control mechanisms, not only 2PL. In this section, we look at optimistic and multi-version concurrency control.

Concurrency Control in a Non-replicated System   With optimistic concurrency control, a transaction's writes are done in a private workspace, and then, at the end of the transaction, a validation phase checks for conflicts, and if none are found, then the private workspace is written into the shared database. One mechanism is backward validation, where the validation of transaction T checks whether there was any concurrent transaction that already performed validation and wrote a data item that was read by T. If this is the case, T has to abort.

Multi-version concurrency control is used in connection with snapshot isolation. Each write operation generates a new version of a data item. We say a data version commits when the transaction that created the version commits. Versions can be used to provide read operations with a snapshot. The read operation of a transaction T_i reads the version of a data item that was the last to commit before T_i started. With this, a transaction reads from a snapshot as of transaction start time. Snapshot isolation has to abort one of two concurrent transactions that want to update the same data item. Commercial systems set write locks to detect conflicts when they occur and abort immediately. However, conflicts can also be detected at commit time similar to the mechanisms for optimistic concurrency control.

Concurrency Control in a Replicated System   The challenge of distributed concurrency control is to ensure that all replicas decide on the same serialization order. Primary copy approaches can simply rely on the (non-replicated) concurrency control mechanism at the primary and then forward write operations or writesets in FIFO order. The concurrency control tasks at secondaries are then quite straightforward. The extensions for an update anywhere approach are often more complicated.

In the particular case of strict 2PL, no extensions to the protocol itself are needed. However, distributed deadlock can occur. For optimistic and snapshot isolation concurrency control the question arises how to perform validation. Validation of all transactions could be performed at one central site. Alternatively, each replica could perform validation. However, in the latter case, the validation process needs to be deterministic to make sure that all replicas validate transactions in the same order and decide on the same outcome. For that purpose, many replication approaches use a total order multicast to send the relevant validation information to all replicas. Total order multicast is provided by group communication systems [13]. It guarantees that all members of a group receive all messages sent to the group in the same total order.

Optimistic Concurrency Control   Figure 12.11 sketches a replica control protocol based on optimistic concurrency control and a central scheduler that performs validation for all transactions. A transaction is submitted to any replica and executed locally according to standard optimistic techniques. A read operation (lines 1-2) accesses the last committed version of the data item. Data items are tagged with the transaction that was the last to write them. A transaction keeps track of all data versions read in the read set RS. A write (lines 3-5) creates a local copy which is added to the transaction's writeset WS. An abort (lines 6-7) simply means to discard both read and writeset. Upon a commit request, the read and writesets are sent to the scheduler (line 8) which performs validation (lines 9-12). It checks whether the readset of the currently validated transaction overlaps with the writesets of any concurrent transaction that validated before. If yes, it tells the local replica to abort the transaction. Otherwise it forwards the writeset to all replicas using a FIFO multicast. The replicas apply them (lines 13-20). A write $w(x)$ of this transaction becomes now the last committed version of x (line 17). Validation and applying the writeset is performed in the same serial order. The protocol description hides several technical challenges when such an approach should really be implemented in a database system. Firstly, one has to determine whether two transactions are concurrent. For that some timestamp mechanism must to be used, which can compare transactions that are local at different replicas.

Snapshot Isolation   Figure 12.12 sketches a replica control protocol based on snapshot isolation and using total order multicast. A transaction executes locally (lines 1-4) reading the last committed snapshot as of start time and creating new versions upon write operations. Abort simply means to discard the writes (lines 5-6). At the end of transaction only the writeset is multicast in total order (line 7). Validation now checks whether this writeset overlaps with the writesets of any concurrent transaction that validated before (line 8). No information about reads needs to be sent, since in SI conflict, leading to abort (lines 9-11), is only considered between write operations. If validation succeeds, remote transactions have to create the new versions (lines 13-16). Transactions are committed serially to guarantee that all replicas go through the same sequence of snapshots. The advantage over the optimistic concurrency control protocol is that read operations remain completely

Upon: $r_i(x)$ for local transaction T_i {*let T_j be the last to update x and commit*}
1: add x^j to read set RS_i
2: **return** x^j

Upon: $w_i(x, v_i)$ for local transaction T_i
3: create local copy x^i of x and add to write set WS_i
4: $x^i := v_i$
5: **return** ok

Upon: abort request for local transaction T_i
6: discard RS_i and WS_i
7: **return** abort

Upon: commit request for local transaction T_i
8: send (RS_i, WS_i) to central scheduler

Upon: receiving (RS_i, WS_i) from replica R {*validation at central scheduler*}
9: **if** $\exists T_j, T_j || T_i \wedge WS_j \cap RS_i$ **then**
10:     send $abort(T_i)$ back to R
11: **else**
12:     multicast WS_i to all replicas in FIFO order

Upon: receiving WS_i for any transaction T_i from central scheduler in FIFO order
13: **for all** $w_i(x, v_i)$ in WS_j **do**
14:     **if** T_i remote transaction **then**
15:         create local copy x^i of x
16:         $x^i := v_i$
17:     write x^i to database
18: commit T_i
19: **if** T_i local transaction **then**
20:     **return** ok

Upon: receiving $abort(T_i)$ for local transaction from central scheduler
21: discard RS_i and WS_i
22: **return** abort

Fig. 12.11 Update Anywhere Protocol based on Optimistic Concurrency Control and Central Scheduler.

Upon: $r_i(x)$ for local transaction T_i
1: **return** committed version x^j of x as of start time of T_i

Upon: $w_i(x, v_i)$ for local transaction T_i
2: create version x^i of x and add to write set WS_i
3: $x^i := v_i$
4: **return** ok

Upon: abort request for local transaction T_i
5: discard WS_i
6: **return** abort

Upon: commit request for local transaction T_i
7: multicast WS_i to all replicas in total order

Upon: receiving WS_i for any transaction T_i in total order
8: **if** $\exists T_j, T_j || T_i \wedge WS_j \cap WS_i$ **then**
9:     discard WS_i
10:     **if** T_i local transaction **then**
11:         **return** abort
12: **else**
13:     **if** T_i remote transaction **then**
14:         **for all** $w_i(x, v_i)$ in WS_i **do**
15:             create version x^i of x
16:             $x^i := v_i$
17:     commit T_i
18:     **if** T_i local transaction **then**
19:         **return** ok

Fig. 12.12 Update Anywhere Protocol based on Snapshot Isolation and Total Order Multicast.

local. The local replica makes sure that all reads are from a committed snapshot. For validation they don't play any role.

Fault-Tolerance   Both the optimistic and the pessimistic protocol above use multicast primitives. If the multicast primitive provides uniform reliable delivery, then we can consider these protocols as eager: a transaction only commits locally when it is guaranteed that the writeset will be delivered at all replicas and when the global serialization order of the transaction is determined. Therefore, when a transaction

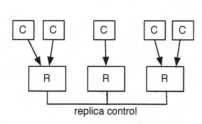

Fig. 12.13 Kernel-based Architecture.

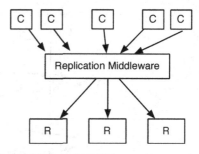

Fig. 12.14 Central Middleware.

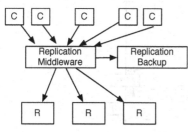

Fig. 12.15 Central Middleware with Backup.

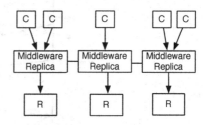

Fig. 12.16 Middleware Replica for each Database Replica.

commits locally it will commit in the same order at all other available replicas. If the above protocols use a multicast without uniform reliable delivery, they have the characteristics of a lazy protocol: a transaction might be committed at a replica that fails and the other replicas do not receive the writeset.

12.4.4 Architectural Alternatives

There exist two major architectural design alternatives to implement a replication tool. Our description of protocols so far followed a *kernel-based* or *white box* approach, where the replica control module is part of the database kernel and tightly coupled with the existing concurrency control module. A client connects to any database replica which then coordinates with the other replicas. The database system is replication-aware. Figure 12.13 depicts this architecture type.

Alternatively, replica control can be implemented outside the database as a *middleware* layer. Clients connect to the middleware that appears as a database system. The middleware then controls the execution and directs the read and write operations to the individual database replicas. Some solutions work with a purely *black-box* approach where the underlying database systems that store the database replicas do not have any extra functionality. Others use a *gray-box* approach where the database system is expected to export some minimal functionality that can be used by the middleware for a more efficient implementation of replica control. For instance, the database system could collect the writeset of a transaction in form of the set of records the transaction changed and provide it to the middleware on request. A

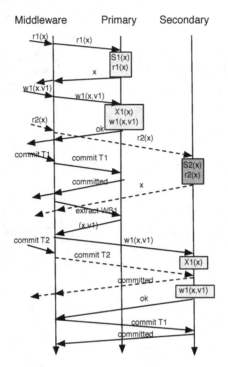

Fig. 12.17 Execution of a lazy primary-copy protocol with a central middleware.

middleware-based approach has typically its own concurrency control mechanism which might partially depend on the concurrency control of the underlying database systems. There might be a single middleware component (centralized approach) as in Figure 12.14, or the middleware might be replicated itself. For example, the middleware could have a backup replica for fault-tolerance (Figure 12.15). Other approaches have one middleware instance per database replica, and both together build a replication unit (Figure 12.16). A transaction can then connect to any middleware replica.

Figure 12.17 depicts an example execution of a lazy, primary copy protocol based on a central middleware. There is an update transaction T_1 and a read-only transaction T_2. All requests are sent to the middleware. T_1 (solid lines) is executed and committed at the primary. T_2 (dashed lines) is executed at any replica (in the example the secondary). After T_1 commits, the middleware extracts the writeset, and executes the write operations at the secondaries. The proper order of execution of these write operations and the local concurrency control mechanisms at the database replicas (here strict 2PL) guarantees the same serialization order at all replicas.

Discussion   Kernel-based approaches have the advantage that they have full access to the internals of the database. Thus, replica control can be tightly coupled with concurrency control and it is easy to provide concurrency control at the record level across the entire replicated system. Writeset extraction and application can be made highly efficient. In contrast, middleware-based protocols often have to partially re-implement concurrency control. Before execution of a particular statement, they often only have partial information of which records are exactly accessed (as SQL statements can contain predicates). This results often in a coarser concurrency level (e.g, table-based). If the database system does not export writeset functionality, writesets need to be extracted via triggers or similar procedures, which often is much less efficient than a kernel-based extraction. Fault-tolerance of the middleware is a further major issue. Depending on how much state the middleware manages, it can be complicated. Finally, the middleware represents a level of indirection, increasing the total number of messages.

However, middleware-based systems have many advantages. They can be used with 3rd-party database systems that do not provide replication functionality and whose source-code is not available. Furthermore, they can potentially be used in heterogeneous environments with different database systems. They also present a nicer separation of concerns. In a kernel-based approach, any changes to the concurrency control implementation might directly affect the replica control module. For middleware-based approaches this is likely only the case with major changes in the functionality of the underlying system.

12.4.5 Cluster vs. WAN Replication

We have already mentioned in the introduction that replication is done for different purposes, and in different settings. When replication is used for scalability, then the replicas are typically located in a single cluster. Read access to data items can then be distributed across the existing replicas while write operations have to be performed on all replicas. If the read ratio is high, then an increasing load can be handled by adding more replicas to the system. In a LAN, message latency is low and bandwidth high. Thus, the number of messages does not play a major role. Hence, a transaction can likely have several message rounds and a middleware can be interposed without affecting performance too much. Furthermore, there is no need for lazy update anywhere replication as the gain in efficiency is not worth the low degree of consistency that it provides. Finally, the write overhead should be kept as low as possible as it determines how much the system can be scaled. Thus, asymmetric replication will be better than symmetric replication.

Often, replication serves the purpose of fast local access when the application is geographically distributed. In this case, replicas are connected via a WAN. Thus, message latency plays an important role. In this context, lazy update anywhere might be preferable as it does not have any message exchange within the response time of the transaction. The price for that, namely conflict resolution and temporary inconsistency, might be acceptable. It might also be possible to split the application into partitions and put a primary copy of each partition close to the clients that are most likely to access it. This would provide short response times for most transactions without inconsistencies. One has to make sure that clients don't have to send several rounds of messages to a remote replica or a remote middleware. They always should be able to interact with their local site or send transaction requests in a single message to remote sites. The influence of symmetric vs. asymmetric replication will likely play a minor role in a WAN setting. The larger message sizes of asymmetric replication might be of disadvantage.

Replication for fault-tolerance can deploy replicas both in a LAN and a WAN. In LANs, typically eager protocols are used to keep replicas consistent. When a replica fails, another replica can take over the tasks assigned to the failed replicas in a transparent manner. Replicas can also be distributed across a WAN, typically with lazy propagation. When a catastrophic failure occurs that shuts down an entire location, a replica in a different location can take over. As catastrophic failures seldom occur, weaker consistency is acceptable for the advantage of having better performance during normal processing.

12.4.6 Degree of Replication

So far, we have assumed that all replicas have a full copy of the database, referred to as full replication. In *partial* replication, each data item of the database has a physical copy only on a subset of sites. The replication degree of a data item is the number of physical copies it has (see Chapter 5 for partial replication).

Partial replication serves different purposes. We mentioned above that for cluster replication, the ratio of write operation presents a scalability limit. Ideally, if a single system can handle C transactions per time unit, than a n-node system should be able to handle nC transactions. However, write operations have to be executed at all replicas. Thus, if write operations constitute a fixed fraction of the submitted workload, increasing the workload means increasing the absolute number of write operations each replica has to perform. This decreases the capacity that is available to execute local read operations. At some level of load, adding new sites will not increase the capacity available for further operations, and thus, throughput cannot be increased beyond this point. In the extreme case with 100% write operations and symmetric replication a replicated system does not provide any scalability as it can handle C transactions just as the non-replicated system.

When using partial replication in a cluster environment, read operations are executed at a single replica, as in full replication. Write operations now only need to be executed at replicas that have a copy of the data item accessed. For instance, if each data item has only two copies, then only two write operations need to be performed. Assuming again 100% write operations and symmetric replication, n replicas can handle $nC/2$ transactions (assuming data copies are distributed and accessed uniformly). With less write operations, it scales appropriately better. The important point is that when the replication degree is fixed to a constant (e.g., 2 or 4), then the system can scale without facing a limit from contention for writing. In contrast, if the replication degree increases with the number of sites in the system (e.g., n, $n/2$), then there is a scalability limit.

In a WAN environment, having a data item replicated at a specific geographic location decreases communication costs for read operations but increases communication and processing costs for update transactions. In this context, the challenge is to place data copies in such a way to find a trade-off between the different factors.

Partial replication has several challenges. Finding an appropriate replication degree and the optimal location for the replicas is difficult. Concurrency control has to be adjusted. When a client accesses a data item, a replica needs to be located. This is not necessarily the local replica. Also, partial replication might lead to distributed queries if no site has data copies of all data items accessed by the query.

12.4.7 Recovery

Recovering failed replicas and letting new replicas join the system is an important task. A joining replica has to get the up-to-date state of the database. This can be done by transferring a copy of the entire database to the joining replica. For a replica that had failed and now rejoins, it is also possible to only receive fresh copies of the data items that were actually changed during the downtime. Alternatively, it could receive and apply the writesets of the transactions it has missed during its downtime. This state transfer can take place offline or online. With *offline* transfer, transaction processing is interrupted until the transfer is completed. Using *online* recovery, transaction execution continues during state transfer. In this case, one has to make sure that the recovering replica does not miss any transactions. For a given transaction, either its changes are contained in the state transfer, or the joining replica receives its updates after the transfer is complete.

12.5 Existing Systems

12.5.1 Early Work

Database replication had its first boom in the early 80s. The book "Concurrency Control and Recovery in Database Systems" [7] provides a formalism to reason about correctness in replicated database systems. The term 1-copy-serializability was created and is still used today. Early work on replication took as baseline concurrency control mechanisms of non-replicated systems, extended them and combined them with replica control [7, 9]. Failure handling – both site and network failures – were a major research issue [6, 1]. Basically all these approaches used eager replication and provided strong correctness properties in terms of atomicity and isolation. In 1996, Gray et al. [20] indicated that these traditional approaches provide poor performance and do not scale as they commit transactions only if they have executed all their operations on all (available) physical data copies. Also, execution is often serially, leading to extremely long response times.

12.5.2 Commercial Systems

Since then, many new replication solutions have been developed. Commercial systems often provide a choice of replication solutions. High-availability solutions often implement a simplified version of primary-copy. In these approaches, all transactions (update and read-only) are submitted to the primary. The secondary only serves as a backup. Writeset propagation to the backups can be eager or lazy. In case the primary fails, clients are automatically redirected to the backup which becomes the new primary. Typically, any active transaction is aborted. Otherwise, clients can continue their requests as if no failure had occurred.

Lazy replication solutions, which allow looser consistency when reading at a replica, are often provided for WAN replication. Sophisticated reconciliation techniques are offered for update anywhere, based on timestamps, site priority, values or arithmetic functions. Both distributed and centralized reconciliation mechanisms exist. Eager update anywhere protocols are rarely found in commercial systems.

12.5.3 Lazy Replication Made Serializable

Some research efforts analyzed the correctness of lazy primary copy protocols where different data items have their primary copies on different sites [14]. In such a scenario, global serializability can be violated even if each site implements strict 2PL. In order to avoid incorrect executions some solutions restrict the placement of primary and secondary copies to avoid irregularities [8, 34]. The main idea is to define the set of allowed configurations using graphs where nodes are the sites and there are edges between sites if one site has a primary copy and the other a secondary copy of a given data item. Serializability can be provided if the graph has certain properties (e.g., it is acyclic). Others require to propagate updates along certain paths in the graph.

12.5.4 Cluster Replication

Group Communication   Work in this direction started with approaches that explore the use of group communication and was based on kernel-replication (such as Postgres-R [25, 47] or the state machine approach [37]). Different tasks, such as transaction execution and data storage, can further be distributed [16]. Many other followed, e.g., [2, 22, 23, 26, 47, 27]. They provide different concurrency control mechanisms, differ in the interface they provide to the clients of the database system (JDBC interface vs. procedural interface), the way they interact with the group communication system, etc. They also consider recovery and failover mechanisms.

Middleware-Based Systems   A lot of work has designed replication protocols that are especially targeted for middleware-based replication. There exist several approaches based on group communication [35, 10, 29, 36]. They often assume one middleware replica for each database replica and middleware replicas communicate with each other via multicast. They are typically all eager protocols.

Other solutions have a single middleware, possibly with a backup [3, 39]. Both eager and lazy approaches have been proposed. There is also considerable work that focuses less on the replica control itself but on issues such as load distribution and query routing [41, 32, 18, 4, 17, 48]. In lazy approaches one has a wide range of options when to actually propagate updates to other replicas, e.g., only when the freshness level goes below a threshold acceptable for queries. Load can be distributed according to many different strategies. Dynamically deciding on the number of replicas needed to handle a certain load has also been considered [19].

In [11], the authors provide an interesting discussion of the gap between the replica control protocols proposed by the research community, and the technical challenges to make them work in an industrial setting.

12.5.5 Other Issues

Approaches such as [40, 46, 28, 30, 44] take the specifics of WAN replication into account. They attempt to keep the number of message rounds low or accept weaker levels of consistency. Many approaches touch on partial replication, such as [17, 46, 45, 43, 44]. The particular issue of session consistency is discussed in [15].

12.5.6 Related Areas of Research

Many other techniques widely used in database systems can actually be considered some form of replication although they are not identified as such by research. In regard to scalability, materialized views are internal replicas of data that have been reorganized and processed in such a way so as to speed up certain queries that no longer need to be processed but can be answered directly from the materialized view. Materialized views can be seen as a special form of lazy primary copy replication (in some cases even update anywhere replication), where a materialized view is not a copy of a specific data item but an aggregation over many data items (i.e, table records) of the database. Thus, this makes change propagation considerably more complex [21].

Parallel databases use both partitioning and redundant data allocation across disks and memory. Replica control algorithms look somewhat different as there is not an independent database engine at each node but the system is treated as a single logical unit (regardless of whether the hardware is intrinsically parallel such as a multi core processor or it is an actual cluster of machines).

In regard to fault-tolerance, the log of a database is a form of replication [33]. All changes to the database are replicated onto stable storage in form of redo and undo logs. When a server fails, a new server instance is started, reading the log in order to recreate the state of the database. Fault tolerance is also achieved through redundant hardware and RAID disks [12] which provide replication at a lower level.

Database caching has been explored extensively for performance improvements [31, 5, 38]. The database cache usually resides outside the database system and caches the most frequently used data items. It is used for fast query execution while updates typically go directly to the database backend. Consistency mechanisms are in place but often involve discarding outdated copies.

12.6 Conclusions

This chapter provides a systematic overview of replica control mechanisms as they occur in replicated databases. We started with a two-parameter characterization providing example protocols based on 2-phase-locking for each of the categories that help to understand the trade-offs between the different categories. Furthermore, we provided an overview of correctness criteria that are important in the context of database replication. Finally, we discuss several other parameters of the replica control design space such as the number of message rounds, writeset processing, concurrency control mechanism, the replication architecture and the degree of replication assumed. We provide a comparative analysis how these parameters influence the performance, design and applicability of a given replica control protocol for certain application and execution environments.

Acknowledgements This work was supported in part by the Natural Sciences and Engineering Research Council of Canada (NSERC), the Spanish National Science Foundation (MICINN) under grant TIN2007-67353-C02, the Madrid Regional Research Council (CAM) under the AUTONOMIC project (S-0505/TIC/000285), and the European Commission under the NEXOF-RA project (FP7-216446).

References

1. Abbadi, A.E., Toueg, S.: Availability in partitioned replicated databases. In: ACM Int. Symp. on Principles of Database Systems (PODS), pp. 240–251 (1986)
2. Amir, Y., Tutu, C.: From Total Order to Database Replication. In: IEEE Int. Conf. on Distributed Computing Systems (ICDCS), pp. 494–506 (2002)
3. Amza, C., Cox, A.L., Zwaenepoel, W.: Distributed Versioning: Consistent Replication for Scaling Back-End DBs of Dynamic Content Web Sites. In: Endler, M., Schmidt, D.C. (eds.) Middleware 2003. LNCS, vol. 2672, pp. 282–302. Springer, Heidelberg (2003)
4. Amza, C., Cox, A.L., Zwaenepoel, W.: A comparative evaluation of transparent scaling techniques for dynamic content servers. In: IEEE Int. Conf. on Data Engineering (ICDE), pp. 230–241 (2005)
5. Bernstein, P.A., Fekete, A., Guo, H., Ramakrishnan, R., Tamma, P.: Relaxed-currency serializability for middle-tier caching and replication. In: ACM SIGMOD Int. Conf. on Management of Data, pp. 599–610 (2006)
6. Bernstein, P.A., Goodman, N.: An algorithm for concurrency control and recovery in replicated distributed databases. ACM Transactions on Database Systems (TODS) 9(4), 596–615 (1984)
7. Bernstein, P.A., Hadzilacos, V., Goodman, N.: Concurrency Control and Recovery in Database Systems. Addison-Wesley, Reading (1987)
8. Breitbart, Y., Komondoor, R., Rastogi, R., Seshadri, S., Silberschatz, A.: Update propagation protocols for replicated databases. In: ACM SIGMOD Int. Conf. on Management of Data, pp. 97–108 (1999)
9. Carey, M.J., Livny, M.: Conflict detection tradeoffs for replicated data. ACM Transactions on Database Systems (TODS) 16(4), 703–746 (1991)
10. Cecchet, E., Marguerite, J., Zwaenepoel, W.: C-jdbc: Flexible database clustering middleware. In: USENIX Annual Technical Conference, FREENIX Track, pp. 9–18 (2004)
11. Cecchet, E., Candea, G., Ailamaki, A.: Middleware-based database replication: the gaps between theory and practice. In: ACM SIGMOD Int. Conf. on Management of Data, pp. 739–752 (2008)

12. Chen, P.M., Lee, E.L., Gibson, G.A., Katz, R.H., Patterson, D.A.: Raid: High-performance, reliable secondary storage. ACM Comput. Surv. 26(2), 145–185 (1994)
13. Chockler, G., Keidar, I., Vitenberg, R.: Group communication specifications: a comprehensive study. ACM Computer Surveys 33(4), 427–469 (2001)
14. Chundi, P., Rosenkrantz, D.J., Ravi, S.S.: Deferred updates and data placement in distributed databases. In: IEEE Int. Conf. on Data Engineering (ICDE), pp. 469–476 (1996)
15. Daudjee, K., Salem, K.: Lazy database replication with snapshot isolation. In: Int. Conf. on Very Large Data Bases (VLDB), pp. 715–726 (2006)
16. Elnikety, S., Dropsho, S.G., Pedone, F.: Tashkent: uniting durability with transaction ordering for high-performance scalable database replication. In: EuroSys Conference, pp. 117–130 (2006)
17. Elnikety, S., Dropsho, S.G., Zwaenepoel, W.: Tashkent+: memory-aware load balancing and update filtering in replicated databases. In: EuroSys Conference, pp. 399–412 (2007)
18. Gançarski, S., Naacke, H., Pacitti, E., Valduriez, P.: The leganet system: Freshness-aware transaction routing in a database cluster. Information Systems 32(2), 320–343 (2007)
19. Ghanbari, S., Soundararajan, G., Chen, J., Amza, C.: Adaptive learning of metric correlations for temperature-aware database provisioning. In: Int. Conf. on Autonomic Computing, ICAC (2007)
20. Gray, J., Helland, P., O'Neil, P.E., Shasha, D.: The dangers of replication and a solution. In: ACM SIGMOD Int. Conf. on Management of Data, pp. 173–182 (1996)
21. Gupta, A., Mumick, I.S.: Maintenance of materialized views: Problems, techniques, and applications. IEEE Data Engineering Bulletin 18(2), 3–18 (1995)
22. Holliday, J., Agrawal, D., Abbadi, A.E.: The performance of database replication with group multicast. In: IEEE Int. Conf. on Fault-Tolerant Computing Systems (FTCS), pp. 158–165 (1999)
23. Jiménez-Peris, R., Patiño-Martínez, M., Kemme, B., Alonso, G.: Improving the scalability of fault-tolerant database clusters. In: IEEE Int. Conf. on Distributed Computing Systems (ICDCS), pp. 447–484 (2002)
24. Jiménez-Peris, R., Patiño-Martínez, M., Alonso, G., Kemme, B.: Are quorums an alternative for data replication? ACM Transactions on Database Systems (TODS) 28(3), 257–294 (2003)
25. Kemme, B., Alonso, G.: Don't be lazy, be consistent: Postgres-R, a new way to implement database replication. In: Int. Conf. on Very Large Data Bases (VLDB), pp. 134–143 (2000)
26. Kemme, B., Alonso, G.: A new approach to developing and implementing eager database replication protocols. ACM Transactions on Database Systems (TODS) 25(3), 333–379 (2000)
27. Kemme, B., Pedone, F., Alonso, G., Schiper, A., Wiesmann, M.: Using optimistic atomic broadcast in transaction processing systems. IEEE Transactions on Knowledge and Data Engineering (TKDE) 15(4), 1018–1032 (2003)
28. Leff, A., Rayfield, J.T.: Alternative edge-server architectures for enterprise javaBeans applications. In: Jacobsen, H.-A. (ed.) Middleware 2004. LNCS, vol. 3231, pp. 195–211. Springer, Heidelberg (2004)
29. Lin, Y., Kemme, B., Patiño-Martínez, M., Jiménez-Peris, R.: Middleware based data replication providing snapshot isolation. In: ACM SIGMOD Int. Conf. on Management of Data, pp. 419–430 (2005)
30. Lin, Y., Kemme, B., Patiño-Martínez, M., Jiménez-Peris, R.: Enhancing edge computing with database replication. In: Int. Symp. on Reliable Distributed Systems (SRDS), pp. 45–54 (2007)
31. Luo, Q., Krishnamurthy, S., Mohan, C., Pirahesh, H., Woo, H., Lindsay, B.G., Naughton, J.F.: Middle-tier database caching for e-business. In: ACM SIGMOD Int. Conf. on Management of Data, pp. 600–611 (2002)
32. Milan-Franco, J.M., Jiménez-Peris, R., Patiño-Martínez, M., Kemme, B.: Adaptive middleware for data replication. In: Jacobsen, H.-A. (ed.) Middleware 2004. LNCS, vol. 3231, pp. 175–194. Springer, Heidelberg (2004)

33. Mohan, C., Haderle, D.J., Lindsay, B.G., Pirahesh, H., Schwarz, P.M.: Aries: A transaction recovery method supporting fine-granularity locking and partial rollbacks using write-ahead logging. ACM Transactions on Database Systems (TODS) 17(1), 94–162 (1992)

34. Pacitti, E., Minet, P., Simon, E.: Fast Algorithm for Maintaining Replica Consistency in Lazy Master Replicated Databases. In: Int. Conf. on Very Large Data Bases (VLDB), pp. 126–137 (1999)

35. Patiño-Martínez, M., Jiménez-Peris, R., Kemme, B., Alonso, G.: MIDDLE-R: Consistent database replication at the middleware level. ACM Transactions on Computer Systems (TOCS) 23(4), 375–423 (2005)

36. Pedone, F., Frølund, S.: Pronto: A fast failover protocol for off-the-shelfcommercial databases. In: Symposium on Reliable Distributed Systems (SRDS), pp. 176–185 (2000)

37. Pedone, F., Guerraoui, R., Schiper, A.: The Database State Machine Approach. Distributed and Parallel Databases 14(1), 71–98 (2003)

38. Perez-Sorrosal, F., Patiño-Martinez, M., Jimenez-Peris, R., Kemme, B.: Consistent and scalable cache replication for multi-tier J2EE applications. In: Cerqueira, R., Campbell, R.H. (eds.) Middleware 2007. LNCS, vol. 4834, pp. 328–347. Springer, Heidelberg (2007)

39. Plattner, C., Alonso, G.: Ganymed: Scalable replication for transactional web applications. In: Jacobsen, H.-A. (ed.) Middleware 2004. LNCS, vol. 3231, pp. 155–174. Springer, Heidelberg (2004)

40. Rodrigues, L., Miranda, H., Almeida, R., Martins, J., Vicente, P.: Strong Replication in the GlobData Middleware. In: Proceedings Workshop on Dependable Middleware-Based Systems (part of DSN02), pp. 503–510. IEEE Computer Society Press, Los Alamitos (2002)

41. Röhm, U., Böhm, K., Schek, H.J., Schuldt, H.: FAS - a freshness-sensitive coordination middleware for a cluster of OLAP components. In: Int. Conf. on Very Large Data Bases (VLDB), pp. 754–765 (2002)

42. Saito, Y., Shapiro, M.: Optimistic replication. ACM Comput. Surv. 37(1), 42–81 (2005)

43. Schiper, N., Schmidt, R., Pedone, F.: Optimistic algorithms for partial database replication. In: Shvartsman, M.M.A.A. (ed.) OPODIS 2006. LNCS, vol. 4305, pp. 81–93. Springer, Heidelberg (2006)

44. Serrano, D., Patiño-Martínez, M., Jiménez-Peris, R., Kemme, B.: An autonomic approach for replication of internet-based services. In: Int. Symp. on Reliable Distributed Systems (SRDS), pp. 127–136 (2008)

45. Serrano, D., Patiño-Martínez, M., Jiménez, R., Kemme, B.: Boosting database replication scalability through partial replication and 1-copy-SI. In: IEEE Pacific-Rim Conf. on Distributed Computing (PRDC), pp. 290–297 (2007)

46. Sivasubramanian, S., Alonso, G., Pierre, G., van Steen, M.: Globedb: autonomic data replication for web applications. In: Int. World Wide Web Conf (WWW), pp. 33–42 (2005)

47. Wu, S., Kemme, B.: Postgres-R(SI): Combining replica control with concurrency control based on snapshot isolation. In: IEEE Int. Conf. on Data Engineering (ICDE), pp. 422–433 (2005)

48. Zuikeviciute, V., Pedone, F.: Conflict-aware load-balancing techniques for database replication. In: ACM Symp. on Applied Computing (SAC), pp. 2169–2173 (2008)

Chapter 13
Practical Database Replication

Alfrânio Correia Jr., José Pereira, Luís Rodrigues, Nuno Carvalho, and Rui Oliveira

Abstract This chapter illustrates how the concepts and algorithms described earlier in this book can be used to build practical database replication systems. This is achieved first by addressing architectural challenges on how required functionality is provided by generally available software componentes and then how different components can be efficiently integrated. A second set of practical challenges arises from experience on how performance assumptions map to actual environments and real workloads. The result is a generic architecture for replicated database management systems, focusing on the interfaces between key components, and then on how different algorithmic and practical optimization options map to real world gains. This shows how consistent database replication is achievable in the current state of the art.

13.1 Introduction

This chapter illustrates how the concepts and algorithms described earlier in this book can be used to build practical database replication systems. Hereafter a practical database replication system is a system that has the following qualities:

- It can be configured to tune the performance of multiple database engines and execution environments (including different hardware configurations of the node replicas and different network configurations).
- It is modular: the system provides well defined interfaces among the replication protocols, the database engines, and the underlying communication and coordination protocols. Thus, it can be configured to use the best technologies that fit a given target application scenario.
- Its modularity is not an impairment to performance. In particular it provides the hooks required to benefit from optimizations that are specific to concrete database or network configurations.
- It combines multiple replica consistency protocols in order to optimize its performance under different workloads, hardware configurations, and load conditions.

B. Charron-Bost, F. Pedone, and A. Schiper (Eds.): Replication, LNCS 5959, pp. 253–285, 2010.

To achieve these goals we have defined an architecture based on three main blocks:

- replication-friendly database,
- group communication support, and
- pluggable replica consistency protocols.

First of all, to achieve modularity without losing performance, the system needs to have replication support from the database engine. As we will see later in this chapter, the client interfaces provided by a Database Management System (DBMS) do not provide enough information for replication protocols. The replication protocols need to know more about the intermediate steps of a transaction in order to achieve good performance. Secondly, we will focus on group communication-based replication protocols. A Group Communication Service (GCS) eases the implementation of replication protocols by providing abstractions for message reliability, ordering and failure detection. In this chapter, we will discuss some details that need to be addressed when applying GCS to practical database replication systems. Finally, we will describe the replication protocols, how they interact with the other building blocks and show how they can be instantiated using different technologies. The achievements described here are the result of our experience in architecting, building and evaluating multiple instantiations of our generic architecture [9, 13].

The rest of the chapter is structured as follows. An architecture for practical database replication is presented in Section 13.2. Then, we devote a separate section to each main component of the architecture. In detail: Section 13.3 describes how to offer replication-friendly database support; Section 13.4 presents the necessary communication and coordination support to the pluggable replication protocols, which are described in Section 13.5. Section 13.6 presents an evaluation of several consistent database replication protocols on top of the described architecture. Section 13.7 concludes the chapter.

13.2 An Architecture for Practical Database Replication

In the following paragraphs we will briefly describe a generic architecture for practical database replication. The architecture, illustrated in Figure 13.1, is composed of the following building blocks:

- The *Application,* which might be the end-user or a tier in a multi-tiered application.
- The *Driver* provides a standard interface for the application. The Driver provides remote accesses to the (replicated) database using a communication mechanism that is hidden from the application, and can be proprietary.
- The *Load Balancer* dispatches client requests to database replicas using a suitable load-balancer algorithm.
- The *DBMS, or Database Management System,* which holds the database content and handles remote requests to query and modify data expressed in standard SQL.

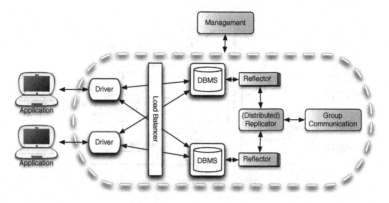

Fig. 13.1 Generic architecture for replication.

- *Management tools,* which are able to control the Driver and DBMS components independently from the Application using a mixture of standard and proprietary interfaces.
- The *Reflector* is attached to each DBMS and allows inspection and modification of on-going transaction processing.
- The *Replicator* mediates the coordination among multiple reflectors in order to enforce the desired consistency criteria on the replicated database. This is a distributed component that communicates using the group communication component.
- The *Group Communication* supports the communication and coordination of local replicators.

An important component of the architecture is the interface among the building blocks, which allows them to be reused in different contexts. The interfaces exposed by the reflector and group communication service are detailed in Sections 13.3 and 13.4 respectively. To support as much as possible off-the-shelf and third party tools, the call-level and SQL interfaces, and the remote database access protocol adhere to existing standards. For instance, the architecture can be easily mapped to a Java system, using JDBC as the call-level interface and driver specification, any remote database access protocol encapsulated by the driver and a DBMS, and an external configuration tool for the JDBC driver.

The generic architecture can be instantiated in several ways, for example, multiple logical components can be provided by multiple or by a single physical component. Figure 13.2 illustrates three relevant instantiations of the architecture.

The first instantiation, illustrated in Figure 2(a), is denoted as the in-core variant. In this case, the reflector is provided within the same physical component as the DBMS, where replication and communication components can be installed to control replication. Typically, such a variant is possible when the DBMS is augmented with replication support. Examples of protocols that need this support are [24, 31].

The second instantiation, illustrated in Figure 2(b), is denoted as middleware variant. In this scenario, clients connect to a virtual DBMS which implements the

256   A. Correia Jr.

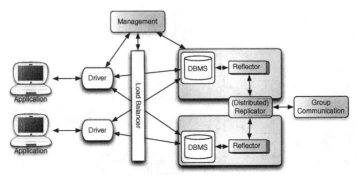

(a) In-core architecture for replication.

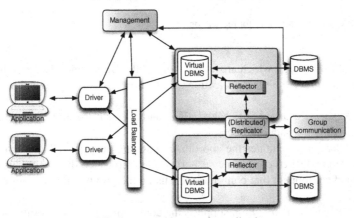

(b) Middleware architecture for replication.

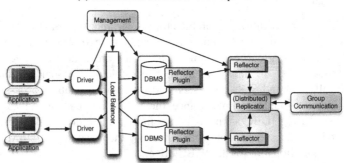

(c) Hybrid architecture for replication.

Fig. 13.2 Different instantiations of the generic architecture.

reflector interface. The virtual DBMS itself is implemented using the client interfaces provided by the real DBMS. The work presented in [26] exploits this approach. A commercial product that also implements this approach is Sequoia [11].

A hybrid approach can also be achieved by adding to the database the necessary hooks to export information about ongoing transactions by means of a reflector plugin. This plug-in interacts with the distributed replication protocol which runs on a different process. This solution is depicted in Figure 2(c).

13.3 Reflector: Replication-Friendly Database Support

A key component in the architecture is the reflector. The purpose of this component is to export a replication-friendly database interface to the replicator (described later in Section 13.5). In this way, the database replication protocols can be implemented independently of the specific DBMS system being used at deployment time, thus promoting the design and implementation of database replication protocols that can be used in a wide range of configurations.

The independence between a specific DBMS system and the replication protocols is achieved by augmenting the standard database interfaces with additional primitives that provide abstractions that reflect the usual processing stages of transactions (e.g. transaction parsing, optimization and execution) inside the DBMS engine. Naturally, the implementation details of the replicator vary depending on the specific DBMS instance and the architecture chosen. In this section we outline the replicator interface and the rationale for its design.

13.3.1 Reflection for Replication

A well known software engineering approach to building systems with complex requirements is reflection [27, 25]. By exposing an abstract representation of the systems' inner functionality, the later can be inspected and manipulated, thus changing its behavior without loss of encapsulation. DBMS have long taken advantage of this, namely, on the database schema, on triggers, and when exposing the log.

Logging, debugging and tracing facilities are some examples of important add-ons to DBMS that are today widely available. The computation performed by such plug-ins is known as a computational reflection, and the systems that provide them are known as reflective systems. Specifically, a reflective system can be defined as a system that can reason about its computation and change it. Reflective architectures ease and smooth the development of systems by encapsulating functionality that is not directly related to the application domains. This can be done to a certain extent in an ad-hoc manner, by defining hooks in specific points of a system, or with support from a programming language. In both cases, there is a need for providing a reflective architecture where the interaction between a system (i.e. base-level objects) and its reflective counterpart is done by a meta-level object protocol and the reflective computation is performed by meta-level objects. These objects exhibit a meta-level programming interface.

Previous reflective interfaces for database management systems were mainly targeted at application programmers using the relational model. Their domain is therefore the relational model itself. Using this model, one can intercept operations that modify relations by inserting, updating, or deleting tuples, observe the tuples being changed and then enforce referential integrity by vetoing the operation (all at the meta-level) or by issuing additional relational operations (base-level).

A reflection mechanism for database replication was also recently proposed in [42]. In contrast to the approach described in this section, it assumes that reflection is achieved by wrapping the DBMS server and intercepting requests as they are issued by clients. By implementing reflection this way, one can only reflect computation at the first stage (statements), i.e. with coarse granularity. Exposing further details requires rewriting large portions of DBMS functionality at the wrapper level. As an example, Sequoia [11] does additional parsing and scheduling stages at the middleware level. In theory, this approach could be more generic and suitable to reflect black-box DBMSs. In practice, this is not the case, since DBMS do not offer the exact same interface. Therefore, the wrapper must be customized for each DBMS. Moreover, this approach can introduce significant latency by requiring extra communication steps and/or extra processing of requests.

Furthermore, some protocols are concerned with details that are not visible in the relational model, such as modifying query text to remove non-deterministic statements, for instance, those involving NOW() and RANDOM(). Also, one may be interested in intercepting a statement as it is submitted, whose text can be inspected, modified (meta-level) and then re-executed, locally or remotely, within some transactional context (base-level).

Therefore, a target domain more expressive than the relational model is required. We propose to expose a transaction object that reflects a series of activities (e.g. parsing) that is taking place on behalf of a transaction. This object can be used to inspect the transaction (e.g. wait for it to commit) or to act on it (e.g. force a rollback). Using the transaction object the meta-level code can register to be notified when specific events occur. For instance, when a transaction commits, a notification is issued and contains a reference to the corresponding transaction object (meta-object). Actually, handling notifications is the way that meta-level code dynamically acquires references to meta-objects describing the on-going computation.

13.3.2 Processing Stages

The reflector interface abstracts transaction processing as a pipeline [17]. This is illustrated in Figure 13.3. The replicator acts as a plug-in that registers itself to receive notifications of each stage of the pipeline. The notifications are issued by the reflector as meta-objects, where each meta-object represents one processing stage. The processing stages are briefly described below. The replicator is notified of these processing stages in the order they are listed bellow:

- The *Parsing stage* parses the received raw statements and produces a parse tree;
- The *Optimization stage* transforms the parse tree according to various optimization criteria, heuristics and statistics to an execution plan;

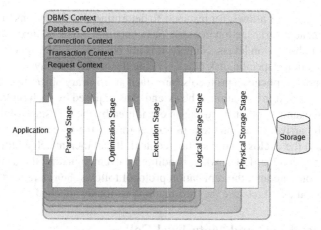

Fig. 13.3 Major meta-level interfaces: processing stages and contexts.

- The *Execution stage* executes the plan and produces object-sets (data read and written);
- The *Logical Storage stage* deals with mapping from logical objects to physical storage;
- The *Physical Storage stage* deals with block input/output and synchronization.

In general, the reflector will issue notifications at the meta-level (to the registered replicator) whenever computation proceeds from one stage to the next. For instance, if a replication protocol needs to ensure that all the requests are deterministic, it needs to be notified on the Parsing stage to modify the initial statement and remove non determinism; when the computation reaches the Execution stage, it will produce a set of read and written data that is reflected, issuing a notification. The interface thus exposes meta-objects for each stage and for data that moves through them.

13.3.3 Processing Contexts

The meta-interface exposed by the processing pipeline is complemented by nested context meta-objects, also shown in Figure 13.3. These context meta-objects show on behalf of whom some operation is being performed. In detail, the *DBMS* and *Database* context interfaces expose meta-data and allow notification of life-cycle events. *Connection* contexts reflect existing client connections to databases. They can be used to retrieve connection specific information, such as user authentication or the character set encoding used. The *Transaction* context is used to notify events related to a transaction such as its startup, commit or rollback. Synchronous event handlers available here are key to consistent replication protocols. Finally, to ease the manipulation of the requests within a connection to a database and the corresponding transactions one may use the *Request* context interface.

Events fired by processing stages refer to the directly enclosing context. Each context has then a reference to the next enclosing context and can enumerate all enclosed contexts. This allows, for instance, to determine all connections to a database or the current active transaction in a specific connection. Some contexts are not valid at the lowest abstraction levels. Namely, it is not possible to determine on behalf of which transaction a specific disk block is being flushed by the physical stage.

Furthermore, replication protocols can attach an arbitrary object to each context. This allows context information to be extended as required by each replication protocol. As an example, when handling an event fired by the first stage of the pipeline signaling the arrival of a statement in textual format the replication protocol gets a reference to the enclosing transaction context. It can then attach additional information to that context. Later, when handling an event signaling the availability of the transaction outcome, the replication protocol follows the reference to the same transaction context to retrieve the information previously attached.

13.3.4 Base-Level and Meta-level Calls

An advantage of reflection is that base- and meta-level code can be freely mixed, as there is no inherent difference between base- and meta-objects. For instance, a direct call to meta-level code can be forced by the application programmer by registering it as a native procedure and then using the CALL SQL statement. This causes a call to the meta-level code to be issued from the base-level code within the *Execute* stage. The target procedure can then retrieve a pointer to the enclosing *Request* context and thus to all relevant meta-interfaces. Meta-level code can callback into base level in two different situations. The first is within a direct call from base-level to issue statements in an existing enclosing request context. The second option is to use the enclosing *Database* context to open a new base-level connection to the database.

A second issue when considering base-level calls is whether these also get reflected. The proposed interface allows to disable reflection on a case-by-case basis by invoking an operation on context meta-objects. Therefore, meta-level code can disable reflection for a given request, a transaction, a specific connection or even an entire database. Actually this can be used on any context meta-object and thus for performance optimization. For example, consider a replication protocol, which is notified that a connection will only issue read-only operations, and thus ceases monitoring them.

A third issue is how base-level calls issued by meta-level code interact with regular transaction processing regarding concurrency control. Namely, how conflicts that require rollback are resolved in multi-version concurrency control where the first committer wins or, more generally, when resolving deadlocks. The proposed interface solves this by ensuring that transactions issued by the meta-level do not abort in face of conflicts with regular base-level transactions. Given that replication code running at the meta-level has a precise control on which base-level transactions are scheduled, and thus can prevent conflicts among those, has been sufficient to solve all considered use cases. The implementation of this simple solution resulted in a small set of localized changes within the DBMS.

13.3.5 Exception Handling

The DBMS handles most of the base-level exceptions by aborting the affected transaction and generating an error to the application. The proposed architecture does not change this behavior. Furthermore, the meta-level is notified by an event issued by the transaction context object; this allows meta-level to cleanup after an exception has occurred.

Most exceptions within a transaction context that are not handled at the meta-level can be resolved by aborting the transaction. However, some event handlers should not raise exceptions to avoid inconsistent information on databases or recursive exceptions, namely, while starting up or shutting down a database, while rolling back or after committing a transaction. In these cases, any exception will leave the database in a panic mode requiring manual intervention to repair the system. Furthermore, interactions between the meta-level and base-level are forbidden and any attempt of doing so, puts the database in panic mode.

Exceptions from meta-level to base-level calls need additional management. For instance, while a transaction is committing, meta-level code might need to execute additional statements to keep track of custom meta-information on the transaction before proceeding, and this action might cause errors due to deadlock problems or low amount of resources. Such cases are handled as meta-level errors to avoid disseminating errors inside the database while executing the base-level code.

13.3.6 Existing Reflector Bindings

In this section we discuss how the reflector interface was implemented in three different systems, namely, Apache Derby, PostgreSQL, and Sequoia. These systems represent different tradeoffs and implementation decisions and are thus representative of what one should expect when implementing the architecture proposed in this chapter.

Apache Derby Binding Apache Derby [3] is a fully-featured database management system with a small footprint developed by the Apache Foundation and distributed under an open source license. It is also distributed as IBM Cloudscape and in Sun JDK 1.6 as JavaDB. It can either be embedded in applications or run as a standalone server. It uses locking to provide serializability. The initial implementation of the Reflection interface takes advantage of Derby being natively implemented in Java to load meta-level components within the same JVM and thus closely coupled with the base-level components. Furthermore, Derby uses a different thread to service each client connection, thus making it possible for notifications to the meta-level to be done by the same thread and thus reduced to a method invocation, which has negligible overhead. This is therefore the preferred implementation scenario. The current implementation exposes all context objects and the parsing and execution stages, as well as calling between base-level and meta-level as described in Section 13.3.4.

PostgreSQL Binding   PostgreSQL [39] is also a fully-featured database management system distributed under an open source license. It has been ported to multiple operating systems, and is included in most Linux distributions as well as in recent versions of Solaris. Commercial support and numerous third party add-ons are available from multiple vendors. It currently provides a multi-version concurrency control mechanism supporting snapshot isolation. The major issue in implementing the interface is the mismatch between its concurrency model and the multi-threaded meta-level runtime. PostgreSQL uses multiple single-threaded operating system processes for concurrency. This is masked by using the existing PL/J binding to Java, which uses a single standalone Java virtual machine and inter-process communication. This imposes an inter-process remote procedure call overhead on all communication between base and meta-level. Furthermore, the implementation of the reflector interface in PostgreSQL uses a hybrid approach. Instead of directly coding the reflector interface on the server, key functionality is added to existing client interfaces and as loadable modules. The meta-level interface is then built on these. The two-layer approach avoids introducing a large number of additional dependencies in the PostgreSQL code, most notably in the Java virtual machine. As an example, transaction events are obtained by implementing triggers on transaction begin and end statements. A loadable module is then provided to route such events to meta-objects in the external PL/J server. The current implementation exposes all context objects and the parsing and execution objects, as well as calling between base-level and meta-level as described in Section 13.3.4. It avoids base-level operations blocking meta-level operations simply by modifying the choice of the transactions to be terminated upon deadlock detection and write conflicts.

Sequoia Binding   Sequoia [11] is a middleware system for database clustering built as a server wrapper. It is primarily targeted at obtaining replication or partitioning by configuring the controller with multiple backends, as well as improving availability by using several interconnected controllers. Nevertheless, when configured with a single controller and a single backend, Sequoia provides a state-of-the-art JDBC interceptor. It works by creating a virtual database at the middleware level, which reimplements part of the abstract transaction processing pipeline and delegates the rest to the backend database. The current implementation exposes all context, parsing and execution objects, as well as calling from meta-level to base-level with a separate connection. It does not allow calling from base-level to meta-level, as execution runs in a separate process. It can however be implemented by directly intercepting such statements at the parsing stage. It neither avoids base-level operations interfering with meta-level operations, and this cannot be implemented as described in the previous sections as one does not modify the backend DBMS. It is however possible to the clustering scheduler already present in Sequoia to avoid concurrently scheduling base-level and meta-level operations to the backend, thus precluding conflicts. This implementation is of great interest when with a closed source DBMS that does not natively implement reflector interfaces.

13.4 GCS: Communication and Coordination Support

All database replica consistency protocols require communication and coordination support. Among the most relevant abstractions to support database replication we may identify: reliable multicast (to disseminate updates among the replicas), total order (to define a global serial order for transactions) and group membership (to manage the set of currently active replicas in the system).

A software package that offers this sort of communication and coordination support is typically bundled in a package called a *Group Communication Toolkit*. After the pioneer work initiated two decades ago with Isis [8], many other toolkits have been developed. Appia [28], Spread [2], and JGroups [5] are, among others, some of the group communication toolkits in use today. Therefore, group communication is a mature technology that greatly eases the development of practical database replication systems.

At the same time, group communication is still a hot research topic, as performance improvements and wider applicability are sought [47, 43, 33, 35, 34]. Furthermore, group communication is clearly an area where there is no one solution that fits all application scenarios. For instance, just to offer total order multicast, dozens of different algorithms have been proposed [15], each outperforming the others for a specific setting: there are protocols that perform better for heavily loaded replicas in switched local area networks [18], others for burst traffic in LANs [22], others for heterogeneous wide-area networks [40], etc. More details about the primitives offered by a group communication toolkit can be found in Chapter 3 and Chapter 6.

Therefore, having a clear interface between the replication protocols and the GCS has multiple practical advantages. To start with, it allows to tune the communication support (for instance, by selecting the most appropriate total order protocol) without affecting the replication protocol. Furthermore, given that different group communication toolkits implement different protocols, it should be possible to re-use the same replication protocols with different group communication toolkits.

To address these problems we have defined a generic interface to group communication services that may be used to wrap multiple toolkits. The interface, called *Group Communication Service for Java*, or simply jGCS, has been designed for the Java programming language and leverages several design patterns that have recently become common ground of Java-based middleware. The interface specifies not only the API but also the (minimum) semantics that allow application portability. jGCS owns a number of novel features that makes it quite distinct from previous attempts to define standard group communication interfaces, namely:

- jGCS aggregates the service in several complementary interfaces, as depicted in Figure 13.4, namely a set of *configuration interfaces* (namely, GroupConfiguration, ProtocolFactory and Service), a *message passing interface* (Data), and a set of *membership interfaces* (Control). The configuration interface specifies several opaque configuration objects that encapsulate specifications of message delivery guarantees. These are to be constructed in an implementation dependent manner to match application requirements and then supplied using some dependency injection technique. The message passing interface exposes a straightforward in-

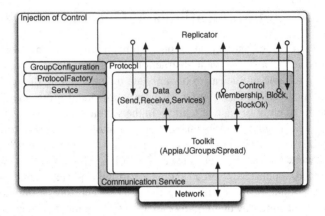

Fig. 13.4 Components of the GCS.

terface to sending and receiving byte sequences, although concerned with high
throughput, low latency and sustainable concurrency models in large scale applications. Finally, a set of membership interfaces expose different membership
management concepts as different interfaces, that the application might support
or need.

- jGCS provides support for recent research results that improve the performance
  of group communication systems, namely, *semantic annotations* [34, 35, 33] and
  early delivery [32, 45, 43, 41].
- the interface introduces negligible overhead, even when jGCS is implemented as
  wrapper layer and is not supported natively by the underlying toolkit.

13.4.1 Architectural and Algorithmic Issues

In this section we discuss the main features that must be provided by the group
communication toolkit to cope with the requirements needed by database replication
protocols. As proof-of-concept, we implemented the presented features in the Appia
group communication toolkit.

Optimistic Uniform Total Order   The notion of optimistic total order was first
proposed in the context of local-area broadcast networks [32]. In many of such networks, the spontaneous order of message reception is the same in all processes.
Moreover, in sequencer-based total order protocols the total order is usually determined by the spontaneous order of message reception in the sequencer process.
Based on these two observations a process may estimate the final total order of
messages based on its local receiving order and, therefore, provide an optimistic
delivery as soon as a message is received from the network. With this optimistic
delivery, the application can make some progress. For example, a database replication protocol can apply the changes in the local database without committing it. The

commit procedure can only be made when the final order is known and if it matches the optimistic order. If the probability of the optimistic order matching the final order is very high, the latency window of the protocol is reduced and the system gains in performance.

Unfortunately, spontaneous total order does not occur in wide-area networks. The long latency in wide-area links causes different processes to receive the same message at different points in time. Consider a simple network configuration with three nodes a, b, and s such that network delay between nodes a and b is $2ms$, and network delays to and from node s are $12ms$. Assume that process a multicasts a message m_1 and that, at the same time, the sequencer process s multicasts a message m_2. Clearly, the sequencer will receive m_2 before m_1, given that m_1 would require $12ms$ to reach the sequencer. On the other hand, process b will receive m_1 before m_2, as m_1 will take only $2ms$ to reach b while m_2 will require $12ms$. From this example, it should be obvious that the spontaneous total order provided by the network at b is not a good estimate of the observed order at the sequencer.

To address the problem above, a system can be configured to use a total order protocol such as SETO [29]. SETO is a generalization of the optimistic total order protocol proposed in [43] and operates by introducing artificial delays in the message reception to compensate for the differences in the network delays. It is easier to describe the intuition of the protocol by using a concrete example. Still considering the above simple network configuration, assume also that we are able to provide to each process an estimate of the network topology and of the delays associated with each link. In this case, b could infer that message m_1 would take $10ms$ more to reach s than to reach b. By adding a delay of $10ms$ to all messages received from a, it would mimic the reception order of a's messages at s. A similar reasoning could be applied to messages from other processes.

When configured to use this protocol, the group communication toolkit delivers the original message as soon as it is received (network order). Notifications about optimistic total order and final uniform total order are later delivered, indicating that progress can be done regarding a particular message.

Primary Partition Support   Partitions in the replica group may happen due to failures in the cluster (network, switching hardware, among others). In asynchronous systems, virtual partitions (indistinguishable from physical partitions) may happen due to unexpected delays. A partitionable group membership service allows multiple concurrent views of the group, each corresponding to a different partition, to co-exist and evolve in parallel [4, 16]. In the context of database replication, this is often undesirable as it may lead to different replicas processing and committing conflicting updates in a uncoordinated form. A partition in the group membership can then easily lead to the *split-brain* phenomenon: the state in different replicas diverges and is no longer consistent. In contrast, a primary-partition group membership service maintains a single agreed view of the group at any given time, delivering a totally ordered sequence of views (processes that become disconnected from the primary partition block or are forced to crash and later rejoin the system).

In our implementation, primary partitions are defined by majority quorums. The initial composition of the primary partition is defined at configuration time, using standard management interfaces. The system remains alive as long as a majority of the previous primary partition remains reachable [23, 6]. The dynamic update of the primary partition is coordinated and has to be committed by a majority of members of the previous primary. This is deterministic and ensures that only one partition exists at a time. Using this mechanism, a replica that belongs to a primary partition can move to a non-primary partition when a view changes. In this case, the replication protocol only gets notified that the group has blocked and does not receive any view while it is not reintegrated in a primary partition.

13.4.2 Existing GCS Bindings

Open source implementations of jGCS for several major group communication systems have been already developed, namely, Appia [28], Spread [2] (including the FlushSpread variant), and JGroups [5]. All these bindings are open source and available on SourceForge.net.[1] Besides making jGCS outright useful in practice, these validate that the interface is indeed generic. These implementations are described in the following paragraphs.

Appia Binding   Appia [28] is a layered communication support framework that was implemented in the University of Lisbon. It is implemented in Java and aims at high flexibility to build communication channels that fit exactly in the user needs. More details about Appia are described in Section 13.4.1.

The implementation of GCS is built directly on Appia's protocol composition interfaces as an additional layer. GCS configuration objects thus define the micro-protocols that will be used in the communication channels. Each service identifies an Appia channel and messages are sent through the channel that fits the requested service. As Appia supports early delivery in totally ordered multicast, this is exposed in the GCS binding using the ServiceListener interface. Appia implements all extensions of the ControlSession, depending on the channel configuration.

JGroups Binding   JGroups [5] is a group communication toolkit modeled on Ensemble [19] and implemented in Java. It provides a stack architecture that allows users to put together custom stacks for different view synchronous multicast guarantees as well as supporting peer groups. It provides an extensive library of ordering and reliability protocols, as well as support for encryption and multiple transport options. It is currently used by several large middleware platforms such as JBoss and JOnAS.

The JGroups implementation of GCS also uses the configuration interface to define the micro-protocols that will be used in the communication channel. JGroups can provide only one service by the applications, since configurations only support

---

[1] GCS and its bindings are available in http://jgcs.sf.net

one JGroups channel per group communication instance. JGroups implements all extensions of the ControlSession.

Spread Binding   Spread/FlushSpread[2] is a toolkit implemented by researchers of the Johns Hopkins University. It is based on an overlay network that provides a messaging service resilient to faults across local- and wide-area networks. It provides services ranging from reliable message passing to fully ordered messages with delivery guarantees. The Spread system is based on a daemon-client model where generally long-running daemons establish the basic message dissemination network and provide basic membership and ordering services, while user applications linked with a small client library can reside anywhere on the network and will connect to the closest daemon to gain access to the group communication services. Although there are interfaces for Spread in multiple languages, these do not support the Flush-Spread extension, which provides additional guarantees with a different interface.

The Spread and FlushSpread implementations of GCS use the configuration interface to define the location of the daemon and the group name. The implementation to use (FlushSpread or just Spread) is also defined at configuration time. In Spread, the quality of service is explicitly requested for each message, being thus encapsulated in Service configuration objects.

13.5 Replicator: Pluggable Replication Protocols

The replicator is a distributed component responsible for coordinating the interaction among all DBMS replicas in order to enforce the consistency of the replicated database. It directly interfaces with the reflector and relies on the GCS module for all communication and replica membership control, as shown in the Figure 13.5.

It is within the replicator that the replica consistency protocols are implemented. The module is built around four process abstractions that are able to express most,

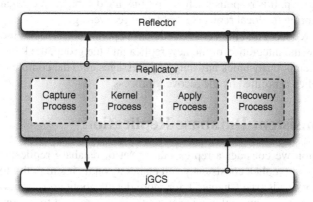

Fig. 13.5 Replicator architecture.

if not all, database replication protocols. These are the Capture, Kernel, Apply and Recovery processes and are described next.

Capture Process   The capture process is the main consumer of the reflector events. It receives events from the DBMS, converts them to appropriate events within the replicator and notifies the other processes. In particular, it receives a transaction begin request and registers the current transaction context. For instance, for update transactions, the capture process may instruct the reflector to receive the write and read sets of the transaction when the commit request is performed. Using this information, it may construct an internal transaction event that carries the transaction identification along with the corresponding read and write sets. It then notifies the kernel process which, in turn, is responsible for distributing the transaction data and enforcing the consistency criterion.

Kernel Process   This process implements the core of the replica consistency protocol. In general, it handles the replication of local transactions by distributing relevant data and determining their global commit order. Additionally, it handles incoming data from remotely executed transactions. The local outcome of every transaction is ultimately decided by the kernel process, in order to ensure a target global consistency criterion. To execute its task, the kernel process exchanges notifications with the capture and apply processes, and interfaces directly the GCS component.

Apply Process   The apply process is responsible for efficiently injecting incoming transaction updates into the local database through the reflector component. To achieve optimum performance, this implies executing multiple apply transactions concurrently and, when possible, batching updates to reduce the number of transactions. This needs however to ensure that the agreed serialization order is maintained.

Recovery Process   The recovery process intervenes whenever a replica joins or rejoins the group. It is responsible for exporting the database state when acting as a donor or to bring the local replica up-to-date if recovering.

Both the recovery and the kernel modules cooperate closely with the GCS module. To allow the integration of the new replica into the group, the kernel module is required to temporarily block any outgoing messages until the complete recovery of the new replica is notified by the recovery process.

13.6 Consistent Database Replication

In this section we consider a representative set of database replication protocols providing strong replica consistency and elaborate on their suitability to handle demanding workloads (see Chapter 1 for more details about consistency models for replication). We start by analyzing each protocol with respect to its contention path and concurrency restrictions. Then we compare their performance using a common test-bed, implemented as plug-ins for the replicator component of our architecture, using the industry standard TPC-C benchmark and workload.

Database replication protocols differ greatly in whether transactions are executed optimistically [31, 24] or conservatively [37]. In the former, a transaction is executed by any replica without a priori coordination with other replicas. It is just before committing that replicas coordinate and check for conflicts between concurrently executed transactions. Transactions that would locally commit may end up aborting due to conflicts with remote concurrent transactions. On the contrary, in the conservative approach, all replicas first agree on the execution order for potentially conflicting transactions ensuring that when a transaction executes there is no conflicting transaction being executed remotely and therefore its success depends entirely on the local database engine. Generally, two transactions conflict if both access the same *conflict class* (e.g. table) and one of them updates it.

As expected, both approaches have their virtues and problems [21]. The optimistic execution presents very low contention and offers high concurrency levels. However, it may yield concurrency-induced aborts which, occasionally, may impair the protocol's fairness since long-running transactions may experiment unacceptable abort rates. On the contrary, the conservative approach does not lead to aborts and offers the same committing opportunities to all transaction types. The resulting degree of concurrency heavily depends on the granularity of the defined conflict classes. Fine conflict classes usually require application-specific knowledge and any labeling mistake can lead to inconsistencies.

Another crucial aspect of database replication protocols is whether replication is active or passive. With active replication each transaction executes at all replicas while with passive protocols only a designated replica actually executes the transaction and the state updates are then propagated to the other replicas. Active replication is required for structural or system wide requests, such as the creation of tables and users, and desired for update intensive transactions. The passive approach is otherwise preferable, as it confines the processing to a single replica, is insensible to non-deterministic requests, and allows for more concurrency.

In the following sections we discuss and compare five consistent database replication protocols: a conservative and two optimistic passive replication approaches, an active replication protocol (inherently conservative regarding transactions execution), and a hybrid solution that combines both conservative and optimistic execution as well as active and passive replication. In all cases we consider a common practice that only update transactions are handled by the replication protocols. Queries are simply executed locally at the database to which they are submitted and do not require any distributed coordination. The discussion on the impact of this configuration in the overall consistency criterion has been discussed elsewhere [30].

Our analysis is focused on dynamic aspects, namely on the queuing that happens in different parts of the system and on the amount of concurrency that can be achieved. Then, we contrast the original assumptions underlying the design of the protocols with our experience with the actual implementations using the TPC-C workload [21].

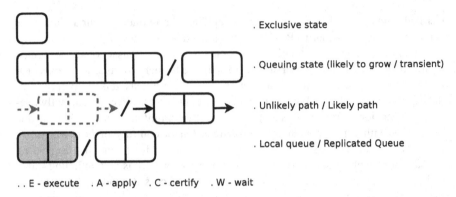

. Exclusive state

. Queuing state (likely to grow / transient)

. Unlikely path / Likely path

. Local queue / Replicated Queue

. . E - execute   . A - apply   . C - certify   . W - wait

Fig. 13.6 Notation.

Figure 13.6 introduces the notation used to represent the state maintained by the protocol state-machines. Given the emphasis on dynamic aspects, we use different symbols for states that represent queuing and for states in which at most a single non-conflicting transaction can be at any given time. We show also which queues are likely to grow when the system is congested. When alternative paths exist, due to optimistic execution, we show which is the more likely to be executed. We make a distinction between local and replicated queues and identify relevant actions: execute, apply, certify, and wait.

At the core of all these protocols is an atomic (or total ordered) multicast. For all of them we use a consistent naming for queues according to the use of the *atomic mcast* primitive. Queue Q0 is before the atomic mcast, Q1 is between the atomic mcast and its delivery, and Q2 is after the delivery.

Some of the discussed algorithms [36, 31] have been originaly proposed using atomic primitives with optimistic delivery. The goal is to compensate the inherent ordering latency by allowing tentative processing in parallel with the ordering protocol. If the final order of the messages matches the predicted order then the replication protocol can proceed, otherwise the results obtained tentatively are discarded. Protocols with this optimistic assumption use messages in Q1. Queue Q1 has messages with tentative order. In contrast, messages in Q2 have a final order.

13.6.1 Replication with Conservative Execution

We consider the Non-disjoint Conflict Classes and Optimistic Multicast (NODO) protocol [36] as an example of the conservative execution. In NODO data is a priori partitioned in conflict classes, not necessarily disjoint. Each transaction has an associated set of conflict classes (the data partitions it accesses) which are assumed to be known in advance. In practice, this requires the entire transaction to be known before it is executed, precluding the processing of interactive transactions.

NODO's execution is depicted in Figures 13.7 and 13.8. The former shows exchanged messages and synchronization points whereas the second focuses on its

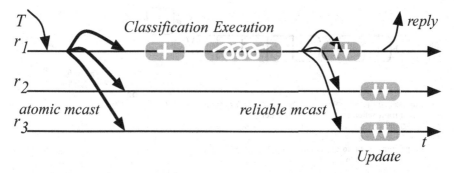

Fig. 13.7 Conservative execution: NODO.

dynamic aspects. When a transaction is submitted, its identifier (id) and conflict classes are atomically multicast to all replicas obtaining a total order position. Each replica has a queue associated with each conflict class and, once delivered, a transaction is classified according to its conflict classes and enqueued in all corresponding queues. As soon as a transaction reaches the head of all of its conflict class queues it is executed. In this approach, a transaction is only executed by the replica to which it was originally submitted.

Clearly, the definition of the conflict classes has a direct impact on performance. The fewer the number of transactions with overlapping conflict classes, the better the interleave among transactions. Conflict classes are usually defined at the table level but can have a finer grain at the expense of a non-trivial validation process to guarantee that a transaction does not access conflict classes that were not previously specified.

When the commit request is received, the outcome of the transaction is reliably multicast to all replicas along with the replica's updates (write-set) and a reply is sent to the client. Each replica applies the remote transaction's updates with the parallelism allowed by the initially established total order of the transaction.

The protocol ensures 1-copy serializability [7] as long as transactions are classified taking into account read/write conflicts. To achieve 1-copy snapshot isolation [26] transactions must be classified taking into account just write/write conflicts.

A transaction is scheduled optimistically if there is no conflicting transaction already ordered (Q2). This tentative execution may be done at the expense of an abort if a concurrent transaction is later on ordered before it.

Figure 8(a) shows the states that a transaction goes through upon being submitted by a client. Assuming that group communication is the bottleneck, the time spent in the queue waiting for total order (Q1) is significant enough compared to the time taken to actually execute such that it is worthwhile to optimistically execute transactions (transition 2 instead of transition 1). This makes it possible that when a transaction is finally ordered, it is immediately committed (transition 4). Assuming that the tentative optimistic ordering is correct, a rollback (transition 3) is unlikely.

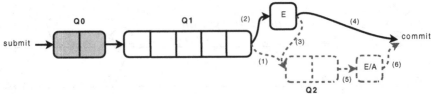

1 - Final Delivery (optimistic execution not started (unlikely) or remote)
2 - Submit transaction to optimistic execution
3 - Final Delivery (missed order and then rollback (unlikely))
4 - Final Delivery (correct order)
5 - Submit transaction to execution in order
6 - Execution finished in order

(a) Assuming that atomic mcast is the bottleneck.

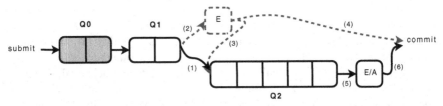

1 - Final Delivery (optimistic execution not started or remote)
2 - Submit transaction to optimistic execution (unlikely)
3 - Final Delivery (missed order and rollback (unlikely, but it doesn't matter))
4 - Final Delivery (correct order)
5 - Submit transaction in order
6 - Execution finished in order

(b) Assuming that transaction execution is the bottleneck.

Fig. 13.8 States, transitions, and queues in NODO.

On the other hand, if the transaction execution is the bottleneck, then queuing will happen in queue Q2 and not in queue Q1. Thus if Q2 is never empty, then no transaction in queue Q1 is eligible for optimistic execution. This scenario is depicted in Figure 8(b): The optimistic path is seldom used and the protocol boils down to a coarse-grained distributed locking approach, which has a very large impact on scalability. Notice that if there are k (disjoint) conflict classes, there can be at most k transactions executing in the whole system.

Experiments using the TPC-C workload show that in a local area network, group communication is not the bottleneck. Figure 13.13 shows the NODO protocol saturating when there are still plenty of system resources available.

13.6.2 Replication with Optimistic Execution

To illustrate the optimistic execution approach we consider two protocols: Postgres-R (PGR) [24] and Database State Machine (DBSM) [31]. In both protocols, transactions are immediately executed by the replicas to which they are submitted without

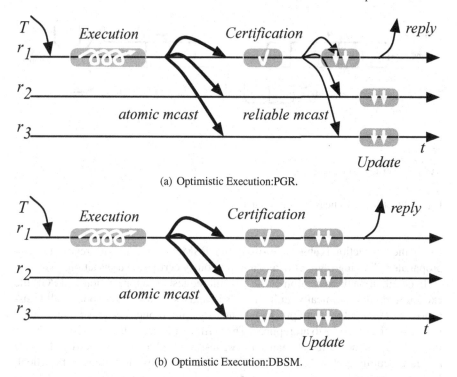

(a) Optimistic Execution:PGR.

(b) Optimistic Execution:DBSM.

Fig. 13.9 Optimistic executions: PGR and DBSM.

any prior global coordination. Locally, transactions are synchronized according to the specific concurrency control mechanism of the database engine.

The messages exchanged and the synchronization points of the execution of these protocols are depicted in Figure 13.9. The dynamic aspects are depicted in Figures 13.10 (PGR) and 13.11 (DBSM). Upon receiving a commit request, a successful transaction is not readily committed. Instead, its changes (write-set) and read data (read-set) are gathered and a termination protocol initiated. The goal of the termination protocol is to decide the order and the outcome of the transaction such that a global correctness criterion is satisfied (e.g. 1-copy serializability [7] or 1-copy snapshot isolation [26]). This is achieved by establishing a total order position for the transaction and certifying it against concurrently executed transactions. The certification of a transaction is done by evaluating the intersection of its read- and write-set (or just write-set in case of the snapshot isolation) with the write-set of concurrent, previously ordered transactions. The fate of a transaction is therefore determined by the termination protocol and a transaction that would locally commit may end up aborted.

These protocols differ on the termination procedure. Considering 1-copy serializability, both protocols use the transaction's read-set in the certification procedure. In PGR, the transaction's read-set is not propagated and thus only the replica exe-

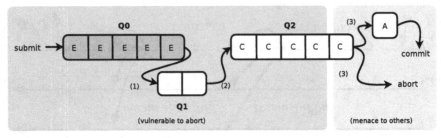

1 - Multicast
2 - Final Delivery
3 - Commit/Abort due to Certification

Fig. 13.10 States, transitions, and queues in PGR.

cuting the transaction is able to certify it. In DBSM, the transaction's read-set is also propagated allowing each replica to autonomously certify the transaction.

In detail, upon the reception of the commit request for a transaction t, in PGR the executing replica atomically multicasts t's id and t's write-set. As soon as all transactions ordered before t are processed, the executing replica certifies t and reliably multicasts the outcome to all replicas. The certification procedure consists in checking t's read-set and write-set against the write-sets of all transactions ordered before t. The executing replica then commits or aborts t locally and replies to the client. Upon the reception of t's commit outcome each replica applies t's changes through the execution of a high priority transaction consisting of updates, inserts and deletes according to t's previously multicast write-set. The high priority of the transaction means that it must be assured of acquiring all required write locks, possibly aborting any locally executing transactions.

The termination protocol in the DBSM is significantly different and works as follows. Upon the reception of the commit request for a transaction t, the executing replica atomically multicasts t's id, the version of the database on which t was executed, and t's read-set and write-set. As soon as t is ordered, each replica is able to certify t on its own. For the certification procedure, t's read-set and write-set are checked against the write-sets of all transactions committed since t's database version. If they do not intersect, t commits, otherwise t aborts. If t commits then its changes are applied through the execution of a high priority transaction consisting of updates, inserts and deletes according to t's previously multicast write-set. Again, the high priority of the transaction means that it must be assured of acquiring all required write locks, possibly aborting any locally executing transactions. The executing replica replies to the client at the end of t.

In both protocols, transactions are queued while executing, as would happen in a non-replicated database, using whatever native mechanism is used to enforce ACID properties. This is queue Q0 in Figures 13.11 and 13.10.

The most noteworthy feature of both protocols is that since a transaction starts until it is certified, it is vulnerable to being aborted by a concurrent conflicting transaction that commits. On the other hand, from the instant that a transaction is certified until it finally commits on every node, it is a menace to other transactions which will be aborted if they touch a conflicting item. Latency in any processing stage is thus bound to increase the abort rate. A side-effect of this is that the resulting system, when loaded, is extremely unfair to long running transactions.

In the DBSM, the additional latency introduced by replication is in the atomic multicast step, similarly to NODO (Q1) in Figure 8(a). This is an issue in WANs [20] and can be addressed with optimistic delivery. PGR [24] does not use optimistic delivery. In clusters, latency comes from exhausting resources within each replica as queues build up in Q0 and Q2. It is thus no surprise that any contention whatsoever makes the abort rate increase significantly.

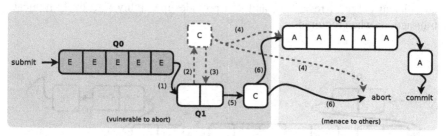

1 - Multicast
2 - Certify Optmistically (unlikely)
3 - Final Delivery, missed order and then rollback (unlikely, but it doesn't matter)
4 - Final Delivery, correct order
5 - Certify in order
6 - Commit/Abort in order

Fig. 13.11 States, transitions, and queues in DBSM.

13.6.3 Active Replication

Active replication is a technique to build fault-tolerant systems in which transactions are deterministically processed at all replicas. Specifically, it requires that each transaction's statement be processed in the same order by all replicas. This might be ensured by means of a centralized or a distributed scheduler.

Sequoia [12], which was built after C-JDBC [10], for instance, uses a centralized scheduler at the expense of introducing a single point of failure. Usually, any distributed scheduler would circumvent this resilience problem but would require a distributed deadlock detection mechanism. To avoid distributed deadlocks, one might annotate transactions with conflict-classes and request distributed locks through an atomic multicast before starting executing a transaction. In contrast with NODO, however, a reliable message to propagate changes would not be needed as transactions would be actively executed. In both approaches, the consistency criteria would be similar to those provided by NODO.

The case against active replication is shown in NODO [36]: unbearable contention with high write ratio. This technique additionally has the drawback of requiring a parser to remove non-deterministic information (e.g. random() or date()), thereby leading to re-implementing several features already provided by a database management system.

The active replication pays off when the overhead between transferring raw updates in a passive replication is higher than re-executing the statements. And of course, it makes it easy to execute DDL statements.

13.6.4 Hybrid Replication

Akara [20] pursues a hybrid approach: it ultimately enforces conservative execution to ensure fairness while leveraging the optimistic execution of transactions to attain an efficient usage of resources, and still provides the ability to actively replicate transactions when required.

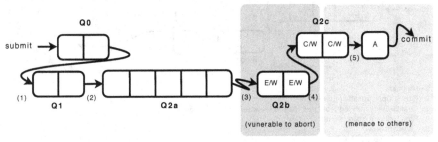

1 - Pre-classification and multicast
2 - Final Delivery
3 - Scheduler: scheduled to run optimistically or wait if remote or active
4 - Optmistic execution finished or simply next in line
5 - Next in line

Fig. 13.12 States, transitions, and queues in Akara.

Figure 13.12 depicts the major states, transitions, and queues of the protocol. For the sake of simplicity, as in Section 13.6.1, we assume conflict classes correspond to tables (typical case) and that all transactions access at least a common table (interesting cases).

Upon submission, transactions are classified according to a set of conflict classes and totally ordered by means of an atomic multicast. Once ordered, a transaction is queued into Q2a waiting to be scheduled. Progression in Q2a depends on an admission control policy. When a transaction reaches the top of Q2a it is transferred to Q2b and then executed. Transactions run while in Q2b are said to be executed optimistically as they may end up aborting due to conflicts with concurrent transactions in Q2b or Q2c. After execution, and having reached the top of Q2b, a transaction is transferred to Q2c. When a transaction reaches the top of Q2c it may be ready to commit (it may also need to abort due to conflicts). If it is ready to commit, its changes are propagated to all other replicas and the transaction commits. Otherwise, the transaction is forced to re-execute conservatively by imposing its priority on any locally running transaction.

The Akara protocol maximizes resource usage through the concurrent execution of potentially conflicting transactions by means of an admission control mechanism. It is worth noticing however that an admission policy that only allows to execute non-conflicting transactions according to their conflict classes makes Akara a simpler conservative protocol like NODO. The key is therefore to judiciously schedule the execution of each transaction in order to exploit resource availability thus reducing contention introduced by a conservative execution while at the same time avoiding re-execution. In [20] a simple policy that fixes the number of concurrent optimistically executed transactions is adopted. More sophisticated policies taking into account the actual resource usage or even dynamic knowledge of the workload could be used.

The mix of conservative and optimistic executions may lead to local deadlocks. Consider two conflicting transactions t and $t\prime$ that are ordered $< t, t\prime >$ and scheduled to run concurrently (both are in Q2b). If $t\prime$ grabs a lock first on a conflicting data item, it prevents t from running. However $t\prime$ cannot leave Q2b before t without infringing the global commit order.

If both transactions have the same conflict classes and, of course, are locally executed at the same replica, the proposed solution is to allow t' to overtake t in the global commit order. Notice that when a transaction t is totally ordered this ensures that no conflicting transaction will be executed concurrently at any other replica. Therefore, if t's order is swapped with that of $t\prime$ with the very same conflict classes then it is still guaranteed that both t and $t\prime$ are executed without the interference of any remote conflicting transaction. In the experiments conducted with the TPC-C (Section 13.6.5), for example, the likelihood of having two transactions with the very same conflict classes is more than 85% of the occurrences.

Finally, the protocol also allows transactions to be actively executed, thus providing a mechanism to easily replicate DDL statements and to reduce network usage for transactions with very large write-sets. A transaction t marked as active is executed at all replicas without distinction between an initiating or a remote replica, and its execution is straightforward. When t can be removed from Q2a, it is immediately moved to Q2b, and so forth, until it gets to Q2c. When t can proceed from Q2c, it is executed with high priority, committed, and then removed from Q2c. Active transactions are not executed optimistically to avoid different interleaves at different replicas.

13.6.5 Evaluation

To evaluate the protocols we use a hybrid simulation environment that combines simulated and real components[44]. The key components, the replication and the group communication protocols, are real implementations while both the database engine and the network are simulated.

In detail, we use a centralized simulation runtime based on the standard Scalable Simulation Framework (SSF)[1], which provides a simple yet effective infrastructure for discrete-event simulation. Simulation models are built as libraries that can be reused. This is the case of the SSFNet [14] framework, which models network components (e.g. network interface cards and links), operating system components (e.g. protocol stacks), and applications (e.g. traffic analyzers). Complex network models can be configured using these components, mimicking existing networks or exploring particularly large or interesting topologies.

To combine the simulated components with the real implementations the execution of the real software components is timed with a profiling timer [38] and the result is used to mark the simulated CPU busy during the corresponding period, thus preventing other jobs, real or simulated, from being attributed simultaneously to the same CPU. The simulated components are configured according to the equipment and scenarios chosen for testing as described in this section.

The database server handles multiple clients and is modeled as a scheduler and a collection of resources, such as storage and CPUs, and a concurrency control module. The database offers the reflector interface (Section 13.3) and implements multiversion concurrency control.

Each transaction is modeled as a sequence of operations: i) fetch a data item; ii) do some processing; iii) write back a data item. Upon receiving a transaction request each operation is scheduled to execute on the corresponding resource. The processing time of each operation is previously obtained by profiling a real database server.

A database client is attached to a database server and produces a stream of transaction requests. After each request is issued, the client blocks until the server replies, thus modeling a single threaded client process. After receiving a reply, the client is then paused for some amount of time (thinking time) before issuing the next transaction request.

To determine the read-set and write-set of a transaction's execution, the database is modeled as a set of histograms. The transactions' statements are executed against this model and the read-set, write-set and write-values are extracted to build the transaction model that is injected into the database server. In our case, this modeling is rather straightforward as the database is very well defined by the TPC-C [46] workload that we use for all tests. Moreover, as all the transactions specified by TPC-C can be reduced to SPJ queries, the read-set extraction is quite simple.

Clients run an implementation that mimics the industry standard on-line transaction processing benchmark TPC-C. TPC-C specifies five transactions: *NewOrder* with 44% of the occurrences; *Payment* with 44%; *OrderStatus* with 4%; *Delivery* with 4%; and *StockLevel* with 4%. The *NewOrder*, *Payment* and *Delivery* are update transactions while the others are read-only.

For the experiments below we added to the benchmark three more transactions that mimic maintenance activities such as adding users, changing indexes in tables or updating taxes over items. Specifically, the first transaction *Light-Tran* creates a constraint on a table if it does not exist or drops it otherwise. The second transaction *Active-Tran* increases the price of products and is actively executed. Conversely, *Passive-Tran* does the same maintenance activity but its changes are passively propagated. These transactions are never executed in the same run, have a probability of 1% and when are executing the probability of the *NewOrder* is reduced to 43%.

The database model has been configured using the transactions' processing time of a profiled version of PostgreSQL 7.4.6 under the TPC-C workload. From the TPC-C benchmark we only use the specified workload, the constraints on throughput, performance, screen load and background execution of transactions are not taken into account.

We consider a LAN with 9 replicas. In the LAN configuration the replicas are connected by a network with a bandwidth of 1Gbps and a latency of $120\mu s$. Each replica corresponds to a dual processor AMD Opteron at 2.4GHz with 4GB of memory, running the Linux Fedora Core 3 Distribution with kernel version 2.6.10. For storage we used a fiber-channel attached box with 4, 36GB SCSI disks in a RAID-5 configuration and the Ext3 file system.

We varied the total number of clients from 270 to 3960 and distributed them evenly among the replicas and each run has 150000 transactions.

Experimental Results   In what follows, we discuss the queues for each protocol described in previous sections. For the NODO approach, we use the simple definition of a conflict class for each table, which can be easily extracted from the SQL code. We do not consider finer granularity due to the possibility of inconsistencies when labeling mistakes are made. Figures 13.13 and 13.14 compare the DBSM, PGR and NODO.

The DBSM and PGR show a throughput higher than 20000 *tpm* (Figure 13(a)). In fact, both present similar results and the higher the throughput the higher the number of requests per second inside the database (Figure 13(b)). These requests represent access to the storage, CPU, lock manager and to the replication protocol. Clearly, the database is not a bottleneck. In contrast, the throughput presented by NODO is extremely low, around 4000 *tpm*, and its latency is extremely high (Figure 13(c)). This drawback can be easily explained by the contention observed in Q2 (Figure 13(d)).

Unfortunately, with the conservative and optimistic approaches presented above, one may have to choose between latency and fairness. In the NODO, for 3240 clients, 2481 transactions wait in Q2 around 40 *s* to start executing (Figure 14(a)). In contrast, an optimistic transaction waits 1000 times less and the number of transactions waiting to be applied is very low.

The abort rate is below 1% in both optimistic approaches as there is no contention and the likelihood of conflicts is low in such situations (Figure 14(b)). However, to show that the optimistic protocols may not guarantee fairness, we conducted a set of experiments in which one requests an explicit table level locking on behalf of the *Delivery* transaction thus mimicking a hotspot. This is a pretty common situation in practice, as application developers may explicitly request locks to improve performance or avoid concurrency anomalies. In this case, the abort rate is around 5% and this fact does not have an observable impact on latency and throughput but almost all Delivery Transactions abort, around 99% (Figure 14(c)).

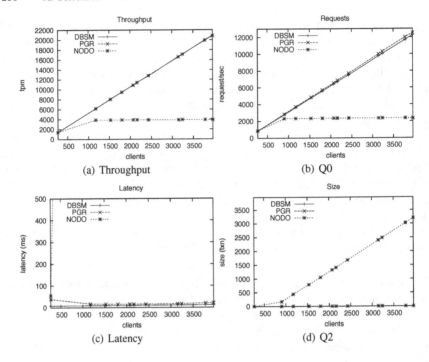

Fig. 13.13 Performance of DBSM, PGR and NODO.

In [21], a table level locking is acquired on behalf of the *Delivery* transaction to avoid flooding the network and improve the certification procedure. Although the reason to do so is different, the issue is the same.

In all the experiments, the time between an optimistic delivery and a final delivery were always below 1 *ms*, thus excluding Q1 from being an issue.

To improve the performance of the conservative approach while at the same time guaranteeing fairness, we used the Akara protocol. We ran the Akara protocol varying the number of optimistic transactions that might be concurrently submitted to the database in order to figure out which would be the best value for our environment. This degree of optimistic execution is indicated by a number after the name of the protocol. For instance, Akara-25 means that 25 optimistic transactions might be concurrently submitted and Akara-n means that there is no restriction on this number.

Table 13.1 shows that indefinitely increasing the number of optimistic transactions that might be concurrently submitted is not worth. Basically for Akara-n, latency drastically increases and as a consequence throughput decreases. This occurs because the number of transactions that fails the certification procedure increases. For 3240 clients, more than 89% of the transactions fail the certification procedure (i.e. in-core certification procedure like in PGR, see Section 13.6.2). Furthermore, after failing such transactions are conservatively executed and compete for resources

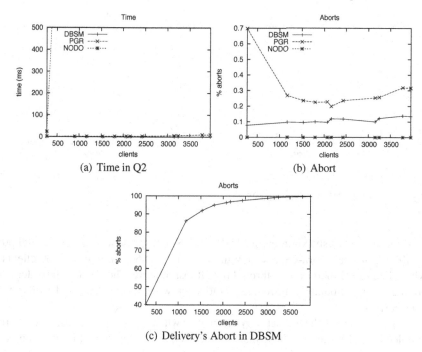

Fig. 13.14 Latency vs. abort rate (DBSM, PGR and NODO).

Table 13.1 Analysis of Akara.

	Lat (ms)	Tput (tpm)	Unsuccess(%)
Akara-25	178	16780	2
Akara-45	480	16474	5
Akara-n	37255	3954	89
Akara-25 with Light-Tran	8151	9950	21
Akara-25 with Active-Tran	109420	1597	21
Akara-25 with Passive-Tran	295884	625	22

with optimistic transactions that may be executing. Keeping the number of optimistic transactions low however reduces the number of transactions allowed in the database and neither is worth. After varying this number from 5 to 50 in steps of 1, we figured out that the best value for the TPC-C in our environment is 25.

In what follows, we used the DBSM as the representative of the family of optimistic protocols thus omitting the PGR. Although both protocols present similar performance in a LAN, the PGR is not worth in a WAN due to its extra communication step.

Figure 13.15 depicts the benefits provided by the Akara-25. In Figure 15(a), we notice that latency in the NODO is extremely high. In contrast, the Akara-25 starts degenerating after 3240 clients. For 3240 clients the latency in the DBSM is about 9 *ms*, and in the Akara-25, it is about 178 *ms*. This increase in latency directly af-

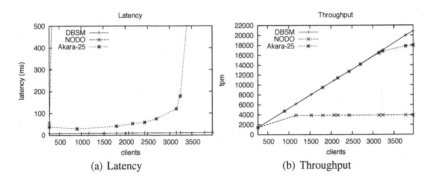

(a) Latency   (b) Throughput

Fig. 13.15 DBSM, NODO and Akara-25.

fects throughput as shown in Figure 15(b). The NODO presents a steady throughput of 4000 *tpm*; the Akara-25, a steady throughput of 18605 *tpm* after 3960 clients; while the DBSM increases its throughput almost linearly. The DBSM starts degenerating when the database becomes a bottleneck what was not our goal with these experiments.

Table 13.1 shows the impact on performance when the maintenance activities are handled by our protocol. These maintenance activities represented by the transactions *Active-Tran* and *Light-Tran* are actively executed and integrated in runs with the *Akara-25*: *Akara with Active-Tran* and *Akara with Light-Tran*, respectively. In order to show the benefits of an active execution in such scenario, we provide a run named *Akara with Passive-Tran* in which the updates performed by the *Active-Tran* are atomically multicast. The run with the *Passive-Tran* presents a latency higher than that with the *Active-Tran* as the former needs to transfer the updates through the network. However, both approaches have a reduced throughput and high latency when compared to the normal Akara-25 due to contention caused by a large number of updates.

The run with the *Light-Tran* does not have a large number of updates but its throughput decreases when compared to the Akara-25 due to failures in the certification procedure. This is caused by the fact that the transaction *Light-Tran* mimics a change on the structure of a table and thus requires an exclusive lock on it.

In a real environment, we expect that maintenance operations occur with a rate lower than 1% and so they should not be a problem as the optimistic execution of other transactions might compensate the temporary decrease in performance.

13.7 Conclusions

This chapter addresses the existing trade-offs when implementing database replication in different environments. It shows that database replication in practice is constrained by a variety of architectural, algorithmic, and dynamic issues.

To address these issues, a generic architecture that supports legacy database management systems without compromising the performance that can be achieved in native implementations is described. Then, a communication abstraction that encapsulates distributed agreement and supports a range of implementations and advanced optimizations is presented. Finally, a modular approach to implementing replication protocols is put together and evaluated, showing how different algorithmic choices match assumptions on system dynamics and performance.

The experimental results reported here point out that a successful practical application of database replication, in particular, when strong consistency is sought, depends on a combination of factors. Namely, that the architectural approach to interfacing the database server dictates which replication algorithms are feasible; and that the availability of different communication primitives directly impacts the efficiency of different algorithms in a particular setting. By taking these factors into account, it is possible to achieve good performance in face of variable workloads and environments.

Acknowledgements This work was partially supported by the GORDA (FP6-IST2-004758) and the Pastramy (PTDC/EIA/72405/2006) projects.

References

1. http://www.ssfnet.org/
2. Amir, Y., Danilov, C., Stanton, J.: A low latency, loss tolerant architecture and protocol for wide area group communication. In: IEEE/IFIP International Conference on Dependable Systems and Networks (2000)
3. Apache DB Project. Apache Derby version 10.2 (2006),
   http://db.apache.org/derby/
4. Babaoglu, O., Davoli, R., Montresor, A.: Group membership and view synchrony in partitionable asynchronous distributed systems: Specifications. Operating Systems Review 31(2) (1997)
5. Ban, B.: Design and implementation of a reliable group communication toolkit for Java (1998), http://www.cs.cornell.edu/home/bba/Coots.ps.gz
6. Bartoli, A., Babaoglu, O.: Selecting a "primary partition" in partitionable asynchronous distributed systems. In: IEEE International Symposium on Reliable Distributed Systems (1997)
7. Bernstein, P., Hadzilacos, V., Goodman, N.: Concurrency Control and Recovery in Distributed Database Systems. Addison-Wesley, Reading (1987)
8. Birman, K.P., van Renesse, R.: Reliable Distributed Computing with the Isis Toolkit. IEEE Computer Society Press, Los Alamitos (1993)
9. Carvalho, N., Correia Jr., A., Pereira, J., Rodrigues, L., Oliveira, R., Guedes, S.: On the use of a reflective architecture to augment database management systems. Journal of Universal Computer Science 13(8) (2007)
10. Cecchet, E., Marguerite, J., Zwaenepoel, W.: C-JDBC: Flexible database clustering middleware. In: USENIX Annual Technical Conference (2004)
11. Continuent. Sequoia v2.10 (2007), http://sequoia.continuent.org
12. Continuent. Sequoia 4.x (2008), http://sequoia.continuent.org
13. Correia Jr., A., Pereira, J., Rodrigues, L., Carvalho, N., Vilaça, R., Oliveira, R., Guedes, S.: GORDA: An open architecture for database replication. In: IEEE International Symposium on Network Computing and Applications (2007)
14. Cowie, J., Liu, H., Liu, J., Nicol, D., Ogielski, A.: Towards realistic million-node Internet simulation. In: International Conference on Parallel and Distributed Processing Techniques and Applications (1999)

15. Défago, X., Schiper, A., Urbán, P.: Total order broadcast and multicast algorithms: Taxonomy and survey. ACM Computing Surveys 36(4) (2004)
16. Dolev, D., Malki, D., Strong, R.: A framework for partitionable membership service. In: ACM Symposium on Principles of Distributed Computing (1996)
17. Garcia-Molina, H., Ullman, J., Widom, J.: Database Systems The Complete Book. Prentice-Hall, Englewood Cliffs (2002)
18. Guerraoui, R., Kostic, D., Levy, R., Quema, V.: A high throughput atomic storage algorithm. In: IEEE International Conference on Distributed Computing Systems (2007)
19. Hayden, M.: The Ensemble System. PhD thesis, Cornell University, Computer Science Department (1998)
20. Correia Jr, A., Pereira, J., Oliveira, R.: AKARA: A flexible clustering protocol for demanding transactional workloads. In: International Symposium on Distributed Objects and Applications (2008)
21. Correia Jr., A., Sousa, A., Soares, L., Pereira, J., Moura, F., Oliveira, R.: Group-based replication of on-line transaction processing servers. In: Maziero, C.A., Gabriel Silva, J., Andrade, A.M.S., de Assis Silva, F.M. (eds.) LADC 2005. LNCS, vol. 3747, pp. 245–260. Springer, Heidelberg (2005)
22. Kaashoek, M., Tanenbaum, A.: Group communication in the Amoeba distributed operating system. In: IEEE International Conference on Distributed Computing Systems (1991)
23. Keidar, I., Dolev, D.: Totally ordered broadcast in the face of network partitions. In: Dependable Network Computing, Kluwer Academic Publishers, Dordrecht (2000)
24. Kemme, B., Alonso, G.: Don't be lazy, be consistent: Postgres-R, a new way to implement database replication. In: VLDB Conference (2000)
25. Kiczales, G.: Towards a new model of abstraction in software engineering. In: IMSA Workshop on Reflection and Meta-level Architectures (1992)
26. Lin, Y., Kemme, B., Jiménez Peris, R., Patiño Martínez, M.: Middleware based data replication providing snapshot isolation. In: ACM SIGMOD (2005)
27. Maes, P.: Concepts and experiments in computational reflection. In: ACM International Conference on Object-Oriented Programming, Systems, Languages, and Applications (1987)
28. Miranda, H., Pinto, A., Rodrigues, L.: Appia: a flexible protocol kernel supporting multiple coordinated channels. In: IEEE International Conference on Distributed Computing Systems (2001)
29. Mocito, J., Respicio, A., Rodrigues, L.: On statistically estimated optimistic delivery in large-scale total order protocols. In: IEEE International Symposium on Pacific Rim Dependable Computing (2006)
30. Oliveira, R., Pereira, J., Correia Jr, A., Archibald, E.: Revisiting 1-copy equivalence in clustered databases. In: ACM Symposium on Applied Computing (2006)
31. Pedone, F., Guerraoui, R., Schiper, A.: The database state machine approach. Journal of Distributed and Parallel Databases and Technology (2002)
32. Pedone, F., Schiper, A.: Optimistic atomic broadcast. In: Kutten, S. (ed.) DISC 1998. LNCS, vol. 1499, pp. 318–332. Springer, Heidelberg (1998)
33. Pedone, F., Schiper, A.: Handling message semantics with generic broadcast protocols. Distributed Computing 15(2) (2002)
34. Pereira, J., Rodrigues, L., Monteiro, M.J., Oliveira, R., Kermarrec, A.-M.: NeEM: Network-friendly epidemic multicast. In: IEEE International Symposium on Reliable Distributed Systems (2003)
35. Pereira, J., Rodrigues, L., Oliveira, R.: Semantically reliable multicast: Definition, implementation and performance evaluation. IEEE Transactions on Computers, Special Issue on Reliable Distributed Systems 52(2) (2003)
36. Patiño-Martínez, M., Jiménez-Peris, R., Kemme, B., Alonso, G.: Scalable replication in database clusters. In: Herlihy, M.P. (ed.) DISC 2000. LNCS, vol. 1914, p. 315. Springer, Heidelberg (2000)
37. Jiménez Peris, R., Patiño Martínez, M., Kemme, B., Alonso, G.: Improving the scalability of fault-tolerant database clusters. In: IEEE International Conference on Distributed Computing Systems (2002)

38. Pettersson, M.: Linux performance counters, `http://user.it.uu.se/~mikpe/linux/perfctr/`
39. PostgreSQL Global Development Group. Postgresql version 8.1 (2006), `http://www.postgresql.org/`
40. Rodrigues, L., Fonseca, H., Veríssimo, P.: Totally ordered multicast in large-scale systems. In: IEEE International Conference on Distributed Computing Systems (1996)
41. Rodrigues, L., Mocito, J., Carvalho, N.: From spontaneous total order to uniform total order: different degrees of optimistic delivery. In: ACM Symposium on Applied Computing (2006)
42. Salas, J., Jimenez-Peris, R., Patino-Martinez, M., Kemme, B.: Lightweight reflection for middleware-based database replication. In: IEEE International Symposium on Reliable Distributed Systems (2006)
43. Sousa, A., Pereira, J., Moura, F., Oliveira, R.: Optimistic total order in wide area networks. In: IEEE International Symposium on Reliable Distributed Systems (2002)
44. Sousa, A., Pereira, J., Soares, L., Correia Jr., A., Rocha, L., Oliveira, R., Moura, F.: Testing the dependability and performance of GCS-based database replication protocols. In: IEEE/IFIP International Conference on Dependable Systems and Networks (2005)
45. Sussman, J., Keidar, I., Marzullo, K.: Optimistic virtual synchrony. In: Symposium on Reliability in Distributed Software (2000)
46. Transaction Processing Performance Council (TPC). TPC benchmark C Standard Specification Revision 5.0 (2001)
47. Vicente, P., Rodrigues, L.: An indulgent uniform total order algorithm with optimistic delivery. In: IEEE International Symposium on Reliable Distributed Systems (2002)

Index